For Honour and Fame

ALSO BY NIGEL SAUL

Richard II
English Church Monuments in the Middle Ages:
History and Representation

For Honour and Fame

Chivalry in England, 1066–1500

NIGEL SAUL

THE BODLEY HEAD
LONDON

Published by The Bodley Head 2011

2 4 6 8 10 9 7 5 3 1

Copyright © Nigel Saul 2011

Nigel Saul has asserted his right under the Copyright, Designs
and Patents Act 1988 to be identified as the author of this work

First published in Great Britain in 2011 by
The Bodley Head
Random House, 20 Vauxhall Bridge Road,
London SW1V 2SA

www.bodleyhead.co.uk
www.vintage-books.co.uk

Addresses for companies within The Random House Group Limited can be
found at: www.randomhouse.co.uk/offices.htm

The Random House Group Limited Reg. No. 954009

A CIP catalogue record for this book
is available from the British Library

ISBN 9781847920522

The Random House Group Limited supports The Forest Stewardship Council® (FSC®),
the leading international forest certification organisation. All our titles that are printed on
Greenpeace approved FSC® certified paper carry the FSC® logo. Our paper procurement
policy can be found at: www.randomhouse.co.uk/environment

Typeset in Monotype Dante by Palimpsest Book Production Limited,
Falkirk, Stirlingshire

Printed and bound in Great Britain by
Clays Ltd, St Ives PLC

For my wife

Preface

To write about chivalry in medieval England is to embark on a voyage through a world at once glamorous and violent, alluring and yet elusive. For many, chivalry evokes images of knights in shining armour, menfolk competing for the attention of a fair lady, pennons and streamers fluttering from castle battlements. Much of this picture is a product of the nineteenth-century romanticisation of the Middle Ages – the kind of re-creation that gave us Waterhouse's 'Lady of Shalott' and Viollet-le-Duc's rebuilding of Carcassonne. Its roots lay in an idealised view of the medieval past which grew up in reaction to the horrors of the grim industrialisation of the time. The real medieval world was altogether less lyrical and more down-to-earth than the fanciful re-creation. Nonetheless, we know enough about the cultural achievements of the Middle Ages to be aware that the image of the fully accoutred mounted knight was one which attracted and captivated contemporaries. The tales of King Arthur and his Knights of the Round Table inspired a whole genre of vernacular romance literature. The prowess of the knights of the Hundred Years War was celebrated in Froissart's *Chronicle*, one of the most compelling narrative accounts of the medieval period. From the early twelfth century the knightly class dominated the secular landscape of western Europe, spawning an aristocratic culture which was shaped in their heroic image and reflected their martial values. It is that richly layered chivalric world, which has done so much to influence our own view of the Middle Ages, which is the subject of this book.

Over a quarter of a century ago another book was published which was to be the point of departure for all modern studies of chivalry. This was Maurice Keen's *Chivalry*, an ambitious, pioneering work which rescued chivalry from the hands of lyrical escapists and placed it firmly in the forefront of medieval studies. The aim of the present volume is to build on the foundations which Keen laid and to do so by engaging with his legacy more specifically in the context of medieval England. The book will accordingly concern itself with how chivalry shaped both the practice of kingship in England and the expectations which people had of their kings, with how it spawned a rich and distinctive aristocratic culture, and how its values infused aristocratic codes of behaviour and personal piety. It will look, too, at the knights and gentry at home, at their changing role in society and their place in local office-holding and administration. It will look at the architecture of chivalry, at the castles and fortifications which were the outward face of the aristocratic elite and proclaimed its militant values. It will look at aristocratic women and their relationship with chivalric culture. Finally, it will attempt a consideration of what the legacy of chivalry might be to us today.

Chivalry was the value system and behavioural code of the secular aristocratic elite of the Middle Ages. Studying it focuses our attention on the social group which made the biggest and most forceful impact on the contemporary world. It affords us the opportunity to explore a world at once colourful and visual, mannered and polite, prickly and violent. It introduces us to a society whose values were very different from our own.

Acknowledgements

I would like to record my appreciation to Will Sulkin and Kay Peddle of The Bodley Head for their careful and patient work on the preparation of this book. I am especially grateful to Will Sulkin for his meticulous editorial work, which has added greatly to the book's distinction.

Contents

List of Illustrations

Colour-washed drawing of a kneeling knight, added *c.* 1250 to a Westminster psalter of the early thirteenth century (*British Library/ Bridgeman Art Library*)

Sir Geoffrey Luttrell being armed by his wife and daughter-in-law, from the Luttrell Psalter, *c.* 1335–45 (*British Library/Bridgeman Art Library*)

Odo, Bishop of Bayeux, at the Battle of Hastings, from the Bayeux Tapestry (*Bridgeman Art Library*)

Tomb effigy attributed to William Marshal, Earl of Pembroke, in the Temple church, London (*Chris Christodoulou*)

The chancel, Stoke d'Abernon church, Surrey, third quarter of the thirteenth century (*author*)

The Round Table in the hall of Winchester Castle, late thirteenth century (*John Crook*)

Rubbing of the brass of Sir Hugh Hastings (d. 1347), Elsing church, Norfolk (*Jon Bayliss*)

Tile showing a knight with a couched lance, Ottery St Mary Church, Devon (*author*)

Cross–slab grave cover, Salford Church, Bedfordshire, early fourteenth century (*author*)

The 'English saints' window, Heydour Church, Lincolnshire, c. 1360 (*author*)

Tattershall Castle, Lincolnshire, the keep, c. 1430–50. To one side of the castle, and out of view, is the church, which Lord Cromwell rebuilt at the same time (*the late Nicholas More*)

Dover Castle, Kent, the keep, c. 1170–88 (*John Goodall*)

Cooling Castle, Kent, entrance gate to the inner courtyard, c. 1380 (*author*)

Warkworth Castle, Northumberland, the keep, late fourteenth century (*John Goodall*)

Drawing of the brass of Joan, Lady Cobham (d. 1434), Cobham Church, Kent (*Society of Antiquaries*)

Tomb of Reginald, Lord Cobham KG (d. 1361), Lingfield church, Surrey (*author*)

Drawing of the brass of Robert Wyvill, Bishop of Salisbury (d. 1375), in Salisbury Cathedral (*Edward Kite*)

The chantry chapel of Richard Beauchamp, Earl of Warwick (d. 1439), St Mary's Church, Warwick (*author*)

Drawing of the Battle of Shrewsbury from the Beauchamp Pageant, c. 1490 (*British Library, Shaun Tyas*)

Sir William Chamberlain KG (d. 1462), from the east window of East Harling church, Norfolk (*Jon Bayliss*)

Portrait relief of Sir Thomas Lovell, attributed to Pietro Torregiano, c. 1516–20, Westminster Abbey Museum (*Dean and Chapter of Westminster Abbey*)

Introduction: Chivalry and History

One of the most attractive drawings to have come down to us of a medieval knight is a colour-washed sketch in a thirteenth-century psalter commissioned for Westminster Abbey. Probably the work of an artist associated with the court, it presents an idealised image of a Christian warrior. The young tyro is shown kneeling with his arms outstretched and his hands open. He is dressed in a mail hauberk, over which is draped a linen surcoat bearing the emblem of the *cross patée*. From his belt is suspended a sword in a scabbard, and through his left arm passes a lance with a pennon attached. Behind him, leaning over the battlements of a tower, a page is seen handing him his helm while, to one side, a warhorse rears up and begins to canter forward.

The scene is deliberately conceived in a void. The knight, suspended in mid-air, turns away from, and not towards, the page handing him his helm. The warhorse is caught in the act of tripping over his left foot. Little or no relationship is established between the various elements which make up the drawing.

The effect of this artistic licence is to present the knight in visionary terms: to invest him with the aspirations and idealism of his age, to make him an image of human perfection. He is like Chaucer's Knight, 'a verray parfit gentil knyght', 'a worthy man', a lover of 'trouthe and honour'. Greed and avarice, and the other vices of which knights stood accused, find no place in his nature. His ideals are the Christian ones of truth and justice, righteousness and peace. He exemplifies everything that might be considered best in his order.

A very different image of knighthood is presented in the dedication miniature of the Luttrell Psalter, *c.* 1335–45. In the famous arming scene, Sir Geoffrey Luttrell, who commissioned the volume, is shown being fitted out for war. He is depicted astride a richly caparisoned charger, reaching out to receive his helm from his wife, while his daughter-in-law, to one side, prepares to hand him his shield. The emphasis in this scene is less on the visionary aspects of knighthood than on the insignia of status and rank. Heraldry figures prominently. Sir Geoffrey's arms, *azure a bend argent between six martlets argent*, are shown everywhere – on his surcoat, the enormous ailettes behind his shoulders, his pennon, even on the fan-like crest of his helm. His warhorse has them blazoned on its saddle, on its exotic fancrest and its long flowing trapper. Family heraldry appears on the clothing of the two female figures. On Lady Luttrell's gown are the arms of Luttrell impaling those of her natal family of Sutton (*or a lion rampant vert*), and on the gown of Luttrell's daughter-in-law, Beatrice Scrope, those of Scrope (*azure a bend or, a label of five points argent*) impaling the arms of Luttrell. What is narrated in this miniature is a story of lineage and dynasticism, not just idealism and knightly vocation.

Yet beneath the rich surface glitter of the picture there is a deeper meaning. The key to this is found in the juxtaposition of the image with the text of the manuscript. The miniature is placed at the end of Psalm 109 and opposite most of Psalm 110. Linkage with this second psalm is provided not only by position but by the presence of heraldic border patterns of repeated martlets, for Luttrell, and lions, for Sutton. The theme which ties together text and miniature is that of lordship. It is established in the opening words of the psalm, 'Dixit dominus domino meo . . .' ('And the Lord said to my lord'), and is picked up in the imagery of the initial 'D', in which God the Father (the heavenly lord) is shown in conversation with an enthroned King David (the earthly lord), who sits at his right hand. A connection was thus made by the artist between biblical lordship and Sir Geoffrey's own lordship. Sir Geoffrey's knighthood is placed in a hierarchy of lordship which finds a role for knighthood in the divinely ordained scheme of things.[1]

The two miniatures are separated in time by some three-quarters of a century, and iconographically they differ sharply. Yet they project the same concern – the concern to invest the knight with an ethical quality, to make him more than a simple warrior or bearer of arms and to surround him with an aura of charisma and mystique. Knighthood is represented as noble and dignified, a divinely ordained estate, a bulwark of society against disorder. It is this quality of knighthood, this aristocratic ethic, which we recognise as chivalry, a word derived from the French *chevalier*, a knight.

Yet if we recognise chivalry when we see it, it is tantalisingly hard to define precisely. Indeed, it is tempting to say that it is almost beyond definition. Medieval chivalry was more an outlook than a doctrine, more a lifestyle than an explicit ethical code. It embraced both ideology and social practice. Among the qualities central to it were loyalty, generosity, dedication, courage and courtesy, qualities which were esteemed by the military class and which contemporaries believed the ideal knight should possess. Chivalry meant different things to different people; like beauty, it was found in the eye of the beholder. For the heralds, whose primary task was to recognise coats of arms, its essence lay in the display of armorial charges on a shield, in the attesting of ancestral descent through the multiplication of quarterings. For the clergy, whose concern was to direct knighthood to the Church's own ends, it was more a religious vocation, the responsibility of knights to wage war in a just cause, pre-eminently the recovery of the Holy Places from the infidel. For the legists, whose goal was to bring order to the brutal realities of war, it was a legal construct intended to curb military excess, a set of moral guidelines to distinguish proper behaviour from improper. For the writers of romances – lovers of stories but also moral instructors – it was about the attainment of virtue through ennobling feats of arms to win the favour of a lady. For others again, the knights themselves, it was about what Sir Thomas Malory in the fifteenth century called 'dedys [deeds] full actuall' – fighting on horseback, jousting in tournament lists and the achievement of manliness through prowess. For the intellectuals and theorists, whose aim was making sense of human society, chivalry – *chevalerie* in French – was the way to describe the military and aristocratic elite, a social order, the second estate of God's creation.

The divergent perceptions of contemporaries find an echo in the diversity of approaches to the subject in modern scholarship. To some writers – especially those who approach the subject from the standpoint of political and military history – chivalry boils down to a rationalisation of knightly practice; it is a way of describing the camaraderie which developed between knights as they practised the arts of fighting and jousting on horseback. To others, it is a more court-based affair, centring on the code of manners which characterised and regulated the polite society of courtiers and aristocracy. To others again, it is the set of conventions which limited the horrors and excesses of war by prescribing an ethical basis of reasonable conduct between knights. For yet others again, it is essentially the rough and ready business of tit-for-tat justice which, so far from limiting violence, actually spread it by embodying an honour code which prescribed retaliation for every minor affront.

What cannot be disputed is that chivalry, in the sense of an aristocratic value system, had a wide influence across medieval society. Because the aristocracy constituted the social as well as the military elite, and for this reason were culturally dominant, their value system impinged on areas far beyond the military. The influence of chivalry was felt in political life, in social behaviour, in the conduct of disputes, in funerary rituals, even in architecture and design. If chivalry lay somewhere between ideal and reality, between codification and practice, its impact on the culture of society was both real and substantial.

Yet, strangely, chivalry has figured relatively little in most general accounts of medieval England. In virtually all writing on military history, it is the more down-to-earth business of the organisation of war which dominates.[2] The raising of troops, the impressment of shipping, the hiring of mercenaries, the assembling of indentured retinues – it is these practical, administrative matters which have commanded historians' attention. What, in particular, has attracted discussion is the levying of taxation for war, because this was connected with the emergence of parliament and thus with the rise of representative government. Chivalry, for all the importance it had in shaping contemporary attitudes – indeed, in shaping the conduct of war – has been strangely neglected. Much of the explanation for this oversight is to be found in its elusiveness as a historical phenomenon. Chivalry does not feature in the administrative sources which form the staple source material of the political and institutional historian. As the Dutch scholar Johan Huizinga wrote nearly a century ago: 'Combing the records in which chivalry is little mentioned, [historians] have succeeded in presenting a picture of the Middle Ages in which economic and social points of view are so dominant that one tends at times to forget that, next to religion, chivalry was the strongest of the ideas which filled the minds and hearts of those men of another age.'[3] The rise of cultural history in the twentieth century has gone some way to remedying this intellectual imbalance. Nonetheless, there is still a much larger literature on the origins and early history of chivalry than on its later development and its interaction with the broader culture of society.

The main aim of the present book, therefore, is to present an account of English aristocratic society in the Middle Ages which puts chivalry centre-stage. The intention is to range broadly across chivalric practice and experience to illuminate the relationship between chivalry and the main political, military, social and artistic currents of the day. At the heart of the book is a series of narrative chapters tracing the history of chivalry in England from the eleventh century to the early sixteenth, while interspersed with these are thematically organised discussions of such issues as the organisation of war, the role of chivalry in the field, the relationship between chivalry and violence, and the influence of chivalry on art and literature. Chivalry provided the writers and artists of the Middle Ages with both a rich narrative repertory and an inexhaustible store of visual motifs. It would be misleading, however, to reduce the history of chivalry to a superficial romp through episodes of glitz and glamour. Within chivalry there were tensions and inconsistencies, and these were picked up and commented on by contemporaries. So the debates of the day about chivalry and chivalric conduct will figure nearly as much as the valorous deeds of the knights themselves. Chivalry was not a movement or institution cut off from the mainstream of society; on the contrary, it formed part of the wider ethos and value system of society. It was central to the identity of the English medieval elite. The medieval aristocracy were shaped in a chivalric image. When knights went off to war, they did so in one capacity as subjects acknowledging their obligations to their king, yet they did so in another as adventurers questing 'for honour and fame'.

I

The Origins of English Chivalry

The Chivalric Conquest

Chivalry, however it is defined, is associated first and foremost with the estate of knighthood and with fighting on horseback. The word knight, though Germanic in origin, carries the same meaning as the French *chivalier*, a knight, and both are connected with *cheval*, a horse. *Chevalerie*, the nearest contemporary approximation to 'chivalry', carries with it resonances of skill in the art of horsemanship.

The arrival in England of chivalry in the sense of fighting on horseback can be dated very precisely. It was introduced by the Normans in 1066. In the period before the Norman invasion the English do not appear to have employed this technique: at the battle of Hastings, as in every other conventional setpiece military encounter, they fought on foot. The difference between the English fighting style and that of the Normans can be seen clearly in the Bayeux Tapestry. The two lines of soldiers in the battle scenes are virtually indistinguishable in terms of attire: they both wear mail hauberks with short sleeves and conical helms with long extensions over the nose. Where the two sides can be told apart is in their deportment and tactics. The English are shown fighting on foot wielding axes, while the Normans – or the Norman elite – fight on horseback wielding lances and sometimes swords. The sharply contrasting military traditions of the two sides influenced their whole approach to warfare. In battle the English had been accustomed to lining up in a strong defensive formation; at Hastings, therefore, Harold arrayed his men along the full length of a wide south-facing ridge. The Normans, on the other hand, tended to think more in offensive terms. The mobility given to them by the use of mounts allowed them to use shock tactics against their adversaries. At Hastings, after his infantry had failed to dislodge the English, William finally secured victory when his knights lured the English down the hill, using the ruse of the feigned retreat, then turned on their pursuers and destroyed them.

It is not altogether clear why the English had failed to develop the skills of cavalry warfare. Culturally they had close connections with Normandy, and many of the English elite, like Harold himself, would have witnessed Norman knights in action. It is hardly as if the English were not practised in the arts of horsemanship. They regularly used horses for rapid movement on campaign and in Anglo-Saxon society costly mounts were valued as symbols of status. Once on the field of battle, however, it was their practice to dismount. It is possible that this choice of tactic was related to their training in the main battle weapon they used – the axe – which was best wielded on foot. However, of greater importance perhaps was the fact that the adversaries they most often encountered, the Danes or Vikings, themselves fought on foot, offering little incentive for the development of new tactics.

If the Norman Conquest brought with it a new way of fighting and an assertive new ruling elite, it also brought a new code of honour, a more humane set of values governing the conduct of war. With the Normans came chivalry in the sense of an aristocratic ethic of restrained behaviour, an assumption on the part of the elite that they would treat one another with respect. In the period to 1066 the English had shown themselves exceptionally brutal in their treatment of losers in war and civil strife. Noblemen who found themselves at the mercy of their opponents had to reckon with the prospect of death or mutilation. By the late eleventh century that was not the Norman way of doing things. The Norman revolution involved not only a revolution in military technology; it also involved a revolution in the conduct of war. The English found themselves the beneficiaries of a medieval proto-version of the modern Geneva Convention.

The point can be illustrated by looking at two incidents which occurred soon after the conquest. The first took place at Dover when William was in the process of subduing the port after his victory.[1] On the arrival of the Norman army at the town the English defenders, demoralised by news of Harold's defeat and death, decided immediately to capitulate, despite the natural strength of the position they were defending. As they were about to yield, however, some Norman troops eager for booty set fire to the town. 'The duke,' noted his biographer William of Poitiers, 'not wishing those to suffer who had begun negotiations with him for surrender, paid for the rebuilding of their houses and made good their other losses; and he would have severely punished those who had started the fire if their numbers and base condition had not prevented their detection.' Duke William's name is not usually associated with compassionate treatment of the English in the years after the Conquest. In his conduct of hostilities, however, he behaved humanely – in contrast to the standards which the English themselves had applied before 1066. He imprisoned, but he rarely executed, and ensured the security of the non-combatants in his power.

The second incident occurred in 1068 when William was subduing the last embers of English resistance in the West Country. The citizens of Exeter had risen in rebellion, rejecting his rule and refusing to give him their fealty. William immediately set off for the south-west, and the citizens, hearing this, sent a delegation to meet him and to offer hostages. As William drew near with his army, they had second thoughts. Worried about possible Norman retribution, they retreated behind the walls and resumed resistance. William, infuriated by this volte-face, ordered one of the hostages to be blinded in view of the defenders. The siege came to its inevitable end not long afterwards. Once William's men began mining the walls, the inhabitants knew that they would have to give in. Accordingly they surrendered, coming out with their books and treasures, and threw themselves on the king's mercy. William pardoned them, 'refrained from seizing their goods, and posted a strong and trustworthy guard at the gate, so that the rank and file of the army could not break in and loot the city'.² William was simply applying the rules of war with which he had become familiar in Normandy. Once a formal surrender had been made, the citizens should be accepted into the king's peace and protected from pillage. There was no possibility that the Norman soldiery would be allowed to plunder and take booty.

The Normans' attitude stands in stark contrast to that of the English, who had always been used to taking the lives of those they had defeated in war. When Harold Godwinson had overcome Hardrada and the invading Norwegians at Stamford Bridge in 1066, he put the fleeing survivors to the sword without mercy. A century before, his predecessors had acted in the same way towards defeated Vikings: the sequel to a pitched battle had invariably been wholesale slaughter of the survivors; there was no question of the exercise of mercy. The fact that the Vikings were usually pagan doubtless encouraged and, to some extent, legitimised this policy. Yet the English were no less ruthless in their treatment of their fellow nationals on the losing side in domestic disputes. Internal feuding and political competition were invariably accompanied by blood-letting.[3] In 1016, when Earl Uhtred of Northumbria submitted to Cnut, offering hostages for good conduct, he was nonetheless executed. Twenty years later, when Alfred Æthling, Æthelred II's son, was arrested by Godwin, King Harold's father, he was so badly mutilated that he died soon afterwards. In 1041, when Earl Eadwulf approached King Harthacnut under a safe conduct, the king broke the terms of his promise and had the earl killed. The conduct of English queens in their treatment of foes was no better. In 1064 Edith, Edward the Confessor's queen, had Gospatric, an enemy of her brother Tostig, tricked and killed at her husband's court. Brutality was woven into the fabric of Anglo-Saxon political life. Where the notorious King Æthelred had led, early in the century, with the St Brice's Day massacre of the Danes in England, his kinsmen and associates, English or Anglo-Scandinavian, followed. Such behaviour was part of the tradition in which English aristocrats had been brought up. It was their way of doing things.

But it was not the Normans' way. The Normans were no less rough, tough and aggressive than the English, yet they did not routinely resort to savagery in their treatment of well-born opponents. The reason is, in large part, to be found in developments which had occurred in continental warfare in the earlier part of the eleventh century. The nobility and knights were by this time beginning to appreciate the value of treating one another in such a way as to permit mutual self-preservation. The reason for this was, paradoxically perhaps, that on the continent warfare was far more widespread than in England. In northern France and the surrounding areas of Normandy, Brittany and Anjou at the turn of the millennium disorder was endemic. Lords and castellans were constantly fighting one another, jostling for supremacy, position and power. The extensive construction of castles – a practice unknown in pre-Conquest England – led to more protracted campaigning as military outcomes were increasingly deter-mined by drawn-out sieges. In circumstances like these it was in everyone's interests to agree a set of conventions which limited the impact of hostilities on participants and their followers. An escape route had to be found from what was rapidly becoming a Hobbesian world in which life was nasty, brutish and short. The informally agreed solution was to trade property, strategic assets or political favour against the grant to a prisoner of his life. Through the offering of something of value in return for mercy, an incentive was given to a captor to spare a prisoner in his grasp, although there was never any prospect of a nobleman thinking twice before thrusting a sword into someone of inferior rank to himself. But for those with assets to trade or favours to grant, the new arrangements had the appeal of combining financial gain with self-preservation.

Against this background, a body of conventions came into existence which limited the barbarism of war while allowing it to go on. Behind this development, however, lay a second change, one perhaps still more far-reaching: the rise of a money economy. A systematic regime of property exchange – which later became ransoming – could only operate in a cash-rich society. In the early Middle Ages this had not been the situation in Europe. The supply of money was actually contracting, and in some parts of the continent there was a retreat to a barter economy. In the early ninth century, when Charlemagne had gone campaigning in Saxony, his aim had been to enslave captives: to make human beings his marketable commodity. By the late eleventh century, however, Europe had begun to turn the corner; the days of contraction were over and the economy was on the mend. Trade was expanding, new towns were being established, and the bounds of cultivation being pushed forward. People were buying and selling both locally and across long distances. In consequence, Europe was being transformed from a society of gift exchange into a monetised economy centring on market mechanisms. The effects of this seismic shift were felt not only in matters of consumption but in values and social customs. War could be absorbed into the workings of a monetised economy with benefits to all who took part in it. And because those who led in war – the nobles and knights – comprised the social as well as the military elite, the effects were felt more generally across society. A new ethic was called into being which underpinned relations between the members of Europe's upper classes.

And yet, as an ethic, this proto-chivalry was not actually as new as it seemed. There were elements embedded in the code which long predated the late eleventh and twelfth centuries. The qualities of prowess, loyalty, courage and largesse, central to the later definition of chivalry, had been esteemed by Europe's warrior elites for centuries. In a sense they were universal qualities. In all societies which have been dominated by military elites, whether in Europe or Asia, it has been the heroic qualities associated with leadership in war to which the highest respect has been paid. The martial qualities which defined twelfth-century chivalry were precisely the qualities which had been celebrated centuries before in such poems as the *Battle of Maldon*, written *c.* 1000. They were not so different in character from the heroic values and brave deeds celebrated in *Beowulf* and the Scandinavian sagas. A key element in twelfth-century chivalry was the emphasis on a knight's loyalty, the obligation on him to stand by his lord, to fight with him to the death. It is precisely this quality which is captured in the *Battle of Maldon*. Faced by a Viking onslaught, the ealdorman Byrhtnoth dies surrounded by his military household, all of them preferring death to the ignominy of flight.[4]

What was novel in the years around 1100 was the grafting onto this ancient code of a range of qualities which softened and civilised the conduct of war. To the manly qualities of honour, courage and prowess were now added the humane ones of courtesy and magnanimity, mercy and generosity. A commander who in earlier times, having captured a castle, would have promptly despatched the garrison, now granted them their lives. Once a formal surrender agreement had been made he would allow the garrison free egress, release the castellan on condition of good behaviour, and grant the prisoners their freedom.[5] In this way, he would win praise for his actions, enhancing his repute at the same time as encouraging imitation by others and promoting a currency of honourable conduct. The chronicler Orderic Vitalis, a perceptive observer of Anglo-Norman society, praised King William Rufus for going above and beyond the bounds of political prudence in his magnanimity to his enemies. Rufus's release of his enemy Helias of la Flèche in 1099 attracted the widespread admiration of those who wrote about his career.[6] It was considered a great act of courtesy.

A by-product of England's absorption into the emergent world of chivalry was to heighten the sense of difference between the English, or

Anglo-Normans, and the non-English peoples of the British Isles. Before 1066, socially and culturally the peoples of the British Isles had all belonged to much the same sort of world. They all fought using the same tactics and the same weapons. Their warfare was marked by savagery and brutality. Their forces burned, raped and pillaged in campaigns of devastation. In battle, when they had rounded up their prisoners, they carried them off to slavery back home. Those whom they could not enslave they immediately killed or mutilated. They neither gave quarter, nor did they show mercy or humanity to the defeated or innocent. Internal wars were conducted according to the same rough and ready rules. When one side gained the edge over the other, victory was accompanied by bloodletting and mutilation.

By the twelfth century, when the Normanised English had renounced the inhuman methods of the past, the fighting of war in this way by the non-English peoples of the British Isles struck contemporaries as barbaric. Of the conduct of the Scots on their invasion of England in 1138, Orderic Vitalis wrote, 'A ferocious army of Scots invaded England with the utmost brutality and gave full rein to their brutality, treating the people of the borders with bestial cruelty. They spared no one, killing young and old alike, and even butchered pregnant women by savagely disembowelling them with their swords.'[7] Another chronicler, Henry of Huntingdon, wrote in a similar vein, accusing the Scots of murdering pregnant women, impaling children on their spears and butchering priests at their altars. The Scots' conduct of war seemed to the English unnaturally cruel and barbaric. Their treatment of non-combatants caught up in hostilities came across as pitiless and scarcely Christian. The English chroniclers of the twelfth century began to articulate a new view of the Celtic peoples as culturally inferior to themselves. William of Malmesbury, a writer exhibiting all the condescension of the literati, saw them as barbarians who lacked the polish and civilisation of the English.

Back in the age of Bede, five centuries before, the Celtic peoples had been admired by the English for their cultural achievements. By the eleventh and twelfth centuries that was no longer the case: culturally and economically, they had fallen behind their neighbours. Wales, Scotland and Ireland lacked towns and cities, fairs and markets – the attributes of a developed economy. Its people were poorer and more shaggy-looking, and their houses mere hovels. The

English were conscious of their own increase in wealth and material prosperity, and their Celtic neighbours seemed underdeveloped by comparison. In the highlands to the north and west the European monetised economy petered out, and in the non-English parts of the British Isles the infrastructure allowing for the ransoming and exchange of prisoners hardly existed. In England the attitudes and institutions of chivalry could develop; in the Celtic lands they could not.

The Rise of the Mounted Knight

If chivalry in one sense involved a revolution in the rules governing war, in another it involved a revolution in the actual fighting of war. Chivalry and the art of fighting on horseback went together. The words chivalry, *cheval* and *chevalier* are cognate, and *chevalerie* was the collective term which contemporaries used to describe a group of mounted knights. The richly accoutred knight was England's first cavalier. How had the rise of mounted warfare come about? And how did it lead to a social as well as a military revolution?

The earliest references to European cavalry warfare are to be found back in the sixth and seventh centuries in the lands of the Frankish kings. The Franks, unlike most of their fellow Germanic tribesmen, appear to have mastered the technique of fighting on horseback. As early as 507 reference is made to them deploying mounted units on campaign. In that year the Merovingian ruler Clovis published an edict regulating the taking of fodder and water for the use of his men's horses. In the eighth century mounted units were a regular feature of the forces of the Emperor Charlemagne and his father.

The emergence of cavalry encouraged the development of a social elite for one very straightforward reason: it greatly increased the cost of warfare, so that only the rich could then afford it. A mounted warrior needed a horse – one specially bred and trained – and that was expensive. Ideally, he needed a second horse, lest the first was killed beneath him. He also needed ample numbers of servants, stable boys and esquires to attend to his own necessities and those of his horses. There was a further factor: a warrior needed, above all, the leisure time to devote to regular training and exercise, essential if he were to master the difficult art of fighting on horseback. By the tenth century the knight's need for expensive, full-time training appears to have become so pressing that he was released from the daily grind of tilling the soil and was supported instead either by the grant of a piece of land, tilled by a dependent tenantry, or by the provision of residence in his lord's household.

By itself, however, the rise of this new method of fighting would not have led to the appearance of the body of attitudes we associate with chivalry. The art of fighting on horseback, as we have seen, originated well before the development of chivalry in its mature form. More than cavalry fighting itself, it was developments in combat tactics which provided the stimulus to the growth of a culture which enveloped knights in mystique. In the second half of the 1000s a new way was developed of using the lance as an offensive weapon.[8] Until this period the lance or spear had been used in any number of ways: it had been carried, gripped at roughly the point of balance, with the right arm extended, so as to deliver an underarm blow; it had been carried high in the air to deliver an overarm thrust, as shown in the Bayeux Tapestry; or it had been used as a projectile, hurled at the enemy from close quarters. To these well-established methods of delivery in the eleventh century was added a fourth: horse, rider and lance all gathered into what has been called a human projectile. Here, the knight, with his lance tucked tightly under his right armpit and his left arm handling the reins, would charge at his opponent to deliver a massive hammer blow at the moment of impact. If this lethal manoeuvre was to be effective, a much heavier lance would be needed; a light wooden lance would simply shatter on impact. The knight would also need a much more solid saddle bow if he were not to be swept from his seat by the shock of contact. All the essential elements – weapon, saddlery and tactics – appear to have come together in the second half of the eleventh century. And when that moment arrived, the mounted warrior acquired an unprecedented level of destructiveness. He had become the Sherman tank of medieval warfare and commanded the marvelling attention of contemporaries.

At the same time, he found himself needing yet more hours of training and exercise. By the early twelfth century he was beginning to find these in tournaments. It is no coincidence that around the time that these developments were occurring we hear the first mention of these events. They were to become one of the central institutions of medieval chivalry, places where knights perfected their technique while simultaneously gaining in repute and developing a collective identity. The origins of tournaments are to be found in continental Europe in the late eleventh century.[9] The earliest such events appear to have been held on the borders of France and the Holy Roman Empire in the area of Valenciennes and Tournai. In 1095, in what may be the first reference to such a gathering, Count Henry III of Brabant is reported to have been killed in a joust before his household and that of the castellan of Tournai, whom he was visiting. Early the next century, Count Charles of Flanders is said by his biographer to have enjoyed travelling to France with his knights to take part in tournaments in order to enhance his reputation and the power and glory of his county.

Tournaments may have come into being as a by-product of the so-called Peace Movement of the eleventh century. At a time when reformist churchmen were struggling to curb the lawlessness of fighters in areas where princely authority was weak, organised fights provided knights with a way of refining their skills while technically remaining within the letter of the law. Early tournaments bore little if any resemblance to the carefully choreographed encounters of later centuries. They were serious affairs – mock battles fought between teams of a hundred or more knights on each side who fought until they had driven their opponents from the field. The word tournament, coined to describe such events, meaning 'to revolve' or 'to whirl around', conveyed exactly what they were like. After the initial change, the knights engaged in a heaving melee, using their swords to unhorse members of the opposing team. The rise of the tournament coincided almost exactly with increased use of the technique of charging with the couched lance. The rough and tumble of the tournament provided ambitious young tyros with precisely the training they needed to master this challenging tactic.

By the 1120s and 1130s tournaments were being held at sites all over mainland Europe and in England. The keenest of the young bachelors, like William Marshal, made their round of the tourneying circuit every year, showing off their prowess while perfecting their fighting techniques. As the men engaged and bonded with one another, so they developed modes of thought and habits of conduct which bound them together as a group. They established a brotherhood in arms which transcended the ties of lordship, family and ethnic identity. Tournaments can thus be seen as a key institution in both nurturing and sustaining the culture and the performance of chivalry. At the same time they introduced young knights to the role which money could play in the regulation of military conduct. Early in the history of tourneying a convention was developed that if a combatant was taken prisoner, he could secure his release by paying a ransom to his captor. It was also accepted that the captor was entitled to claim the armour and horse of his captive as legitimate spoils of battle. In these respects the conventions of tourneying precisely anticipated the conventions which came to apply in the conduct of war more generally.

A minority of those who made the round of the tournament circuit were wealthy aristocrats, the sons of kings or the lords of territories like Count Charles of Flanders. A much larger proportion, however, were men of lesser means who were looking to make a name for themselves. In earlier times, men of this sort would scarcely have been regarded as noble at all. They were considered merely 'free', inferior in blood to the better-born aristocrats. Such jobbing soldiers might enjoy a limited distinction because they were skilled in horsemanship, something which raised them above those who fought on foot; however, they hardly warranted mention in the same breath as the grander knights. In the course of the eleventh century this situation began to change. The lesser – that is, the landless – knights rose in status and esteem, attaining a rough equality with their betters. This major social shift proved the precursor to the final stage in the evolution of chivalry – the merging of the greater and the lesser knights to form a single elite group defined by military leadership. When this last development occurred, chivalry in its fully developed form may be said to have arrived.

The gradual rise in status of the lesser knights can be traced in the changing use of words – in fact, just two words, both of them Latin – *miles* meaning 'knight', and *dominus* meaning 'lord'. The one travelled down the social scale, while the other travelled up. In the eleventh century *dominus* moved rapidly down the scale. Originally used to describe members of the elite, by 1100 it was being applied more widely, describing first barons and castellans and later mere knights. By the end of the twelfth century quite humble knights were described as *dominus* – or lord – in witness lists to charters. *Miles*, on the other hand, travelled in the opposite direction. A classical Latin word meaning 'soldier' entirely devoid of connotations of rank, it came to be applied to men who were considered *domini*. *Miles* was acquiring honorific associations which in earlier times it had lacked. As the martial values of prowess and courage with which it was associated spread throughout aristocratic society, so the title was applied to those in higher social levels. What this development indicates is that knighthood and social status were fusing together. The greater and the lesser knights were merging into a single group, clothing themselves in an elite identity which marked them from those in lower ranks.

Why the social elevation of the *milites* occurred is not altogether clear. One possible explanation is that it was linked to the spread of seigneurial castles across northern and central France, which was happening at this time. Castles were of little use to their owners unless they were staffed and defended by permanent and mobile garrisons. When members of the knightly warrior class took on garrison duty, they climbed a step or two up the social ladder. Typically these men were provided with board and lodging in the castle, and perhaps also paid a fee. Living in close proximity to the lord, they found something of that lord's superiority rubbing off onto them. In status, if not in economic means, they acquired a degree of parity with the older nobility.

The outward and visible sign of the formation of a single knightly class was its ceremony of admission. Knighthood, a form of chivalric Freemasonry, was equipped with its own initiation rite. The act of dubbing, or making, a knight is first recorded in the later eleventh century. Outwardly it had much in common with the ancient ritual of the delivery of arms to a young vassal on coming of age. Like the warrior of the early Middle Ages, the apprentice knight was invested by a senior knight or relative with a sword and belt, the symbols of his station. Around 1065 a young Norman knight, Robert of Rhuddlan, was girded with a sword by King Edward the Confessor of England, at whose court he was living. In 1086 the future King Henry I, a younger son of the Conqueror, was girded with hauberk, helmet and swordbelt by Archbishop Lanfranc. In 1100 Count Fulk of Anjou was to recall how, at Pentecost forty years before, he had been girded with a sword by his uncle, Count Geoffrey of Anjou.

What distinguished the knighting ceremony from the established giving of arms was the semi-ritualistic character of the later event. It was much more than a coming of age. The most impressive knightings could be occasions of some grandeur. John of Marmoutier gives this account of the knighting in 1128 by King Henry I of a later Geoffrey of Anjou on the eve of his marriage to Matilda, the king's daughter:

> On the great day, as required by the custom for making knights, baths were prepared for use. After having cleansed his body, and come from the purification of bathing, the noble offspring of the count of Anjou dressed himself in a linen undershirt, putting on a robe woven with gold and a surcoat of a rich purple hue. His stockings were of silk, and on his feet he wore shoes with little golden lions on them. His companions, who were to be knighted with him, were all clothed in linen and purple. He left his privy chamber and paraded in public, accompanied by his noble retinue. The horses were led, arms carried to be distributed to each in turn . . . He wore a matching hauberk made of double mail . . . To his ankles were fastened golden spurs. A shield hung from his neck on which were golden images of lioncels . . . he carried a sword from the royal treasure, bearing an ancient inscription over which the superlative Wayland had sweated with much labour and application in the smiths' forge.[10]

A generation later, the English scholar John of Salisbury gave an idealised description of another knighting in his *Policraticus* (*Statesman's Book*). John saw his ceremony beginning in traditional fashion with the girding of the new knight 'with the belt of a soldier'. At its climax, however, John introduced a novelty: John's knight was to walk in solemn procession to a church, where he would place his sword on the altar, dedicating both himself and his sword to the service of God.[11]

It can hardly be supposed that all twelfth-century knightings took the elaborate liturgical form which John of Salisbury thought fitting. John's description represented more the aspirations of the ecclesiastical reformers of knighthood than day-to-day reality. For the most part, knightings remained firmly secular in character. On some occasions, however, they could be staged on a grand enough scale. Writing in the 1130s, Geffrei Gaimar was to recall a mass knighting which King

William Rufus had carried out at the feast inaugurating the new Westminster Hall at Whitsun 1099. 'The knighting was so splendid,' he wrote, 'that people will talk of it for evermore. The king dubbed [men] in such style that the whole of London was resplendent with knights. And what am I to say about such a feast? Simply that it was so magnificent that it could not possibly have been more so.'[12] By Gaimar's time the knighting ceremony was beginning to mark the knight's entry into a charmed circle, his admission into the company of the blue-blooded. The knight was no longer a jobbing soldier, a mere warrior; he was on his way to becoming a figure of standing and status.

In the mid- to late twelfth century all the elements which were to coalesce in medieval chivalry gradually came together. Nobility, knighthood and courtesy fused to create an aristocratic ethic which surrounded knights with charisma and mystique. In the early 1200s men actually began to talk about chivalry – and in about 1220 an anonymous author could write of an 'order of chivalry' (*L'Ordene de Chevalerie*). Chivalry was an aristocratic ethos which had its origins in the broad open landscapes of northern France and the Low Countries. In its embryonic form it was introduced into England by the Normans after 1066. It was to attain its full flowering a century or two later in the cosmopolitan world of the Angevin and Plantagenet kings. In later medieval England it was to become one of the decisive influences in the shaping of aristocratic culture.

2

Chivalry and Empire, 1066–1204

The Normans who introduced the new culture of chivalry to England were one of the most dynamic and assertive peoples of medieval Europe. In just a couple of generations they not only conquered England, they established social and political ascendancy over much of southern Italy and Sicily, provided the leadership of the First Crusade and were instrumental in the creation of the crusader kingdom in the east. In the British Isles they carried William I's conquest forward across the Severn and the Wye into south Wales, while individual Normans settled in southern Scotland at the behest of King David I, among them the ancestor of Robert Bruce. Wherever the Normans went, they took with them their religious and cultural values. From the Cheviots to the deserts of Syria, from the borders of Brittany to the toe of Italy, the Normans were agents for the dissemination of brave new ideas on how things should be done.

The effect of the events of 1066 was to create an entirely new polity in north-western Europe, a polity of unprecedented size and resources, the combined dominion of England and Normandy. The creation of this regional superpower naturally aroused the enmity and distaste of the kings of France. The dukes of Normandy were nominally vassals – that is to say, feudal tenants – of the French kings. Back in the 1040s Henry I of France had actually assisted the young Duke William in his struggle with his unruly barons. As a result of the conquest of England, however, the duke was transformed into an overmighty subject, a potential challenger to French royal supremacy – and that right on the king's doorstep in the Seine valley. Within ten years of 1066 it became a key aim of French policy to undermine the Norman (and later the Angevin) position in France – indeed, to sever the link between Normandy and England altogether. The struggle between the two powers was to be a long and bitter one, and it was conducted by fair means and foul. Whenever there were dissensions within the Anglo-Norman or Angevin elites, the French exploited them ruthlessly. Before 1066 England had only intermittently been involved in continental military entanglements. Wars had generally been forced on her by invaders from without, usually from the north. In the wake of the Norman Conquest the position changed: the new realm was constantly engaged in war – war in defence of the state created by the Conquest. There was no shortage of military activity to occupy the attentions of the new Anglo-Norman knightly class. England became a country geared to meeting the manpower, financial and logistical demands generated by the strategic needs of her new masters.

Money, the Sinews of War

The constant military pressure created an intense demand for knights, and the heyday of the Anglo-Norman rulers witnessed a seller's market for the professional mounted combat soldier. According to the chronicler William of Malmesbury, in England King William Rufus's needs were such that 'sellers sold to him at their own prices and knights fixed their own rates of pay'.[1] The position was much the same on the other side of the Channel in Normandy. Rufus's elder brother, Duke Robert, who held the duchy, cast far and wide to find knights. When, by the mid-1090s, he found himself running short of money to pay their wages, he turned in desperation to his brother. Anxious to enlist on the Pope's great crusade to the east, Robert pawned Normandy to his sibling for 10,000 marks to finance his retinue.

Knights seeking employment had no difficulty finding suitable openings in the Anglo-Norman world. According to William of Malmesbury again, William FitzOsbern, a close ally of the Conqueror, was said to be almost reckless in the amount that he spent on knights.[2] Among the rulers of the day, King William Rufus was particularly famous for his liberality. Suger, abbot of Saint-Denis near Paris and a shrewd observer of the contemporary scene, described Rufus as 'that wealthy man, a pourer out of English treasure, a wonderful merchant and paymaster of knights'.[3] According to William of Malmesbury once again, 'knights flocked to him from every region this side of the Alps and he bestowed funds on them lavishly'.[4] Liberality, a chivalric virtue, was also, for Rufus, a virtue born of necessity. In the late eleventh and twelfth centuries the successful ruler was the free-spending ruler, one who had the means to hire and reward knights. The amount that Rufus spent on recruiting knights caused astonishment among his contemporaries. In 1094 he was described as showering gold, silver and lands on the knights he weaned away from their allegiance to his brother Robert. In 1095 he sent his younger brother Henry, the future Henry I, to Normandy 'with ample funds' to lure yet more knights to England. In 1097 and 1098 he took knights into his pay from France, Brittany, Flanders and Burgundy. After he became king on his brother's death in 1100, Henry was just as lavish. In 1103 he entered into a treaty with the count of Flanders, whereby the count in return for an annual pension of £500 was to supply him with 1,000 knights in England against invasion or rebellion, 1,000 knights to serve in Normandy or 500 knights in Maine.[5]

Renowned though they both were for the scale of their spending on knights, neither Henry I nor Rufus actually showed much interest in putting their men to the test in battle. Henry fought just two field battles in the course of his long career, and Rufus none at all. Rufus usually achieved his ends by the more convenient, if less chivalric, tactic of bribery. According to William of Malmesbury, in 1088 Rufus secured the castles of Saint-Valery and Aumale in Normandy 'by his usual methods, by bribing the men in charge'.[6] Henry was resourceful in a slightly different way. In the words of the same chronicler, Henry 'preferred to fight with policy rather than with the sword; he triumphed, if he could, without spilling blood'.[7] Contemporary thinking on strategy was anyway sceptical of risking all in an armed engagement; the outcome was too uncertain. In reality, neither king found himself often needing to resort to arms: he could achieve virtually all he wanted by relying on the sheer power of his reputation. The knowledge of his wealth and his capacity to hire mercenaries was enough to make an adversary think twice before taking him on.

Where did all these mercenary knights come from? Certain areas proved especially fertile as recruiting grounds.[8] Many knights came from the poorer, pastoral peripheries of the Norman-Angevin empire, such as Wales and Brittany. According to William of Malmesbury,

Henry I employed Bretons 'because those people are so poverty stricken in their homeland that they earn their pay by gold in service abroad'. The large and increasingly overcrowded cities of Flanders also proved good recruiting territory, as Henry I's treaty showed. Flemings were employed by the rebels of 1173–4 and by King John in the winter of 1215–16 in his campaign in the north of England. William of Ypres, King Stephen's main mercenary captain, was a Fleming. Towards the end of the twelfth century, soldiers from Brabant, adjoining Flanders, figured with particular prominence in the armies of the Angevin and French kings. In 1174 Henry II crossed from France to England to confront his adversaries 'with a mounted retinue and a crowd of Brabanters'. In 1191 a force mobilised on Richard I's behalf by his chancellor in England, William Longchamp, included Brabanters and hired Flemish mercenaries. One of Richard's most celebrated commanders in the east was his mercenary captain Mercadier, the so-called 'prince of the Brabanters'.

A good number of the knights taken on by the Anglo-Norman and Angevin kings were retained as permanent members of the king's household. The king's extended household was, in one of its guises, an essentially military body. In the administrative records it was usually referred to as the *familia regis*, to distinguish it from the *domus*, the more courtly establishment ministering to the king's domestic needs. By the time of Edward I (reigned 1272–1307) it was a body of several hundred men, mostly knights and esquires, the numbers expanding and contracting in line with the king's military commitments. The household provided the core element of all the king's armies. In 1298, when Edward I launched a major invasion of Scotland, the household provided no fewer than 800 men, over a quarter and perhaps as much as a third of all the cavalry. In a very real sense, the English army was simply the king's household in arms writ large.

The situation in Edward I's reign corresponded in all essentials to that of the late eleventh and twelfth centuries. At the heart of every royal army in the Anglo-Norman and Angevin periods were the knights of the king's household. Orderic Vitalis, a chronicler with a special interest in military matters, provides many insights into the organisation of the army in the campaigns of the Anglo-Norman period.[9] He says that in the war of Sainte-Suzanne in Normandy, which stretched over the years 1084–6, the Conqueror left the task of mopping up resistance in neighbouring Maine to the troops of his household. In his account of Rufus's reign he tells us that the king's household was active in the campaign in the Vexin, which followed the king's acquisition of Normandy from his brother, and that it supplied garrisons for castles in Maine. For the long reign of Henry I (1100–35) he provides more detailed comment. Orderic says that members of the household were active in the campaigns of 1105 and 1106 which led to the king's decisive victory over his brother at Tinchebrai. He also records that the household played a key role in the campaigns of 1118 and 1119 against the king of France and Robert's son William Clito. He shows how the king's household knights were used to provide manpower for castle garrisons, explaining that, when King Henry was suppressing a rebellion led by Waleran, count of Meulan, he dispersed his household men across castles at Gisors, Evreux, Bernay and elsewhere. Occasionally, Orderic provides an indication of the numbers involved. He says that in 1119 there were 200 knights in one detachment of the household, suggesting an overall strength considerably higher. In his account of 1124 he reports that 300 knights, supported by horsed archers, were mobilised to deal with a rebel force led by Count Waleran.

It is likely that many of the household knights were mercenaries with little or no land to their name; a few at least, however, were quite senior men. On Orderic's evidence, Alan the Red, count of Brittany, William de Warenne, Richer and Gilbert de Laigle, all magnates of high rank, served for spells in a household capacity. Men of this standing would have acted as corps commanders, leaders of the contingents which provided the backbone of the larger royal army. Although rich and well born, they would have seen nothing demeaning in serving at the king's command. On the contrary, they would have regarded it as a path to chivalric distinction and a convenient means of gaining access to the king's ear, the fountainhead of patronage and favour.

The armies of the Anglo-Norman and Angevin kings were thus highly professional bodies kept in the field by a steady flow of money from the royal treasury. Yet it has often been thought, largely on the evidence of Domesday Book, that the true basis of knightly obligation in this period was not money, but land. A picture has been painted of knights serving in the royal host in return for grants of lands from superiors, part of which they might in turn grant to sub-tenants, and there is certainly evidence that feudal contractual structures of land-holding were crucial to the functioning of society in this period. The reciprocal ties of sponsorship and service forged between lord and vassal were to form the basis of all landholding law for a long time to come. What is not so clear, however, is the proportion of knights in the king's host provided through this system of landed obligation. The provision of knight service finds surprisingly little mention in the writings of Orderic Vitalis, William of Malmesbury and the other chroniclers; and Orderic for one was particularly attentive to matters of military organisation. It seems, on the whole, more likely that the Anglo-Norman and Angevin kings chose to meet their needs from a pool of professionals on whom they could call rather than from feudal tenancies. In the field highly trained mercenaries or household knights would always be of more value to a commander than ill-trained or ill-equipped part-timers.

If feudalism as a contemporary reality had little in common with textbook theory, it is nonetheless unwise to dismiss it as a mere figment of the historical imagination. The quotas notionally provided by feudal landholdings were actually of very considerable value to the king – and the emphasis should be on 'value'. Commuted for cash, they could be a lucrative source of revenue to the king's treasury. Feudalism is most convincingly understood as a rich, almost infinitely exploitable nexus of financial privileges. At every point in the feudal landholding structure there was a right or obligation which could be turned into money. As early as 1100 it is recorded that the king was taking money payments in lieu of personal military service – the payments known as scutage (literally 'shield money'). Henry I, in his Coronation Charter of 1100, disavowed his predecessor's collection of scutage, though he was soon to go back on his promise. Other payments could be realised from the rights of ownership which a lord retained over an estate after he had granted it to a tenant. When a feudal tenant died and his son took his place, the lord was entitled to a sum known as relief, a succession duty. In the event that a tenant died leaving a son under age, the lord was entitled to take his lands into temporary custody – wardship – allowing him access to the income of the estate for the duration of the minority. If the tenant died leaving not a son but a daughter or daughters, the lord could make money from the sale of the marriages or alternatively use the daughters' marriages as a source of patronage. Should he find himself faced with an emergency need for cash, for example to pay for a knighting ceremony, feudal custom also allowed him to levy a tax known as an aid on his tenants.

In all these ways and others, feudal tenurial structures could be made to yield money for those fortunate enough to have tenants holding from them. The system was of the greatest value to the greatest lord, the king. As the person at the apex of the feudal pyramid, the king could also profit from his subjects' needs by charging for the various privileges and perquisites they were always seeking. If money-raising under the Normans and Angevins looks more like a system of irregular plundering than a modern system of public taxation, it still worked. It provided the king with an effective way of securing his share of the huge wealth of the upper classes.

In the twelfth century the revenues yielded by such payments could be very considerable. In 1129–30, the first year for which figures survive, Henry I's exchequer accounted for receipts of £23,000, a massive sum by the standards of the day. Of this amount, just over £11,000 was accounted for by the king's lands (the royal demesne) and an astonishing £10,000 by feudal windfalls and other incidental payments. Among the receipts in this latter category were sums of £1,000 for 'an agreement' with the king (no details given) paid by Robert FitzWalter, and 1,000 marks (£666) paid by William de Pont de l'Arche for the marriage of Robert Mauduit's daughter and the office of king's chamberlain, which Robert held.[10] To these incidental sums could be added the yield from the geld – the ancient land tax, which was likewise very considerable, albeit by the twelfth century in decline. Kings used the income from this assortment of sources to hire the best knights available, the professionals who made their living from soldiering. The renown of such knights ensured that their names would be well known to the king and his household officers. Usually they had made their reputations on the tournament circuit. The most celebrated knight of the late twelfth century, and certainly the most familiar to us today, was William Marshal (often referred to by his official title of 'the Marshal'), the younger son of a baron who rose to be regent of England in the minority years of Henry III. Shortly after his death in 1219 the Marshal's life story was written up as a poem at the dictation of an esquire in his service.[11] It opens a remarkable window onto the world of chivalric values at the turn of the twelfth and thirteenth centuries.

The Life of William Marshal

William Marshal was born around 1147, the fourth son by his second marriage of John FitzGilbert the Marshal, a middling baron with lands in Berkshire and the Thames valley. At the age of about twelve, the boy was found a place in the household of his mother's cousin, the wealthy Norman baron William de Tancarville, whose estates lay in the lower Seine valley. The farming out of youngsters to others was standard practice in medieval aristocratic society. In 1167 William was knighted by his master and fought for him in a skirmish near the border. The next year he transferred to the service of another relative, his uncle Patrick, earl of Salisbury. He was already gaining a formidable reputation as a tourneyer, regularly unhorsing opponents and taking prizes and ransoms. In 1168 his loyalty and skill on campaign in Poitou brought him to the attention of Henry II's queen, Eleanor of Aquitaine. It was through Eleanor's patronage that in 1169 he was awarded responsibility for the training in arms of her son, the king's heir, Henry the Young King.

Royal service was to be of crucial significance in promoting William's social advance, because it gave him access to perhaps the most prestigious knightly entourage of his day. Henry the Young King was a popular if highly impressionable young man. Each year he took William, his 'dearest friend' as he called him, as his companion on the tourneying circuit of northern France, spending freely of his allowance from his father as he did so. Service with the Young King was not without its pitfalls and hazards. In 1173 the ambitious royal heir rose in rebellion against his father, and William appears to have got caught up in the struggle, although his biographer understandably says little of the episode. After 1174, when agreement was reached between father and son, restoring peace to the Angevin world, William and the Young King threw themselves back into the tournament circuit. For the next decade William regularly attended three, four or five tournaments each year, enhancing his reputation at the same time as growing rich on prize money. By 1180 he had the means to maintain his own establishment of knights.

The sheer scale of his success aroused jealousy among his less talented rivals. In 1182, as criticism mounted, some malcontents levelled accusations against him of feathering his own nest at the expense of his employer. For a year or so he was banished from the Young King's household, and he had to seek a livelihood with other lords. Before long, however, he was welcomed back. In 1183 he was at the Young King's side when the latter died at the castle of Martel on the Dordogne. It was to the Marshal that the dying prince entrusted the sacred charge of going on his behalf on crusade to the Holy Land.

From 1184 to 1186 William was in the Latin east, waging war against the infidel. On his return he was awarded a position in the household of the king himself. This was another crucial appointment. At the king's side he had immediate access to the fountainhead of royal favour. In 1189, when Henry II died, he managed apparently effortlessly the transition to the regime of his successor, Richard the Lionheart, and scooped up yet more rewards. Shortly after the new king's accession William was granted a prize of almost unimaginable value – the hand in marriage of Isabel de Clare, heiress to the earldom of Pembroke, one of the richest inheritances in the land. Secure in landed wealth, he was set on the path that would take him to a position of supreme importance in national affairs and ultimately to the regency in 1216.

In twenty years William had risen from obscurity to the very top of the feudal aristocracy. The foundations of his remarkable career were found in the specific circumstances of the time. In the later twelfth century it was perfectly possible for a talented young knight to turn a career in errantry into a career in royal service. Sideways switches of this kind posed no problem in a socially fluid world where men could move freely between households and across the frontiers of lordships and polities. Undoubtedly luck played a part in the Marshal's ascent: he seems always to have been in the right place in the right company at the right time. More remarkable still than his good fortune, however, was his vaulting ambition. He was immensely competitive; he played to win. In tournaments he mastered one of the most difficult tactics of the day – grabbing the reins or bridle of the other knight's horse as it charged past – to attract and impress the crowd. More than most tourneyers, he aimed to make money from his exploits on the circuit. At a tournament at Eu in Normandy in 1178 or 1179 he seized as many as ten horses from his victims as prizes. Over a two-year period in the 1180s he and a partner took captive no fewer than 103 knights. At Anet in Normandy in 1179 he pre-empted a group of fellow tourneyers by immediately accepting the surrender of some knights sheltering in a barn, thereby depriving his companions of any chance of a ransom.

William Marshal was endowed with virtually all the qualities which contemporaries esteemed in a knight. He had the soldierly virtues of courage, strength, vigour and boldness. At the same time, he possessed the complementary qualities of charm, courtesy and affability. He made the consummate courtier. Yet alongside the many attributes which attracted admiration, he had a hard-headed side – he was relentlessly assertive; he was always in search of advancement. The generosity for which he was famed could sometimes be a cloak for naked self-interest. There is little sign that he was touched to any degree by the softer side of chivalry.

Yet, despite the impression given by his career, there was no paradox or inconsistency in the values by which William set store. If contemporaries associated courtesy with courts and courtliness, they also accepted that ambition and careerism could flourish in the same setting. Some twelfth-century commentators regarded courts as places where men competed ruthlessly to climb the greasy pole. To recognise this is not to suggest that polite behaviour among knights was necessarily artificial or contrived: politeness came naturally to men who frequented courts. It is, however, to suggest that courtesy and politeness, when coupled with energy and a degree of canniness, could assist an ambitious young man seeking to make his way in the world. In the 'civilised' courtly societies of the twelfth century, the setting of the so-called Twelfth-Century Renaissance, such qualities could be harnessed to serve the cause of self-advancement. It is this lesson, above all, which we learn from the career of William Marshal.

'The most remarkable man of his time' [12]

The qualities which brought fame and wealth to William Marshal were displayed still more clearly in the person of his patron Richard the Lionheart. In the eyes of most of his contemporaries Richard was quite simply the greatest princely ruler of his day. On the Third Crusade he completely overshadowed his fellow ruler King Philip II of France. He attracted the admiring attention even of his Arab enemies: Ibn al-Athir paid tribute to him as the most remarkable man of his time.[13] An energetic and ambitious ruler, he cut a figure not just on the Angevin but on the European stage. Famously he spent only five months of his reign in England, yet his influence on the development of kingship in England was immense. Almost without effort he reshaped Angevin and English kingship in his chivalric image. It was against his style that the kingship of all England's later rulers was to be judged. His successors on the throne of England were placed under a heavy burden of emulation.

Richard was born at Beaumont Palace, Oxford, in 1157, the second surviving son of Henry II and Eleanor of Aquitaine.[14] From an early age he established himself as his mother's favourite. His relations with his strong-willed and assertive father were turbulent, Richard suspecting Henry of favouring his brothers. In 1173 Richard played a key role in the rebellion of Henry the Young King against their father, which the king of France helped aggravate. In 1184 he rose in rebellion a second time, on this occasion over a plan to reapportion the Angevin lands to the advantage of his younger brother John. In July 1189 he was in rebellion yet again, and in alliance with the French king, when he received news of his father's death at Chinon (6 July).

Despite his record of filial disloyalty, Richard succeeded to an un-divided inheritance, encountering no opposition from rivals. The task to which he gave his immediate attention was that of organising a large-scale crusade to the east. Two years before, Jerusalem had fallen to Saladin following the Latins' defeat at the Horns of Hattin. With this setback the very existence of the Latin kingdom established by the First Crusade in 1100 was called into question, and help was urgently needed. After a year's preparation Richard set off in the summer of 1190 at the head of a well-equipped force numbering at least 6,000 men. He took a land route across France to Marseilles, where a fleet sent ahead from England awaited his arrival. From Marseilles he sailed down the west coast of Italy to Sicily, where he overwintered, and then on to Cyprus, which he conquered following a dispute with the local ruler. He dropped anchor off the great Muslim-held city of Acre in June 1191. Acre had been subjected to a half-hearted siege by a Christian army for over a year. Within a month of his arrival, however, Richard had reduced the place. The morale of the Christian forces, which had fallen to a low ebb, was immediately lifted.

Richard's next aim was to attempt the recovery of Jerusalem. He realised, however, that before he could advance on the Holy City he needed to take possession of the coastline, essential if the delivery of supplies was to be assured. Accordingly, in the late summer of 1191 he embarked on a long march south down the littoral across barren, sun-scorched countryside to the city of Jaffa. Constantly harried by enemy cavalry, he scored a major victory over Saladin at Arsuf (7 September) and arrived at Jaffa after a gruelling nineteen days on 10 September. With his lines of communications secure, he could now think of advancing on Jerusalem. What concerned him, however, was that, even if he took the city, he would have difficulty holding on to it because his resources were inadequate and his supply lines very extended. In December, in appalling weather, he marched to within twelve miles of the city and gazed at its distant skyline. His army was eager for an assault, but he knew that even if he breached the walls prolonged occupation of the city would be impossible. Reluctantly, he pulled back. The following year, after leading a foray deep into Egypt, he advanced on Jerusalem a second time. Again, he had to accept that an assault, however tempting, would be strategic folly. In September 1192 Richard opened negotiations with Saladin on a truce, reaching agreement on terms which guaranteed freedom of access for pilgrims to the Holy Places, and the following month embarked on the long journey home. Although Richard had failed in his primary objective of recapturing Jerusalem, he had nonetheless succeeded in stabilising the crusader state. The fact that the kingdom was to survive for another hundred years was due in no small part to his endeavours in the field.

If Richard's achievements on crusade read like a Greek epic, the story of his journey back to Europe has more of the character of stage farce. One accident after another was to dog his steps. In late November 1192 he was forced by bad weather to abandon his passage across the Mediterranean and resort instead to the difficult land route across the Alps. Worse still, in December, as he was emerging from the Alpine foothills, he was arrested by his old adversary Leopold, duke of Austria, who nursed a grievance against him from the crusade, and handed over to the emperor of Germany. For over a year the terms of Richard's release were the subject of tortuous negotiations between representatives of the Angevin and imperial governments. At the beginning of 1194, however, a ransom of no less than 100,000 marks was finally agreed; arrangements were set in motion in England to raise the money, and in February Richard was set free.

Once back in his dominions Richard embarked on the massive task of recovering the territories which had been lost to the French in his years of absence. In the north and west of France the situation was particularly serious. In Normandy Philip had conquered most of the area east of the Seine; in Touraine and Poitou he had taken possession of the castles of Loches and Châtillon-sur-Indre, while in Aquitaine the barons had raised the banner of revolt. Richard set about responding to these challenges with energy. In May he stabilised the frontier in the Seine valley and upper Normandy, moving south to relieve French pressure on castles in Touraine. When he felt that he had strengthened his position sufficiently, he agreed to a truce with the French at Tillières.

The following year the struggle resumed. In July or August Philip destroyed Richard's castle of Vaudreil, south of Rouen, while Richard retaliated by attacking Philip's lands further south. In 1196 Richard and Philip reached an agreement at Louviers, whereby Richard recovered virtually all the lands that he had lost except for border territories in Normandy. Philip, however, would not give up. In 1198 he returned to the fray, but Richard worsted him in an engagement at Gisors, in the course of which the French king was unhorsed and thrown into the River Epte. The contest between the two kings only ended when Richard was killed by a crossbow bolt at Chalus-Chabrol in the Limousin in April 1199.

Richard's military career – although, like Henry V's later, brought to a premature end – was one of the most outstanding of the Middle Ages. Richard showed himself to be a brilliant commander, a master of the art of siegecraft and a charismatic leader of men. He did not fight many battles because he did not need to. He could always rely on achieving his objectives by other means. In accordance with contemporary practice, he put his trust in the reduction of castles, the wasting of enemy lands and the outwitting or outmanoeuvring of his adversary's forces, rather than in the hazard of battle. But he was never lacking in bravery. Richard was a Napoleon of his age. His military genius was recognised across Europe and beyond.

The effect of his reign in England was to strengthen the Angevin dynasty's identification with chivalric and knightly values. Richard's two most able immediate predecessors, Henry I and Henry II, had both in their different ways been very successful in arms. Richard's achievements, however, were of an altogether greater order. What distinguished Richard was that he made a virtue rather than a necessity of war.[15] He showed how war, particularly crusading war, could strengthen and legitimise kingship. From his reign on, not only was the waging of war to figure more prominently in the expectations that people had of their kings; success or otherwise in arms was to be the test by which a king's exercise of his duties was to be measured. For Richard's successors, his was the career against which theirs would be judged.

Richard's magic was to work its effect in various ways. In the first place, the memory of his achievements was to live on after him. His struggle in the east with his rival Saladin was to become legendary, with poems and tales written in celebration of it.[16] And, if Richard's genuine achievements on crusade were not enough, new ones were soon added to them. A story which gained wide circulation concerned a legendary personal encounter with Saladin. According to this yarn, Richard accepted a challenge from Saladin to a duel, riding a horse which had been given to him by his Muslim opponent. The gift was a trick: the horse was a colt born to the mare which Saladin was going to ride, and the plan was that when the mare whinnied the colt would lie down, leaving Richard at his opponent's mercy. However, Richard was forewarned of the danger by an angel. Preparing for the duel by stuffing his colt's ears with wax, he entered the lists. When Saladin's mare whinnied and the colt did not react, Richard, taking advantage of his opponent's discomfiture, unhorsed him and chased him from the field. In 1251 Henry III was to commission a wall painting of the story to decorate a chamber of his palace at Clarendon in Wiltshire, and a series of floor tiles depicting the duel were laid at Clarendon, the Tower of London and elsewhere. The episode quickly became popular enough to enjoy wide literary and artistic circulation.

Another story which enjoyed wide popularity told of the king's captivity in Germany. Its origins concerned his nickname – Coeur de Lion – which was a contemporary sobriquet. According to this tale, the king of Germany's daughter fell in love with Richard when he was in prison and spent some agreeable nights with him. When the girl's father learned of the liaison, he planned Richard's murder by having a hungry lion introduced to his cell. But Richard, armed only with silk handkerchiefs, was able to kill the lion by thrusting an arm down the beast's throat and tearing out its heart – which he then proceeded to sprinkle with salt and eat in front of the astonished king and his court. To the period of Richard's imprisonment also belongs the famous story of Blondel, the fictitious minstrel who is said to have discovered the king's whereabouts by singing songs outside castle after castle until at last he heard the king answering back. Legend gathered around Richard's name, it seems, almost spontaneously.

Nonetheless, the growth of the subsequent cult owed more than a little to Richard's own encouragement. Richard was a master of the art of self-promotion, aware that his image needed careful burnishing and manipulation. He took care to keep his subjects well informed of his diplomatic coups and victories in the field abroad and was one of the first English kings regularly to use newsletters. Whenever he scored a major triumph, he made sure to publicise it. On his way to the east in 1191 he wrote to the justiciar William Longchamp justifying his seizure of the kingdom of Cyprus. Seven years later, when back in Normandy, he described his victory over King Philip and the French on the bridge at Gisors. These semi-official documents were circulated and copied into the chronicles.

Richard also took care to ensure that his achievements were sympathetically reported by those accompanying him in the field. In the work of Ambroise, the minstrel who travelled with him on the Third Crusade, he secured a full and sympathetic account of his exploits in the east. Ambroise tells the story of how, when Emperor Isaac of Cyprus asked to be spared being fettered in iron, Richard fettered him in silver chains. The story, presumably fed to Ambroise, was one calculated to emphasise Richard's power and make him appear a new Caesar. Richard, with his eye for publicity, was well aware of the importance of the grand gesture. When he set off on the crusade, he took the sword Excalibur with him. By assiduous self-promotion he ensured widespread support for himself in his dominions. In England, in the course of time, he became a popular hero.

By one very practical measure Richard strengthened the identification of the knightly class with his own values: he authorised the reintroduction into England of tournaments. Tourneying had been viewed disapprovingly by Henry II, who had banned the activity in England on the grounds that it encouraged disorder. Accordingly, knights who wanted to gain fighting experience had been obliged to go abroad – as William Marshal had done.

In 1194, according to William of Newburgh, Richard reversed his predecessor's policy, introducing a system of licensing.[17] Five places in England
were designated official tournament sites: the fields between Salisbury
and Wilton in Wiltshire, between Warwick and Kenilworth in Warwickshire,
between Brackley and Mixbury in Northamptonshire, between Stamford
and Wansford in Lincolnshire, and between Blyth and Tickhill in
Nottinghamshire. A fee was charged for a licence to hold a tournament,
and each participant paid according to his rank.[18] According to William
of Newburgh, Richard's purpose in encouraging tournaments was to
improve the quality of the English knights so as to make them the equal
of their French counterparts. So successful was the measure that within
a decade or two, in the well-informed opinion of William Marshal, thirty
English knights were the equal of forty French.

Through the enduring power of his reputation and through the
efforts he made to disseminate his values, Richard became the agent
of a major shift in English monarchical style. In the years after his
death the values of the English monarchy were increasingly shaped
along the lines which Richard himself had championed. The sheer
scale of his achievements, across so wide a field, brought lustre to
his line; at the same time, his achievements placed his successors
under a heavy burden of emulation. Richard's style of kingship was
considered the model to which all who came after him on the throne
should aspire. Young kings or kings-to-be from this time on were
judged by how far they lived up to his exacting standards. In the
1270s, after his accession, the youthful Edward I was greeted approvingly: he was said to 'shine like a new Richard'. When in the next
generation Edward II was held up for reproach, it was said that, had
he practised arms, he would have excelled Richard in prowess. In
funerary eulogies, when tributes were paid to deceased kings, as to
Edward I in 1307, it was conventional for the deceased ruler, providing
he deserved it, to be compared to the Lionheart in bravery.[19] Richard
had succeeded in raising the prestige of the Angevin royal line, and
he had achieved this principally through his achievements in arms.
By virtue of his influence, the English monarchy was gradually transformed into a chivalric monarchy. Chivalric values were henceforth
the values with which the most successful of England's kings were
to be associated.

3

The Making of Chivalric Culture,
1100–1250

In medieval aristocratic society, chivalric activity and cultural expectation went hand in hand. The chivalric lifestyle of the aristocracy
found its mirror in literature, just as literature found much of its
inspiration in chivalry. In the romance writing lapped up by the aristocracy, the themes most commonly dealt with were the performing
of brave deeds, the knightly quest for honour and the love of a
knight for his lady. These were themes with an immediate appeal to
an aristocracy which defined itself as a military elite, but because that
aristocracy was also a social elite, they found a wider audience among
those influenced by elite tastes – the humbler knights, esquires and
lesser gentry, even in some cases townsmen. Chivalric culture played
a key role in shaping the culture of medieval society as a whole. This
was true not only of literature, but also of architecture and the visual
arts.

The emergence of a distinct chivalric culture can be traced to the
early twelfth century. Europe was at this time experiencing an immense
intellectual awakening. The most striking manifestation of this was
the rediscovery, through Arabic translations, of some of the writings
of Greek antiquity. Underlying and informing the new mood, however,
was something deeper – a fresh outlook on the world, an outlook
with its roots in theology. European teaching of the early Middle Ages
had emphasised the hopelessness of humanity's prospects on Earth.
To early medieval writers, humans were fallen creatures whose fate
rested with the Almighty. In the twelfth century that pessimism was
gradually laid aside and thinkers invested humankind with a new
dignity and a new power. Through the application of reason, it was

argued, the individual human could understand the mind and will of God and bring order to his own experience. To such thinkers as Peter Abelard the whole universe appeared intelligible and accessible, with humanity occupying a fitting place in it. At the same time the deity himself was humanised and made more approachable, quite different from the terrifying God of judgement of earlier times. For women a new role model was found in the Virgin Mary, whose cult was encouraged by St Bernard and the Cistercians, and who was seen as a mediatrix between humanity and the Almighty. In literature the new outlook of the time found expression in troubadour lyrics, which showed a range of tenderness and emotion altogether unprecedented in the poetry of the earlier Middle Ages.

It was against this background that the emergent culture of chivalry took shape. Chivalry, tempered and refined by the new mood of the twelfth century, transformed the knight from a mere warrior into an idealised figure. In earlier times the warrior had been preoccupied with the struggle for survival in a fallen world. The knight of the twelfth century was altogether freer and happier. He was given a role to perform in a divinely ordained hierarchy, that of protecting the other two orders of society, the clergy and the labouring classes. He was invested with nobility, good fortune and charisma. Influenced by the twelfth-century cultural awakening, the culture of chivalry was richer, subtler and more diverse than the culture of earlier centuries. It complemented heroism with a range of literary and artistic references that invested it with an emotional intensity which in an earlier age would have been inconceivable.

In its broadest sense English chivalric culture took four main forms. Three of these were related: the first, a fondness for the new literature of Arthurian romance, the so-called Matter of Britain, which attained its first flowering in the writings of Geoffrey of Monmouth; the second, a taste for Anglo-Norman romance, the vernacular poetry which conferred legitimacy on baronial aspirations by dealing with the exploits of local dynastic heroes and legendary figures in a family's past; and the third – implicit in and associated with the second – a fascination with England's history, arising from the new aristocracy's appetite to learn more about its adoptive country. The fourth and last was different. This was the development of a language of visual symbolism, the most striking manifestation of which was heraldry.

Together the four can be said to have formed the main elements of a culture marked by a liking for romance, heroism and display.

Arthur and the Matter of Britain

Although chivalric literature was to find its most characteristic expression in the stories of King Arthur and the Knights of the Round Table, it did not have its origins there. Before the rise to popularity of the Arthurian genre there was an earlier tradition of writing, the *chansons de geste*. The *chansons* dealt with the familiar themes of honour, bravery and struggle; however, they lacked the romantic ingredient of a quest for a lady. They stood halfway between the early medieval heroic literature and the later romance literature, into the common stock of which they were eventually to merge.

The *chansons de geste* took as their main subject matter the battles and heroic achievements of the Emperor Charlemagne and his paladins. They centred on three great themes – the defeat of Roland at Roncesvalles, the deeds of Guillaume d'Orange, count of Toulouse, and the rebelliousness of the northern French barons under Charlemagne's successors. In the form in which they have come down to us, the *chansons* are mostly of early twelfth-century date; the traditions they drew on, however, originated in works of Charlemagne's own time in the late eighth and ninth centuries. Two of the cycles, those based on the *Chanson de Roland* and the *Chanson de Guillaume*, deal with broadly the same subject, the wars between the Franks and the Muslims in southern France and Spain in the eighth century. The *Chanson de Roland*, the finer of the poems, is built around two connected episodes in that conflict: Charlemagne's retreat from Spain and the death of his commander Roland, and Charlemagne's subsequent revenge on the manipulative Baligant and Ganelon, who were largely responsible for Roland's death. Ganelon, the story goes, was sent on an embassy to Spain after Roland had offended him, and arranged for the Muslims to fall on the emperor's rearguard under Roland's command in the Roncesvalles pass. Events unfolded entirely as planned: the Franks, on entering the pass, saw not one but five armies confronting them; Roland's close friend Oliver begged him to summon Charlemagne by blowing his great ivory horn; Roland, however, refused and fought alone, overcoming four of the armies and falling just before the fifth attacked. It is a story of bravery and faithfulness. Before long the narrative had acquired its stock pantheon of heroes, with Roland the valiant being contrasted with Oliver the wise. Scenes from the story were represented in stone on the front of Verona cathedral and in stained glass in an aisle window at Chartres cathedral.

The *chansons* took a real historical figure – the Emperor Charlemagne – and spun around him a series of invented martial episodes; fact and fiction were woven as warp and weft in the cycle. Roland, the supposed duke of the Breton march, may or may not have had a real historical existence; Oliver apparently had none at all. In the body of literature which came to supplant the *chansons*, the Arthurian romances, the blurring of fact and fiction was taken much further. Arthur, an early British leader with a shadowy existence in the Welsh annals, was placed at the centre of an exotic pseudo-historical fantasy world and credited, along with his knights, with a fictitious career of gallantry and brave deeds. The heroic Arthur was perhaps the most brilliant and original literary creation of the Middle Ages. He was the brainchild of an obscure Welsh clerk, Geoffrey of Monmouth, in his *The History of the Kings of Britain* (*Historia Regum Britanniae*), written in the 1130s.[1] This was destined to become a medieval bestseller.

Geoffrey claimed to have found the source material for his history in 'a very ancient book in the British tongue' given to him by his friend Walter, archdeacon of Oxford. The appeal to an 'ancient' source was simply an authenticating device designed to confer legitimacy on Geoffrey's supposed history. Geoffrey's book, written in Latin, was quite manifestly a work of fiction, as a number of his more sober-minded contemporaries, such as the chronicler William of Newburgh, pointed out. Geoffrey traced the history of Britain through a sweep of 1,900 years from Brutus, great-grandson of the Trojan Aeneas and founder of the kingdom, to the last British king, Cadwallader, who, harassed by plague and war, surrendered it to the Saxons in the seventh century. Brutus, according to Geoffrey, came to Britain following the fall of Troy and, after beating off the giants who inhabited the island, established his capital at London, which he called Trinovantium or New Troy. After his death, the kingdom was divided between his sons, with Loegria, the part corresponding to England, passing through a succession of rulers, among them Bladud, the founder of Bath, and Lear, who foolishly trusted his daughters, until it descended to Uther Pendragon, the father of Arthur.

At this point Geoffrey let his imagination run riot. Arthur, he said, was born of the adulterous union, engineered by Merlin, of Uther and Ygerna, duchess of Cornwall. At the time of his accession, Britain was under attack from the Saxons. Through Merlin's counsel and his own prowess, Arthur turned the tables on the invaders, driving them from Britain and pursuing campaigns of conquest in Scotland, Ireland and Gaul. He was about to challenge the might of imperial Rome itself when he heard of the treachery of his nephew Mordred, who had seized Queen Guinevere. Returning to England, he pursued Mordred to Cornwall and engaged him in battle, slaying him but suffering mortal injury himself. Carried mysteriously by boat to Avalon, he surrendered his crown to his nephew Constantine. Later, the British were driven back to Wales, but an angelic voice told a later king, Cadwallader of the eventual return of the Britons and their recovery of the kingdom they had lost.

Geoffrey found the raw material for his *History* not, as he claimed, in one 'ancient book' but in a whole variety of sources. Some of these were works of authority, such as Bede's *Ecclesiastical History* and the chronicles of the two British writers Gildas and Nennius; others, however, were legendary. In the rich seams of Celtic mythology, with which he was familiar, he was able to search for fictions which, reworked and suitably embellished, he could turn into an exotic story of national origins. Central to Geoffrey's literary ambition was the elevation of the British – that is to say, the Welsh and the Bretons – as a nation. He wrote against the background of a major resurgence of Welsh power, which in the 1130s saw two princes, Morgan and Iorwerth ap Owain, sweep down from the mountains and establish lordships based on the previously English-held castles of Caerleon and Usk.[2] Morgan, who remained in occupation of Caerleon for some twenty years, was actually to style himself on one occasion in a charter a king. Just when Geoffrey was penning his *History*, then, there was once again a Welsh princely ruler holding court in the very place where, centuries before, Arthur himself had held sway. Geoffrey may have been responding to this mood of Welsh excitement and antici-pation when he penned his description of Arthur's magnificent court at Caerleon, at which he had received the homage of the subject princes of Britain.

Geoffrey's readers were able to enjoy his *History* without necessarily subscribing to, or even being aware of, his Welsh agenda, which was largely hidden. For a good many of his contemporaries, the most noticeable quality of Geoffrey's work must have been its universality: it gave an account of English origins which set English legitimacy within the Virgilian context of the fall of Troy. Whatever his readers' understanding of his work, it certainly enjoyed an immediate popularity. It circulated in hundreds of copies and was paid the compliment of generating a massive secondary literature.[3] A copy of it was owned by Walter Espec, lord of Helmsley in Yorkshire and founder of Rievaulx Abbey. In the 1140s Geffrei Gaimar produced a French version to serve as the first part of his *Estoire des Engleis*. There were copies in cathedral and monastery libraries as well as in baronial halls and chambers. Interest in Geoffrey's work was as keen in continental Europe as in England, and he attracted an extensive following, not least among the Cistercians of northern France and the Low Countries.

Part of the reason for Geoffrey's enormous popularity was that he offered his readers not so much a historical record as a mirror of their own times. He drew reassuringly on contemporary assumptions, attitudes and ideas. In Geoffrey's *History* Arthur's kingship was presented as a version of twelfth-century kingship. Arthur did all the things that twelfth-century kings did: he gave generous gifts and rewards to his knightly followers; he summoned a feudal host; he held ceremonial crown-wearings at the great seasonal festivals. According to Geoffrey, Arthur made his court the international model for refined courtly behaviour; the noblest men in Europe, he wrote, sought 'to conduct themselves, in matters of dress and the bearing of arms, in the manner of Arthur's knights'. Much the same could have been said of the appeal to the European nobilities of the courts of William Rufus and Henry I. Likewise Arthur's conquests evoked contemporary parallels. Arthur had conquered Gaul, Scotland and Italy; Geoffrey's readers would have recalled William of Normandy extending his dominion over Brittany and Maine before taking on the conquest of England. Geoffrey took the familiar aristocratic world of his lay readers but projected it back, making it altogether grander, more exotic and more alluring as he did so.

Geoffrey's *History* is perhaps best regarded as a version of a foundation myth. The peoples of early medieval Europe had a longing for vivid historicising accounts which explained and legitimated national origins. The *History* may be interpreted as one of the most impressive and successful of such narratives. Not only did it recount and explain; it also amused and entertained. Its original association with the British or Welsh was quickly lost sight of as it took on an overlapping identity with their neighbours, the English. The latter, uniquely among the peoples of the British Isles, actually lacked a foundation myth of their own. The best narratives which they could come up with – and these rather underwhelming – were the stories of Hengist and Horsa in Bede. Conscious of their weakness in the historically aware twelfth century the English appropriated the cult of Arthur, adapting it to their needs. Thus Arthur was reinvented as an honorary Englishman; he was provided with an English burial place, Glastonbury Abbey; his court of Camelot was located in an English castle at Tintagel in Cornwall; and his sword Excalibur was mysteriously given into the hands of an English king, Richard the Lionheart. By the late thirteenth century Arthur was clothed in his new identity as a champion of English chivalric kingship. In the reign of Edward I his cult was made the means to mobilise the English knightly class in support of a new English-led bid to establish a British kingship.[4]

If Arthurianism developed in one direction as an English foundation myth, it developed in another into something broader and more cosmopolitan. By a process of literary osmosis Geoffrey's stories of Arthur and his knights were turned into the genre of European literature known as the Matter of Britain. There were three Matters which formed the mainstay of romance writing in the Middle Ages – the Matter of Rome, the Matter of France and the Matter of Britain. With myths of Celtic origin already in circulation on the continent, Arthur quickly became a figure of broad international appeal. The treatment of Arthur by later writers differed in certain important respects from Geoffrey's. In Geoffrey's hands, the world of Arthur had been violent and masculine, in this regard bearing the heavy imprint of the old *chansons de geste*. His Arthur was constantly waging war, ravaging the countryside and slaughtering his enemies. Geoffrey showed little interest in the emotional life of his characters. Later continental writers developed those aspects of his work which Geoffrey himself had left undeveloped. The role of women, for example, was expanded and given greater emphasis. Most important of all, new heroes were introduced. Where Geoffrey had identified only three of Arthur's knights by name, later writers were to mention others who had featured in ancient accounts – Sir Tristan and Sir Gawain – and they introduced an entirely new one, Sir Lancelot. Arthur himself was now overshadowed by those nominally in his service. It was the courtier knights on whom attention was henceforth to be focused, not the king to whom they owed allegiance.

The first person to attempt a reworking of the *History* was the Jersey-born poet Wace, whose *Roman de Brut*, completed in 1155, was a loose vernacular translation of it.[5] Wace was a pioneer in the imaginative use of Geoffrey's material. He adapted it freely, developed it in new directions and introduced new stories of his own. It was Wace who, crucially for the future, invented the Round Table, Arthur's ingenious device for seating his knights without provoking quarrels over precedence. Wace also shifted the balance of Arthur's conquests to outside England, thus locating him on both sides of the Channel, not just in Britain. Wace may be said to have paved the way for the groundbreaking work of the French writer Chrétien de Troyes some twenty years later.

Chrétien was perhaps the ablest and most significant of the French romance writers of the Middle Ages. Very little is known about his career beyond what he tells us himself – that he came from Troyes, that Marie de Champagne was his patron, and that Philip, count of Flanders, was a dedicatee of one of his works. His five surviving romances – *Eric et Enide*, *Cliges*, *Lancelot* or *Le Chevalier de la Charrette*, *Yvain* or *Le Chevalier au Lion*, and *Perceval* or *Le Conte du Graal* – are all highly original works which show qualities of elegance, maturity and inventiveness. *Le Chevalier de la Charrette* broke new ground in introducing the story of the adultery of Lancelot and Guinevere into the Arthurian cycle, while *Le Conte du Graal* attempted the first serious exploration of the Grail legend. Where earlier works had confined themselves to straightforward celebration of chivalric values, Chrétien subjected these to scrutiny, exploring such themes as love and adultery, actuality and aspiration, ambition and spiritual fulfilment. The sanguinary violence of Geoffrey's *History* was softened and toned down. In Chrétien's hands the underlying assumptions of the new, more civilised, aristocracy were subjected to searching analysis and debate.

Through the works of Chrétien, and through the thirteenth-century collection known as the Vulgate Cycle, which brought together the stories of the Grail and the death of Arthur, the Arthurian corpus passed into the European literary mainstream.[6] Yet Chrétien's own treatments of Arthurian themes appear to have aroused little enthusiasm in England. Only a few English texts, notably the *Ywain and Gawain*, directly reworked Chrétien's oeuvre.[7] In England Arthur's unique historical positioning appears to have had a limiting effect on the ways in which writers interpreted themes relating to his career. In England Arthur was seen not as a fictional or idealised creation but as a real historical figure with an actual existence in the remote past. He took his place among the Nine Worthies, or Heroes, alongside the likes of Charlemagne and the crusader Godfrey de Bouillon. He was the hero – almost the father – of the nation. One fourteenth-century Cornish knight was to claim that his ancestors had actually received their arms from the historical Arthur.[8] Stories of Arthurian knighthood were accordingly treated less freely, and in less abstract fashion, than in France. They tended to be located in specific historical settings – principally Glastonbury and Windsor – whereas writers from outside England happily located the king in a variety of periods and settings. For English writers and readers Arthur was a national hero, a kingly exemplar, a heroic figure from their nation's distant past. He had a specific place in the history of their country; he was a figure with a significant local as well as cosmopolitan appeal.

'Neither all lies, nor all true': Romances and the Myths of Family History

The rise of fictionalising histories like Geoffrey of Monmouth's formed part of a larger literary phenomenon which saw the production in England of epics and romances in French for a mainly noble audience – French, or Anglo-Norman, being the English upper-class vernacular. We have already seen how the eleventh- and early twelfth-century *chansons de geste* developed the idea of treating the career of a real historical character – Charlemagne – as a factual core around which to spin fictional narratives of bravery and heroism. In the next generation, Anglo-Norman romances were to rely on much the same technique. Using the poetic form, they took a real or imagined historical character and fashioned around him fanciful stories which would appeal to a noble audience. Geoffrey's original *History* had been written in prose chronicle form, which helped to give it the semblance of historical verisimilitude; the poetic form, which was often used for romance writing, allowed the creation of a more fictional atmosphere.

The genre known as romance comprised the principal secular literature of entertainment in the Middle Ages. Less heroic than the *gestes* and epic narratives and less lyrical than the Breton lays, it was a genre essentially recreational in function.[9] Chaucer described it as the 'storial thyng that toucheth gentillesse'.[10] Its rise coincided with the emergence of a newly self-conscious courtly aristocratic ruling class in northern Europe. It was this aristocracy whose members provided the main patrons and audience of the new genre;[11] it was likewise the exploits and preoccupations of the aristocratic class which provided its main subject matter. In England the romance rose to popularity in the years after the Norman Conquest. This was a period of precocious development for Anglo-Norman literature. The scale of literary activity owed something to the multiculturalism of post-Conquest England, to the meeting and intersection of two vernacular literatures – English and French – and the creative challenges to which this gave rise.[12] It owed something too to the encouragement of a leisured and intellectually curious aristocratic patron class who were looking for a literature which reflected their values and aspirations. If writers were tempted sometimes to refashion the outlook of their audiences through what they wrote, nonetheless they had to write what their audiences wanted to hear.

Among the most important twelfth-century romances are two by a clerk who lived in the Welsh border country – Hue de Rotelande (Rotelande probably being Rhuddlan in Dyfed). Hue's *Ipomedon*, which he says he wrote at Credenhill near Hereford, is a poem of some 10,500 lines about a wandering knight, Ipomedon, who undertook a series of adventures to prove his worth to his lady.[13] Hue wrote a sequel, *Protheselaus* (c. 1190), of nearly 13,000 lines, in which he told of the adventures of Ipomedon's younger son.[14] Hue's tales, which are set in Apulia and Calabria, are a heady mix of the familiar romance motifs of unrequited love, three-day tournaments and unrecognised brothers. Serious issues are considered along the way, among them questioning of obsessive love, distaste for the violence of warfare and exploration of personal identity. Hue, however, offers his observations in a humorous parody that verges on the burlesque. He tells us that he wrote *Protheselaus* for Gilbert FitzBaderon, lord of Monmouth, who was related on his mother's side to the powerful de Clare family. Gilbert seems to have been typical of the enlightened patron class of the age. Hue tells us that he had a personal library in Monmouth Castle which was well stocked with works in both Latin and French. Like Walter Espec of Helmsley, Gilbert delighted in listening to tales of the fabulous and amusing.[15]

Two other romances of the late twelfth century, *Boeve de Haumtone* and *Waldef*, have English settings, respectively Southampton and East Anglia. *Boeve* survives in two thirteenth-century fragments, totalling 4,000 lines. An epic-style romance, it tells how Boeve (or Bevis), ten-year-old son of the earl of Hampton, is deprived of his patrimony and sold by pirates to the king of Armenia, whose daughter he falls in love with, and how on his escape he returns home to recover his inheritance before dashing off again to rescue the lady from her abductors. The naming of Boeve's horse, Arundel, suggests that the poem may have been written as a tribute to William d'Albini, lord of Arundel.[16] *Waldef*, incomplete but still running to 22,000 lines, likewise dwells on the theme of exile and return, in this case of an English king, but combines it with a parallel story of a divided family and a quest for lost sons. The narrative is lively and fast-moving but also violent and amoral. It is possible that it draws on a tenth- or eleventh-century saga, now lost. *Waldef* is the least courtly of all the romances of this period.

The most important surviving romance from the thirteenth century is *Gui de Warewic*, a 13,000-line octosyllabic work, written in the early to mid-thirteenth century. This narrates how the humble Guy won the hand of Felice, the earl of Warwick's daughter, by performing brave deeds in her honour, but later repented of his violent past, embarked on a pilgrimage to the Holy Land and on his return lived out his remaining years as a hermit at Guy's Cliffe by the River Avon. The story has a strong historical streak and probably draws on fragmentary pre-Conquest traditions about the family's past. It provides

a foundation myth for the earls of Warwick and may have been written
to reinforce the earls' reputation at a time when their fortunes were
suffering decline.[17] The poem enjoyed wide popularity in the Middle
Ages and survives in a dozen or more manuscripts. When translated
into English metrical verse in the fourteenth century, it went on to
reach a still wider audience.[18]

Another Anglo-Norman romance with a strong family context is
Fouke Fitzwarin, which survives in a fourteenth-century prose version
representing an original octosyllabic romance of the previous century.[19]
The story has its origins in the partly verifiable history of the Fitzwarin
family of Whittington in Shropshire. The eponymous Fulk is sent as
a young boy to the court of Henry II, where he quarrels with the
future King John, is stripped of his inheritance and condemned to the
life of an outlaw. The poem traces the story of his struggles with John
and his men, his exploits in the greenwood, his life on the move and
eventually his reconciliation with the tyrant and one final adventure
involving a giant in Ireland. With its emphasis on the struggle of good
against evil, and its hero an outlaw figure, the poem bears many
similarities to the Robin Hood legends, which are likewise rooted in
the social conditions of the early thirteenth century.

Such romances were almost certainly written by chaplains connected
with the aristocratic patrons whose families or distant ancestors formed
the subject matter of the work. The principal themes considered were
the challenges and preoccupations of aristocratic society – a son
confronted with a rival to his inheritance, an esquire yearning for the
hand of a distant or superior lady, a young bachelor seeking revenge
after years of refuge abroad. Such age-old themes not only made for
good adventure stories, they formed the stuff of life in a competitive
honour-based society. The world of insular romance was thus a very
different one from that imagined in the febrile fictionality of Arthurian
romance. The Arthurian tales focused on courts and courtliness. Even
when they were not about King Arthur himself, they were about
knights in his service. Implicitly they lent legitimacy to the notion of
effective centralised monarchy. The Anglo-Norman romances, by
contrast, were concerned not so much with courts as with lordship
and landholding, inheritance and dynastic progression. The romances
showed the closest interest in those situations and administrative processes which resulted in challenges to royal authority. Typically, the

hero of the romances was a landless bachelor who found himself deprived of his lands and facing a struggle to get them back. The themes of marriage and family were important in many of the stories; love, however – at least in the chivalric sense – typically was not. What the subject matter of the romances suggests is that their audience was found in baronial and knightly society, not in the polite ambience of royal courts. The world of the romances was one in which heroes blended into local history and in which the heroes' lives were structured around ancestry and a sense of place. It is partly the emphasis on the hero's lands which gives the romance literature its powerful sense of locality. All the romances show a strong affinity with a particular corner of England, be it Southampton or Warwick, Shropshire or East Anglia. What the poet sought to create was a fiction which combined a feeling for family and place with a storyline which addressed the concerns and challenges of aristocratic society.[20]

A Sense of the Past

The keen interest which the Anglo-Norman aristocracy took in the past was to develop in a number of directions in the course of the twelfth century. It led, on the one hand, to a fashionable interest in fictional romance and ancestral myth-making, while on the other it found expression in a curiosity about the early history of England itself. The twelfth century was probably the first to witness a substantial lay readership for history.

This lively interest in England's past was the product of a very specific set of historical circumstances. The Anglo-Norman aristocracy whose forebears had conquered England in 1066 knew very little about the country over which they had established mastery. The first generation of settlers had remained essentially Norman in outlook, unsurprisingly since they held lands on both sides of the Channel. By the second and third generations, however, there was a shift in outlook as they came to regard themselves as more English than Anglo-Norman. A natural consequence of this shift of identification was a desire to learn more about England's past – and to establish contact with that past in such ways as to legitimise the present. The cataclysm of the Conquest thus became a powerful stimulus to historical research. Oddly, the Anglo-Saxons had left very little historical writing for later generations to build on: Bede's *Ecclesiastical History* and the *Anglo-Saxon Chronicle* were the only two sources of value. The learned men of the twelfth century, therefore, had to undertake the bulk of their research themselves. Sometimes they worked in association with patrons in the lay aristocracy: William of Malmesbury, the greatest historian of the period, dedicated his *Historia Novella* to Robert, earl of Gloucester, while Ailred of Rievalux was encouraged in his writing by his friend Walter Espec, lord of Helmsley. Sometimes they wrote principally to establish the antiquity of their own monastic houses or cathedral churches.

Much of the historical writing of the twelfth century took the form of conventional chronicles. William of Malmesbury's various works – his *Gesta Regum*, *Gesta Pontificum* and *Historia Novella* – and Henry of Huntingdon's *Historia Anglorum* were all conceived in the established chronicle tradition. These were lengthy prose works in elegant Latin which looked in their different ways to classical antiquity for their models. One remarkable historical work, however, stands apart from this tradition. It is Geffrei Gaimar's *Estoire des Engleis*. Gaimar's work is important for two reasons. First, it was written in French and not Latin, and is therefore likely to have been read by a predominantly lay audience; and, second, it is in octosyllabic rhymed couplets rather than prose. The *Estoire* is deserving of respect as the first known verse romance history of England.

Disappointingly little is known about Gaimar himself. He is thought to have been a secular clerk of Norman extraction, and he probably had some connection with Walter Espec of Helmsley, for he says that he obtained a copy of Geoffrey of Monmouth's *History* through Walter's good offices, and he refers to Walter's kinsman Nicholas de Trailly, a canon of York: Nicholas, he says, will vouch for the authenticity of his sources. In his Epilogue he helpfully identifies his patron for us, an aristocratic lady, Constance, wife of Ralph FitzGilbert, who, according to Gaimar, could read French.[21] Constance was connected with another female patron, Alice, widow of Robert de Condet, who commissioned a verse translation of the first nineteen chapters of the Book of Proverbs together with a scholastic commentary, a formidable work of 11,000 lines. Ralph FitzGilbert was a baron of middling rank whose main estates lay in Lincolnshire but who had acquired lands in Hampshire, perhaps through marriage. He was the founder of Markby Priory and a benefactor of the priories of Kirkstead and Stixwould. Gaimar shows himself particularly knowledgeable about those parts of the country in which his patron had interests. In the *Estoire*, then, we have a rare example of a vernacular history written for a patron in chivalric society. We are afforded an exceptional insight into the literary tastes of an elite twelfth-century readership.

Gaimar tells us that he wrote his chronicle in fourteen months, probably between March 1136 and April 1137. His sources were varied. For the earliest period he used Geoffrey of Monmouth's *History*. For the middle period, covering the late fifth to the mid-tenth centuries, he relied on the prose annals of the *Anglo-Saxon Chronicle*. For the century and three-quarters from 959 he wrote largely independently, relying on various sources, some written and some oral; the latter apparently included informants whose ancestors had frequented the court, among them probably Ranulf, earl of Chester.[22] For the post-Conquest period his material is original, if disordered.

Gaimar's *Estoire* is a notably secular work; the affairs of the religious hardly figure at all. Its main concern is with aristocratic culture and politics, and in this area it broke significant new ground. Where Gaimar was innovative was in his portrayal of the kings and noblemen of the past in chivalric terms. He took the chivalric values which he observed in the men around him and projected them back onto the fighting men of earlier times. Thus he pictured King Alfred, an essentially heroic figure, as possessing the chivalric qualities of wisdom, mercy and courtesy. He portrayed the tenth-century King Edgar in similar fashion, adding tellingly that Edgar had been more powerful than any king since Arthur. His strengths as an observer of chivalry are naturally most apparent in his portrayal of figures from the more recent past. In his account of Rufus's reign, he reversed the order of events at one point to highlight the story of Rufus's release of Count Helias of la Flèche as illustrating the king's qualities of mercy and magnanimity. Later, in his treatment of the death of King Malcolm of Scotland, he reports that Rufus took a tough line with Robert Mowbray, the king's slayer, but adds significantly that he refrained from mutilating or executing him, a mark of his chivalry.[23] It has been suggested that Gaimar's portrayal of Rufus in the *Estoire* is probably the first portrait of a chivalrous king in European history.[24] If this is the case, as it may be, then it is significant that the book was written for a baronial family – and, specifically, for the lady of that family. In Gaimar's work we are afforded a valuable insight into the literary and social milieu in which chivalric history was created and represented.

The genre of chivalric historical writing represented by Gaimar's *Estoire* is illustrated by two other French verse chronicles to have come down to us from the late twelfth century. One is Jordan Fantosme's history of the Anglo-Scottish war of 1173–4 and the baronial rebellion of that year, and the other Ambroise's eyewitness account of the Third Crusade.

Jordan's chronicle is constructed in the manner of the old *chansons de geste*. It is a story of heroes and heroism, built around a grand overarching theme, that of the failure of the rebellion against Henry II because of the rebels' excess of pride. The heroes, for all their failings, are surprisingly the rebels, William, king of Scots, and David, earl of Huntingdon. The former, says Jordan, was 'noble' and brave and only drawn into the war with the English because he was ill-advised, while the latter is portrayed in still warmer tones as 'a most estimable man', 'better than any I saw', and someone who would never dream of robbing an abbey or church.[25] It is possible that Jordan was especially sympathetic to Earl David because his doubling as an English noble made him a member of the international chivalric brotherhood.[26]

Ambroise's *Estoire*, written a generation later, is the work of an enthusiastic supporter of the Third Crusade. Ambroise's hero is unsurprisingly the main hero of that crusade, King Richard himself. Ambroise constantly emphasises Richard's bravery: he says that he was 'the bravest man in the world', and that God knew 'his foresight and bravery'.[27] He portrays him as the ideal knight: 'his deeds of chivalry were so great that men marvelled'.[28] He says that his court was magnificent: whenever he feasted, he used only the richest plate: his cups and dishes were of gold or silver, ornamented with figures and animals in bas-relief, or engraved, and studded with precious stones.[29] Ambroise showed himself highly receptive to Richard's propaganda, reproducing stories almost certainly fed to him by Richard himself which magnified the king's achievements. Yet he had little need actually to invent stories. To write romance history of the kind loved by his readers, he had simply to tell the story as it was.

It is not altogether clear how extensive the audience was for works of this sort. In most cases the manuscripts have come down to us in a mere handful of copies. By contrast, there are several dozen copies of Henry of Huntingdon's *History* and significant numbers of William of Malmesbury's main works; of Geoffrey of Monmouth's *History* there are as many as 200 copies.[30] On the other hand, it is hard to judge the popularity of romance history entirely by the somewhat unreliable test of numbers of extant manuscripts. Histories written by clerks for private patrons were bound to survive in fewer numbers than texts written in monasteries, which enjoyed institutional continuity.

An insight into the setting in which these secular histories were composed is provided by the epilogue to Gaimar's *Estoire*, in which the author lists those to whom he feels himself indebted. He mentions seven names: King Henry I; his queen Adeliza; Robert, earl of Gloucester; Walter Espec; a poet called David; Walter, archdeacon of Oxford; and Nicholas de Trailly, canon of York. These are people drawn from a wide cross-section of landowning society, both clerical and lay. Two other men who, on the evidence of their writings, may be judged to have been familiar with Gaimar's text are William of Newburgh, the Augustinian canon and chronicler, and Richard FitzNigel, Henry II's treasurer.[31] At least nine people, therefore, can be associated with a history written for the wife of a middling Lincolnshire baron. In the Middle Ages it was common for texts to circulate freely between readers. In the twelfth century it was also the case that they were listened to more than they were read. A single copy of a poem or history could therefore have reached dozens, perhaps many dozens, of people. There is every reason to suppose that Gaimar's *Estoire* reached a far wider audience than the modest evidence of manuscript survival would suggest. And very likely, the same can be said of the other verse chronicles and romance histories of the time.

The Visual Culture of Chivalry

Aristocratic culture, it has been said, was a culture of display.[32] In the Middle Ages, when literacy was limited, it was through visual display that messages about status were communicated. Great men advertised their greatness before a variety of audiences – tenants, retainers, visitors – in settings as varied as baronial halls, churches and on the highway. They likewise showed off their greatness using a variety of media. They dressed lavishly in public. In the Bayeux Tapestry Duke William of Normandy is shown wearing a garment of high status – a three-quarter-length mantle thrown back over the shoulders and fastened by a clasp at the throat; knights would typically be attired in rich silk robes when they were dubbed at royal knighting ceremonies. It was normal for the well born and the well connected to surround themselves with large households. Becket, when he became Henry II's chancellor in 1155, provoked comment by the size of his retinue, the magnificence of his household and the crowds of servants who attended on him. When lords, both lay and ecclesiastical, built castles, it was as much to proclaim status as to provide themselves with a stronghold. In the Middle Ages great lords had to be seen to be great if they were to remain so. The idea was inherited from the ancient world that outer was the mirror image of inner: inner worth found its reflection in outward splendour. A man's position in the social pecking order would be measured in terms of the richness of his public demeanour.

In the twelfth century there was a steadily increasing range of means by which great men could communicate their social standing. Not only did such men have more money to spend, they felt a greater urge to spend it in ways that affirmed their separateness from others, such as townsmen, who had also acquired more disposable wealth. A notable development of the period was the growing use and refinement of aristocratic insignia. Emblems and devices once deployed in an exclusively military context were now adopted in civilian settings to provide evidence of social status and position.

The wider use of banners or standards provides a good example of the practice. Banners had long been used as rallying points in battle and on the campaign trail. In Roman times the legionaries had gone into battle under standards bearing the symbol of the eagle. At Hastings in 1066 King Harold had fought under the old English standard of the dragon. From around the turn of the eleventh and twelfth centuries the use of banners became more widespread, and in the Angevin world they were sometimes used in knightly investiture ceremonies. The later custom in Gascony, whereby the count took up his sword and banner from the altar of the collegiate church of Saint-Seurin in Bordeaux, was of twelfth-century origin. Banners also acquired greater potency as objects charged with special, often religious, meaning. Banners such as the oriflamme, the national standard of France, were blessed before being taken into battle. In East Anglia knights competed to carry the banner of St Edmund into battle at the head of the retinue of Bury St Edmunds Abbey. By the late twelfth century knights who had won the right to carry a banner were regarded as occupying a high position. They were known as bannerets and considered superior to the main body of knights, the knights bachelor. Banneret was to become a rank in society. By the fourteenth century the square banner was sometimes shown on bannerets' tombs and brasses as a mark of status, as at Lingfield in Surrey.

Military imagery also came to feature significantly on seals. Wax seals had first appeared in the later eleventh century as a way of authenticating charters and other formal instruments. The early seals of kings had shown the monarch sitting enthroned in majesty. In England King Edward the Confessor's royal seal had shown him in such a pose and holding the symbols of his regal authority. Edward's was a one-sided seal. After the battle of Hastings William the Conqueror introduced a seal which was impressed on both sides. On the obverse William was shown, like his predecessor, enthroned in state, while on the reverse he was shown in an altogether new image – armed and on horseback. The new style represented a shift to a more military conception of monarchy. Seals with equestrian images were soon adopted by members of the aristocracy. A charter of Ilbert de Lacy, granting the manor of Tingewick in Buckinghamshire to the Abbey of Holy Trinity, Rouen, had attached to it a seal showing Ilbert as a mounted warrior. By the late twelfth century, as part of the process of the emulation of elite practices by the middling ranks, seals of this sort were adopted by the knightly class. Richard de Lucy, Henry II's justiciar, thought the practice presumptuous. 'It was not the custom of old for every petty knight to have a seal,' he said mockingly, 'it is only kings and great men who should use them.'[33] But the knightly class won the day. Moreover, the process of dissemination did not stop at the boundaries of knighthood. By the thirteenth century esquires and even well-to-do village freeholders were using seal-like devices.

In the position which the figure of the enthroned king occupied on royal seals, on those of the nobility the owner's coat of arms was usually represented. The appearance of coats of arms – in other words, the language of heraldry – was one of the most significant developments in aristocratic culture in the twelfth century and was to be of huge importance for the visual projection of knightly power in the future. Heraldry is best described as a system of identifying individuals by means of a range of hereditary devices placed on a shield. Decorative symbols of various sorts had long been in use on military shields and banners. As we have seen, the Saxons had fought under the dragon device at the battle of Hastings. Where heraldry broke new ground was in making use of a stable set of emblems which could be passed down from generation to generation in a single family. Heraldry, unlike the old dragon device, could be used to display lineage and family identity, and for this reason became the outward and visible sign of nobility. And because the nobility as a social group was characterised by the chivalric lifestyle, it is fair to say that it became the outward and visible sign of chivalry itself.

Most of the early evidence for the use of heraldry in England comes from seals. In one of the earliest surviving devices, that of Waleran, count of Meulan (d. 1166), the count is shown on horseback bearing a chequered coat on his shield, surcoat and banner (c. 1139). The chequered coat had been used a few years before by his maternal uncle Ralph, count of Vermandois (c. 1130), and in the generation to come was to be used by the Franco-Norman counts of Meulan and the English earls of Leicester, Warenne and Warwick.[34] In this way the coat became the hereditary property of a particular family. It was not only valued as a practical means of identification; it had also become a source of family pride.

Heraldry, while developing an early association with seals, actually had its origins in the problems of personal identification on the battle-field. By the early twelfth century the development of armour had reached the point where the mounted warrior was cased from head to toe in a mail suit, his face all but invisible beneath a massive helm and a noseguard. In the thick of the fight it was becoming increasingly difficult for knights to tell combatants on their own side from the enemy. The problem was particularly acute in tournaments, where it was important for knights to know which riders heading in their direction were proper targets for capture and ransom. The problem of recognition was no less serious for those on the sidelines in tournaments – the judges and spectators. The friends of combatants, for example, needed to be able to tell who was who, so that they could cheer on those they supported. A symbolic or geometrical device on a shield or surcoat was a convenient aid to identification. Chrétien de Troyes in *Chevalier de la Charrette* describes how some knightly onlookers pointed out the combatants to the queen: 'Do you see the knight with the gold band across his red shield? That is Governauz de Roberdic. And do you see the other one, who has an eagle and a dragon side by side on his shield? That's the king of Aragon's son . . .'[35]

Heraldry quickly developed a special vocabulary, based on French, to describe the colours and images on coats of arms. There were terms for the ordinaries, or geometric patterns on the shield – the *chief*, *fess*, *bend*, *pale* and *chevron*; and there were special words for the tinctures or colours – *or* (gold) and *argent* (silver) the two metals, and *sable* (black), *gules* (red), *azure* (blue), *vert* (green) and *purpure* (purple), the five colours. At the same time a series of rules was drawn up to regulate the arrangement and depiction of the devices on the shield. For example, it was prescribed that no metal should be laid on a metal, nor any colour on a colour. Likewise, the positions that could be used for heraldic beasts were limited, stylised and given technical appellations. The practical operation of these rules can be illustrated from the royal arms of England. In technical parlance these arms were *gules, three lions passant guardant or*: that is to say, on a red field, three golden lions, facing outwards, with their right forelegs raised. The essential requirement of any coat of arms was that it be clear and easy to recognise and remember. Not uncommonly, as an aid to identification, knights adopted devices which involved a pun on their names. The Trumpingtons of Trumpington in Cambridgeshire, for example, bore *azure crusilly two trumpets or* (blue with crosses, two trumpets gold), and the Septvans of Chartham (Kent) *azure three cornfans or* (silver, three winnowing fans gold). The use of such allusive, or 'canting', devices carried the very practical advantage of reducing the danger of overlapping claims to coats. Before the fifteenth century in England the adoption of arms was unregulated: knights could adopt whatever devices they liked provided they were not already in use. There was always the danger, however, that, in ignorance of each other, two knights could adopt the same coat.

The men whose business it was to recognise, recall and record coats of arms were the heralds. The origins of the office of herald are probably to be found in the staging and ceremony of tournaments. These big occasions brought together great assemblages of people – armourers, minstrels, jongleurs, grooms – all of them lesser servants or artisans who made a living from satisfying the needs of the contestants. In the early days of the tournament the heralds were numbered among this community of hangers-on – indeed, among the humbler members of it. One of their duties was to publicise and proclaim tournaments: they would wander from place to place giving notice of the great event. Later, it seems, they became attached to particular knights and would call out their names and cheer them on as they entered the lists. According to the life of William Marshal, a particularly noisy herald or esquire, Henry le Norreis, greeted the Marshal's appearance at every tournament with the cry, 'God aid the Marshal!'[36] It is likely that the ranks of the heralds overlapped with those of the minstrels. In the account books of Edward I's household the two groups are lumped together under the single heading 'minstrels'.

By the early thirteenth century the heralds were acquiring the duty with which they were later principally to be associated, that of recognising and recording knights' coats of arms. They were the obvious people to take on the task, because they were regularly present at tournaments and knew all the knights. Quite possibly they had some limited involvement as judges or masters of ceremonies: this would explain the later appearance, of the office of king of arms. By the mid-thirteenth century the office of herald was beginning to acquire a degree of formality. Heralds were usually attached to a particular master; they wore his colours or livery; they were regularly paid and entrusted with specific duties. They were rising in status and dignity. Later a hierarchy would be established in the profession, from pursuivant at the bottom to king of arms at the top. It is likely that the earliest surviving treatise on heraldry, the late thirteenth-century *De Heraudie*, was written by a herald.[37]

The role of heralds in the thirteenth century was essentially that of acting as the registrars of chivalry, as the men whose collective memory recorded its visual repertory. They learned the language of heraldry, and they interpreted its rules. Much later they were to acquire the additional power of actually conferring grants of arms on aspirants. This final stage was to come in the fifteenth century, when the need arose to examine and approve the credentials of claimants to armigerous status who lacked the usual military experience. In the early days, however, the heralds' main responsibility was to observe and record: they were witnesses to the nexus of ties linking the worlds of heraldry and tourneying.

Heraldry traced its origins to an aristocratic culture which still largely overlapped with the culture of heroism and fighting. The oral and literary tastes of the nobility centred largely on tales of errantry, courage and prowess. Over time, this culture was to change, and aristocratic insignia, in particular coats of arms, were to develop a larger role as ensigns of civilian status. Once aristocratic symbolism entered into this new and wider role, collectively it took on new associations – with dignity, gentility, social exclusiveness: in a word, with snobbery. Banners and arms became 'tokens of nobleness'. By this route chivalry, which had originated as a practical military code, developed into a code of manners defining a civil elite no longer composed of men exclusively of military experience, but embracing lawyers, civil servants and others of professional origin who sought respectability in the partial embrace of aristocratic culture. It was at this point that chivalry assumed the character of the outward and visible form of social respectability defined in terms of polite knighthood.

4

Knighthood Transformed,
1204–90

In the space of a few months in 1204 the political map of Europe was transformed by King Philip II of France's conquest of Normandy and the adjoining Angevin lands. The great assemblage of dominions which Henry II and Eleanor of Aquitaine had put together and which their son Richard the Lionheart had spent his last years defending had fallen apart. Of all the lands on the continent which King John had inherited on his accession in 1199, only the duchy of Aquitaine in south-west France was left to him.

With the loss of Normandy, and with the ending later of John's attempts to recover it, the period of warfare in which English knighthood had been involved since the Conquest was all but over. English forces were not to find themselves drawn into any large-scale or protracted military struggles until Edward I's reign. The wars of the thirteenth century were generally small. There were minor expeditions to Brittany in 1230 and to Gascony in 1225 and 1253, the last of these led by King Henry III himself; there were various skirmishes on the Welsh borders in the 1240s and 1250s. There were also brief but intense periods of civil war at the end of John's reign and in the 1260s between Henry III and Simon de Montfort. These hostilities apart, however, the thirteenth century was a remarkably peaceful period, perhaps the most tranquil of the Middle Ages. It is against this background of relative military inactivity that we have to view a development of the highest significance in the history of chivalry in England – a fall in the number of knights – a development with far-reaching consequences for English society.

Where Have All the Knights Gone?

That Henry III's ministers were well aware that the number of knights in England was in decline is evident from the fact that from the 1220s they regularly resorted to measures to ensure that those eligible to assume knighthood took up the rank. Knights were still needed for war service or castle duty, even if not on the same scale as before. Accordingly, every decade or so – whenever a military campaign was planned – writs of distraint were issued, ordering those with a certain income to take up the rank or, if not, to pay a fine. The first such writs were issued in November 1224, when the sheriffs were told to ensure that every layman of adult age who held one or more knights' fees and was not a knight took up the rank by the Sunday after Easter. The measure was conceived as part of the wider preparations made for the expedition to Gascony in 1225. Further orders were issued in 1230, 1242, 1253 and 1256.[1] In 1241 the qualification was changed from tenurial to financial. In other words, distrainees were identified not as holders of knights' fees but as holders of lands worth a certain amount, in this case estates worth twenty pounds per annum. Henry III's chief ministers were clearly concerned at the declining response rate to summonses of the knightly host. They appear to have identified the main cause of the problem as the fragmentation of knights' fees and accordingly resorted to a financial qualification as a way of putting pressure on those possessed of the necessary means.

The shortage of knights also revealed itself in the reductions in the quotas of knights owed by the barons – the tenants-in-chief – to the feudal host. At the levels these obligations had been fixed in the late eleventh and twelfth centuries, the quotas were in many cases very high. Some tenants-in-chief owed sixty, ninety or a hundred knights to the king. By the beginning of the thirteenth century it was becoming increasingly difficult for them to muster contingents on this scale. Even in John's reign, when the demand for knights was most intense, the king's officers would often settle in practice for a lesser figure. In 1210, for example, Geoffrey FitzPeter got by with supplying ten knights and not the ninety-eight for which he was theoretically liable, and in 1214 the earl of Devon was allowed to serve with twenty

knights and not the eighty-nine of his formal obligation. The Crown
never publicly gave its assent to a wholesale reduction of the quotas
due from the baronial tenants-in-chief, although it recognised their
increasing unreality by agreeing through a process of piecemeal negotiation to reductions in the quotas owed by some of the most heavily
burdened of those tenants. Richard of Cornwall's quota, for example,
was reduced from one hundred knights to three, John de Courtenay's
from ninety-two likewise to three, and Robert St John's from fifty-five
to five.[2] A number of tenants-in-chief seem to have struck some very
favourable bargains with the king. Peter of Savoy, for example,
succeeded in securing a reduction of his quota from 140 knights to a
mere five. In a few cases it was to emerge that these men could in
fact supply considerably more knights than the totals for which they
accepted responsibility. In 1245 the earl of Winchester turned up for
a Welsh campaign with ten knights instead of the three knights and
one sergeant (or esquire) for which he was theoretically liable.[3]
Nevertheless, if some of the new quotas were on the low side, the
key point remains: that by the 1240s there were far fewer knights in
England than there had been. Both the king and his tenants-
in-chief were aware of the seriousness of the problem. The process
of renegotiation formed part of an attempt to adjust to new
circumstances.

It is unfortunately difficult to tell just how severe the fall in numbers
was, and at what level the number was eventually to stabilise. For
Henry III's reign there are no comprehensive feudal surveys comparable to the *Cartae Baronum* of Henry II's time. There is only one sure
way of arriving at a figure for the period before the reduction began,
and that is by laboriously totting up the references to knights which
occur in the various administrative sources of the day. Certain categories of office in the workings of justice, such as grand assize juries,
were reserved to knights and knights alone. If all the men found in
these capacities are added up, it is possible to arrive at an approximate
figure for the number of knights active in the years 1200–20. For the
later years of the century, the period by which numbers are likely to
have sharply declined, another body of material becomes available –
the rolls of arms compiled by the heralds, which record attendance at
big tourneying events. If we compare the two sets of figures, the
results are instructive. On the evidence of the administrative sources

from the beginning of the century it can be estimated that there were at least 3,600 knights in England, and perhaps nearer 4,000, a figure which comes very close to the notional 5,000 knights of the old feudal quota.[4] But just seventy or eighty years later, if the evidence of the rolls of arms is to be believed, the figure had fallen to no more than 1,250.[5] Nearly two-thirds of England's knightly company had evaporated.

By any standard this was a remarkable decline, and it is hardly surprising that the government should have reacted with urgency by the issuing of writs of distraint. Yet there is evidence that the problem went back much further still. The number of knights in England was already in decline by the later twelfth century. In 1180, in his treatise on court life, Walter Map had commented on the problem of knights falling into debt and risking the loss of their inheritances.[6] A little earlier Richard FitzNigel, in the *Dialogue of the Exchequer*, had made comments in a similar vein.[7] Some at least of the knightly class were evidently in financial difficulties well before the thirteenth century. This crisis was not only serious; it was prolonged.

While contemporaries showed a keen awareness of the problem, they made little or no attempt to reflect on its causes. During the middle of the thirteenth century the government acted on the assumption that the fragmentation of knights' fees, caused by the buying and selling of land, was eating into knightly income, and responded by offering assistance with the costs incurred in fitting out for knighthood. Later, however, their attitude appears to have shifted to the view that knights were unwilling rather than unable to support the rank, hence the policy of issuing writs of distraint. It is probably easier for scholars today to identify what was happening than it was for contemporaries. In broad terms, the main cause of the shrinkage seems to have lain in the series of major social and economic changes sweeping through knightly and aristocratic society at the time.[8] Over the previous century and a half the higher aristocracy had been developing a greatly increased appetite for the display of rank and status. Moreover, they were fortunate in that their incomes had been rising steadily in an expanding economy, so they had the means to indulge their tastes. The knights, their vassals, anxious to keep up, had likewise developed an interest in decking themselves out in finery and the trappings of class. The sharp rise in expenditure to which their ambitions committed them, however, placed a severe strain on their resources. Some of their number were able to afford the expense, while others – principally the less well endowed – became burdened with debt and had to give up the struggle.

The beginnings of this trend towards a more opulent lifestyle are to be found around the turn of the eleventh and twelfth centuries. On both sides of the Channel, top families were developing a taste for a bolder and more forceful and articulate style of grandeur. The households over which they presided became larger and more carefully differentiated by rank. The castles which they built were conceived on a grander and more arresting scale. At the highest levels there was a trend towards the adoption of distinctive items of attire, with earls taking to wearing hats and coronets of estate. Increasingly, rules of behaviour were formulated for those who moved in the company of the greatest magnates. It was specified, for example, that when the lord spoke all should fall silent. At the same time the language of symbolism was extended to distinguish those of noble birth from those endowed merely with freedom. Heraldry was adopted as a means of visual identification by those who could claim to belong to the knightly and aristocratic elite. As the twelfth century wore on, chivalric aristocracy was increasingly suffused with an aura of exclusivity and status.

Where matters of display were concerned, the aristocrats took their cue from the kings and princes whom they served and in whose company they moved. The courts of rulers such as Henry I and Henry II offered a mixture of inspiration and desire for emulation to those who thronged them. On the one hand they provided a model of polite and civilised behaviour, while on the other they inevitably encouraged flattery by imitation. In medieval society it was generally the case that cultural patterns were diffused from the top down. That is to say, if someone in the elite adopted a new lifestyle, then those in the ranks immediately below would shortly take note and imitate the example. It is precisely this kind of downward dissemination which is to be observed at sub-aristocratic level at the turn of the twelfth and thirteenth centuries. Just as the aristocracy had appropriated the trappings and lifestyle of princes, so in turn knights took to appropriating those of aristocrats. In this way knights pitched their bid for admission to a club which had hitherto been occupied only by earls, barons and castellans. In adopting the airs and graces of the elite they were saying, in effect, that they were aspiring to be members of that elite themselves.

The foundations of this process of knightly assertion were laid in the important administrative reforms of Henry II's reign. As a result of the king's introduction of new common-law processes, or assizes as they were known, the knights came to be appointed to a range of administrative positions which had hitherto been the preserve of the aristocracy. Under the Assize of Northampton of 1176 a group of knights from each hundred was charged with reporting to the royal justices those suspected of breaching the king's peace. By the terms of the Grand Assize of three years later, twelve reputable knights of each neighbourhood were required to sit as jurors settling matters of right in disputes over land. By the end of Henry II's reign, as the legal treatise associated with Ranulf de Glanvill makes clear, the knights had become the mainstays of the local administration of justice and the main actors in the proceedings of county courts. Like the barons – the king's tenants-in-chief – they had a recognised stake in the land and bore a responsibility for maintaining its peace. Socially knights were coming to be seen as separate from those who ranked below them, those who were merely free. In the witness list appended to a charter of John, the constable of Chester, issued in 1178 five knights (*milites*) were placed at the beginning and thus awarded precedence over the freemen present.[9] The new exclusivity of the knightly class marked them out as members of the aristocracy.

The new elitism of the knightly class showed itself in all sorts of ways. They began to construct manor houses like those of the aristocracy, built of stone not timber, sometimes including polite withdrawing chambers, as at Boothby Pagnell in Lincolnshire. They took to creating big deer parks in which they could indulge the aristocratic sport of hunting. They built up larger and more hierarchically organised households to minister to their and their family's needs. In some cases they even founded religious houses modelled on those of the nobility, in which they could be buried and where prayers could be offered for their souls. In general, they took to assuming all the trappings of status which the magnates themselves had assumed a century or so before. And their aspirations cost them money. Where once a knight had been able to manage on an income of five to ten pounds a year, he now needed at least twenty pounds a year to maintain himself.

With the economy expanding, those knights endowed with demesnes (home farms) big enough to allow production for the market were well able to support their ambitions. If they found expenditure rising, they could increase their income in line with it. Not all knights, however, were in a position to turn the economic conditions of the day to their advantage. The thirteenth-century knightly class was a biblical house with many mansions. If there were knights with large demesnes which could generate surpluses, there were many more with smaller estates, or with estates which could not easily be turned to market production. It was the knights who fell into this latter category who were the losers in the big thirteenth-century shake-out. Unable to increase their incomes, they had no alternative but to abandon knightly status and sink into the ranks of the merely free. The families who were left constituted a more exclusive group than their predecessors. They were fewer in number but socially more exalted. They were the cream of their class, the leaders of local society.

What was striking about this newly ambitious elite was their self-consciousness. The knights of the twelfth century had been a fairly self-effacing group, scarcely standing out from their neighbours and associates. The knights of the thirteenth century could hardly have been more different, being socially alert, administratively active, and taking a delight in the trappings of status. One particular medium in which they took an interest was the novel science of heraldry. It was in the thirteenth century that the adoption, use and display of heraldry by the knightly class first became widespread.

Knights' adoption of heraldic bearings provides a neat illustration of the pattern which we have observed of the downward diffusion of the trappings of rank. A number of the earliest knightly coats can be shown to have been derived directly from those of the magnates who had developed the science of heraldic blazon in the first place. A whole series of arms, for example, was derived from the arms of Geoffrey de Mandeville, earl of Essex (d. 1144).[10] Geoffrey, a baron active in Stephen's reign, bore a simple and distinctive coat, *quarterly or and gules*. Among those who adopted coats very similar to his were the de Vere earls of Oxford, who were descended from Geoffrey's brother-in-law; the descendants of Roger FitzRichard of Warkworth in Northumberland, who had married Geoffrey's sister-in-law; and the Beauchamp lords of Bedford, who were descended from Geoffrey's wife by her second marriage. A variant of the same arms with a border of *vair* (alternating blue and white) was later to be adopted by John FitzGeoffrey, Henry III's justiciar in Ireland and half-brother to two earls of Essex. A similar pattern of dissemination occurred with the de Clare arms, *or, three chevrons gules*, which were used in the twelfth century by both main branches of the de Clare family, the earls of Hertford and the earls of Pembroke. Among others who adopted variants of the coat were the FitzWalter lords of Dunmow, who were descended from Robert FitzRichard de Clare (d. 1136), and the Montfitchet and Monmouth families, who were descended respectively from the sisters of Richard FitzGilbert of Clare and Gilbert de Clare, earl of Pembroke.

Another common way in which heraldic bearings were disseminated was through the network of a lord's tenants and dependants. Again good examples are afforded by the process of adoption of the de Clare coat. The families of Pecche of Bourne in Kent, Sackville of Fawley in Buckinghamshire, d'Abernon of Stoke d'Abernon in Surrey, and d'Aubigny of Belvoir in Leicestershire, all of which held lands from the de Clares, used coats derived from the familiar de Clare chevrons. In the north Midlands a similar pattern can be seen with the dissemination of the wheatsheaf (or garb) device of the Blundeville earls of Chester. This was adopted by, among others, the de Lacys, hereditary constables of Chester, and the Segraves, a Leicestershire baronial family who held land from the Blundevilles. The practice of adopting – or adopting and adapting – the arms of a feudal superior was one of the main means by which heraldic devices were disseminated among the knightly class.

By the end of the thirteenth century there was scarcely a knight of any consequence in England who had not adopted a coat of arms for himself. Indeed a knight could hardly be considered a knight in any meaningful sense if he had no blazon to his name. The science of heraldry provided the new, more elite knightly class of the day with a repertory of identifying devices which, while strictly practical, also enveloped those who used them in an air of mystique and social exclusivity.

If one way in which the elitism of the new knightly class could find expression was through the medium of heraldry, there was also a second way, and this of a quite different order – namely through the development of the institutions and mechanics of local lordship. It was precisely in these difficult, unstable years of sifting and sorting in the knightly class that the new wealthier knights first actively entered into the role of manorial lord. Back in the twelfth century knights had spent a great deal of their time in magnate households as garrison men, feudal retainers, household officials or some other kind of dependant. Their successors in the thirteenth century, while retaining their links with the lords and in many cases being fee'd by them, were based more in the countryside. They nurtured a growing sense of personal lordship, local identity and proprietorship. Richer and individually more powerful than their twelfth-century predecessors, they were able to reorganise their lands, strengthen their hold over their tenants and develop the apparatus of seigneurial jurisdiction. They were on the way to becoming the 'gentry', as they would be known in later centuries. It was partly to articulate this new sense of themselves as figures of local importance that they were so keen to rebuild their homes, the moated manor house being a highly visible symbol of authority and lordship. It was in the same spirit of seeking witness to local proprietorship that they developed an interest in the parish church. Through the rebuilding of churches and the creation within them of dynastic mausoleums they could articulate an ecclesiastical dimension to their lordship. What the *eigenkloster*, the family monastery, had long done for the identity of magnates, the parish church was shortly to do for knights.

Back in the earliest days of knightly society in England knights had generally been buried in the Benedictine monasteries founded by their baronial superiors, which gave institutional expression to the feudal honours of which they were tenants. These monasteries enjoyed wide popularity as burial places because, as corporate institutions, they could offer uninterrupted intercession for the souls of those buried in them. By the late thirteenth century, however, there was a shift among knightly patrons away from monastic burial and towards interment in parish churches. This shift is evidenced by the increasing number of knightly tomb effigies in parish churches. Whereas in the years to around 1270 relatively few such monuments were commissioned, after that time there was a sharp rise, and the number continued to go up. Among the finest of many excellent examples of such effigies are those at Tickenham in Somerset, Threekingham in Lincolnshire and Stowe Nine Churches in Northamptonshire. Behind the shift to parish church burial lay a much larger shift in knights' outlook on the world. Instead of seeing themselves, as they had, principally as members of feudally defined communities, they now saw themselves as members of communities defined by locality. The area they identified with was the area of their own lordship. In physical terms their world found expression above all in two buildings, the manor house and the parish church usually adjacent to it.

Knightly involvement in church building was in many cases prompted by the need to enlarge church fabrics to create additional space for family burials. This was the case, for example, at Cogenhoe in Northamptonshire, where the nave was rebuilt on an ambitious scale by the lord of the manor, Sir Nicholas de Cogenhoe, in the second half of the century.[11] Sir Nicholas's own effigy is tucked away in a low recess in the wall of the south aisle, where it can still be seen today. A notable feature of the building was the inclusion of a series of shields of arms on the capitals of the nave pillars, displaying the Cogenhoe arms and the arms of families to which the Cogenhoes were related. The placing of the shields in this position is highly unusual and must reflect Sir Nicholas's personal initiative. Doubtless at one time there were also shields of arms in the windows and perhaps also painted on the walls.

At Stoke d'Abernon in Surrey the d'Abernons rebuilt the chancel of their parish church on a lavish scale in the 1250s.[12] On the site of a small Norman apsidal chancel the family raised an elegant two-bay structure, vaulted in stone and with a boss at the intersection of the ribs carved in the shape of a rose, a symbol of the Virgin Mary, patroness of the church. An extensive series of paintings decorated both the walls and the vault, the scheme on the east and south walls, showing tiers of angels, still well preserved. The patron of the work, Sir John d'Abernon I, was represented by a donor figure in a painting on the north side of the chancel arch, facing the nave, above a side altar.

It was relatively unusual in the thirteenth century for a knightly family to undertake the rebuilding of a chancel, for this was the part of the fabric for which the rector was legally responsible. Knightly endeavour was generally concentrated on rebuilding the nave, as at Cogenhoe, or the construction of an aisle or side chapel, as at Curry Rivel in Somerset. At Stoke d'Abernon the need to create burial space almost certainly provided one reason for the rebuilding, as family interments were to be made in the chancel, before the altar, for the next three generations. Indeed, it is for the magnificent brasses of Sir John II and Sir John III, two of the earliest knightly brasses to survive, that the church is chiefly famous today. Yet, for an intended gentry mausoleum, the chancel was not large. By the fifteenth century burial space was running short again, and a new chapel had to be built on the north side of the church. What is remarkable about the chancel at Stoke d'Abernon is not so much its scale as its opulence. What the d'Abernons were interested in was not just providing burial space but creating suitably magnificent surroundings for the celebration of the liturgy. It is noteworthy in this connection that the d'Abernons were actually patrons of the church: they held the advowson, the right of appointing the parson. Almost certainly in this capacity they were responding to the priorities of the Third Lateran Council, which had met in 1215, in ensuring proper decorum in Eucharistic worship. They were acting in a proprietorial fashion not just as lords of the manor but in their role as patrons with responsibilities to the parish.

Servants of the State

By the end of the thirteenth century the knights were well on their way to becoming the gentry of later years, a landed elite of local territorial importance. No longer were they just professional soldiers or tourneyers employed primarily in military households; they were emerging as lordly figures with a stake in the localities where they lived.

The sphere in which their growing importance most immediately registered was that of county office-holding and administration. From Richard the Lionheart's time, as the range and intensity of royal government expanded, a whole series of new offices and commissions was brought into being. In 1194 the office of coroner was created with specific responsibility for holding inquests into dead bodies, four coroners being appointed in each shire from among its 'most loyal and trustworthy knights'. Forty years later, by a division of the sheriff's responsibilities, the office of escheator was created, with responsibility for collecting the feudal revenues of the Crown.

In addition to these offices, there were new groups of justices and local commissioners. By the 1220s county knights were appointed alongside professional lawyers as justices of gaol delivery, trying the prisoners held in gaol awaiting trial between the visits of the judges of the central courts. In the same period knights with particular legal expertise were appointed to act alongside professional justices on the assize circuits. From the 1260s local keepers of the peace, drawn from the ranks of the gentry, were appointed with responsibility for maintaining order. In the fourteenth century these men, armed with additional powers, were transformed into justices of the peace. From the 1290s justices of 'oyer and terminer' were appointed in increasing number to 'hear and determine' particular cases brought for their attention. These men too were members of the knightly class, who worked alongside professional justices. A number of administrative commissions were also brought into being by the needs of late thirteenth-century government. Gentry commissioners, for example, were appointed in each shire to collect taxes whenever a subsidy (or tax) on movable property was granted in parliament, while commissioners of array were appointed to supply the king's need for foot soldiers whenever an expedition abroad was anticipated.

The extensive involvement of the knightly class – and later of the richer esquires – in local administration is illustrative of the phenomenon which has been called self-government at the king's command. This is a term which describes the system whereby the king's government, recognising its lack of coercive power, left the communities of shire knights largely to themselves provided that they met the military and financial needs of the Crown when required to do so. For the knights this was a perfectly satisfactory arrangement. As sheriffs and JPs they could annex royal and public power to their own influence to reinforce their jurisdictional positions locally. The spheres of public and private merged in their hands.

Through their involvement in royal administration, the knightly class was drawn into ever closer association with the Crown and the higher nobility. The responsibilities of the two groups were essentially complementary, with the nobility occupied in government chiefly at the national level, advising and assisting the king and commanding his armies, and the knights discharging duties devolved to them at a lower level. If the responsibilities of nobility and knights were largely separate, the two groups were nonetheless linked both socially and politically. In their exercise of informal social dominance they acted as a single all-encompassing elite.

Because of these developments, it is possible to see England witnessing the gradual emergence of a broad upper class like the *noblesse* found in France and elsewhere in Europe. By *noblesse* is meant a broadly based elite composed of all families of noble descent who maintained their blood purity irrespective of wealth or poverty. Characteristic of a *noblesse* in the pre-modern era is the absence of any formal legal distinctions within the elite group, greater and lesser nobles being treated as one. In representative assemblies members of the *noblesse* normally sat together in one estate, or house, made up of all those of noble and gentle background. The important distinction in such societies was not so much between the greater and the lesser nobility as between the nobility and the trading and labouring classes.

Even the most cursory review reveals resemblances between the *noblesse* of continental polities and the broad elite group emerging in thirteenth-century England. In England, as on the continent, the nobility and knights formed a single elite group defined by their entitlement to the use of a coat of arms. In England, as in Europe, the boundary between the two groups was ill defined, some lords counting as barons, while others of similar wealth did not. In England, again as in Europe, nobles and knights were united in a single chivalric culture forged in war and expressed in literature and visual display. In England, again as elsewhere, nobles and knights were joined in a single social network: they intermarried; they were linked together by ties of kinship, association and retainer; and they moved in the same social circles. In England, as all over Europe, increasing emphasis was placed on social exclusivity.

Yet, in the end, there never was to be a continental-style *noblesse* in England. For all the signs of assimilation between knights and nobility, the two groups remained separate and distinct. In late medieval England, when men spoke of lords, they meant titled lords not country knights. Increasingly the wealthier lords – the magnates – drew apart from their inferiors until in the fifteenth century they formed a separate and exclusive peerage. On the continent there was also to be a drawing apart by the top elite. Nowhere in continental Europe, however, was the distinction between nobles and knights to become as marked as it was in England. On the continent the *noblesse* as nobility embraced all of noble descent. This was not to be the case in England. Why was England exceptional?

The greater part of the answer is to be found in the institutional development of the English parliament. By a quirk of historical development magnates and knights, the upper and lower nobility, found themselves sitting in different houses, the magnates in the Lords and the knights in the Commons. In most though not all continental assemblies no such separation was to occur, magnates and well-to-do knights sitting together as members of the second estate. The process of separation came about largely as a by-product of the Crown's need to secure popular consent to the levying of taxation. Before the late thirteenth century most sessions of parliament were composed only of lords, recipients of individual summonses from the king. By the 1270s, however, as the levying of taxation became more frequent, it was felt that lords, because they attended in a personal capacity, could not bind the community of the realm as a whole, and the assent of a more broadly based representative group was held necessary. Such a group was found in the assembly of elected shire knights, the nucleus of the future House of Commons. By Edward I's reign it was accepted that if a grant of public taxation was to have legal validity, representatives of the knights had to be present. Around the same time the representatives of the larger towns were invited to sit in the Commons alongside the knights. By a parallel and independent process the distinction between knights and lords was reinforced by standardisation of the lists of lords, which meant that the lords took on the character of a hereditary caste.

Whatever the effects of placing knights and burgesses together in the same chamber in promoting social integration – and clearly there must have been some – one thing is clear: England was not to have a continental-style *noblesse*. When the magnates and knights were sorted and separated into two parliamentary houses, they also ended up in two different social groups. The one group, socially the higher, came to constitute a discrete nobility, while the other coalesced into the gentry. The Knights of the Shires in parliament were the knights of the shires back home. Although the knights had more in common culturally with the lords than they did with the burgesses, in terms of status they were not of the same ilk. By the fifteenth century the nobility which the knights had once enjoyed was fast slipping away. The process of growing social exclusivity which had favoured the knights back in the thirteenth century was to count against them two centuries later.

5

Kingship and War, 1272–1327

'The New Richard'

When Edward I succeeded his father in 1272 the throne was occupied for the first time since the Lionheart's day by a chivalric enthusiast. Edward, like Richard, was not just a practitioner of war; he revelled in the chivalric associations of war, and he turned his realm into a country organised for war. Edward had a particular fascination with the cult of King Arthur, which he was probably the first ruler to deploy in the service of the English monarchy. In Edward's reign the connection between kingship and chivalric enthusiasm, which had first been forged by the Lionheart, was drawn still closer. Edward's accession aroused high chivalric expectations. One contemporary hailed the new ruler as shining 'like a new Richard', claiming that he brought 'honour to England by his fighting as Richard did by his valour'.[1] The comparison with the Lionheart was to live on in popular imagining until the end of the reign. In a chronicler's eulogy penned on his death in 1307, it was again with the Lionheart, among others, that Edward was compared.

The future King Edward was born in 1239, the eldest son of Henry III and Eleanor of Provence. Not a great deal is known about his upbringing and early life. It may be significant, however, that one of the earliest references to him reveals him as involved in tourneying. In 1256, the chronicler Matthew Paris reports, he was supplied with suitable weapons and armour to practise his skills at a specially arranged tournament at Blyth in Nottinghamshire.[2] The meeting, according to Matthew's account, proved a bloody one. Tournaments at this time still took the form of rough mass encounters and several of those who took part suffered injury. Edward, however, emerged from the fray unscathed. Whether this was because of his skill or through sheer luck, Matthew does not say.

In 1260 Henry allowed his son and his friends to venture abroad to exercise their tourneying skills. According to one account, they failed to acquit themselves with any distinction, and Edward himself was wounded.[3] Edward was to make a second foray into tourneying on the continent two years later, in the summer of 1262, this time suffering losses with his friends in an encounter at Senlis. Evidently at this stage Edward was little more than an amateur at the sport. By the mid-1270s, however, his reputation stood higher. After returning from crusade in 1274 he was invited by Count Peter of Chalon to stop at Chalon-sur-Saône to take part in a competition which pitched his Englishmen against all comers. This mighty struggle, in which Edward and his men were outnumbered, turned so violent that it acquired the name of the Little War of Chalon. In 1278, after his accession, Edward was invited to take part in another competition, a lavishly staged festival at Le Hem near Amiens.[4] Only his involvement in leading a campaign against the Welsh prevented him from attending.

Edward's experience of tourneying appears to have alerted him to the importance of the sport in assisting in the renewal and remilitarisation of English knighthood. In 1267 he and his brother Edmund and cousin Henry of Almain jointly issued an edict which allowed tournaments to be held again in England after a fifty-year lapse.[5] Henry III, like Henry II, had viewed tournaments with suspicion, regarding them as hotbeds of violence, disorder and political disaffection. Edward's thinking was different. Like the Lionheart, of whose encouragement of tournaments he would have known, he viewed tourneying favourably. He was particularly concerned, as the Lionheart had been, to gain a military edge over the French. Neither Louis IX of France in his later years, nor his successor Philip III, had shown much interest in promoting tourneying, and Edward believed that by encouraging his knights to practise arms he could steal a march on England's old rival. He and his supporters promoted the sponsorship of tournaments and, at least until the 1270s, he took part in them himself. As king, he regularly laid on tournaments and Round Tables to mark such occasions such as royal rites of passage. In 1299 lavish jousting was organised at Canterbury to mark the occasion of his second marriage – to Margaret of France.

In the years immediately before his accession, however, Edward's commitment to chivalric values found clearest expression not so much in tourneying as in crusading. Edward was the first English king to embark on a crusade since the Lionheart in the 1190s, and the last to do so until Henry Bolingbroke, the future Henry IV, in the 1390s.[6] His expedition to the east undoubtedly both added to his reputation and enhanced the glory of the English Crown. The immediate spur for his crusade had been an appeal by the papal legate Ottobuono for military aid for the beleaguered Latin Kingdom of Jerusalem.[7] King Louis of France responded by taking the cross in 1267, and Edward followed suit the following year.

Edward had initially planned to join the French in their diversionary attack on the North African port of Tunis, but after hearing of Louis's death in 1270 and the subsequent French withdrawal from the city, he headed for the Holy Land instead. Edward took with him a modest force, probably consisting of no more than a thousand men, and arrived off Acre in May 1271. With the crusader kingdom already in terminal decline, there was little real difference he could make. He and his men launched two raids, one on Saint-Georges-de-Lebeyne in late June, and the other on Qaqun in November, neither sortie having much effect. In May 1272 the king of Jerusalem, Hugh de Lusignan, agreed to a ten-year truce with Sultan Baibars, the Muslim leader, and shortly afterwards Edward prepared for his return to England. It was probably around this time that the most celebrated episode of the crusade took place – the attempt of a Muslim assassin to kill him. Edward succeeded in fending off the assailant, seizing his poisoned knife and slaying him, but himself suffered a wound in the arm. In a later, semi-fictionalised version of the episode his devoted wife Eleanor saved his life by sucking the poison from the wound. As with the Lionheart, it is significant that legend accumulated around Edward, implying that he was seen as a figure of stature and charisma to whom a good story could easily attach itself.

Edward returned to England on 2 August 1274, his father having died two years earlier, and well before the end of the decade he was engaged in full-scale hostilities on England's borders. In 1277 he launched the first of two brilliantly organised campaigns against the Welsh, attacking Llywelyn of Gwynedd, the last independent Welsh ruler, who had taken advantage of English weakness to expand his power in the Marches, trapping his armies in Snowdonia and forcing him to submit. In 1282, after Llywelyn rejected the terms imposed on him five years before,

Edward launched a second campaign, aiming this time to eliminate Gwynedd altogether. In a brisk autumn campaign he again encircled the principality, cutting off supplies to the Welsh, and Llywelyn was trapped and killed at Irfon Bridge. In 1284, after the last embers of Welsh independence had been extinguished, Edward wiped the principality from the map, absorbing it administratively into England.

It is against the background of this massive English assault on north Wales that we need to view the most remarkable development in the history of chivalry in those years, Edward's promotion of the cult of the mythical British king, Arthur.

Edward was the first monarch since Richard the Lionheart a century earlier to take much of an interest in the legendary Arthur.[8] The Lionheart's enthusiasm is well attested to by Benedict of Peterborough's report that he took Arthur's sword Excalibur with him on crusade, presenting the trophy to King Tancred of Sicily.[9] It is also significant that in Richard's reign Arthur's reputed bones at Glastonbury were exhumed and reinterred, the abbot who performed the act, Henry of Sully, being Richard's cousin. Neither of Richard's two immediate successors, John and Henry III, was to show any great interest in Arthurianism. It was only in Edward's reign, and largely as a result of his efforts, that Arthur's cult was both popularised and accommodated in English court culture. Edward was attracted to Arthur in part by general chivalric sentiment: the cult of the mythical king was a component in the international knightly culture of the day. He was also attracted, however, by considerations of political expediency. Arthur's Britishness could add some legitimacy to his attempts to create a new British kingship in the wake of his absorption into the English state of the last independent Welsh principality.

Edward's interest in Arthur was, not surprisingly, to find its first public expression the year after the first Welsh war. At Eastertide 1278 Edward and his queen visited Glastonbury Abbey on a tour of the West Country. What happened there is described by the Glastonbury chronicler Adam of Domerham:

> On the Tuesday, in the twilight of the day, the lord king ordered
> the tomb of the famous King Arthur to be opened. There were
> then discovered, in two coffins painted with their likenesses and
> their coats of arms, the bones of the said king of marvellous size

and of Queen Guinevere, of great beauty . . . An inscription was written above each figure. On the next day, Wednesday, the king took the king's bones, and the Queen Guinevere's, wrapped them in precious cloths, put them back in the chests, sealed them with their seals, and ordered the same tomb to be placed before the high altar, retaining the heads and cheeks outside, for the devotion of the people, and placing the following writing with them:

These are the bones of the most noble King Arthur, which on the 19th April in the year of Our Lord 1278 were placed here by the illustrious King Edward of England in the presence of Queen Eleanor (and other notables).[10]

Following Edward and Eleanor's visit an impressive new tomb was made for the two bodies in the place which the king specified, immediately before the high altar. The tomb was destroyed when the abbey was dissolved in 1539 and no trace of it now remains. Its appearance, however, can be reconstructed from the detailed description given by the Tudor antiquary John Leland in his *Assertio*. On Leland's evidence, the tomb took the form of a plain black marble chest, supported on four crouching lions, one at each corner, with a sculpted panel of Arthur at the head.[11] It was thus very different in appearance from most English royal monuments of the day and was probably designed to evoke associations with antiquity via the porphyry sarcophagi of kingly burials in southern Europe. What is striking is that this design was to be picked up, early in the next century, on Edward's own monument in Westminster Abbey. Edward's simple dark marble tomb chest is strikingly austere in the context of English royal funerary commemoration, and the intention may have been to evoke comparison with Arthur's tomb at Glastonbury. Although the tomb chest was made some years after Edward's death, it almost certainly reflects his own plans. Even in death, Edward wanted to be seen to stand in lineal succession to the celebrated Arthur.

In the tourneying context Edward's Arthurianism found clearest expression in his encouragement of the form of knightly encounter known as the round table. Round tables were a type of knightly competition of early thirteenth-century origin which swept to popularity in the second half of the century.[12] Matthew Paris's description of one of these events at Walden in Essex in 1252 gives some indication of their character, suggesting that large numbers of knights were involved, probably in a knockout competition. Typically the arms used were blunted lances rather than sharpened weapons – at Walden an unfortunate error over weapons led to a fatality.[13] Round tables were fairly mannered events, not rough melees like the old-style tournaments. A reference to seating at a round table at Warwick in 1257 implies that chairs, or at least stands, were used at some stage for the ease of onlookers.[14]

Five round tables are known to have been staged in Edward's reign, three of them noted by the chroniclers. The first, and probably the grandest, was held in 1279, when Roger Mortimer, a friend of the king and a Welsh Marcher lord, held a round table at Kenilworth, inviting no fewer than a hundred knights and a hundred ladies to attend. Edward himself was present, and at the end his sister-in-law presented Mortimer with some barrels which appeared to contain wine but which, when opened, were found to be full of gold. It has been suggested that Mortimer's motivation in holding the round table was to associate himself with Arthur, from whom he claimed descent through his Welsh mother.[15]

Edward sponsored two of his biggest round tables in non-English parts of the British Isles. The first of these was held in 1284 at Nefyn in the Lleyn peninsula, in the wake of his conquest of Snowdonia. It was attended by both English and foreign knights, and the main event was a contest between two teams, one headed by the earl of Lincoln and the other by the earl of Ulster. The second was an event held at Falkirk in Scotland in 1302, covered in less detail by the chroniclers, perhaps because of its remoteness, but apparently held to commemorate Edward's victory over Wallace near the town four years before.

Edward's interest in the Arthurian institution of the Round Table is most powerfully represented for us today by the great table probably commissioned by him in 1285.[16] The table still survives in the hall of Winchester Castle and is the grandest piece of wooden furniture to have come down to us from the Middle Ages. It consists of an enormous circular timber frame with a planked surface, measuring eighteen feet (5.5 metres) in diameter and weighing three-quarters of a ton. It is fashioned entirely of oak and fastened with wooden pegs, except in the joints of the felloes (which form the rim), where iron nails were used. The table rested on twelve big legs, now lost, the heavy centre steadied by a pillar possibly of stone but more probably of timber.

No documentary evidence survives to indicate when the Winchester round table was made. Tree-ring evidence, however, points to a date somewhere between 1250 and 1350, most probably between 1250 and 1300. The plausible suggestion has been made that the table was commissioned in the 1280s as part of preparations for a visit made by Edward I to Winchester in September 1285, in the course of which a round table tournament was held.[17] Winchester was a city rich in Arthurian associations. According to Geoffrey of Monmouth, it was at Winchester that Arthur's father, Uther Pendragon, was acclaimed king, while according to the thirteenth-century *Mort Artu* it was near Winchester that Arthur's final battle against the evil Mordred was fought. Edward had convened a council meeting at Winchester for September 1285, in connection with which a mass knighting was arranged, and round table tourneying may have been staged as a festive accompaniment to this. Conceivably the magnificent table was used as the setting for a feast hosted by the king in honour of leading participants in the tournament and visiting dignitaries.

One other major chivalric event in Edward's reign was invested with a powerful Arthurian colouring, and that was the Feast of Swans held at Westminster on Whit Sunday 1306. This celebrated gathering was conceived as part of Edward's programme for the renewal of English knighthood. The immediate context was provided by the knighting of the king's son, the future Edward II. In the presence of a massive assembly of magnates and knights in St Stephen's Chapel, the now aged king bestowed knighthood on his son, and the latter then knighted no fewer than three hundred tyros of his own age. Afterwards, when the company adjourned to the palace for dinner, two large roasted swans were brought in on a tray covered with a lattice of gold. Over these delicacies the king swore two oaths, one to avenge himself on the new Scots leader Robert Bruce, and the other to go again on crusade to the Holy Land. The young Prince Edward then joined in the oath-taking, swearing that he would not sleep two nights in the same place until he had fulfilled his father's undertaking against the Scots. All the other knights apparently followed suit.

The making of a vow at a great feast, when the diners were well lubricated, was to become a familiar trope in the rituals of late medieval chivalry. In 1454 at the Feast of the Pheasant at Lille the duke of Burgundy swore to go on crusade, a commitment later to return to haunt him. Over time, the gesture was to become hackneyed. There can be little doubt, however, that to those present in May 1306 the vows represented an opportunity to re-enact and live out Arthurian fantasy. Arthur and his knights, as the romances related, had all pledged themselves by vow to high and perilous enterprises. In the *Conte de Graal* of Chrétien de Troyes, Sir Perceval, in Arthur's hall, swore that he would never sleep two nights in the same place till he had achieved the object of his quest. In the *Queste del Saint Graal*, after the Grail, covered with white samite, had floated into Arthur's hall, first Sir Gawain and then the other knights vowed to search for a year and a day until they had seen the vessel again. Vowing to commit oneself to a noble cause at a feast, if not actually doing so, was one way in which knights could re-enact and embrace the Arthurian fantasy. That contemporaries were alert to the associations implied by the Feast of Swans is indicated by the chronicler Langtoft's observation that nothing like this occasion had been seen since Arthur's feast at Caerleon.[18]

In the mythological culture of Edward's court the theme of Arthurian romance was also picked up in architecture – which in this context means principally castle architecture, for Edward's reputation was as a castle builder. The most striking Arthurian allusions are to be found at the grandest of the king's castles, Caernarfon, begun in 1283 and still incomplete at the king's death. Caernarfon was a structure which made use of exceptionally wide-ranging historical imagery.[19] Its site had strong mythological associations with the Emperor Constantine. According to Welsh legend, Magnus Maximus, allegedly the father of Constantine, dreamt of a beautiful maiden living in a castle with multicoloured towers at the mouth of a river. His envoys tracked down the fortress and he was able to marry the maiden. In 1283, according to one chronicler, the body of Magnus Maximus was actually discovered when the castle's foundations were being dug. Against this background, it is not surprising that the castle's architecture was replete with references to an imperial and Constantinian past. Carvings of eagles were placed on top of the West, or Eagle, Tower, and bands of stone of contrasting colour were used in the main walls in imitation of the Theodosian walls at Constantinople.[20]

Sinadon (Snowdon) or Segontium (the Roman name for the town) had long been familiar to readers and writers of Arthurian romance as the birthplace of Perceval and where Arthur had sat at the Round Table. At the same time, according to Geoffrey of Monmouth, in a heroic conflation of as many as three historical Constantines, Arthur himself was none other than the grandson of the emperor. In these circumstances of mythological profusion it would be surprising indeed if Caernarfon's architecture had not made visual reference to the mythical and the fantastic. As it was, it made such reference in abundance. Its geometrical ground plan, its surfeit of turrets – no fewer than three on top of the Eagle Tower – and its battlements carved with figures all proclaimed the world of romance, investing the castle with a mystique and aura unique among the castles of north Wales.

By exploiting a heady mix of history and myth at Caernarfon, Edward strove to present himself to his subjects as the new Arthur, the heir to the Arthur of legend. At the same time, by a complementary strategy he made an audacious attempt to deprive the Welsh of their own claim to Arthurian legitimacy. In the wake of his conquest of Snowdonia he made the Welsh hand over to him the regalia of Llywelyn's princely dynasty. Among the items which the Welsh were forced to surrender was what they claimed to be Arthur's crown. The seizure of so precious a relic made a considerable impact on contemporaries. According to one account, 'the crown of the famous Arthur, which had been held by the Welsh in such honour for so long, was now translated against their will to the glory of the English'.[21] The writer appears to have seen the loss of the crown as depriving the Welsh of an object central to their national identity. In 1284 Edward arranged for his eldest son Alfonso to present the regalia to the shrine of St Edward the Confessor in Westminster Abbey, although in the event this does not appear to have happened. Possibly, because of the regalia's importance, it remained in the king's personal collection of relics.

In almost everything that he did as king Edward mixed convention with political calculation. This was certainly true of his engagement with the cult of Arthur. Edward's interest in Arthur and his court had its origins in an aristocratic culture which revelled in myth, legend, history and pageant. Edward lived and breathed this culture and was steeped in its values. In the 1290s he commissioned a series of paintings of the Maccabean victories of ancient Israel for the Painted Chamber at Westminster, attesting to the martial ethos of his court.[22] His sheer absorption in chivalry, however, was not something which stood in the way of him appreciating how it could be made to serve immediate political needs. Edward's ambition was to create an imperial, British-wide kingship. He had conquered Wales by 1283 and by the time of his death was halfway to conquering Scotland. The attraction which Arthur had for him was that he was a British, and not an English, king. By laying claim to Arthur's inheritance Edward could likewise lay claim to historical legitimacy for his imperial ambitions. In Wales it was easy enough for him to clothe himself in the mantle of Arthurianism: there were myths about Arthur to be exploited and there were relics which he could seize and carry away. In Scotland, however, the task was more difficult. Yet Edward showed himself nothing if not resourceful. In a letter which he sent to the Pope in 1301 justifying his claims he accorded Arthur an honoured place. Arthur, he said, had conquered Scotland and had installed a subject king there; this king had performed service to Arthur at the great Whitsun feast which he had held at Caerleon. Arthurianism, ever open to invention, could easily be manipulated and reinterpreted. It could be made to serve English monarchical needs, just as the cult of Charlemagne had been made to serve French royal needs. In the Arthur of historical myth could be found a new Arthur, the Arthur of political legitimation. It was this Arthur which Edward put to such effective use in his monarchical propaganda.

The Revival of English Knighthood

By the middle years of his reign Edward enjoyed a reputation as one of Europe's greatest and most distinguished princely rulers. With the death of St Louis in 1270 and the collapse of Hohenstaufen rule in Germany twenty years earlier, he faced few rivals in distinction. He was the arbiter of chivalry in Europe, with aspirant knights of all nationalities and allegiances vying to be dubbed by him. To some he must actually have seemed like Geoffrey of Monmouth's Arthur, whose court was likewise a magnet for Europe's young noblemen.

Edward's grandiose ambitions gathered pace in the second half of his reign. Encouraged by his successes in Wales, he embarked in the 1290s on the much greater task of subduing Scotland. In the northern kingdom, however, resistance was to be both fiercer and better organised than in Wales because it was supported by the resources of an effective state. Under a succession of inspirational leaders, notably Robert Bruce from 1306, the Scots were to conduct an increasingly effective guerrilla war. Edward scored significant triumphs in the field, notably at Falkirk in 1298, but was never able to convert these into subjugation of the country as a whole. The war which he had unleashed in 1296 dragged on through his successor's reign and on into that of his successor in turn. To add to Edward I's problems, the English were also faced with wars against the French, who took advantage of his problems to make encroachments into Aquitaine.

It is the intense military activity of Edward's later years which helps to explain his concern to expand the ranks of English knighthood. Edward needed large numbers of well-trained, well-equipped knights who could undertake regular campaigning in difficult terrain. Edward's wars were fought across a wider theatre and on a larger scale than any English wars for three-quarters of a century. From 1296 until 1314 there were expeditions to Scotland or to the Scottish Borders almost every year. Some of these involved armies of very considerable size. The force which Edward led to Falkirk in 1298 was, on the evidence of the payrolls, almost certainly the largest, numbering some 30,000– 35,000 men; the cavalry contingent alone accounted for about 3,000 men, 110 of them high-status knights banneret.[23] In 1300 the force which Edward led to besiege Caerlaverock Castle was another of considerable size, numbering perhaps 10,000–12,000 men, some 850 of them cavalry of the king's household. In 1303, for the campaign which he led to the Moray Firth, Edward mustered 7,500 foot soldiers and perhaps 280 heavily armed knights. In Edward II's reign much the biggest force was that which was defeated at Bannockburn in 1314. This was a force on a scale to match some of Edward I's largest, numbering at least 15,000 men, about 2,500 of them cavalry. In 1322 perhaps as many as 2,000 cavalry took part in a campaign against the Scots to protect the northern border. Edward I's earlier wars against the Welsh, while they had been fought on a more limited scale, had again involved large forces. The army which Edward led in 1277 is known to have numbered some 15,000 men.

Edward's need for knights – or, rather, for knights and serjeants (esquires) – meant that he had to be flexible and imaginative in his approach to recruitment. There had been a major contraction in the ranks of the knightly class since the early thirteenth century. Overall, as we have seen, numbers had fallen from a total of perhaps 4,000 at the end of the twelfth century to some 1,250 three-quarters of a century later. The number of militarily active knights had almost certainly fallen further still. It has been estimated that by Edward I's reign there were no more than about 500–1,000 fighting knights at most. A major disincentive to service were the start-up costs which a knight faced in fitting out for war. To take to the field, a knight had not only to equip himself with armour and weapons, which might cost ten to twenty pounds; he also needed a big warhorse – a destrier – which might cost between fifty and sixty pounds or more. If the knight was summoned to fight in a theatre where there was little prospect of profit, such as Scotland, he might well feel that the expenditure did not justify the return. In the long peace of Henry III's reign knights' fighting skills had atrophied; there had been little or no call for their services. In Edward I's reign the position was very different. Knights were in great demand. So where did the king find his men, and how did he overcome their reluctance to fight?

One initiative of Edward's, which, perhaps surprisingly, brought only mixed results, was pay for military service. Hitherto, the barons or tenants-in-chief – those who held their lands directly from the king – had performed their service as a matter of obligation. The duty of attending on the king with an agreed quota of knights was one which followed from the act of homage which they performed for their lands. However, the quotas for which they were nominally liable had been negotiated down in the thirteenth century and by the 1280s were quite inadequate for the king's needs. The challenge which Edward faced was to find a way of coaxing the tenants-in-chief into attending with knightly vassals over and above those for which they were contractually liable.

The means on which he alighted in the 1280s to achieve this end was the offer of pay. With the novel resource of parliamentary taxation at his disposal, he had no difficulty in finding the money. He launched his initiative in April 1282, when he issued writs to six earls and 152 others inviting them to serve in the second Welsh war in return for pay.[24] The writs provoked what appears to have been a considerable crisis. The responses to the king's invitations were overwhelmingly negative. At a council meeting in April Sir Robert Tiptoft, one of the king's household knights, was replaced in command of the forces in south Wales by the earl of Gloucester, and in May the king was forced to replace the summonses with new ones which made no mention of pay. The reasons for the baronial hostility, a seemingly extraordinary act of self-denial, can only be guessed at. It is possible that there was concern that entitlement to booty and captured lands might be threatened if royal pay were accepted. It is equally conceivable that there was a more generalised concern about loss of status and independence among the landed classes. Whatever the reasons, baronial feelings ran high enough to dissuade Edward from further innovation. On only one subsequent occasion did he again offer pay. This was in the winter of 1297/8, when a group of earls and barons was tempted into serving on these terms for three months on the Scottish Borders.

As an alternative to pay Edward experimented with a very different approach, that of making appeals directly to the knights on the basis of their wealth. In other words, instead of summoning the knights through their lords, as traditionally, the king summoned all knights with lands of a certain value directly to fight as part of the fealty owed to him. Since Henry II's time, by the Assize of Arms all free men in England had been under obligation to possess arms and military equipment appropriate to their rank. Edward now aimed to impose a more specific obligation to perform cavalry service on those who had the means to afford the equipment needed. In 1282 he summoned all knights with lands worth at least twenty pounds per annum who were not already at the Welsh war to attend the campaign. In 1296 he issued summonses to serve in Scotland to all those whose lands were worth forty pounds per annum, the level at which landholders were obliged to assume knighthood. In 1300 he issued yet another summons to those with lands worth forty pounds to attend for service in Scotland. On this last occasion, however, he encountered opposition from the baronage and was obliged to withdraw the order. The great men of the realm were growing concerned that Edward was becoming too exacting in his demands and insisted that henceforth he issue only conventional summonses. Edward had to back down again, and no more qualification-based summonses were issued for the remainder of his reign. Later calls for service took the form of either traditional feudal summonses or appeals to his subjects' oaths of fealty and allegiance.

Edward's failure to alter significantly the composition of his forces by adjusting the letters of summons suggests that what contributed most to successful cavalry recruitment at the time was actually a quite different factor, a general remilitarisation of English knighthood. In other words, more effective in boosting turnout than wielding the big stick over the barons was the subtler tactic of mixing stick and carrot. While it can hardly be doubted that compulsion assisted in recruitment for a few campaigns – some of those in Scotland, for example – more productive overall in improving participation were the king's measures to raise the status of knighthood and make it a rank worth assuming.

The king's own chivalric impulses played a major role in achieving this objective. His active participation in crusading, his staging of tournaments and round tables, and his encouragement of Arthurianism all contributed in their different ways to a popularisation of knightly values. The impact of the revival of knighthood was felt most immediately in Edward's own circle. It is evident, for example, in the rapid rise in the number of household knights receiving the king's pay. Outside the royal entourage its effects were spread countrywide by those with the closest ties with the county elites – pre-eminently by the king's household knights, and the magnates and their retainers. In the reigns of the first two Edwards it was the magnates' own retinues – in particular, those of the earls of Lancaster and Pembroke – which took the lead in providing the teams around which the main tournaments were organised. A commitment by a retainer to undertake military service on his lord's behalf was now typically written into the indentures which stated the retainer's terms of service.[25] The greater willingness of the knightly class to offer military service attested to the new pride which they felt in their martial calling and their readiness to see in it an expression of traditional chivalric ideals. By one inspired measure Edward was able to extend his achievement into the reign of his successor. This was the mass dubbing at the Feast of Swans, at which the future Edward II was knighted and some 267 aspirant knights with him.[26] Edward, nearing death, took every precaution to ensure that his achievement in renewing English knighthood would live on after him. It is a tribute to his success that no fewer than 84 per cent of the 854 knights in the Parliamentary Roll of Arms drawn up in his son's reign can be shown to have been militarily active.[27]

The keenness which members of the knightly class were to show in entering into their obligations can be gauged from the length of some of their careers in arms. In some cases these extended over several decades, even across reigns. The knights of the royal household naturally had the most impressive records. Sir Robert Tiptoft, for example, after seeing service in the baronial wars of Henry III's reign, served Edward loyally in the wars in Wales and Gascony, and before his death in 1298 was preparing for service in Scotland. Sir William Latimer, another household knight, won his spurs on Edward's crusade in the early 1270s, and later served the king in Wales, Scotland and Gascony.[28] A number of magnate retainers had records scarcely less distinguished. Sir John de la Rivière, a retainer of Earl Aymer de Valence, fought in virtually every campaign between 1297 and 1314, while Sir Ralph de Camoys, a dependant of the Despensers, served even longer, from 1297 into Edward III's reign.[29] The greatly enhanced military awareness of these years can be sensed in the spread of heraldry as a form of decorative adornment. By the early fourteenth century displays of heraldic blazons were found not only in the rolls of arms, which celebrated knightly achievement and solidarity, but on tomb monuments, in stained-glass windows and in the spaces above castle and abbey gateways. Some of the richest displays had their origins in the solidarities forged on campaign. At Norbury church in Derbyshire, c. 1298–1306, the arms of the patron, Sir Henry Fitzherbert, figure in the chancel windows alongside some two dozen others, those of magnates and knights all linked by their service in the Scottish wars.[30]

In the mid-thirteenth century the knights had transformed themselves into a small but elite group decked out in the trappings of a borrowed aristocratic lifestyle. They had strengthened their identity with an involvement in warfare which allowed them to develop martial traditions and a shared chivalric mentality. Within families traditions of military service were being built up which contributed to the formation of a closely knit military class. It was this intense militarisation, which originated in the Edwardian wars, which lay behind the great English achievements to come in the Hundred Years War.

Chivalry at Bay?

For some 200 years a characteristic of chivalric society had been the magnanimous treatment of political captives and opponents. When kings had put down rebellions, they had treated those at their mercy with respect. They did not starve them, mutilate them or put them to death; after a show of stern disapproval, they received them into their peace and granted them their lives.

This code of behaviour had been introduced by the Normans in 1066.[31] In pre-Conquest times murder, execution or mutilation had been the fate which awaited those who had failed in rebellion against a king; mercy and compassion were rarely, if ever, shown. After the Norman Conquest, rebellion was still identified with treason and was accordingly considered an act of betrayal, but typically the punishment exacted was forfeiture and imprisonment, not loss of life. In the Norman period it was not unknown for luckier rebels to be allowed to flee abroad.

In the late thirteenth century, however, these chivalric conventions began to break down. Rebels who failed in a challenge to a ruler found themselves treated much more harshly than hitherto. The trend towards brutalisation began in the reign of Edward I and continued into that of his successor.[32] The respect which knights had once shown to each other began, in certain circumstances, to dissolve.

The first rebel to feel the full impact of the tough new approach was Dafydd, brother of Llywelyn, the Welsh prince who had led the revolt against the English in 1282. Dafydd was captured in 1283 and sentenced to a gruesome death. He was to be drawn to the scaffold because he was a traitor, hanged for his homicide, had his bowels burned because he had committed his crimes at Easter and, finally, was quartered because he had plotted the king's death. In August 1305 an equally gruesome fate was administered to the Scottish leader William Wallace, who had been captured earlier that month and been brought down to London for punishment. He too was condemned to suffer the multiple penalties of a traitor. He was drawn to his place of execution at Smithfield, hanged and disembowelled, had his entrails burned in front of him and was beheaded. His remains were then quartered. His head was placed on London Bridge, while the quarters were sent to towns in northern England and in Scotland as a warning to others.[33] In the summer of 1306 similar horrific penalties were visited on those involved in Robert Bruce's uprising who had the misfortune to fall into English hands.[34] One of the victims was John, earl of Atholl, Edward's own kinsman, the first earl put to death by an English king since 1076.

In the next reign, that of Edward II, the penalties inflicted on the non-English resistance leaders Dafydd and Wallace were to be inflicted on the king's internal enemies as well. In the wake of the rebellion of Thomas, earl of Lancaster in 1322, dozens of magnates and knightly rebels were executed as traitors. Lancaster himself, being of royal blood, was let off with beheading. His fellow rebels, captured at Boroughbridge, were condemned to far worse fates. Bartholomew Badlesmere, a Kent knight, was dragged by a horse through Canterbury to a crossroads outside the town, where he was hanged and afterwards beheaded.[35] To terrorise the realm into submission, Edward adopted the tactic of despatching the condemned for execution in the areas where they had exercised lordship. The reaction of contemporaries was one of horror. The Lanercost chronicler was aghast at the king daring to execute his nobles 'without holding a parliament or taking the advice of the majority'.[36] In the next few years the country was to become locked in a cycle of ever-escalating violence. In 1326, when Edward II was overthrown, his ally, the younger Despenser, was subjected to the same treatment as he had meted out to his own enemies. He was drawn to the gallows at Hereford, hanged and disembowelled, and finally put out of his misery by beheading. Four years later, Roger Mortimer, Queen Isabella's paramour, who with the queen had been responsible for the king's overthrow, was in turn arrested and subjected to a traitor's death.

What were the causes of this sudden and shocking descent into barbarity? There had been no comparable outbreak in the wake of the baronial wars of the 1260s; nor had there been in the aftermath of the war of Henry III's minority before that. In the 1260s the royalists had hardly shown themselves generous or merciful in their treatment of their Montfortian opponents; their harshness, indeed, had been a factor in delaying reconciliation between the two sides. Yet apart from the premeditated slaying of de Montfort himself at Evesham in 1265 they had confined themselves to seizing and plundering the rebels' lands. They had not engaged in extended and extensive bloodletting of the kind that was to be seen later. Nor did they indulge in such acts of stigmatisation as the reversal or defacement of their opponents' coats of arms.[37]

To a large extent Edward I's toughness towards defeated rebels can be explained in terms of his legalism. The treatment which he meted out to the resistance leaders Dafydd and William Wallace was rooted in his view of their military activity. In Edward's eyes the two men were rebels engaged in an illegal war against their rightful lord, a lord who enjoyed overlordship over their respective peoples. Their own view was the contrary one that they were fighting an entirely just war between two equal and independent polities. Edward's rejection of his opponents' claims allowed him to dispense with the normal conventions dictated by the laws of war and to punish them as traitors.

Edward II, in his treatment of his domestic enemies, was simply following the precedent set by his father. Where one king had blazed a trail in the exaction of legal rigour, it was easy for another, particularly a rather ungenerous one, to follow. The younger Edward was assisted in his task by the emergence in the fourteenth century of a professional judiciary entirely dependent for promotion on royal patronage and favour.[38] In both the words and the actions of such senior judges as Sir Geoffrey le Scrope the emphasis was on the subject's obligation of unquestioning obedience to the king.

There was another factor, however, which almost certainly had a bearing on the treatment of rebels, and this was the loss of Normandy in 1204. In the century and a half in which England and Normandy had been joined under the same ruler or the same dynasty, the duchy had offered a refuge to anyone rebelling against royal authority in England. As long as there was a Norman bolt-hole to which malcontents could flee to escape justice, the king could never bring the full force of his authority to bear on those who opposed him. By the late thirteenth century, however, with Normandy lost and England an island state again, the position was very different. The full rigour of the law could again be exacted. As the author of the *Vita Edwardi Secundi* was to observe, for an islander to rebel against his king was like a chained man trying his strength against his prison warder.[39] If chivalry as theatre and display was to enjoy its full flowering in the fourteenth and fifteenth centuries, the same could not be said of chivalry as clemency; the days of royal and aristocratic moderation had passed.

6

Edward III and Chivalric Kingship, 1327–99

With the beginning of the French wars of Edward III's reign, a new era was to open in the story of chivalric knighthood in England. The memories of the military defeats and political disappointments of Edward II's reign were banished to the past, and king and nobility joined together in pursuit of glory abroad. A key turning point was the great English victory at Crécy in 1346. Crécy was one of the most significant battles of the later Middle Ages. Not only did it set the seal of divine approval on Edward III's kingly regime and his claim to the French Crown; it paved the way for a new and closer accommodation between chivalric culture and the English monarchy. In the eyes of later generations Edward III was the perfect king whose example his successors would do well to follow. Like Richard the Lionheart before him, Edward was to place all who ruled after him under a heavy burden of emulation.

The Road to War

The conflict with the French which we recognise as the Hundred Years War, although developing into a war for the Crown, originated in something lesser – a dispute over the status of Aquitaine. Since 1259 the kings of England had held the duchy of Aquitaine, in south-west France, as vassals of the French kings, a subordinate relationship which limited the autonomy of the king's government in the duchy in several important respects. In the first place, the king-duke was prevented from conducting an independent foreign policy because of the requirement that his actions and priorities accord with those of the French; second, he was constrained in his dispensation of justice by the possibility that aggrieved subjects would appeal against him to the French *parlement* in Paris. In the reigns of the first two Edwards the consequences of these restrictions on sovereignty became steadily more apparent. A major reason for this was that the social and political conditions of the duchy encouraged disputes which dragged in the ducal government: boundaries and jurisdictions were ill defined; nobles and towns were assertive and independent, and the king-duke's officials often high-handed in their dealings with plaintiffs. In an age when the dispensation of justice was a key element in the exercise of lordship, and the number of litigants who sought judgments in his courts a measure of a lord's power, the French king was well placed to undermine the foundations of the duke's government in Bordeaux.

Disputes between the kings of England and France over the status of Aquitaine had led to the French confiscating the duchy twice in the seventy years following the making of the terms in 1259. In 1294 Philip IV had declared the duchy confiscate in the wake of a dispute over navigation rights with Edward I, while thirty years later Charles IV resorted to confiscation in a border dispute with Edward II. By 1337, when Philip VI confiscated the duchy for the third – and, as it was to happen, for the last – time, it was clear that things could not go on as they had.

Edward's bid for the French Crown was conceived as a way of circumventing the interminable disputes about the status of Aquitaine. Edward saw his bid as a means by which he could skirt round all the complex arguments arising from his vassal status by claiming to be the rightful king of France himself. In the circumstances of the time, he had ample grounds for his claim. In 1328 Charles IV, the last of Philip IV's three sons, had died, like his brothers without surviving issue, and there was no obvious successor. Invoking the Salic Law, the French council had awarded the crown to Philip's nephew, Philip, count of Valois, who became Philip VI, ignoring Edward's claim through his mother, Philip IV's daughter. Edward, after initially failing to challenge this decision, assumed the title of king of France at a ceremony at Ghent in January 1340. To draw attention to his new style, he quartered the fleur-de-lys of France on his shield with the lions of England. The Hundred Years War was therefore in a technical sense a chivalric dispute, a quarrel between two knights over the right to bear a particular coat of arms. Small wonder, in the circumstances, that Edward III should have been so keen to seek combat with his adversary on the field of battle.

Edward's early campaigns against the French in the Low Countries between 1338 and 1340 had brought him little in the way of strategic advantage. Despite being kept well supplied with money by the English exchequer, he suffered constant shortages of cash, with massive payments to his allies virtually bankrupting his treasury, while the French added to his problems by refusing to give battle. By the autumn of 1340 all that he had to show for his efforts was a naval victory over the French at Sluys off the Flemish coast, a significant triumph but not one that altered the balance of power between the two sides.

A year or two later Edward was to enjoy no greater success in the field in Brittany, where he opened a second front in alliance with the pro-English duke, John de Montfort. By the end of 1343 Edward's military challenge to the French king seemed in danger of petering out. Yet it was essential that he achieve a major victory in the field if he were to vindicate his claim to the French Crown. In the mid-1340s a fresh opportunity arose with the eruption of internal political dissension in France. Within eighteen months he was to win a victory which would both transform his military fortunes and result in the creation of a new style of chivalric kingship in England.

Crécy and the Fortunes of War

Edward's intentions for the campaign which was to reach its climax at Crécy have been much debated. There can be little doubt, however, that the king's main aim was to unleash an assault of such ferocity on French territory that Philip of Valois would have to meet him in battle. The conditions of the day favoured Edward. Philip had suffered 'exceeding blame' for his failure to engage Edward in the Low Countries, while his economic policies, which included debasement of the currency, were causing impoverishment among his subjects. It was whispered that 'the king of England should better have obtained the realm of France than the king who held it' and that it was 'better to be ruled well by an Englishman than badly by a Frenchman'.[1] There was a considerable well of discontent here which Edward could exploit. One particular dispute in Normandy played into his hands. Here a quarrel had broken out between two lords of the Cotentin, Godfrey de Harcourt, lord of Saint-Sauveur, and Robert Bertrand, marshal of France and brother of the bishop of Bayeux. In the spring of 1343 Harcourt attacked and burned two of the bishop's manors. The French king's officials reacted vigorously to this affront, seizing Saint-Sauveur and arresting Harcourt's confederates. Harcourt fled first to Brabant and then to England. Edward was thus provided with an ally who could help him raise Normandy. In the summer of 1345 he began mobilising his resources for a major invasion of France the following year.

Edward landed at Saint-Vaast-la-Hougue in the Cotentin around dawn on 12 July 1346. His army of some 14,000–15,000 was the largest to be taken to France at any one time in the Middle Ages. Simply transporting it across the Channel placed massive demands on English shipping. The moment he disembarked Edward received Godfrey de Harcourt's homage for his Norman lands, an act implying recognition of his claim to be king of France. At the same time Edward declared that the persons and goods of all who would enter into his obedience should be protected from harm or molestation on pain of life and limb. He wanted to ensure due order and stability in his rear as he advanced into France to seek out his adversary and engage him in battle.

Edward's army headed south and east divided into three divisions, the largest under the king himself, the other two under his son, the Black Prince, and the leading earls. The three divisions marched separately along a broad front, so as to spread devastation over the widest possible area as they went. After taking Carentan and Saint-Lô they marched towards Caen, the largest city in Normandy after Rouen. At Caen the French were taken completely by surprise and a relief force led by the duke of Normandy arrived too late to be of assistance. The town surrendered after only three days. Bartholomew Burghersh, one of the English commanders, put the death toll at 5,000, 'so that, praise be to Our Lord, our business has gone as favourably as it could'.[2] Edward did little to curb the plunder that followed: he wanted to show other towns the consequences of disobedience to his will.

From Caen Edward moved rapidly east to the Seine valley, covering seventy miles in less than a week. The French king by this time had brought his army to Rouen. Anxious that he still lacked the manpower to confront his adversary, he ordered the destruction of the bridges over the Seine, forcing Edward to march upstream to Paris. Edward was by now concerned that he might be pinned on the west bank of the Seine by the French, with his line of retreat blocked off. At Poissy, however, his men repaired a bridge over the river, allowing him to cross. Philip, thrown onto the defensive, issued a series of challenges to Edward, offering to meet him in single combat – challenges to which Edward responded with ambiguous replies. The English king wanted to choose his own site for the engagement which would settle their dispute: one where his men could employ the strong defensive formation which they had perfected in war over the previous twenty years.

From Poissy he headed north to find a crossing point over the River Somme. He needed to transfer his army to the far bank to make contact with the fleet bringing him supplies and to gain a clear line for possible retreat. With the help of a local informant he found a crossing at Blanchetacque, downstream from Abbeville, near the mouth of the river. A small French force was guarding the bank opposite. At low tide on 24 August Edward's men stormed across, driving back the French and taking possession of much-needed food supplies. The main French host was by now only fourteen miles away, near Abbeville, and battle could no longer be averted. Edward took up position near the village of Crécy, in the English-held county of Ponthieu, on a site reconnoitred by Harcourt, the earl of Warwick and Sir Reginald Cobham. The site was carefully chosen; there is a distant possibility, indeed, that it may have been identified as a potential battlefield nearly fifteen years before by Burghersh, when seneschal of Ponthieu. It gave Edward precisely the setting that he needed to meet the French on his own terms. Stretching north-east–south-west it took the form of a broad, flat-bottomed valley, narrowing at each end so as to limit the opportunities for French advance and retreat, and with a steep bank on the east blocking off escape in that direction. Provided the English could achieve their ambition of routing the French cavalry, the site had the potential to be a killing field. Small wonder that Edward was described as being 'merry and delightful' on the eve of battle.[3]

The contest was fought on the late afternoon of 26 August. Edward drew up his army at the end of the valley in three divisions, each deployed in column. The men-at-arms – the knights and esquires – were dismounted. Before the entire line small pits were dug, to trip up the enemy horses. A number of Philip's advisers, observing the English dispositions, recommended delaying until the next day to allow time for reorganisation. Philip, however, normally a cautious man, ordered an immediate advance. His force of 4,000–6,000 Genoese crossbowmen were the first to move forward. They opened fire, but rapidly found themselves outmatched by the enemy longbowmen, who could fire further and faster with deadly effect. Collapsing under the hail of arrows, they broke ranks and fled, having achieved nothing. The main French cavalry line now tried to advance, but fared no better. As arrows flew, 'thicker than rain' it was said, horses reared and bolted, throwing their riders and causing havoc in the French ranks. The French, scarcely lacking in bravery, mounted no fewer than three general assaults on the English, each ending in failure. Philip tried rallying his men, but in vain. By nightfall the English were in possession of the field. Among the dead were the blind king of Bohemia, a close ally of Philip; the king's brother, the count of Alençon; his nephew the count of Blois; the count of Flanders; and seven more counts and viscounts. The French had lost the cream of their military elite. English casualties were few.

Edward's triumph at Crécy constituted one of the most remarkable battle outcomes of the Middle Ages. French dominance of European arms to this date had been so complete that observers might well have predicted a victory for Philip. Yet the English triumph was not altogether unheralded. For some twenty years the English had been practising and honing the tactics which now brought them success. The use of the longbow in English armies can be traced back to the reign of Edward I, when it began to supplant the, till then, traditional crossbow. The idea of combining dismounted men-at-arms with archers was a tactic which had been developed in the Scottish wars of the 1330s. It was first attempted in the Stanhope Park campaign of 1327, failing then because of the Scots' refusal to engage, but was subsequently employed to greater effect at Dupplin Moor in 1332 and Halidon Hill the following year. Use of the combined defensive formation against the French is first recorded at the battle of Morlaix in

Brittany in 1342, when the earl of Northampton deployed it success-fully against Charles of Blois. At Morlaix Northampton had employed another tactical device which was to be used again at Crécy. This was the digging of pits covered with vegetation in front of the line against advancing horses. It was an idea which the English had picked up from the Scots, who had used it against them at Bannockburn.

A major weakness of the armies of Edward I's day had been their poor mobility, a problem caused by the presence of a large and cumber-some infantry corps. In Edward III's reign this difficulty was overcome by replacing a proportion of the infantry by a smaller number of lightly armed mounted archers. The new force could be used both to give protection to the knights in battle and to act in a raiding and foraging capacity on the march. Thanks to the presence of the mounted archers Edward III's armies in France were considerably faster moving than his grandfather's had been in Scotland.

If the adoption of new tactics was a major contributor to the English success at Crécy, only slightly less important was the accumulated military experience of many of those who fought in the battle. Among the men-at-arms and commanders in particular there was a body of experience which stretched back to the proving ground of the Scottish wars of the 1330s. The five earls involved at Crécy had all fought at Halidon Hill in 1333 and had subsequently served regularly in Scotland and on the early campaigns in Flanders. The great majority of Edward's commanders had also seen service in the winter campaigning in Brittany of 1342–3. The earl of Northampton brought to the field of Crécy memories of the battle of Morlaix, as did his lieutenants on that occasion, Sir Richard Talbot and Sir Hugh Despenser. A sizeable minority of the knights had careers which went back further still. Sir Robert Morley and Sir Bartholomew Burghersh, for example, had both served since 1315, while the sub-marshal of the army, Sir Thomas Ughtred, had begun his career at Bannockburn the year before that.

It was not only experience which these veterans brought to the business of fighting in France; it was something still more valuable – the experience of fighting in close teams. A notable characteristic of some of the larger retinues which fought at Crécy was their consider-able stability of composition. Of the seventy-two men known to have accompanied the earl of Northampton, well over half had fought under him before, most of them in Brittany, some half-dozen or so in the

Low Countries or Scotland before that. Only seven of the thirty-six identifiable knights in the earl's retinue at the battle were entirely new to his service. It was a similar story with the king's retinue, which formed the core element of the largest of the three divisions. At the heart of the king's company was a group of knights – Sir Richard Talbot, Sir Michael de Poynings, Sir Reginald Cobham and Sir Thomas de Bradeston among them – who had been at his side since the Scottish wars of the early 1330s.

The cohesiveness of so many of the larger retinues takes on added significance when viewed in relation to the organisational structure of the army. The Crécy force was made up of two main elements – the mixed retinues of men-at-arms and archers assembled by captains who had contracted to supply a certain number of men for an agreed term of service, and infantrymen raised independently by the commissions of array in the shires and the Welsh Marches. The mixed retinues were a relative novelty, a pragmatic response to the twin challenges of finding a way of raising mounted archers without imposing unacceptable costs on local communities, and supporting them in the field when the king was not present in person. The solution, of using captains experienced in raising men-at-arms to raise archers too, was one which proved extremely convenient for the Crown. It had the special attraction of devolving onto others a range of responsibilities which would otherwise have to be borne by royal officials.

The use of mixed retinues, however, brought a further advantage – an advantage almost certainly unforeseen at the start and which emerged only as a by-product of administrative reorganisation. In the field it made for much greater operational integration. The retinues were made up of soldiers of complementary skills – archers balancing men-at-arms, and infantrymen cavalry. Hitherto these groups had been raised and organised separately, and had undergone their training separately. Once they were raised together, the relationship between them began to change: they discovered the advantages of cooperating, which paved the way for tactical cooperation in the field.

It has often been assumed that the men-at-arms and archers at Crécy fought separately – the men-at-arms in the centre, and the archers on the wings. Such a hypothesis, however, is inherently improbable. To break up a mixed retinue in this way would have been to throw away all the advantages brought by the experience of training and fighting as a group. It would also have been tactically foolish: archers were lightly armed and would have been dangerously exposed without support from men-at-arms and spearmen. The most likely reconstruction is that the men-at-arms and archers, deployed in their established companies, were intermingled.[4] The task of the men-at-arms was close combat, and that of the archers, once their lethal volleys had been unleashed, to back up the men-at-arms, wielding swords or clubs alongside them. The close inter-relation of men-at-arms and archers was thus of crucial importance in contributing to the English success at Crécy. Behind that lay the use of mixed retinues in which the two elements gained experience in working together in combined companies.

If the cohesiveness of Edward's force was thus the second factor which made it so effective at Crécy, one last reason played some part in the English success – the king's encouragement of the culture and institutions of chivalry. Edward's absorption in chivalry helped both to enhance the prestige of his court and to strengthen the ties which bound him and his knightly companions together. Edward actively encouraged his magnates and knightly entourage to live and breathe the chivalric high life. From the moment of his assumption of power in 1330, tournaments – or hastiludes – had been held almost monthly in summer and on the major feast days in winter, giving a total of perhaps ten or eleven events a year, each lasting between two and four days. Edward's household knights were as active as he himself in sponsoring tournaments. Sir William Clinton, later earl of Huntingdon, sponsored such an event at Dartford in 1331 and Sir Robert Morley another at Stepney a few months later. Some of the grander tournaments were associated with important moments in the life of the royal family. The birth of the king's son Edmund of Langley was accompanied by lavish jousting in 1341, while in 1355 the baptism of Thomas of Woodstock and the churching of Queen Philippa were both marked by what were said to be 'great festivities and grand hastiludes'.

The influence of Low Countries chivalry can be detected in the growing enthusiasm for inaugurating tournaments with elaborate processions in which women were participants as well as men. A theatrical, even a festive, quality can be detected in many of the grander events of the day. On some occasions the knights took to the lists in exotic and colourful disguises. At a tournament in 1343 organised by Sir Robert Morley the knights dressed up as the Pope and twelve of his cardinals, while in 1359 another company dressed as the mayor and aldermen of London. There is a strong overlap between the theatricality of such jousting and the play-acting entertainments which formed a regular feature of the court's seasonal festivities.[5] Extravagant dressing-up was common to both. In 1347 Edward donned an exotic green animal outfit for both a joust in which he took part and for that year's Christmas festival at court.

For all the fantasising that went with these events, however, jousting was an activity with a strictly practical purpose: it was both a substitute and a preparation for war. The regime of training which it provided was rigorous. Those who participated could suffer injury, on occasion death. At a tournament at Northampton in 1342 Henry of Grosmont's brother-in-law Sir John de Beaumont was killed and 'many nobles wounded or otherwise mutilated'. At Woodstock in 1389 the young John Hastings, earl of Pembroke, the last of a distinguished line, was killed jousting, to the dismay of onlookers. Tourneying contributed to the formation of the knightly esprit de corps that was so important an ingredient in Edward's military success. Remarkably perhaps, even the donning of disguises in tourneying served a practical purpose. It made for equality between competitors by ensuring that a lesser knight did not defer to the superior blood of his rival. In 1334 at a major tournament at Dunstable the king appeared under the arms of the Arthurian knight Sir Lionel. On several later occasions he appeared wearing the arms of members of his household entourage. Participating incognito in the manner of Arthurian heroes was a way of linking the fantasy world of romance to the practical world of preparation for war.

Chivalry, the Order of the Garter and Windsor

The chivalric junketings which glamorised Edward's court were to reach their climax in the months following the king's return from France. Edward sailed back to England in mid-October 1347 after receiving the submission of the citizens of Calais. In the ten months which followed he attended tournaments at Bury St Edmunds,

Reading, Windsor, Lichfield, Eltham and Canterbury.[6] On each occasion, according to the exchequer accounts, he appeared splendidly attired. For the tournament at Lichfield he and his retinue were dressed in colourful robes of blue and white. Huge sums were spent on livery badges and special costumes for all the lords and ladies gathered to watch the spectacle.

This intense tourneying forms the backcloth to what in retrospect appears the most significant chivalric event of these years – the establishment of the Order of the Garter. This celebrated knightly company was to become the most illustrious and important of the chivalric orders of the Middle Ages. In the fifteenth century it was to be emulated by many new companies in continental Europe, notably the Order of the Golden Fleece of the dukes of Burgundy. The Garter, however, was always the most highly regarded of them all. A major reason for its success was its association with a monarchy riding high on the back of chivalric achievement.

The precise date of the order's foundation is not known. The only direct statement to have come down to us is in a later prologue to its statutes which says that it was founded in the twenty-third year of Edward's reign – that is to say, between 25 January 1349 and 24 January 1350. On the evidence of the royal accounts, it seems almost certain that the first formal meeting of the order was convened in this period, in conjunction with a tournament held at Windsor on 23 April 1349. Since one of the founder knights listed in the prologue is known to have died before 2 September 1349, and two others died in the same year, probably victims of the Black Death, the order must have been constituted before the end of August 1349. There seems a strong likelihood that the Windsor tournament of April that year was the occasion when the statutes were published and the first companion knights inducted.

The order was conceived as a confraternity of twenty-four companion knights, to whom the king and the Black Prince were added, bringing the total to twenty-six. Overall, the ethos of the company was strongly military. Great emphasis was placed in the statutes on knightly endeavour and loyalty to the king as superior of the order. Knights were to be chosen for election on the basis of their personal worthiness, their martial renown and the unblemished nature of their reputations. A distinctive feature of the arrangements was found in the religious dimension to the foundation. Edward provided for the order to be linked institutionally to the chapel in the lower ward of Windsor Castle, which was to serve as its religious and ceremonial centre. Here Masses were to be said for the souls of deceased knights, while the memory of those same knights was kept alive by the placing of stall plates above their seats on their deaths. The connection between the order and the chapel was a witness to the dedication of the member knights to a Christian knighthood.

The twenty-four founder knights were drawn principally from the ranks of those who had contributed to the victory at Crécy. Twenty of the group can be shown to have taken part in the battle, and two of the others – Sachet d'Abrichecourt and Henry d'Em – could conceivably have been present. The two remaining knights, Henry of Grosmont and the Captal de Buch, had helped by leading or taking part in the subsidiary action in Aquitaine. The establishment of the order was thus simultaneously an act of thanksgiving and a reward for those who had served on the campaign. Yet at the same time it was something more: it was an institutional symbol of Edward's vindicated claim to the French Crown. The enigmatic symbol of the Garter finds its meaning in this context. The famous Garter legend 'Honi soit qui mal y pense' (Shame on him who thinks ill of it), significantly in French, referred to Edward's claim; implicitly it condemned all who questioned it. The device of the Garter had been used on pennons and streamers in the course of the Crécy–Calais campaign. Now in the wake of the spectacular victory it was adopted as the motto device of the new company.

The creation of the order drew on, and formalised, a whole variety of impulses which had been circulating at Edward's court for some time. The idea of a chivalric company of fixed membership obviously originated in the Arthurian concept of the Round Table. The strong play-acting element was heavily indebted to the *ludi* – courtly entertainments – which probably lay behind much of the theatrical side of late medieval chivalry. The seeming novelty of the adoption of a device and motto can be traced to the practice of some of the tourneying teams of the day. In Lincolnshire in the mid-1340s such a team used the motto 'Better is war than peace.'[7] The order itself appears to have originated as a pair of evenly matched tourneying teams. The complement of twenty-four knights was probably arrived at as two teams of twelve, one under the king, the other under his son, the two corresponding to the two pairs of stalls in which the knights were seated in the chapel.[8]

One big difference, however, can be detected between Edward's earlier endeavours and the order as established in 1349 or 1350. All of Edward's earlier chivalric impulses had found expression in the context of his Arthurianism. Edward's obvious fascination with the cult of Arthur had manifested itself in a whole variety of ways. As we have seen, in 1334 the king had appeared in the lists wearing the arms of 'Sir Lionel', the arms ascribed to Sir Gawain in fictive armorial tradition. Four years later he was to name his third-born son Lionel, again evoking associations with Arthur and the Knights of the Round Table. In 1331 he and Queen Philippa had visited Glastonbury Abbey in Somerset to see the reputed tomb of King Arthur. In 1344 he had actually announced his intention 'to found a Round Table in the same manner that the Lord Arthur, once king of England, had relinquished, to the number of 300 knights'. The accounts of the king's exchequer record that he embarked on the construction of a vast hall in the upper ward of Windsor Castle to accommodate the proposed company. The foundations of this hall were excavated in 2006.[9] Right to the very moment of his departure for Crécy, Edward was reflecting on the mythical associations of King Arthur's court, particularly as they related to Windsor. It is possible that he was seeking to promote Windsor, his birthplace, as a new Arthurian cult centre over the rival claims of Glastonbury, Caerleon and Winchester. In this context his choice of the bishop of Winchester as prelate of the order could have been a gesture intended to assist in the transfer of Winchester's claims to Windsor.[10] Windsor was to be the new Camelot, home to the most honourable and esteemed knightly company in the realm.

When he founded the Order of the Garter, however, Edward was to some extent turning his back on the legendary world of Arthurian romance. It would be an exaggeration to say that he rejected it completely: the cult of Arthur was never wholly abandoned at Edward's court. It is likely, for example, that the motet *Sub Arturo*, in which the king is identified with Arthur, was composed for the Garter celebrations of 1358.[11] Yet Arthur was never again to occupy the position of prominence in English royal myth-making that he once had. The search for appropriate chivalric legitimising models was to move in new directions. Where literary precedent had once been the dominant factor influencing the king's ideas for an order, there was now to be a new force – the lordship and protection of political sainthood. At some stage in the planning for the Order of the Garter Edward made the crucial decision to associate his new institution with the cult of St George.

The king's need for the patronage of a saintly sponsor had become apparent once he had settled on the idea of linking the order to the chapel in the lower ward at Windsor. Arthurian patronage could no longer be accommodated within the new structures envisaged, for Arthur was a secular figure. What the company required was the patronage of a Christian saint, and St George came with all the right credentials. A soldier martyr killed in the Diocletian persecutions of the early fourth century, he legitimised both Edward's martial ambitions and his plans for a new European role for his monarchy. St George owed his fame to his miraculous appearance to the First Crusaders at the siege of Antioch in 1098. His dramatic intervention, setting the crusaders on their victorious course to Jerusalem, made him the natural protector of a Christian knighthood dedicated to recovery of the Holy Places. By the thirteenth century he was being credited in James de Voragine's *Golden Legend* with a range of miraculous feats – enduring a protracted martyrdom of seven years, overcoming a dragon in combat, and springing to the defence of the Virgin, who armed him with a shirt of mail, a lance, shield and warhouse. The attractions of St George to Edward III were his martial repute, his cosmopolitanism and above all his ability to transcend national boundaries and allegiances. He attracted devotees and admirers all over Europe. He was acclaimed as the exemplar of chivalry in France, Hungary, Italy and the Empire. His cult attracted followings in the courts of Paris, Avignon and Anjou. His espousal by Edward attested to the outward-looking internationalising ambitions of his monarchy; it lent a legitimising touch to his bid for a place at Europe's monarchical top table.

At the same time it did something else: it paved the way for a bid by the English king to appropriate the cult for his own exclusive use. Edward was aiming, in effect, to nationalise St George, while simultaneously preserving something of his universality. Edward's entry into what amounted to a saints' war with the French injected a new

ideological element into the political struggle between the two countries. Evidently concerned that the French might launch a bid to hitch
the saint's cult to their own national cause, he moved to take it over
himself. The measure of his success is found in the strength of the
saint's identification with English martial effort in the years to come.
At Agincourt seventy years later it was under St George's banner that
a later soldier king, Henry V, was to triumph over the French in battle.
When, nearly two centuries later still, Shakespeare was to make Henry
declare at Harfleur, 'God for Harry! England and St George!' he
switched Agincourt for the harbour town, but he faithfully reproduced
the spirit of the scene.

It is easy to conceive of Edward as the genius whose imaginative
flair gave birth to the Order of the Garter. To credit Edward alone with
that idea, however, would be to overlook the involvement of other
significant figures. One such who was almost certainly involved was the
king's cousin Henry of Grosmont, earl of Derby, later duke of Lancaster.
Duke Henry was one of the most distinguished noblemen of his day,
a soldier, politician and diplomat of distinction. His knowledge of
Europe's courts and their culture was unmatched by that of anyone
else in England. In 1343 he had assisted the Castilian king Alfonso XI in
his operations against the Moorish-held city of Algeciras. A decade later
he had travelled to Prussia and Lithuania to aid the Teutonic Knights
in their crusades against the Slavs. Duke Henry was an authority on all
matters chivalric and relating to the practice of arms. His influence can
almost certainly be detected in the final form assumed by the Order of
the Garter.

It may well have been Duke Henry who suggested the idea of
replacing a larger, looser order with an elite fellowship of twenty-four
knights. King Alfonso of Castile had recently founded an elite
company, the Order of the Band. This was a model for the Garter in
being a relatively small company, all of whose members were bound
in close relation to the king, so conceived, as the Garter was to be,
as a buttress of royal power. Significantly, the order also made use of
an item of personal attire as its device, in this case a sash worn over
the shoulder. During his visit to Castile Duke Henry could hardly
have failed to notice the existence of the new company; indeed, it is
very likely that many of its members were with him at the siege of
Algeciras. The information which he brought back about the Castilian

king's initiative could have been significant in shaping Edward's own ideas.

It is also possible that Duke Henry suggested that St George be made patron of the order. The hypothesis is prompted by the inclusion of the saint on a brass with which the duke was associated, that of Sir Hugh Hastings at Elsing in Norfolk. Sir Hugh, the younger brother of the earl of Pembroke, was another commander involved in the operations of 1346. Edward had entrusted him with the leadership of a force in Flanders charged with distracting and diverting the French while he himself landed in Normandy. Sir Hugh had died in July 1347 after contracting dysentery at the siege of Calais. Duke Henry acted as one of his two executors and was almost certainly involved in the design of his brass.[12] This magnificent memorial, one of the most opulent of its day, is rich in chivalric reference, and Duke Henry himself is represented in one of the side shafts of the canopy. The figure of St George is shown in the canopy pediment itself, riding triumphantly over a stricken dragon. If the inclusion of the saint – remarkable for this early date – is indicative of the duke's interest in his cult, then it is conceivable that he was responsible for its encouragement at court. It may be worth remembering that the duke had visited Avignon in the course of the negotiations of 1344, in which case he would have seen Simone Martini's frescoes of St George and the dragon in the porch of the cathedral there.

Edward's achievement in harnessing the ideas and initiatives of his magnates to his own essentially personal vision of a national chivalric company is a mark of his genius as a ruler. In the decade to come, once the terrible scourge of the Black Death had passed, his thoughts were to return to Windsor, the castle where his order was based. As a result of the creation of a college of priests to serve the order's Chapel of St George, the court had lost the use of the residential apartments in the lower ward. To make good this loss, Edward embarked in the 1360s on the construction of an entirely new set of apartments in the upper ward.

This project was to be much the largest secular building programme of its day. The new apartments, luxuriously fitted out, were ranged round three courtyards high up overlooking the river.[13] The king's lodging consisted of a grand six-chamber sequence of rooms, and the queen's of a five-chamber sequence. The route by which visitors processed to the king's rooms was stretched out to create an impression of space and grandeur. Visitors were admitted through the left-hand of two entrances from the ward into a big staircase hall; they were then taken, by a circuitous route, along a gallery to the south of the main courtyard to a second staircase; they went up this staircase, and then made their way round a long first-floor gallery finally to the lodging. A novelty of the castle's planning was the placing of the hall, chapel and great chamber sequentially along the main front, the three rooms linked for effect externally by a system of uniform fenestration. The cost of the building programme was enormous. Over an eighteen-year period Edward spent no less than £51,000 on the project, some of it met from the profits of war. The functions which the magnificent new castle was to perform were both practical and symbolic. Windsor was to be simultaneously a great residential palace and a stage setting for the pageantry of monarchy. Its dramatic site high on a bluff above the river, along with its exotic skyline, invested it with romance and mystery. It had already figured in an episode in Chrétien's Arthurian romance, *Cligès*.[14] Windsor was to be a monument to chivalry, a witness in stone to the antiquity and traditions of the English monarchy, the capital of a legendary kingdom reborn.

Meanwhile Edward was still enjoying many of the fruits of success in war. His commanders were continuing to win notable victories in the field. In 1356 his son the Black Prince, exceeding even his father's achievement at Crécy, captured the French king at Poitiers and brought him captive to London. In 1360, however, after a stalled campaign in northern France, Edward decided to reach a settlement with the French. By the terms of a treaty negotiated between the two sides at Brétigny, in return for surrendering his claim to the French Crown, he was awarded large parts of south-west France in full sovereignty. The treaty represented the summit of Edward's achievements in war. Over the next decade his political grasp slowly weakened. He sank into lassitude and senility, preyed upon by an avaricious mistress, Alice Perrers, at the same time as his son fell victim to a debilitating illness. The new French king, Charles V, taking advantage of the English collapse, reopened the war, clawing back many of the territories ceded at Brétigny. By the time of Edward's death in 1377 little was left of his earlier gains beyond Calais and its march and the area around Bordeaux. Nonetheless the memory of his triumphs lived on. His tomb epitaph, composed in the mid-1380s, hailed him as 'the glory of the English, the flower of kings past, the pattern for kings to come'. The chronicler Walsingham, a little later, said that he 'had been among all the kings and princes of the world renowned, beneficent, merciful and august, and given the epithet "the Favoured One" on account of the remarkable favour through which he distinguished himself'.[15] To Froissart, 'Edward had had no equal since the time of King Arthur . . . The kingdom of England was grief-stricken' on his death.[16] At his funeral in Westminster Abbey Edward was given an appropriately chivalric send-off: a knight decked out in the royal arms offered up a shield at his burial place. Edward's place in England's pantheon of royal heroes was assured.

Chivalric Kingship and its Legacy

Edward's posthumous reputation was to be of considerable significance in shaping the character of English late medieval kingship. Through his remarkable triumphs in war Edward established a new paradigm of militant chivalric rule.[17] English history in the late Middle Ages was to be in a very real sense a negotiation with the memory of his achievements. For as long as the pursuit of external war was considered the foundation of good kingship and success in war the measure of God's blessing on the kingdom, Edward's kingship was the exemplar for others to follow.

The nature of Edward's legacy can be seen in a tract written nearly a century after his death, William Worcester's *Boke of Noblesse*. Worcester, a conservative longing for the good old days, wanted to persuade Edward IV to renew national self-confidence through war with the French. In support of his argument, he appealed to the memory of Edward's achievements. 'Edward,' he wrote, 'was the most famous knighte of renomme,' and 'notwithestanding [his] great conquestis and batailes . . . he never atteyned to that souvraine honoure but by valiauntness of Englishe men.'[18] Edward, for Worcester, was not only a king who provided a model of martial achievement; he was also the creator of a united nation in which king and people worked together for the common good.

At roughly the time that Worcester was writing, a parliamentary petition calling for better government likewise invoked the memory of Edward's achievements. The petition recalled the 'immortal fam of . . . Edward III, wiche diffyed kowertyse, avansed manhode, and magyfied trouthe. This noble prince, this princely knyght, this knyghtly conqueror so loved, drad and obbeyed the prynce of prynces, the knyght of knyghts and conqueror of al conquests, that not only encreased his olde renomye, but also made his subjects loved and drad in al strange lands.' Edward was seen here as worthy of admiration not only for his conquests and the renown these brought, but also for the peace and good government, indicative of God's blessing, which came in their wake. Chancellor Alcock made much the same point in 1472, when he replied to another petition from the Commons. 'It is nat wele possible,' he said, 'nor hath ben since the Conquest, that justice, peax, and prosperite hath continued any while in this lande in any Kings dayes but in suche as have made werre outward.' Among the examples he cited in support of this view was the reign of Edward III. 'Werre outward', in the form practised by Edward III, was accordingly seen as a prerequisite for good governance and national renewal. Kingship and knighthood went together. In Froissart's words, in England 'the whole community of the land is always more inclined to war than peace'.[19] England had become 'this seat of Mars'.

The first king who had to engage with Edward's legacy was his grandson and heir, Richard II, who succeeded in 1377. The burden of popular expectation which greeted the accession of the ten-year-old monarch was considerable. Not only was he seen by his subjects as stepping into the shoes of two great Edwards – Richard's father, the Black Prince, who had died in 1376, and Edward III himself; he was also acclaimed for his name Richard, which linked him directly to the Lionheart. The earliest indications which the young king afforded of his character were certainly promising. He commanded admiration for the calmness and courage with which he dealt with the first great test of his reign, the Great Revolt of 1381, when he was brought face to face with the rebels at Mile End and Smithfield. By the mid-1380s, however, there were signs that his early promise was not going to be fulfilled. Richard showed little interest in pursuing a foreign policy of the kind associated with his father and grandfather. When called on by the Commons in 1383 to cross the Channel to challenge the French with an army, he declined. Two years later, when he did finally take the field, it was, more modestly, against the Scots. His government faced a serious difficulty in the mid-1380s in that the exchequer was short of money, but even in the 1390s, when the coffers were full, he refused to fight; he preferred to negotiate for peace. In 1396 he agreed to a twenty-eight-year truce with the French which effectively brought the war to an end for a generation.

Richard's vision of kingship, as it was articulated in the 1390s, thus contrasted sharply with that established by Edward III and, before him, by the Lionheart. Richard had little sympathy with the traditional view of war as an instrument of national renewal, believing, as the Westminster chronicler explained, that it weakened kings by forcing them to barter with their subjects for taxes.[20] In Richard's view, it was the king's sovereign authority which alone brought order to a realm, with the Crown itself becoming the focus for the emotions which had earlier gone into war. When Richard achieved untrammelled power, as he did after crushing his baronial opponents in 1397, he ruled not so much in partnership with his subjects as in opposition to them. His goal was what he called peace, which to him was attained not through success in war but through the rigorous exaction of obedience.[21]

Richard's authoritarian vision of kingship found expression in his attitude to tournaments. He was no less enthusiastic about these events than his father and grandfather had been; the use which he made of them, however, was very different. Where his grandfather had used tournaments to provide his knights with rigorous training and to celebrate his victories, Richard used them as occasions for drawing attention to his majesty. Tournaments are known to have been held in Richard's reign at Westminster in 1385, at Smithfield in 1386, May and October 1390, and 1397, and at Windsor in 1399; in addition, there was smaller-scale jousting each Garter Day at Windsor. The aspect of these events which Richard chose to highlight was more the ceremonial than the practical. Instead of participating in them himself, as his grandfather had done, he watched; he looked down on them from on high. Like Henry VII in Bacon's famous description, he was 'a princely and gentle spectator'. At his hands tourneying was made a vehicle for the cultivation of a kingship of distance.

Richard, in other words, while no great enthusiast for arms, did not entirely reject the culture that went with them. On the contrary, he relished – he revelled in – chivalric display. But at the same time he manipulated and transformed it. Where Edward had used tourneying to bond with his nobles, Richard used it to promote distance and hierarchy. He made it a stage setting for ceremonies which focused on and exalted his own person as king. Lavish jousting accompanied each of his two marriages, in 1382 and 1397. Walsingham speaks of hastiludes lasting days on end after his marriage to Anne of Bohemia in 1382. Knighthood was manipulated in such a way as to highlight the crown as the source of dignity and honour. When Richard visited Ireland in 1395 he made a point of bestowing knighthood on the four Irish high kings and, according to one account, had them wait on him at dinner. In the 1380s, alongside the male institutions of the Order of the Garter, he developed a sorority, or sisterhood, to which aristocratic ladies were appointed, so as to promote a more civilian atmosphere at his court. In elections to the Garter itself, enjoyment of royal favour counted increasingly as a factor. In 1383 and 1385 Thomas Mowbray and Robert de Vere, two of Richard's friends, were elected, although neither was particularly distinguished in arms. In the 1390s John, Lord Beaumont, Sir William Scrope, Thomas Holand, earl of Kent, Sir Simon Felbrigg and Sir Philip la Vache were all elected to the order as a result of royal favour. By manipulating the Garter, as through ceremonialising knighthood, Richard reordered the institutions of chivalry to serve the needs of his new-style monarchy. Chivalry was presented in its new role as a buttress of hierarchy. Tournaments were made theatrical settings for the display of royal majesty. Attention was focused on the king as the source of patronage and honour.

In other circumstances, and at a different time, Richard's vision of kingship might perhaps have succeeded. In the circumstances of the 1390s, however, it was to end in failure. In 1399 Richard was deposed. In March of that year, following the death of his uncle John of Gaunt, the king had seized the estates of the duchy of Lancaster, parcelling them out among his supporters and sentencing Gaunt's son, Henry Bolingbroke, to exile. In June, while Richard was in Ireland, Bolingbroke returned and quickly attracted wide support. Richard's ministers offered little resistance, and by the time the king returned to Wales in late July his cause was lost. In parliament on 30 September Richard was removed from the throne and the Crown awarded to Bolingbroke. Richard's sterile emphasis on the prerogative of kingship proved no substitute for the genuine solidarity between a king and his nobles forged by war and chivalric brotherhood.

The reasons for Richard's downfall were many. The brittleness of the king's personality, the divisiveness of his rule and the narrowing of his circle of advisers all contributed to an erosion of support for him. Yet beneath the short-term and personal factors there was a deeper problem. Richard had set himself completely at odds with the model of chivalric kingship developed over the previous fifty years by Edward III and the Black Prince. Edward's achievement had been to forge an alliance between the Crown and the political class based on a shared commitment to the pursuit of external war. Edward's bid for the French Crown was supported by the nobility because they believed that in upholding his own rights he was upholding their own. Aggressive war strengthened monarchical rule by generating feelings of solidarity between the king and the chivalric class. Edward's genius in creating a national chivalry, expressed in his foundation of the Order of the Garter, helped to harness an otherwise decentralised and individualistic chivalry to the service of kingly rule. The assumptions of Edwardian kingship – that war strengthened the Crown and that kings achieved greatness in war – were rejected by Richard. His own conception of monarchy – that of a lofty ruler commanding obedience from his subjects and drawing strength from the prerogative – proved no substitute. It failed to engage the support of the political and fighting classes. In the century and a half after Edward III's victory at Crécy, it was clear that his vision of kingship would provide the benchmark against which that of his successors would be judged. Richard's supplanter, Henry IV, a one-time crusader, more than measured up to the expectations of his subjects. He was everything that the unwarlike Richard was not. He stood for the highest chivalric ideals of the day.

7

War, Fame and Fortune

In the autumn of 1386 a series of hearings was convened in the Court of Chivalry to determine who had the better right to bear the arms *azure a bend or*: the Cheshire knight Sir Robert Grosvenor, or his challenger, the former royal treasurer Sir Richard Scrope of Bolton in Yorkshire. Each claimant brought along his friends, associates and military companions to give witness statements – depositions – on his behalf. These statements, preserved in the official record of the case, afford vivid insights into the military experience of the English knightly class in the fourteenth century.

Among the deponents who gave evidence in the refectory of Westminster Abbey on 15 October 1386 was one who, on retiring from active service, was to have a distinguished civilian career. This was Sir Richard Waldegrave of Bures St Mary in Suffolk, twelve times MP for that county and speaker in the parliament of November 1381. Waldegrave, aged forty-eight and by his own account armed for a quarter of a century, recalled episodes from a career which had taken him all over Europe and the Near East.[1] He said that he had seen Sir Richard Scrope bearing the arms to which he laid claim 'in the expedition of the late king before Paris' – that is, Edward III's campaign to Reims and Brétigny in the winter of 1359–60. He also said that he had seen Sir William Scrope attired in the said arms with a label 'beyond the Great Sea in the company of the earl of Hereford at Satalya, at a parley which was held between the king of Cyprus and Takka, lord of Satalya', so locating him at the capture of the port of Satalya in southern Turkey by King Peter of Cyprus in 1361. He added that he had seen the banner of Sir Henry Scrope displayed at 'Balyngham Hill' and on the expedition into the Pays de Caux which the duke of Lancaster commanded – referring, respectively, to an English raid into the Pas-de-Calais and Lancaster's expedition in Lower Normandy, both in 1369.

Sir Richard Waldegrave was hardly unique among the deponents in the range and diversity of his military experience. A few of those who gave evidence had even longer campaigning memories on which to draw. One esquire, Nicholas Sabraham, a man otherwise unknown to history, claimed to have served 'in Prussia, Hungary, at Constantinople, at the Bras de St Jorge and at Messembria' – and that was before mention of his service in Scotland and France.[2] Sir William Moigne, a Huntingdonshire knight, had taken part in virtually every significant campaign in the Hundred Years War from the mid-1340s. He described how he had seen Sir William Scrope using the arms *azure a bend or* at the siege of Calais in 1347, where he had daringly intercepted relief supplies which the French were trying to smuggle in, 'so that every Englishman spoke of him with great honour'. He said that he had seen Sir Richard using the arms 'before Paris' – that is, on the Reims–Brétigny expedition of 1359–60. Finally, he declared that he had seen members of the family using the arms 'in Gascony and Spain' – by which he meant during the Black Prince's invasion of Castile on behalf of Pedro the Cruel in 1367, in which Moigne had taken part.[3]

It would be wrong to suppose that military experience on this scale was normal among the English knightly class in the fourteenth century; men like Waldegrave and Moigne stood out precisely because of the sheer length of their careers. Nonetheless, large numbers of knights and esquires were still fulfilling the aristocracy's traditional role of service in war. Sir Maurice Bruyn, another of the witnesses in 1386, who said that he had been armed for forty-eight years, recalled that he had seen members of the Scrope family using the disputed arms on campaigns in which he had participated in theatres as far apart as Scotland, Tournai, Brittany and France.[4] Yet another deponent, Sir William Lucy, supported his own statement by reference to a career which had begun at Sluys in 1340, continued through the battles of Crécy and Poitiers and the Reims–Brétigny expedition, and took in crusading service in Prussia after the coming of peace.[5] Nor was this degree of experience altogether new. In the early years of the century many knights had chalked up equally impressive records in the Scottish wars. Sir Nicholas de Valers of Down Ampney in Gloucestershire, to name but one, had enlisted for every campaign against the Scots between 1298 and 1310 and had served in the Holy Land before that.[6] In some cases traditions of active service were carried on from generation to generation. No fewer than six generations of the Poynings family of Poynings in Sussex saw service in the field in the fourteenth and fifteenth centuries. So why did these men show such enthusiasm to take up arms?

The Fortunes of War

One explanation is to suppose that they were motivated by the traditional chivalric appeal of fame, honour and glory. It was in these terms that the chronicler Jean Froissart pictured the battles of the Hundred Years War, presenting them as exquisitely choreographed encounters between knights driven by their quest for honour and renown. A quite different interpretation is to see the knights as moved less by idealistic motives than by an appetite for material gain. K. B. McFarlane suggested that the men who enlisted for service 'made no pretence of fighting for love of king or lord, still less for England or for glory, but [were concerned solely] for gain'.[7] In other words, they went off to France for the same reason that in the eighteenth century their descendants were to go off to India – to line their pockets, to seek not only fame but fortune.

How are we to decide between these alternatives? As McFarlane himself pointed out, there is no shortage of evidence to support the view that money played a part in motivating knights to fight. There is the well-attested fact that the majority of ransoms were paid to English knights for the simple reason that the English won all the main battles. It is indicative of the businesslike outlook of the English military class that when, in 1421, a brotherhood-in-arms agreement was made between two English esquires, most of the terms related to the division of ransom profits between the two men.[8] It is worth adding in this connection that the costs of the Hundred Years War fell principally on the French. Apart from some enemy raids on Channel ports in the fourteenth century, the war was fought predominantly on French, not English, territory. Even allowing for the fact that in the end the English were expelled from France, the English soldiery still managed to reap rich rewards, taking ransoms even in the last years of the war. Back in the thirteenth century the English knightly class had been highly reluctant to take up arms in support of its kings' attempts to recover the Angevin possessions in France. After the heady victory of Crécy, however, opposition to overseas military service melted away. There were prizes to be won, towns to be sacked, prisoners to be taken and ransomed. War could be made to pay.

The willingness of the knightly class to participate is even more striking given that service was now voluntary. In the early fourteenth century governments had struggled to think up schemes to compel landholders to enlist for service.[9] As late as 1344 Edward III was setting up a complex scheme whereby every landholder on a sliding scale of income up to £1,000 a year was under obligation to find troops in approximate proportion to his wealth. A five-pound landholder was to provide an archer, a twenty-five-pound one a man-at-arms, and so on. This elaborate scheme was a major part of the package of measures which the king took to provide himself with an army for his expedition to France two years later. Yet, for all its apparent success, it was not a model which was repeated. In the course of the 1346 expedition the king was to win his mighty victory over the French at Crécy. In the exhilarating aftermath of the battle knightly attitudes to participation in the war were transformed. Schemes to extend the basis of obligation could be abandoned and forgotten.

That overseas war was now approached in a more businesslike way appears to be indicated by the highly distinctive methods of recruitment put in place from the 1340s. The time-honoured and often ineffective routines of issuing summonses to tenants-in-chief to provide feudal knight service and landowners to bring men-at-arms were now set aside. The responsibility for raising men was devolved instead to captains, usually bannerets or nobles, who would enter into agreements – called indentures – with the Crown to provide contingents of a certain size and composition for service abroad in return for payment of wages from the exchequer. The indenture system was originally introduced for expeditions in which the king was not personally involved. This was because, if the king were not present, then no household officers would be present either, and an alternative system of control and administration would need to be set up. Indentures provided both exchequer and household with a means of managing an army abroad without the need for the king to be with it. Indentures were first used to provide an entire army in 1337, when Edward sent a substantial force into Scotland. Over time the terms of service laid out in the documents became standardised: typically, the precise composition of the force would be specified and, with it, the terms and conditions of the men's service and the arrangements for payment. Thus in April 1347 Sir Thomas Ughtred indented to serve the king in France for a year with a force of twenty men-at-arms, six of them knights, and twenty mounted archers, wages to be paid quarterly, the first instalment in advance when Ughtred and his men reached the coast. In many later contracts provision was made for division of the spoils of war, with all towns and castles captured being reserved to the king.

The great attraction of the indenture system to the Crown was that it devolved responsibility for recruitment – so often in the past a headache for the king's household – to a third party. For the most part, contracting captains appear to have volunteered their services in sufficient number to satisfy the king's needs. Only when the tide of war turned badly against the English, as it did in the mid-fifteenth century, is there evidence of a shortage of possible candidates. Typically what captains did on entering into a commitment with the Crown was arrange to meet their obligations by entering into sub-contracts with soldiers below them. In 1380, for example, Sir Hugh Hastings made no fewer than twenty-four indentures with men who contracted to serve under him on Thomas of Woodstock's expedition to Brittany.[10] These sub-contracts were modelled on the one into which the captain himself had entered, specifying the length of service, theatre of war, size of retinue and, crucially, arrangements for payment, the terms on this last point replicating the captain's own terms with the king. The commercial character of these indentures – at whatever level they were negotiated – is indicated by the careful attention given in them to all matters financial. From the late four-teenth century, for example, it was common for provision to be made for the division of ransom money, as in the brotherhood-in-arms contract mentioned above of 1421. The sheer popularity of the inden-ture system affords clear evidence that those involved in it saw military service as a source of profit.

What made possible the Crown's capacity to offer payment for service was a sudden increase in the fiscal resources available to the exchequer from the 1340s. In the late thirteenth and early fourteenth centuries the demands of war had led to the development of a comprehensive system of national taxation founded on the principle of the subject's obligation to assist the king in time of need. According to the legal doctrines governing the grant of taxation, in times of 'necessity', which were increasingly identified with war, the king was entitled to ask for the assistance of his subjects, while his subjects, once they had accepted his case, were under obligation to provide it. By the mid-thirteenth century parliament had emerged as the place where the king entered his plea of necessity, and his subjects indicated their acceptance of it. The emergence of parliament as a national forum in which consent could be secured to taxation led to a massive increase in the financial resources of the English state. By the mid-fourteenth century the king was able to collect taxes in two main forms: a levy on movable property, imposed at the rate of one-fifteenth in the countryside and one-tenth in the towns, and the maltolt, a levy on the exports of wool imposed at the rate of forty shillings on each woolsack. The latter tax alone could be counted on to produce some £60,000–80,000 in a good year. When the king had revenues on this scale to disburse on wages, it is small wonder that the military class responded so willingly to his call.

Yet the importance of pay as a factor in recruitment should not be exaggerated. The rates of pay for soldiering in the Middle Ages were not high. They had been fixed at two shillings a day for a knight in the early fourteenth century, and they remained at that level for virtually the whole of the Hundred Years War – and this despite a sharp rise in the general level of wages in the late fourteenth century. Moreover, there is evidence that those who contracted with the Crown at these rates sometimes offered less favourable rates to their own recruits, allowing them to pocket the difference themselves. To cap it all, payments by the exchequer to captains in royal service were often in arrears.

It should also be remembered that a knight's wages did not automatically translate into profit. The costs to a knight of fitting out for war were often considerable. He would need to find several mounts – one would certainly not be enough because it might be lost on campaign – and a good courser might cost up to twenty pounds. In addition, there was the expense of buying arms and armour. A suit of high-quality Milanese armour in the late fourteenth century would cost at least ten, even twelve pounds, perhaps a fifth of a middling knight's annual income. Even though a complete suit was only an occasional expense, it is clear from wills that knights kept adding to their armour collections, acquiring pieces as and when needed. As armour became heavier and more elaborate, as it did in the fifteenth century under the influence of the Italian armourers, so the financial burden which its purchase placed on knights became more onerous.

Where military service brought the prospect of the biggest rewards was in a quite different area: in the winnings to be made on campaign. Profits in the Hundred Years War were realised in three main forms: in straightforward plunder and booty on the march, in the ransoming of prisoners and in grants of land and office in occupied territories. The sheer scale of the booty and prizes sent back to England made an impact on contemporaries from the very earliest days of the war. The chronicler Thomas Walsingham wrote, with pardonable exaggeration, that there was hardly a household in England which had no spoils from the sack of Caen in 1346.[11] The early expeditions of Edward III, with their pillaging of rich towns such as Calais, brought a flood of luxuries into England, and the soldiers made sure to claim their share of the spoils. In 1356 a Cheshire esquire, John Jodrell, and his fellows picked up at Poitiers a silver nief – pouring vessel – belonging to the king of France, and received £8 12s 6d for it two years later. In the campaign of 1370 the towns of northern France were systematically mulcted by Robert Knolles's men: the unidentified town of 'Maiot' alone paid 160 gold francs in protection money. A note of the war loot in Knolles's possession a few years earlier included a silver basin and ewer with a combined weight of seven pounds, four silver chargers and eighteen silver saucers.[12] In the fifteenth-century phase of the war, when restrictions were placed on plundering, the opportunities for freebooting declined somewhat. Nonetheless, Richard Beauchamp, earl of Warwick, who had been present at the sieges of Caen, Pontoise and Meaux, sent a rich haul of jewels and prisoners back to England in 1421 to finance the rebuilding of the south front of Warwick Castle, while Lord Talbot's capture of Le Mans in 1428 yielded him a haul of apparel, horses and armour.[13]

Much greater fortunes were to be made from the collection of ransoms. High ransoms were hardly a novelty in the Hundred Years War; they had been a feature of warfare since the twelfth century. Their number, however, was substantially greater now because of the many English victories. One of the first high-ranking prisoners to be taken was Guy, brother of the count of Flanders, who was captured by Sir Walter Mauny in a raid on Cadzand in 1337. Mauny sold his prisoner to Edward III for no less than £8,000. In 1346 Sir Thomas Holand captured another high-ranking French nobleman, the count of Eu, at Crécy, and received £12,000 for him from the king, while a year later at La Roche Derrien in Brittany Sir Thomas Dagworth captured Charles of Blois and received £5,000. It was a convention of war that when high-ranking prisoners were taken they should be sold to the king for use as bargaining counters in negotiations with the enemy. Other Englishmen waxed rich on the ransoms of more modest captives. In 1356 the earl of Warwick captured the archbishop of Sens, a non-combatant, at the battle of Poitiers, ransoming him for £8,000. In 1361 Sir Hugh Calveley took captive the future constable of France, Bertrand du Guesclin, and ransomed him for 30,000 ecus. In 1365 Sir Matthew Gourney ransomed his most important captive, the wealthy nobleman Jean de Laval, for £5,000. In 1376 Sir John Harleston and Sir Philip la Vache jointly received £2,500 for their shares in two knightly prisoners they had captured.[14] As Edward III's successes multiplied, the trade in ransoms became so substantial that conventions were agreed for the division of money between the interested parties. As a general rule the captain or immediate commander of the man who took the prisoner would claim a third of the ransom, and the king a third of that in turn. Sometimes, however, commanders took bigger shares. In the 1350s the Black Prince's practice was to demand half of all his men's winnings.

Even when the tide of war turned against the English, as it did in the 1370s, opportunities for profit could still be found. Those in the best position to gain were the garrison captains in frontier regions, who could levy patis – protection money – from districts within riding distance of their castles. In 1378 Sir Richard Abberbury and Sir John Golafre made no less than £870 in this way as captains of Brest, while in the 1380s Sir Hugh Calveley, a shrewd entrepreneur, made a large though unquantifiable profit from his tenure of Cherbourg.[15] In the twilight of the Lancastrian phase of the war in the fifteenth century there was the potential to profit from grants of land in the so-called *pays de conquête*. Henry V had provided for the permanent defence of Normandy by granting fiefs there to English tenants on condition of performance of military service. The earls of Salisbury, Warwick and Shrewsbury, to name but a few of the beneficiaries, had all taken fiefs of this kind. It is hard to estimate the value of these concessions to their holders but, according to William Worcester, Sir Andrew Ogard's lordships were worth no less than £1,000 a year to him, while, on the evidence of his accounts, Sir John Fastolf drew an income of at least £400 a year from his own estates.[16] Fastolf was fortunate enough to dispose of his lands before the English collapse. Others were not so lucky.

There can be little doubt that some Englishmen made very substantial fortunes out of the Hundred Years War. John de Coupland, a minor Northumberland gentleman who had the good fortune to capture the king of Scotland at Neville's Cross in 1346, was raised to banneret rank and awarded the substantial fee of £500 a year. He was further promised that he would be awarded landed estates when these became available, and after a couple of years he was granted the Lancashire estates of William de Coucy.[17] Still more remarkable was the career of the Cheshireman Sir Robert Knolles, who rose from obscurity to establish himself as one of the most prosperous soldierly proprietors in England with extensive estates in East Anglia.[18] When he died in 1407, Walsingham celebrated his achievements, writing that 'besides earning fame in war, he built a bridge over the Medway near Rochester, founded a chantry at Pontefract, helped establish a Carmelite house in London, and undertook many other projects which would have exhausted the treasuries of kings'.[19] Other men saw service in war ripen into a relationship of service to their lord in peacetime on returning home. Some of the most distinguished members of John of Gaunt's war retinue prospered under his patronage to become important office-holders in local administration in England.

The achievement of social mobility through success in arms was not, of course, an entirely new phenomenon. William Marshal had climbed the ladder by capitalising on his prowess as a knight back in the twelfth century. In the Marshal's case, the winning of ransom income was just as important as it was for the knights fighting in France two centuries later. Yet there was an important difference between the circumstances of the Marshal's career and those of the knights of the Hundred Years War. In the twelfth century the Marshal had made his name – and his early fortune – on the tournament circuit, not on the field of war. Although he was to see plenty of action in the field from the 1170s, it was from his tourneying successes that he made the bulk of his fortune as a young bachelor. Two centuries later, while tourneying could still make a knight's name, it was on the field of combat that he aimed to make most of his money. The scale of the opportunities for profit offered by the Hundred Years War was altogether new. Contemporary chroniclers recognised this in their enthusiastic reporting of the war. In 1358 Henry Knighton wrote that men 'were made immensely rich and opulent . . . and many who went out as boys and servants came home rich men'.[20]

Yet for all the evidence of the profitability of war, the role of enrichment in knightly motivation needs to be put in perspective. It is easy to be dazzled by the remarkable success stories which make the Hundred Years War appear a period of unalloyed prosperity for English knighthood. The fact that Knolles, Gourney and so many other knights came back laden with riches does not mean that every English knight did so. There is insufficient evidence to allow us to draw up a balance sheet for the fighting class as a whole. However, on even the limited evidence available it is clear that there are dangers in generalising from a few particular, and perhaps not always very representative, cases.

One important qualification which needs to be made is that the profits of war were unequally distributed across the knightly and gentry class. By no means all the gentry felt the trickle-down effect of wages, protection money and ransom income. In those parts of England where there was low military participation, such as the south Midlands, there was little or no war money at all. It was in the counties where recruitment was strongest that the gains were most evident. Cheshire and Lancashire in the north-west, Warwickshire in the Midlands, Gloucestershire and parts of the south-west – these were the main recruiting grounds and therefore the areas in which gains were most apparent. Cheshire and Lancashire were demesne lordships held in the fourteenth century by two of the most important recruiting captains in the war, the Black Prince and John of Gaunt respectively. Sir Robert Knolles, Sir Hugh Calveley, Sir William Mainwaring and Sir Richard and Sir David Cradock, all important commanders, had their origins in the two counties.[21] Some of these men, when they returned home, invested their money in local religious foundations. In Cheshire 'war churches' came to dominate the landscape much as wool or cloth churches did in Gloucestershire and Suffolk. Bunbury, Nantwich and Acton were all substantially rebuilt by rich captains out of the profits of war. Cheshire, however, was exceptional. In no other county of England was such a concentration of military wealth to be found. Even in Warwickshire, the heartland of the Beauchamp earls of Warwick, evidence of the spoils of war was confined to a few castles, Warwick and Maxstoke, and to one great church – St Mary's, Warwick. In Gloucestershire the position was much the same: the Berkeleys' involvement benefited those in the Berkeleys' household and military affinity but relatively few others. In some parts of England the gains of war were felt hardly at all.

It also needs to be remembered that the number of battles at which valuable prisoners were taken was relatively small. Some of the biggest and most spectacular English victories in the Hundred Years War produced hardly any valuable prizes. At Crécy very few high-ranking prisoners were taken, while at Agincourt the number, though larger, was still not substantial. At Crécy the French king, fearing that a scramble for prisoners would distract his men, had ordered that no quarter be given, and Edward III in retaliation had ordered the same. The one battle which proved highly productive of French prisoners was Poitiers.[22] Here not only the king himself but a good number of the nobility and knighthood were rounded up. In general, it seems to have been at the smaller encounters that the most high-ranking prisoners were taken, and these in total did not amount to more than a few dozen. It is true that the big ransom prizes impressed contemporaries by their sheer scale, but they were not productive of a major shift in wealth from one side of the Channel to the other.

One final point needs to be borne in mind: against the undoubted but unquantifiable profits of war should be set the parallel reality of losses. A minority of English captains, particularly in the later phases of the war, fell into enemy hands and had to be ransomed. In 1377 the seneschal of Gascony, Sir Thomas Felton, was captured at Eymet and had to pay 30,000 livres to secure his release.[23] In 1429 John, Lord Talbot, the future earl of Shrewsbury, was captured at Patay and redeemed himself for what he called an 'unreasonable and importable raunceon'. In 1453, at the very end of the war, Robert, Lord Hungerford and Moleyns, was captured at Castillon and had to find £8,000 to win his freedom, a sum which virtually bankrupted his family.[24] Most unfortunate of all was Sir John Hardreshull, who in the course of a long career in the fourteenth century, was captured no fewer than three times; and there is no evidence that he had any gains to set beside his many losses.[25]

Those who suffered large 'importable' losses, as these men did, were admittedly in the minority, but equally those who scooped the biggest ransom prizes were in a minority too. Neither group can be considered representative of the fighting class as a whole. It is perhaps best to imagine a wide spectrum of field experience in the Hundred Years War. On the one hand were those who were winners on the big scale, the men who have left their mark on the records; in the middle those who made only a small profit or just about managed to balance the books, probably the majority; and at the opposite extreme, the losers, those largely invisible men who lost everything when captured. Which group a man found himself in typically depended on a range of factors. The length and regularity of his service might well have a bearing; those battle-hardened veterans who regularly campaigned would be far more likely to experience the roller coaster of gain and loss than the less frequent campaigners who mixed fighting with office-holding at home. Another consideration was the campaign records and policies on the division of spoils of the captains under whom men served. In 1345 Henry of Lancaster's men reaped handsome rewards for themselves on the Gascon campaign because of the duke's policy of keeping hardly any of the gains for himself.[26] The pattern of experience was thus shaped not only by the simple balance of gain and loss but by other factors: the social and geographical background of those who fought, the length of their military experience, their social connections and magnate affiliations. The armies of the Hundred Years War were made up of men whose motives for fighting might well have been mixed.

Attitudes to enrolment could sometimes be influenced by the individual circumstances of those involved. For at least some, war service offered an escape from the prospect of impoverishment or declining status at home. This was most obviously the case in respect of the less well-off Cheshiremen. Cheshire was a lightly manorialised county with a high proportion of freeholders who looked to military experience to maintain their status. For many other participants, war might be more a matter of obligation. A knight or esquire might sign up to serve under a magnate because to do so was expected of one of his rank. For others again, war had the appeal of dice to the gambler: it was irresistible, even addictive, drawing in men who were tempted by the prospect of the big win even if the big win never came. This was almost certainly part of the appeal of war to men like Sir John Hardreshull. For yet others again, war was a source of excitement, exhilaration and adventure. It gave men the opportunity to live out their Arthurian fantasies and experience the crossing and re-crossing of the boundary between romance and reality. Such may have been the spirit in which the likes of Sir Richard Waldegrave went campaigning in distant places like the eastern Mediterranean, where there was no conceivable prospect of gain. Military service, then, sprang from a variety of impulses and circumstances. If, for some, it was the appetite for profit and gain which was the main spur to enrolment, this was by no means the case with all. Other factors, such as romance, a quest for adventure or simply a sense of social obligation might come into play as well.

Whatever the mainspring to action in individual cases, almost all those knights who fought would have felt the power of one central belief: that fighting in war was what was expected of the nobility.[27] To fight in a just cause brought honour and recognition to a knight, enhancing his fame and repute. As Froissart put it, 'brave men [fight] to advance their bodies and to increase their honour'.[28] The idea that to be noble involved some sort of career in arms was central to the medieval conception of chivalry. The point is one which emerges from the depositions in the Scrope–Grosvenor controversy. To those knights who drew on their recollections at the hearings, episodes of little military significance were just as important as the big battles; all lent weight to a man's martial credentials. Chivalric society subscribed to a set of traditional, largely non-material values. Knights were esteemed for their prowess in arms, their loyalty to their lords and their service in the king's wars. Throughout the Hundred Years War military service remained a central element in the collective consciousness of the English chivalric class.

If this view of military service as rooted essentially in a quest for honour appears at odds with the apparent materialism of some of the knightly class, it is worth repeating that there was a variety of motivation. There were adventurers, freebooters, mercenaries, self-seekers and chancers; but there were also warriors, like Chaucer's Knight, for whom financial considerations were largely secondary. Interestingly, it may have been the case that honour was a quality esteemed even by those who were moved principally by a quest for booty and profit. In the medieval view of the world profit and honour might not be opposites; they could go together – the accumulation of profit might be a mark of honour, in some circumstances even a source of honour. If a knight returned home laden with booty, then it followed that he must be a knight of prowess, a knight with boldness of spirit and so, for that reason, a knight of honour. Wealth, in other words, could provide material evidence of martial achievement. Seen in this light, the pursuit of material gain can be accommodated into a much broader framework of chivalric thinking. Military service, the vocation of a nobleman, while for some a source of profit, could for others be a source of honour and renown. And with renown came recognition, employment and promotion, and with these in turn economic and social advancement. Not least among the attractions of war to a man on the social periphery was the opportunity it afforded of entry to the inner circle of aristocratic society.

Chivalry in Crisis

The motivation of knights was a central issue in debates in the late fourteenth century about what appeared to some the decline of the chivalric ideal. Knighthood, by Richard II's reign, was in crisis. On the one hand intense criticism was voiced of the horrors unleashed by the unemployed soldiery and free companies in France during the lulls in the main Anglo-French struggle; while on the other there was concern that the gradual civilianisation of the knightly class was leading to abandonment of the ideal of a knighthood dedicated to upholding right and justice by arms. The critique of knighthood found expression in the works of some of the finest writers of the age, in particular those of Chaucer and Gower; it also figured in sermon literature and in Thomas Walsingham's chronicle. To some well-informed observers it seemed that there was something seriously wrong with the health of the knightly estate.

The scale of the critical assault on the chivalric class was altogether new. In the early fourteenth century there had been criticism of warfare and the evils which it brought. At that time, however, complaint had focused mainly on financial and other burdens on the people, not on knights' misconduct. Poets had grumbled about taxation grinding the peasantry into poverty, while criticism in parliament had concentrated on the effects of prises – compulsory requisitioning – in depriving people of their property. In the late fourteenth century criticism took an altogether different turn. It was both more moralistic and more introspective. John Gower, one of the most eloquent writers, concentrated on the falseness of knights, lambasting them for their self-indulgence, their cruelty and their quest for worldly glory: 'the number of knights increases,' he wrote, 'but their activity decreases; thus honour is empty since it is without responsibility.' In his *Confessio Amantis* (c. 1386–93) he was still more outspoken. Expressing his views through the dialogue between Amans and his confessor Genius, he said that war 'in a worldly cause' violated charity, while even war in a just cause attracted the unscrupulous, benefiting only those who took part in it.[29]

Gower's views were echoed by Chaucer, who, though rarely addressing the rights and wrongs of war directly, nevertheless indicated his unease about knights' conduct. In two short poems, 'Lake of Stedfastnesse' and 'The Former Age', he reflected on the evils of his time, contrasting the misery brought by avarice and profiteering in war with the happiness of earlier times. In *The Canterbury Tales* his views are made clearest in the 'Tale of Melibee', in which the story of an attack on a gentleman's house is made the occasion to discuss the proper response to violence and the use of arms. A powerful statement of the case for restraint is put into the mouth of Prudence, Melibee's wife: 'I conseille yow that ye begynne no were in trust of youre richesses, for they ne suffisen noght werres to mayntene . . . have pees unto youre worshipe and profit.'[30]

Chaucer's and Gower's detachment from knightly values was shared by an associate of theirs who earlier in his career had appeared to be their very embodiment, Sir John Clanvow. Clanvow, a royal household knight, had seen regular service in France in the 1370s, accompanying

Gaunt on his great *chevauchée* (mounted raid) in 1373, and may have
been on his way to a crusade when he died. In a treatise, *The Two
Ways*, a work in which Lollard sympathies have been detected, he
emphatically turned his back on his old ways:

> For the world hold them worshipful that been great warriors and fighters
> and that destroyen . . . many lands and wasten and given much good
> to them that have enough and that dispenden outrageously in meat,
> drink, clothing and building, and in living in ease, sloth and many others
> sins . . . And of such folk men maken books and songs and readen and
> singen of them for to hold the mind of their deeds the longer here
> upon earth . . . But God that is sovereign truth and a true judge deemeth
> them right shameful.[31]

At the other end of the spectrum from those who criticised the
violence and self-indulgence of the knights were those who believed
that knights were not aggressive enough; they were neglecting the
cult of arms; they were becoming too soft. This is the burden of
the complaint which Walsingham made in his chronicle. There was
common ground between the two positions on one point: a cause of
knights' downfall was their love of women. In a famous passage
Thomas Walsingham denounced Richard II's knights for their
cowardice and effeminacy: 'Several of them were more knights of
Venus than of Bellona, more valorous in the bedchamber than on the
field of battle, defending themselves rather with their tongues than
with their spears, being alert in speech, but asleep when martial deeds
were required.'[32] Walsingham, a supporter of the war against the
French, believed that the king's knights should have constituted an
austere military household spearheading the nation's efforts against
the enemy.

To some extent this chorus of criticism was a response to the
English failure in arms in the late fourteenth century. After the renewal
of Anglo-French hostilities in 1369, the tide of fortune had turned
decisively in favour of the French. The accession of Charles V in 1364
had brought to the French throne a vigorous and clear-sighted new
leader, while in England there was a virtual collapse of leadership
with the decline of Edward III and then, in 1377, the succession of a
boy king. In the space of a few years the lands ceded to Edward III

by the Treaty of Brétigny had been whittled away until little more than the Gascon coastal strip was left. Although between 1369 and 1380 a series of taxes had been voted by parliament, there were hardly any military successes to show for them. On the contrary: for two successive summers, in 1385 and 1386, the south-east of England had lived under constant threat of invasion.

This turning of the tide presented English commentators with a problem. How was their nation's appalling failure in arms to be explained? Since, in the commentators' view, the war was a just one, and the king was simply seeking vindication of his rights, there could be only one answer. God's instruments were inadequate – English knights were corrupt and sinful. The nation was being punished for the lapses of those who were supposed to be its champions.

This was an analysis which lent itself conveniently to literary expression because it could be accommodated within the framework of estates satire. This was a literary form which sought to explain the disorder of society in terms of the failure of the estates – social and occupational groupings – to perform their appointed duties. Thus the clergy were criticised for their ignorance, the monks for their luxury, the lawyers for their greed, and so on. The vice for which the knights were invariably condemned was their avarice. Avarice was held to have a unique capacity to transmute, turning love into hate and peace into war. In the twelfth century it had been largely associated with the clergy; by the fourteenth, however, it was associated with all three social groups and in particular with knights. Gower wrote of its corrupting effect on the knightly class: 'The knight whom the sake of gain moves to enter into battle will have no righteous honour . . . I see that honour is now neglected for gold.'[33]

Although the act of forcing criticism of knights into the straitjacket of satire necessarily distorted it, unduly highlighting the role of avarice, the criticism was nonetheless close enough to reality to carry conviction. In an age when it was apparent that there was money to be made from war, it was not difficult to find a minority of English soldiers whose primary motive was profit. More reputable commanders, such as Calveley and Knolles, may have been moved as much by the quest for honour as by money, but for some, particularly among the mercenary community, the spur to action was more base. The worst offender was probably the notorious John Fotheringhay, commander of the fortress of Creil in the 1350s, who held sway over an area thirty miles round his castle and was reputed to have collected 100,000 francs in safe-conduct fees alone. It was men of Fotheringhay's stamp who were held to have brought the chivalric order into disrepute. What Gower and Chaucer said about the money-grubbing of the knightly class was not altogether without foundation.

But what truth was there in the other, very different, accusation, that knights were abandoning the battlefield for the bedchamber? Walsingham's accusation was made in the very specific context of a perceived failure of duty on the part of some of Richard II's chamber knights and appears in his account of the year 1387. It immediately follows a passage describing the opposition of the king's favourites Robert de Vere, Michael de la Pole, Simon Burley and Richard Stury to the proposed expedition of the earl of Arundel to Brittany. In Walsingham's view, the weak and treacherous counsel of these men undermined the earl's efforts and left the realm ill defended at a time of national emergency. A further dimension to Walsingham's criticism is to be found in a scandal which erupted at Richard's court at this time. Walsingham relates later in his account of 1387 that Robert de Vere had obtained an annulment of his marriage to the Black Prince's niece in order to regularise his relationship with one of the queen's ladies-in-waiting, Agnes Lancecrona. The adultery between de Vere and Lancecrona, condemning as it did a lady of royal birth to shame, caused outrage at court and seemed to substantiate the view that the knightly class was distracted and corrupted by love of women.

One way of interpreting Walsingham's complaint is to see it as part of a tradition which criticised the effeminacy of royal courtiers. For centuries it had been a commonplace of moralists that courts were corrupting and the courtiers who thronged them effeminate. In the 1090s some of the more puritanical monkish chroniclers had criticised William Rufus's knights for their long hair, taking this to be a sign of degeneracy and lack of manliness.[34] Walsingham, in castigating Richard's men as 'knights of Venus', was making a point about the degeneracy of the knights of his own time, implicitly setting up a contrast with a lost or imagined past. He wanted to emphasise the difference between the unwarlike knights of Richard's court and what he regarded as the more manly entourage of the king's predecessor, Edward III.

There was a more immediate context, however, for Walsingham's criticism, and this was to be found in the changing character of the king's household. In the later years of Edward III's reign a new body, knights of the chamber, had been created out of the larger and undifferentiated group, knights of the household. The responsibilities of the new knights were more civilian than those of their predecessors: they acted as political go-betweens, diplomatic envoys and administrators of royal estates and castles. The emergence of this new group reflected the less militarised atmosphere of Edward's court in the years after the making of the Treaty of Brétigny, when the household was beginning to lose its character as a household in arms. The knights' institutional affiliation with the chamber, the king's innermost sanctum, was an indication that they operated near the centre of policymaking and power. Richard II's chamber knights were close to him personally as well as physically. They shared his outlook and cultural tastes and his belief that greatness in kingship was to be achieved in peace not war.

What inspired Walsingham's criticism, therefore, was a change in the character and employment of the knights recruited into royal service. No longer were they all military men, soldiers singled out for their prowess; they included administrators, counsellors and diplomats. They were men who played a part in the exercise of civil and political rule. This was a change mirrored in the larger change which occurred in the knightly class at this time. The late fourteenth-century knights, though certainly still men whose standing was determined by their military position, were no longer solely, or even primarily, soldiers. They were administrators, office-holders, magistrates and political managers. This process of transformation had begun in the thirteenth century when a more elite knighthood had emerged with responsibilities in local government and magnate administration. It gathered pace in the next century, when literate skills were more widely disseminated and when many of the knights were acquiring legal knowledge. By the second half of the fourteenth century knights were displacing clerks in holy orders from posts in government which in the past had been virtually monopolised by them. It is no coincidence that it was around the time of the chamber knights' appearance that the top governmental position of chancellor, on which clerks had had a stranglehold, was first given to a knight. By the 1370s knights were just as likely to be found in major administrative positions as on the battlefield or the campaign trail. This was a change which a traditionalist and social conservative like Walsingham found difficult to reconcile with the view of the knightly class as a military estate.

What these controversies about knightly behaviour show is that by the late fourteenth century traditional conceptions of chivalry were coming under strain in the face of changing social conditions. Not only were the old informal restraints on knightly individualism breaking down in the face of greed and acquisitiveness in war; knighthood itself was evolving into a civil magistracy whose members saw it as a duty and privilege to serve king and realm.

One response to this crisis, building on the idea of war waged for the common good, was the development of regulations governing the conduct of an army on the march. The first such regulations in England were published by Richard II in the course of his expedition to Scotland in 1385.[35] Their aim was to instil military discipline by subordinating individual interests to collective action and commands. Thus the pillaging of churches was forbidden, as were the seizure of victuals and the commandeering of lodgings. To ensure the coherence of companies in battle it was insisted that no men were to go ahead of their captain's banner and no one was to break ranks to pillage. As a way of avoiding disputes over prisoners it was prescribed that pledges were to be taken from those surrendering in battle.

The subordination of individual interests to strategic need pointed the way to a more general resolution of the contradictions inherent in late fourteenth-century chivalry. A prerequisite of the containment of the more mercenary and disruptive aspects of chivalry was the development of an aristocratic ethic which stressed the role of knights not only as warriors of the Crown but as servants of the nation and the common good. It was in the defining of this new civil conception of the upper-class ideal that some of the most fruitful thinking about chivalry was to be found in the fifteenth and sixteenth centuries.

8

The Face of Chivalric War

Although chivalry can easily appear the stuff of romance and legend, at its heart there always lay the hard practical business of combat and training. Chivalry was inseparable from the way of life of the *strenuus miles*, the fighting knight. How and how far, then, did its abstract ideals relate to the day-to-day business of fighting? Did chivalry exercise a moderating influence on knightly conduct in the field, or was it little more than a refined abstraction with virtually no bearing on reality? The question is one with major implications for our understanding of how war was perceived and fought in the Middle Ages. Indeed, it is one which prompts reflection on the relation of chivalry to the values of society more generally. Johan Huizinga saw late medieval chivalry as a largely escapist code, a ritualised culture which provided a refuge from the horrors of a self-doubting, crisis-ridden society. R. L. Kilgour, following him, pictured chivalry as 'a sort of game, whose participants, in order to forget reality, turned to the illusion of a brilliant, heroic existence . . . divorced from the duties of everyday life'.[1] These characterisations of how chivalry interacted with society owe much to the fantasising rituals of one particular court, that of Valois Burgundy. If we are to consider the issues in relation to England, two questions immediately present themselves. One relates to the role played by chivalry in shaping the laws of war, that body of conventions which governed the practice of arms by knights. The other is how much influence, if any, chivalry may be said to have had in moderating the conduct of knights in the field.

War and Law

In the Middle Ages, a period when warfare was endemic, the main issue which occupied those who reflected on war in the abstract was not so much what defined or characterised war as what made a war just. It was in this context that the crucial issue of the legitimacy of war was addressed, and it was in the same context that consideration was given to the matter of the correctness or otherwise of knightly conduct in war.

From the late Roman period a succession of theologians had applied themselves to formulating a body of ideas defining the purpose of war in a Christian society and prescribing the terms on which it should be conducted. Their ideas may be summarised as follows. War, it was held, should be fought only for a just cause; it should be waged on valid authority with due proportionality between provocation and response, and it should be directed to the purpose of re-establishing peace. The fifth-century theologian St Augustine laid down the essence of these precepts in his treatise *The City of God*, in which he wrote that 'the object of war is peace'. 'Wars,' he said, 'are defined as just when their aim is to avenge injury, in other words when a people or city against whom war is declared has neglected either to redress the injuries done by its subjects or to restore what these people have wrongfully seized . . . unjust war is robbery.' St Augustine's opinions were refined and elaborated in the thirteenth century by St Thomas Aquinas, and developed still further by the canon lawyers in the century after that. In the late thirteenth century the Dominican Raymond of Penyafort, summarising earlier writing, laid down five main conditions for a just war. He wrote that a war should be just with regard to the persons engaged in it; it should be just with regard both to its object and its cause; it should be just in intention; and it should be waged on valid authority.[2] Other definitions simply rang the changes on these five basic requirements.

To the drafting of a body of rules or customs which governed the actual conduct of war – the practice of fighting and taking prisoners – the theologians contributed remarkably little. The collection of such rules in the form in which it came into existence in the later Middle Ages – the so-called laws of war – was almost entirely a secular creation, a fusion of knightly custom and Roman law as it was studied from the twelfth century onwards. Those who created the rules were generally civil or canon lawyers. The first and most important such writer, John of Legnano, was professor of civil laws at Bologna. The next important writer, a decade or two later, Honoré Bovet, a French clerk, was probably a canonist. The third authority, Christine de Pisan, an educated woman at the court of King Charles VII of France, stands somewhat apart but closely followed the earlier authorities.

The laws of war in the late Middle Ages were constructed on the basis of two principles. The first was that soldiering was a Christian profession, and not in the modern sense a public service. Thus a knight or esquire, when he bore arms in a public quarrel, fought as an individual, and rights were acquired by or against him personally, not against the side for which he fought. The second was that the laws of war were essentially contractual. This was because war was conceived in law as a joint-stock enterprise in which a participating soldier acquired a legally enforceable right to a share of its profits, gained chiefly through plunder and ransom.[3]

The origins of the body of customs which constituted the laws of war were found in both divine and natural law. Divine law sanctioned war as part of the general struggle of good against evil, while natural law, an expression of God's creation, justified war in a right cause. Neither of the two legal systems, however, could supply firm and enforceable rules for the conduct of war. For these, the sanction of positive law was required, which the legists found in the so-called law of nations – the *jus gentium* – originally the common law of the Roman people. The *jus gentium* provided the essential underpinning of the two universal systems of positive law, canon and civil, which in turn provided the law of arms with a set of written prescriptions applicable in the courts. As the English legist Nicholas Rishton wrote in 1405, 'the law and customs of arms are founded in the texts used by the doctors of civil and canon law'.[4] There was no possibility that conflict might arise between the two different-looking systems of written and unwritten law, because the equity of canon and civil laws was the same as that of the *jus gentium*. Both derived their authority from natural reason.

The corpus of canon and civil law, being common to the whole of Christendom, formed the basis for what amounted to an international code of humane conduct in war. In practice, however, this body of doctrine might seem only distantly related to the practical issues likely to arise in the day-to-day conduct of war. The sorts of questions to which a freelance soldier would want answers related to such down-to-earth issues as the right to exact ransom from prisoners and entitlement to compensation for losses incurred in the service of someone other than his liege lord, matters on which Roman law was unlikely to give any clear rulings. Difficult issues such as these could only be resolved by reference to customary practice. Thus resort was had, as and when necessary, to the advice of those with deep expertise in arms – heralds and senior or distinguished knights. The rules enunciated by such experts were considered authoritative enough to carry the force of law. The use of customary principles was not seen as being in conflict with written law, but rather as extending it at certain points. Both written and unwritten law were found due place in a body of rules which conceptually sat somewhere between codified legislation and customary military practice.

How relevant, in that case, was the body of rules to actual conditions in the field? What meaning, if any, did the writings of John of Legnano and Honoré Bovet have to soldiers on *chevauchée* or to mercenaries plundering villages? Soldiers were not theorists. The only rules for which they were likely to have respect were those they had drawn up themselves. A gap between theory and practice could potentially constitute a source of some difficulty. Yet there was one constraint which even the roughest of knights would recognise, and that was the validity of a promise given on oath – in other words, a contract. For if a knight broke a promise made on oath, his name would be dishonoured, and his honour was the quality which he cherished most in the world. In practice, the laws of war, as recognised internationally, had an ideological underpinning in the knights' code of honour just as much as they did in written law; indeed, the knights' code and the written law for most of the time simply confirmed and reinforced one another. Surprisingly perhaps, knights and lawyers were in broad agreement on the laws of war. The main, indeed perhaps the only, thing separating them was that they approached the matter from different perspectives and in different ways. That is to say, the lawyer's expertise in law was grounded in his education and practice in the courts, whereas the soldier's was based on actual experience in the field. If ever the lawyer were in doubt on a point, he would consult his books, whereas the soldier would instinctively turn for help to his friends the heralds. The heralds in fact provided a bridge between the two worlds. They possessed a considerable body of practical expertise in arms while at the same time were well versed in legal theory. In a treatise which took the form of a dialogue between a pursuivant and his instructor, an old herald, the former asks, 'How shall I learn about the law of arms?' to which the instructor replies, 'You will find it in a book called the *Tree of Battles*' – the text on the laws of war by Honoré Bovet.[5] For the most part, there was no big gap between the theory and the practice of the law of arms. The two rested on a body of ideas which was universal. If the lawyers used a language with which they felt at ease, the rules they articulated were understood and accepted by all who found their profession in the exercise of arms.

The range of matters subject to regulation by the law of arms covered a wide spectrum. Many of the regulations were concerned with personal relations, because men fought in a personal capacity, not as stipendiaries of their states. In most of the treatises there were prescriptions on whether or not a war was fought with legitimate princely sanction; what rights non-combatants might have in time of war; what procedures were to be followed before fighting a battle; what rights a prisoner might have on surrendering to a captor; what measures the captor could take if a prisoner owing a ransom defaulted; in what circumstances reprisals could be taken if a truce or peace were broken; and whether a knight or esquire was entitled to bear the coat of arms he was using.[6] Many of these matters related to the enforceability of contracts. The rules governing ransoms, for example, which bulked so heavily in the treatises, turned on contract law. Conceptualising the law of arms as contract law made it comprehensible to a military class to whom the law of contract, the basis of landholding, would have been second nature.

If the body of law described by the legists was to be of any value to those to whom it applied, it had to be internationally enforceable. A knight in the allegiance of one lord had to be confident that he could secure his rights against a knight of a different allegiance. In the pre-modern era there were no international tribunals beyond those represented by the authority of the Pope and the Holy Roman emperor. When knights brought cases under the law of arms, they brought them in tribunals which belonged to, and were controlled by, sovereign princes. And this posed problems. How, for example, was a judgment given in the court of one prince to be executed in the domains of another, where the prince had no influence? In practice, a great deal of flexibility was shown. The courts of one prince would usually show themselves willing to receive pleas from the tribunal of another because mutual recognition suited all concerned. Owing to the difficulties involved, however, knights would usually begin their litigation in a tribunal controlled by their own ruler. Thus in the 1360s Edward III's council resolved a dispute about whether a French prisoner taken by the archer Nicholas de Stanway could legally be a prisoner of war given that the Frenchman was a clerk. Much later, near the end of the French war, Henry VI's council dealt with a claim by a Gascon esquire to rights over a French prisoner taken at Bordeaux.[7] If a case raised issues which could not easily be dealt with by the king's officers or council, it would be heard by a specialist tribunal – in England the Court of Chivalry, in France the Courts of the Constable and Marshal. In both kingdoms these were permanent tribunals open to suitors, who were free to bring cases at any time. In the early fifteenth century, when the English were in occupation of Paris, many cases were brought before the *parlement* there. Process in military tribunals was usually formal according to civil procedures. If a knight secured judgment in his favour, he could usually expect execution by distraint on his opponent's goods and lands.

If these were the broad principles by which the practice of war was regulated in the late fourteenth century, the age of the Hundred Years War, is it possible to say whether any similar conventions can be discerned a century or two before, when chivalry was less formalised?

Very occasionally, Anglo-Norman or Angevin chroniclers use the Latin terms *jus* or *lex* ('right' or 'law') in connection with the conduct of war. Henry of Huntingdon, writing in the mid-twelfth century, says that after the battle of Lincoln in 1141 the city was given over to pillage *hostili lege* ('by military law'), while Ralph of Diss in the 1180s says that Louis VII of France granted a respite to the citizens of Verneuil *lege proposita*.[8] Sometimes a less concrete noun than *jus* or *lex* was employed. The author of the *Gesta Stephani*, speaking of the siege of Bedford in 1138, says that the garrison was granted honourable egress *sub militari . . . conditione* ('on military conditions').[9] At no point, however, do any of the chroniclers offer an explanation of their understanding of these laws or conditions. It is highly unlikely that they could have understood them to be laws in the later sense, because the foundation of late medieval law was Roman law, and at this time the study of Roman law was undertaken mainly in relation to matters of government. Moreover, there is no evidence of treatises on these matters being written before the fourteenth century.

It is thus unlikely that in the twelfth century there was a law of arms governing the nature of war between protagonists in the sense that there was to be later. This is not to suggest, however, that there was no informal body of custom relating to proper behaviour in war. If the term *lex* was rarely employed in the sources, the word *mos*, meaning custom, is encountered more frequently. Orderic Vitalis, for example, notes how Rufus insisted that the defeated rebels at Rochester in 1088 be forced to leave the city to a fanfare of royal trumpets 'as is customary when an enemy is defeated and a stronghold captured'.[10] William of Malmesbury, in similar terms, says that when Robert of Gloucester besieged Stephen's forces at Wareham in 1141 the garrison 'asked for a truce that, as is customary with such people, they might seek aid from the king'.[11] If there were customs regulating the ways in which garrisons or other forces might surrender, there were likewise customs or conventions regulating the ways in which war might begin. In a civil war, such as that between Stephen and Matilda, it was expected that the vassals rejecting the authority of the king performed an act of formal *diffidatio*, or defiance. In such a war those supporting a rebel leader might also be expected to enter into some agreement that they would neither abandon him nor make peace with his adversary without his consent.[12]

Taken together, these customs and rituals point to the existence of a body of rules perhaps less formal than the later laws of war but nonetheless significant in regulating the conduct of soldiers. What appears to have been lacking before the fourteenth century is any evidence that such rules were enforceable. Although officers such as the constable and marshal might exercise authority within an army, it does not seem that they heard appeals of an international nature lodged by actual or erstwhile combatants. That this should have been so is hardly surprising. In the twelfth century there was no law of arms which approximated to the character of international law subject to trial in a court. Such a law only came into existence in the fourteenth century, when customary, canon and civil law all fused together. Until that point there was no possibility of a fully fledged tribunal of the kind we meet later. Codes of military conduct were upheld principally by the protagonists' sense of honour. In a society in which honour was central to a man's self-worth, that may actually have provided just as effective a means of enforcement.

If the law of arms was therefore largely a creation of the late fourteenth century, it was not one which remained fixed in its original fourteenth-century form for the rest of the Middle Ages. On the contrary, its character as an amalgam of written and customary law gave it the capacity to evolve in response to changing circumstances. Well before the end of the fourteenth century differences of view were beginning to emerge between those who codified the law and those to whom it was applied. In general, the legists who drew up and interpreted the law reflected the outlook of kings and princes – who took men-at-arms into their service – in stressing discipline, while the knights themselves inclined to a more independent view of their position. Honoré Bovet was typical of the legists when, in the 1380s, he wrote that only the king had the power both to make war and prevent others from doing so, deducing from this that only those in the king's service or under his licence were entitled to bear arms.[13] This was a view which contrasted sharply with that of a writer of the previous generation, Geoffrey de Charny, a founder knight of the French Order of the Star, who drew up a list of questions concerned with technicalities of the rights and responsibilities of knights in the field, virtually all of them concluding with the question: 'How will it be judged by the law of arms?'[14] Charny seems to have had little sense of the law of arms as a formal written code in the way that Honoré was to have later. For him, it was a rationalisation of the everyday practices and customs of the knightly class as interpreted by members of that class. The knights were beholden to no one but themselves.

Honoré Bovet's treatise had its roots in the outlook of the French monarchy in the years after the defeats at Sluys, Crécy and Poitiers, when it was striving to impose order on the country. His arguments were designed to legitimise Charles V's efforts to discipline the mercenaries and knights errant and showed little sympathy with the old ideal of the knightly class as an independent, privileged elite. His work was written at a time when knights were still fighting as individuals bound by the honour of their brotherhood, yet it provided the intellectual justification for a very different world, the world of national chivalries, in which knights fought as stipendiaries of the state and in which public interests took precedence over private.

'We laid waste the countryside'[15]

The Middle Ages looked for its knightly exemplars in the great heroes of antiquity. In the *chansons de geste* and the vernacular histories the models of ideal knighthood were found in Hector, Alexander, Scipio and Julius Caesar. Chivalry itself was considered an institution of Roman origin. The only difference between contemporary rules of chivalry and the discipline of the Roman armies was held to be that the latter predated the former. The law of arms was simply the common law of the soldiery of the late Roman Empire. Imperial Rome lived on, at least in a military sense, in the barbarian societies which took its place.

At a time when imperial Rome was perceived through the lens of contemporary conditions, it was only natural that guidance on matters of strategy should be found in a text of that era, Vegetius' *De Re Militari*. Vegetius had written in the late fourth century at the encouragement of an imperial patron, probably Emperor Theodosius. His work was intended to offer a programme for Roman military recovery through army reforms based on improvements in recruitment, training and strategy. From the early twelfth century his text was to attract a wide following, both clerical and lay; indeed, it became a medieval bestseller. No fewer than 320 copies have come down to us, ranging in date from the seventh century to the seventeenth. Translations were made into French, Anglo-Norman, German, Spanish, Portuguese and even Hebrew. The first English translation was made in 1408 at the prompting of the Gloucestershire magnate Thomas, Lord Berkeley.[16]

Vegetius' precepts were given in the context of an army of very different composition, recruitment and organisation from those of the Middle Ages, yet they translated well into medieval conditions. Vegetius began by reviewing the principles which should ideally govern the recruitment and training of an army, stressing the need for moral as well as physical qualities in troops. He then offered comment and advice on the workings and administration of an effective fighting force, highlighting the importance of forage and provisions. In his third book he turned to the matter on which his work was to have the greatest impact in the Middle Ages – tactics and strategy. He said that an army's approach to combat should be coherently planned, well ordered and disciplined; the enemy's intentions should be ascertained and effectively countered; battles should be entered into only if the commander was sure of superiority over his adversary; and stratagem and finesse should be employed to wear down an enemy where possible, obviating the need for the commander to deploy his troops. Victories, according to Vegetius, should be won with minimum effort and cost of life. A commander who prepared his position properly should be able to attain his ends without risking battlefield slaughter.[17]

It need hardly be supposed that Vegetius's text was used as an actual handbook of the art of war in the Middle Ages – there is little evidence that it was widely read before the twelfth century – yet its popularity points to the close interest which commanders took in the planning and conduct of war in the late antique and medieval periods. Practical men like Sir John Fastolf and Sir John Astley, both Knights of the Garter, had copies of Vegetius on their shelves.[18] Nor should it be supposed that Vegetius' was the only military text which they had in their possession. From the late thirteenth century a wide politico-military literature came into being, advising spiritual and temporal leaders on aspects of strategy from crusading to the retention of occupied territories. In the late Middle Ages, however, Vegetius was without peer as an authority on matters relating directly to the theory and practice of war. In a sense, the late Middle Ages, the 'Age of Chivalry', was the period of Vegetian war par excellence.

While it can hardly be doubted that Vegetius' text was widely read, there can equally be little doubt that most commanders learned the bulk of their craft on the job. They honed their skills as fighting men in tourneying contests, as apprentice esquires in the service of knights, as knights on their first campaign. They probably only read Vegetius when they were already well experienced. What is interesting, nonetheless, is that both the theoretical and the practical approaches to war embodied the same basic idea: that battles should if possible be avoided. Vegetius was clear on this. Battles, he said, involved high risk. The outcome of a whole campaign could turn on an encounter of two or three hours, 'after which no further hopes were left for the worsted army'. When the stakes were so high, it made sense for a commander to achieve his ends by what Vegetius called 'strategy and finesse'. In practice, such tactics meant waging war by fire and sword: ravaging and wasting, destroying the enemy's towns and villages and depriving him of his resources, undermining the enemy's lordship by exposing his inability to protect his vassals. In the Middle Ages most warfare took the form of such burning and harrying. Battles, though sometimes necessary to force an issue, were rare.

One of the attractions of burning and harrying was that it minimised direct conflict between members of the warrior aristocracy. William of Poitiers reports that William the Conqueror engaged in harrying his enemies because of his reluctance to shed blood – by which he meant his fellow knights' blood.[19] Knightly casualties in medieval war were on the whole quite low. However, the price for this apparently civilised policy was paid by ordinary folk – humble peasantry and townsmen. The burden and the cost of war were thrust firmly onto their shoulders in the form of loss of livestock, burning of crops and destruction of property. The most notorious example of deliberate destruction as an act of policy was William the Conqueror's 'harrying of the north' in the winter of 1069–70. According to the chroniclers, to break English resistance the Conqueror left no village inhabited between York and the River Tees. The terrible destruction wrought was to leave its mark in the entries for 'waste' in Domesday Book compiled nearly twenty years later. In the mid-twelfth century, in the civil war of Stephen's reign, it was again harrying to which the two parties resorted as their chief weapon against their opponents. According to the Gesta Stephani, one notorious baron, Philip of Gloucester, 'raged in all directions with fire and sword, violence and plunder, and far and wide reduced to bare fields and a dreadful desert the lands and possessions not only of those barons who opposed the king, but even of his own king'.[20] Describing the condition of England in 1143, the same chronicler, probably writing in the West Country, painted a grim picture:

> Some ate . . . the flesh of dogs or horses; others, to relieve hunger, fed
> unsatisfied on raw and filthy herbs or roots; some, because the afflic
> tion of the famine was more than they could bear, wasted away and
> died in droves . . . You could have seen villages extremely well known
> standing lonely and almost empty, because the peasants of both sexes

and all ages were dead . . . All England wore an aspect of sorrow and
misfortune, an aspect of wretchedness and oppression.[21]

In the early fourteenth century it was harrying warfare to which the
Scots resorted in their struggle against the English. Raids were regularly
launched across the border, ravaging the landscape, destroying economic
resources, shattering popular morale and gathering up cartloads of
booty to take home. The populace of the northern counties were terri-
fied of the Scots and would abandon their homes at the first word of
their coming. The damage which the Scots did is everywhere evident
in the tax rolls or estate accounts of landowners of the area. In the year
of Bannockburn tithe income from the churches of Northumberland
dwindled almost to nothing.

The English campaigns in France in the Hundred Years War simply
rolled out these tactics all over again. The *chevauchées*, which were a
speciality of English commanders, had the predictable aims of demor-
alising the populace, weakening enemy capacity and forcing the French
leadership to negotiate. The impact of the raids could be devastating.
In 1339 the English and their allies wrought such havoc around Cambrai
that when relief funds were distributed, no fewer than 174 parishes
were found in need of help. On one occasion, Sir Geoffrey le Scrope,
to show a French cardinal the impact of the war, took him to the top
of a tower and pointed to fires raging for fifteen miles into the
distance.[22] On the Crécy–Calais campaign seven years later, Michael
de Northburgh, a clerk of Edward III, wrote, 'The people in the army
rode pillaging and destroying twelve to fifteen miles around every day,
burning many places . . . They fired everything along the coast from
Roche Masse to Ouistreham, the harbour of Caen, a distance of 120
miles.'[23] A decade later, when the Black Prince launched his *chevauchée*
from Bordeaux to the French Mediterranean coast, according to the
Anonimalle Chronicle, no fewer than eleven cities and 3,700 villages
were destroyed.[24] In the 1370s the English were to organise further
plundering expeditions which, while less devastating than their predecessors, still inflicted considerable damage. In 1373–4 John of Gaunt
cut a swathe across France from Calais to Bordeaux.

It can hardly be doubted, on the evidence of contemporaries'
comments, that such expeditions were undertaken with a clear strategic
aim: that of weakening the enemy's ability to make war. Sir John

Wingfield, the Black Prince's steward, hinted as much when he high-lighted the damage inflicted on French royal finances by his master's Mediterranean raid. 'The land and towns which are destroyed in this *chevauchée*,' he wrote, 'found for the king of France each year more for the maintenance of his war than did half of his kingdom, excluding receipts from coinage and the customs in Poitou.'[25] Yet the question arises: was such war chivalric? There can be no doubt that it was both lethal and effective, but did it accord with contemporary expectations of the behaviour of a good knight?

On the evidence of the biography of one of the most celebrated knights of the period, William Marshal, the answer could hardly be clearer: contemporaries not only had no reservations about such war; they actually admired it. What the Marshal's style of war consisted of was not heroic charges or the performing of brave deeds for ladies; it was sudden swoops, swift mounted raids, cunning ruses and surprise attacks on strongpoints. The Marshal had little time for abstract idealism. He was a hard-headed, practical man. He could be devious. In 1188 he advised Henry II to catch the French king unawares by disbanding his men and mustering them again behind the French lines. There were times when his tactics could be underhand. In a sea battle off Sandwich in 1217 he ordered his men to throw potfuls of blinding chalk dust into the eyes of the hapless French. Yet contemporaries held him in high regard. When King Richard wanted to congratulate him on his clever advice, he complimented him as 'molt corteis' ('most courtly'). To those in a position to judge, he was 'the best knight in the world'.[26]

Attitudes to chivalry were no different in the age of the Hundred Years War. Thomas Montagu, earl of Salisbury, one of the great English commanders of the 1420s, could match the Marshal in his ability to spring a trick or two. Retreating to Normandy after the English defeat at Baugé, he faced a difficult river crossing. To get his men across, he ordered all the doors in the villages they passed through to be ripped off, and then, when they reached the river, had them laid on top of the carts to improvise a bridge. Later, by despatching an advance guard disguised as French soldiers, he managed to dupe the city of Le Mans into surrendering to him. Yet to the anonymous journal writer in Paris at this time Salisbury was most chivalrous, 'moult chevalleraux'.[27]

Contemporaries showed no less regard for the tricks of some of the more disreputable characters of the day. Froissart tells of a Hainaulter knight, Sir Eustace d'Abrichecourt, who, he says, performed 'many fine deeds of arms and often succeeded in knightly combat with noble men, nor could anyone stand up to him because he was young, deeply in love and full of enterprise'. His lady love, he adds, would send him horses, love letters and tokens of affection 'because he was so bold and courageous'. Yet, for all his courtesy, d'Abrichecourt 'built up a fortune from ransoms, the sale of towns and castles, the levying of redemptions in the countryside and on houses, and through the safe conducts he provided'.[28] D'Abrichecourt was a ravager and freebooter, and in the areas under his control levied *appatis* – protection money. Yet Froissart saw no inconsistency between the two sides of his character. Nor, apparently, did those who had dealings with him. D'Abrichecourt was married to a niece of the English queen, and his kinsman Sanchet was a founder Knight of the Garter. Later members of his family settled into the English gentry.

A similar story can be told of the famous mercenary captain Sir John Hawkwood. Hawkwood enjoyed a formidable reputation as a soldier. In the 1360s he was a leading light in the free companies which caused havoc in France and Italy, and in the 1370s he took commanding positions in the forces of first Padua and then Florence, winning a crushing victory for the Paduans at Castagnaro in 1387. Hawkwood was an unscrupulous rough-hewn character who lived by his wits. Like the Marshal, he resorted to deception as part of his armoury. More than once when staging a tactical withdrawal he left campfires burning to trick his adversaries into thinking that he was still around. Hawkwood's reputation, even so, was that of a chivalric warrior. Thirty years after his death the Florentines honoured him with a funerary monument showing him on horseback in the image of the perfect knight. In the 1470s his fellow countryman William Caxton was to speak approvingly of 'Syr Iohan Hawkwode . . . and many other whoos names shyne gloriously by their virtuous noblesse and actes that they did in thonour of thordre of chivalry.'[29] There can be no doubt that Hawkwood was seen as a properly chivalrous knight.

Chivalric war was a tough down-to-earth business, and trickery and subterfuge formed part of it as much as colourful jousts and eve-of-battle *pas d'armes*, but contemporaries had no difficulty in accepting its apparent contradictions. If they admired knightly heroism, they were also aware of the careful planning and good provisioning that actually won wars. In the 1450s William Worcester urged the need for good provisioning on the government as a way of saving the English position in Normandy. People regarded the ingenious employment of deceit as evidence of the prudent application of intelligence. Equally, they could rationalise the accumulation of booty as evidence of prowess in arms.

Much more of an issue was the correct treatment of civilians. Although non-combatants were by definition not part of the military class, they found themselves caught up in the trials of conflict and, as often as not, were the principal victims of chivalric war. How, then, could their suffering be justified? How could war be regarded as chivalric and ennobling when the worst sufferings were inflicted on those who were not involved in it? These were difficult questions to which commentators had no simple answers. In the early Middle Ages the Church had made a genuine attempt to protect non-combatants through the Peace of God movement. At a series of councils in the 970s and later, measures were published imposing strong penalties on those who attacked churches or robbed peasants and other unarmed people of their animals. These measures were supplemented in the 1020s by the Truce of God movement, which sought to restrict the lawful exercise of arms to certain days of the week and times of the year. In each case those who breached the decrees were faced with excommunication.

However, as war was waged on an ever larger scale, involving more and more of a ruler's subjects in support of his conflicts, it became increasingly difficult to determine just who non-combatants were. As the pace of social mobility quickened, divisions between the three divinely ordained orders of society became blurred. It was not just the knights who were involved in fighting. At Courtrai in 1302 an army of townsmen had caused a sensation by defeating the massed ranks of the French cavalry. Moreover, when peasants and townsmen were supporting a war, if not by bearing arms then through paying taxes, the notion of involvement began to lose definition.

In the thirteenth century, therefore, the thrust of the Church's policy on non-combatants was to change. Instead of pursuing the complementary initiatives of the Peace and Truce of God, the authorities turned instead to refining and developing the idea of the just war.[30] The leading thinker of the day, St Thomas Aquinas, focused attention on how such a war should be fought and what constraints should be imposed on those who took part in it. His solutions to these problems centred on the doctrine of proportionality. In time of war, he said, all who did not actively oppose force with force enjoyed certain rights, in particular the right to life and, less certainly, the preservation of property and the means of livelihood. Those who were engaged in fighting, he added, should show respect for those who were not. The means which soldiers used in war must respect the participants' proper intention when beginning the war, the aim of which, as St Augustine had said, must be to achieve peace.

Aquinas's attempts to establish the rights of non-combatants were nobly conceived but ultimately doomed to failure. For there was one problem which neither he nor any other authority could circumvent: namely that medieval religious doctrine raised no objection to war provided that it was just. 'We must understand that war comes from God,' wrote Honoré Bovet, 'not merely that He permits war, but that He has ordained it . . . for the aim of war is to wrest peace, tranquillity and reasonableness from him who refuses to acknowledge his wrongdoing.'[31] The devastation of war could thus be seen as a form of punishment, a rod not spared, a means to the end of bringing the wrongdoer to his senses. If non-combatants supported their lord, then they were guilty of sharing in his wrong and were themselves open to punishment. Moreover, it was not only those directly complicit in their ruler's war-making who were exposed in this way. If the king's council, which spoke for the whole national community, decided upon war, then it was the whole of that community which stood open to chastisement.[32] The medieval conception of a *bellum hostile*, a just war undertaken by a sovereign ruler, posed no real impediment to attacks on civilians or their property. In the age of chivalric warfare the non-combatant peasant or townsman was left effectively without legal protection. Chivalry, while moderating some of the worst excesses of war, was an ethic which chiefly benefited the chivalric class itself. Medieval theologians recognised the existence of the problem; it was, however, left to the thinkers of a later age satisfactorily to resolve it.

'When battle was joined'[33]

Wars could be won without battles if the harrying was sufficiently devastating in itself. Geoffrey of Anjou had conquered Normandy

(1136–44) and Emperor Henry VI Sicily (1195), in each case without engaging in battle. In 1203–4 King Philip II of France drove King John out of Normandy and Anjou without once fighting a battle. Great military reputations could be won without the need for the commander ever to clothe himself in battle honours. Richard the Lionheart built up a formidable reputation on the strength of his siegecraft, not his success in battle. William Marshal built up his reputation on his tourneying prowess. He fought just two battles in the course of a career spanning nearly sixty years.[34]

There were, however, circumstances in which battles could not be avoided. Wars in the Middle Ages often revolved around the capturing and securing of strongholds. Battles might be fought as part of a strategy to gain control of such places. In the civil war of Stephen's reign, the battle of Lincoln (1141) was fought as a by-product of Stephen's attempt to win Lincoln Castle. Eventually, as advances in design made castles ever more difficult to take, battles were fought as substitutes for sieges, offering a quicker and more effective way to resolve disputes or secure territory. Battles might also be fought as a way of bringing a conflict or disagreement to a head. In 1346 Edward III deliberately sought battle to draw down the judgement of God on his struggle with King Philip VI for the French Crown.[35]

Medieval commanders' interest in strategy and tactics showed itself not only in the planning of campaigns, but also in the planning and conduct of battles. Medieval battles can easily appear from the sources as little more than bloody and chaotic melees, and there can be no doubt that the sheer press of men and horses could create situations of appalling horror. At Dupplin Moor in 1332 bodies piled up as the Scots infantry, pressing forward, were mown down where their fallen comrades lay dying. At Agincourt there were scenes of carnage as the second and third French columns stalled, and yet more bodies were added to those already on the ground. But the impression of melee may be an imperfect reflection of what actually happened in any battle. Those who recorded events might not have been genuine eyewitnesses to the events they were describing; they may have derived their information from knights or captains who themselves witnessed only part of the unfolding scene. In reality, a great deal of thought usually went into preparing for a battle. There was too much at stake for it to be otherwise.

The battle site would have been chosen with care. It is likely, for example, that Edward III or his officers had identified the Vallée des Clercs at Crécy as a suitable site for an engagement with the French many years before the battle. The relative dispositions of the cavalry and infantry contingents would need to be given careful consideration. Sometimes it was more effective to field knights dismounted than charging the enemy on horseback. In the battle itself it would be necessary to respond quickly to changes in circumstances so as to avert disaster or make the most of an unforeseen opportunity. At Hastings in 1066 it was Duke William's quick thinking in the face of his knights' stalled advance that won the day for the Normans through the ruse of the feigned retreat to deceive the English.

When strategy and tactics counted for so much, what, if any, was the place of chivalry on the field of battle in the Middle Ages? Did it play any significant role, or was it largely an irrelevance in an age of tough hand-to-hand combat?

It is easy to suppose that the considerations which really mattered in determining battle outcomes were factors such as logistics, intelligence, weaponry and tactical dispositions. Vegetius had stressed the importance of proper logistical and tactical preparation for war in his treatise, and the most successful battle commanders were those who paid greatest attention to these matters. Richard the Lionheart, for example, always ensured that his men were well equipped and marched on full stomachs. Edward III made certain that the armies he led to France were all well resourced. Edward was also shrewd in using tactical manoeuvres he had learned from years of combat with the Scots.

On the evidence of Froissart and other chroniclers, it seems that displays of chivalric behaviour were confined largely to the sidelines of military activity. It was a common practice for knights to engage each other in single combat before battle or in the course of a campaign. Some of these encounters might be unplanned. On the eve of Bannockburn in 1314 an English knight, Sir Henry de Bohun, chanced unexpectedly on Bruce himself, engaging in a combat which cost him his life.[36] More usually such encounters were organised in advance. In 1327, while the earl of Moray and Sir James Douglas were besieging Alnwick, there were, according to the *Scalacronica*, 'grand jousts of war by covenant'.[37] The most celebrated of these encounters was to occur in 1346, in the course of the Crécy campaign, when, as the English and French faced each other across the Somme, a French knight challenged any comer to three jousts with him 'for the love of his lady'. Sir Thomas Colville rose to the Frenchman's challenge. He fought two good jousts; the third, however, had to be abandoned when the French knight's shield was broken, and to continue was judged too dangerous.[38] On one occasion a full-blown 'friendly' battle was fought between the two sides. At the so-called Battle of the Thirty, fought near Josselin in Brittany in 1351, thirty English knights met the same number of French, the latter emerging triumphant after a closely fought contest of several hours.[39] In the pages of Froissart much of the fighting of the Hundred Years War is reduced to carefully choreographed encounters of this kind. Even major battles like Poitiers are treated as series of *tableaux vivants* in which knights showed off their courtesy and prowess. Froissart's purpose in recounting battles in this way was to engage and instruct his readers with exemplary tales of knightly conduct. It need hardly be supposed that battles overall unfolded in precisely the manner that he describes. Almost certainly they did not.

Yet to conclude that chivalry had little role to play in the real business of war would probably be to misread the evidence. Chivalry involved more than the enacting of ritualised combat and the performing of brave deeds to impress fair ladies. Its essence was to be found in the regime of training for war – in the honing of fighting skills in the lists, the building of group solidarity in the *tournoi* and the encouragement of bravery in the quest for honour. The sharpening of these skills was crucial to an army's effectiveness in the field. Chivalry, far from being a romanticised fantasy separate from the knight's everyday experience, was absolutely central to it. There was a continuum between the knight's nurturing of his skills in the tournament lists, where the culture of chivalry was rooted, and his actual practice of arms on the battlefield. The skills developed in the lists – those of good horsemanship, the ability to manoeuvre, and mastering the use of weapons when wearing armour – would prove his mainstay in battle and in the field. If the tournament was central to chivalric culture, equally chivalric culture was central to the experience of fighting in war. This was why in the 1330s Edward III and his captains were so keen to encourage tournaments in the run-up to the opening of the long war with France.

Of all the qualities nurtured by chivalry, the hardest to assess are the mental ones of courage, strength of nerve and steadiness under fire. Yet, elusive as these are, they are to be ranked among the most important. It was precisely the quality of mental strength which, in the thick of the melee, kept men going and maintained a force's discipline. The courage which was essential to survival and fulfilment in battle was inseparable from chivalric self-belief. To contemporaries, courage was an aristocratic quality. It was linked with race, blood and lineage. A knight of good lineage would be emboldened in the field by recollection of his ancestors' brave deeds and spurred on in bravery himself by a desire to add to the family roll of honour. Courage, honour and achievement went hand in hand. Honour, the reward for courage, contrasted with shame, engendered by cowardice, an attribute abhorrent to knighthood. A knight who performed brave deeds humbly and without arrogance was a knight who acted chivalrously.

In a closely fought battle, the presence of a body of knights stiffened by chivalric pride could be crucial in turning the tide of events. This is well illustrated by a key encounter in the Lancastrian phase of the Hundred Years War, the bloody battle at Verneuil in southern Normandy in 1424.[40] This battle, which played a crucial role in the consolidation of Henry V's conquest of the duchy, saw a relatively small English force triumph over a much larger multinational 'French' army. On the eve of the encounter the cards seemed to be stacked heavily in favour of the French. The battle site gave them the advantage, the English being forced into an open plain with no strong defensive position, while their opponents were aided by a newly arrived contingent of Lombard cavalry, for which the English horse were no match. Yet in the event the French lost, and lost badly. It was another Agincourt. Something other than pure military strength was involved.

At the beginning of the engagement the French threw in their most powerful force, the Lombard cavalry. The massed charge of the Lombards was devastating, driving straight through the English line and breaking it in two. The only hope for the English was to regroup and advance on the French before the Lombards could charge again. According to the chronicler Waurin, the entire English force moved forward, pausing periodically to release a shout and then resuming its advance. The French likewise moved forward, but now in more ragged array. As the two sides again locked horns, the English took heart from the bravery and inspirational leadership of their commanders. The earl of Salisbury, performing valiantly under his banner, vowed to go on pilgrimage to Jerusalem if he survived the encounter.[41] In another part of the field the duke of Bedford lashed out right and left with his poleaxe. At one point the English standard went down, but a Norman knight, Jean de Saane, plunged into the French line to retrieve it, giving heart to his side. It was this episode which was to prove the turning point in the battle. The English, their resolve strengthened, broke through their opponents' line, and the French retreat turned into a rout. By the time the Lombard cavalry returned, the battle was all but over.

Verneuil was, by any standard, a battle which the French should have won: the English were in a position of disadvantage, unable to deploy the tactical defensive formation which had served them so well in previous battles of the war. There is no indication that their archers were able to wreak their usual havoc. What delivered them victory was quite simply the strength of their morale, which disciplined them and gave them the will to stand and fight. The leadership of Bedford, Salisbury and the other noble captains played a crucial role in events. Schooled in the art of chivalric war and trained in the tourneying lists, these men knew how to deploy the rhetorical apparatus of chivalry in a way which was inspirational to those they commanded.

In a sense, what chivalry did was ritualise war. It created, as part of its culture, a repertory of symbols, actions and devices which could simultaneously glamorise war, mitigate the worst of its horrors and embolden those who took part in it. Ritualising war invested it with a degree of semi-religious mystique. A theatrical aspect was often brought to the formalities which preceded and followed battles. Before the opening of hostilities at Crécy, Edward III rode the length of his front line, white baton in hand, urging his men on against the French. On the eve of Verneuil, Bedford appeared before his men attired in a surcoat with the arms of England and France, symbolising Henry VI's dual monarchy. There were occasions when a conflict arose between this ritualising and the application of shrewd tactical sense. At Conty in 1430 the Hainaulter knight Sir Lewis Robsart, facing defeat by the French, held his ground 'to uphold the honour of his order of chivalry . . . and died gloriously, honourably, and with very few of his company'.[42] Twenty years later at Castillon, the earl of Shrewsbury was to follow a similarly self-destructive course when he stood firm in the face of overwhelming odds.[43] Even in these apparent acts of madness, however, there could be an element of chivalric method. As was to be the case with Sir Richard Grenville's resistance on the ship *Revenge* in 1591, heroism could serve to inspire future generations by etching itself in the national memory.

The penetration of war by chivalric ritual appears to have gathered pace in the early fourteenth century and the period of the Hundred Years War. This is to some extent an impression derived from the writings of Froissart, which presented the war in France in a way likely to appeal to his noble and knightly patrons. Yet it would be wrong to suggest that it is Froissart alone who conveys this impression. In the work of other writers of the day there is evidence of a growing emphasis on reckless heroism. The author of the *Vita Edwardi Secundi*, for example – a clerk – tells how at Bannockburn the young earl of Gloucester plunged into the Scots to meet his death, spurred on by a desire to uphold his honour in the face of charges of cowardice from the king.[44] In the *Scalacronica* Sir Thomas Gray tells how Sir William Marmion, presented with a helmet with a gilded crest by his lady love and told to show it in the most dangerous places, chanced all in an assault on Norham Castle which nearly cost him his life.[45] In his account of the opening phase of the Hundred Years War Jean le Bel describes how some English knights at Valenciennes vowed each to wear a patch over one eye until he had performed a feat of arms worthy of his lady.[46]

Episodes of this kind, if not quite legion by the fourteenth and fifteenth centuries, were certainly not uncommon. They sometimes attracted the criticism of contemporaries. The practice of making vows to perform valorous deeds was satirised in the poem *The Vow of the Heron*, which made fun of those sworn by Edward III at the start of the Hundred Years War. According to the poet, Count Robert of Artois, Edward's French ally, attending a banquet in London, presented the king with a heron, the most cowardly of birds, implying that he was too cowardly to pursue his claim to the French Crown. This act prompted Edward to swear to engage King Philip in single combat within a month, and his knights to follow him in swearing similar bombastic oaths.[47] No satirical comment of this kind is to be found in the literature of earlier periods. On the evidence of chroniclers' accounts, the practice of war in the twelfth century had been altogether more prosaic. There was certainly nothing glamorous or fantastic about the style of war practised by the Marshal. As we read of it in the verse biography narrated by one of his esquires, it was hard-headed, down-to-earth and practical. Chivalric conduct showed itself appropriately enough in the humane treatment of prisoners of rank, ransoms invariably being claimed instead of lives. There is no evidence, however, of those showier aspects of chivalry which were to figure so prominently in the Hundred Years War. The taking of vows, the performing of brave deeds for women, the fighting of friendly jousts on campaign – these are all conspicuous by their absence.

If a reason is to be offered for the more exotic flavour of war in the late Middle Ages, it is probably to be found in the influence of literature. Knights of the fourteenth and fifteenth centuries, soaked in the legends of Arthurian romance, sought to act out the fictions in their own lives. The worlds of reality and the imagination over-lapped. Thus, when in 1360 two French knights jousted with two English knights dressed in vermilion, the latter were almost certainly acting out a scene in Chrétien's Le Conte du Graal, which includes an episode with a 'Vermilion Knight'.[48] The authors of chivalric biography seem to have sensed little or no distance between what they described and the narratives of imaginative experience. John Barbour termed his chronicle of King Robert Bruce a 'romanys'. Both Barbour and Sir Thomas Gray, author of the Scalacronica, wrote that, if the deeds of Edward Bruce in Ireland were to be set down, they would make a fine romance. Robert Bruce himself is known to have read out passages from the romance of Fierabras to his men when in refuge near Loch Lomond.[49] Just as these knightly exemplars sought to model their lives on romance, so those lives in turn became the subject of new romance. Few in chivalric society took make-believe so far as the Burgundian knight Jacques de Lalaing, who spent a whole year in 1449–50 on an island in the River Saône, challenging all comers to a passage of arms. When, however, as in England a century earlier, tournaments were modelled on the Arthurian Round Table and Edward III created a chivalric order with echoes of Arthur's own, it is hardly surprising that aspects of the world of romance should have infiltrated knightly practice. If the fictional and real worlds sometimes gave the impression of fusing into one imaginative whole, there was however no danger of romantic fantasy entirely supplanting military hard-headedness. In that masterpiece of the alliterative revival *Sir Gawain and the Green Knight*, Gawain, facing the challenge of a return blow from the giant Green Knight, showed little hesitation in accepting the aid of a talisman from his host's wife. Whether he was right to do so, given his commitment to the chivalric code, is a question over which he was to suffer agonies of conscience later (and his readers with him). At the time, however, when crisis loomed, he had no second thoughts. Moreover, when he returned to Arthur's court, he encountered no criticism for his conduct from either the king or his fellow knights. The ambivalence of the poem's ending reflects the ambivalence at the heart of chivalry itself.

9

Chivalry and Nobility

Chivalry and nobility went hand in hand. Chivalry idealised the estate of knighthood, while nobility was a way of describing its social exclusiveness. Among the chivalric class in the twelfth and thirteenth centuries, knighthood had been an honour more highly esteemed than nobility. Knighthood involved a solemn act of initiation, while nobility was simply a social condition into which a man had been born. In the late Middle Ages, however, the relative esteem in which the two dignities were held was reversed. Nobility strengthened its appeal while interest in taking up knighthood went into decline. In the late Middle Ages what mattered to people most was the quality of a man's blood. Increasingly, emphasis was placed on distinction of lineage and the importance of armigerous rank as a mark of that attribute. Knighthood was something which could be dispensed with provided birth and bloodline brought evidence enough of distinction.

The Decline of Knighthood

The late medieval decline in knighthood was, in one sense, nothing new. Knighthood had been in decline since the early thirteenth century. It has already been noted how the number of men taking up the rank of knight in England was in free fall from 1200. In the late twelfth century there had been somewhere between 3,600 and 4,000 knights in England. By the second quarter of the following century the number had fallen to somewhere between 1,200 and 1,500. By the 1280s, when Edward I declared war on the Welsh, there were probably no more than 500–1,000 actual fighting knights at the king's disposal. Edward's measures to promote knighthood went some way to reverse the decline, but numbers never fully returned to their earlier levels. Knightly quality was bought at the expense of knightly quantity.

The late medieval decline in knighthood differed, however, in one significant respect from the decline of the thirteenth century. In the 1200s prospective knights had shunned the rank because they could not afford it. As the knightly lifestyle grew more lavish and, as a result, more expensive, the lesser knights were priced out; they sank down into the ranks of the esquires, respectable but not blue-blooded. In the late Middle Ages the position was different. Those who avoided taking up knighthood were more than able to support the rank; they included some of the richest gentlemen in the land. It was just that knighthood no longer held much appeal for them.

Someone typical of the wealthy new refuseniks was the Essex gentleman John Doreward of Bocking. Doreward was the lord of nearly a dozen and a half manors in Essex and East Anglia.[1] He inherited most of his properties from his parents, acquired another property through marriage and added several more by purchase. Overall, the value of his lands must have approached somewhere between £150 and £200 per annum, at a time when the threshold for knighthood was £40. Doreward ranked among the richest non-magnate proprietors in southern England. It is no surprise that he should have been elected no fewer than six times a knight of the shire in parliament for his county. Such was his distinction that on two of those occasions he was elected speaker. Yet socially he remained no more than an esquire; he never took up the rank of knight.

Still more instructive is the case of a contemporary of Doreward, Thomas Chaucer of Ewelme in Oxfordshire. Chaucer was the son of Geoffrey, the poet. His background lay in royal and administrative service rather than in county society.[2] His connections at court, partly a by-product of his father's career, assured him of a good start in life. His mother, Philippa Roet, was a lady-in-waiting to John of Gaunt's second wife, while his aunt Katherine Swynford was Gaunt's third wife. Already before 1399 his clutch of stewardships and other offices, mainly in the duchy of Lancaster, was bringing him a healthy income. His greatest good fortune, however, was to secure the hand in marriage of Maud, daughter of Sir John Burghersh, the co-heiress of the Burghershes of Oxfordshire. This match brought him a string of manors in Oxfordshire, the south Midlands and East Anglia. Like Doreward, alongside whom he sat in parliament, he added to his inherited properties by purchase. From the profits of office-holding, he bought another half-dozen manors in Oxfordshire and the greater part of the Abberbury family's inheritance in Berkshire. By the time of his death in 1434 his income must have approached £1,000 per annum. He was wealthy enough to be a minor baron, let alone a knight, yet he was content to stay at the rank of esquire.

Why would a well-to-do esquire be dissuaded from taking up knighthood? Did the title of knight no longer carry any cachet or exert any appeal? In most well-established county lineages there was probably still an expectation that each new head of the family would take up the rank. Generations of Vernons of Tong in Shropshire, Savages of Bobbing in Kent and Chaworths of Wiverton in Nottinghamshire dutifully became knights, thereby maintaining family tradition. In Sussex not a generation of the Etchinghams of Etchingham appears to have missed out. Even in the top echelons of local society, however, there were backsliders. In Nottinghamshire in the fifteenth century members of the well-endowed Hercy and Strelley families broke with tradition by opting out. In Gloucestershire in the same period members of the no less affluent families of Tracy of Toddington and Veel of Charfield were content with the rank of esquire. Knighthood was no longer, evidently, a prerequisite for position and standing in local society.

One reason for the widespread reluctance to assume knighthood may have been a fear among those qualified that it would involve them in military service they would rather avoid. Assumption of knighthood had always carried with it an expectation of acceptance of the burdens of rank, whether military or administrative. In the thirteenth and fourteenth centuries kings regularly issued distraint writs obliging forty-pound landholders to take up knighthood, hoping in this way to increase the pool of knights for military service. Those with no interest in fighting excused themselves to the sheriff by paying the five-pound exemption fee. From the returns which the sheriffs sent back to the king, it is clear that the great majority of those who paid to be excused were those whose talents lay in administration not soldiering – John Doreward, Thomas Chaucer and their like. They were men for whom a rank primarily associated with soldiering held no appeal.

The burdens to which knighthood might lead, however, constitute only part of the explanation. Behind the flight from knighthood lay a much bigger story – that of the growing preoccupation with blood and lineage in upper-class society. What commanded respect in the fourteenth and fifteenth centuries was not so much knighthood as such – a personal dignity which died with the holder – as the hereditary capacity to receive and support knighthood – a family attribute. Those privileged with admission to the elite were now not only those who had actually taken up knighthood but those entitled, by virtue of birth, to aspire to it. Knighthood as such was replaced as the pre-eminent bond uniting the aristocracy by a growing appreciation of lineage as the essential prerequisite for chivalric distinction. And the outward and visible sign of nobility in this ancestral sense was possession of a coat of arms. Nobility, a quality belonging to the whole family, eclipsed knighthood, an honour personal to the holder.

This shift to emphasis on lineage and nobility is evident right across Europe in the late Middle Ages and particularly noticeable in France and Germany, where noble rank carried with it the privilege of exemption from public taxation. Precisely for this reason, in much of continental Europe nobility became a condition recognised in law, for the authorities had to know who was and was not liable for exemption from tax. No comparable legal definition of nobility was ever achieved in England, and at no point did the English nobility ever consider claiming the fiscal privileges enjoyed by their counterparts elsewhere. Nonetheless, in certain important respects developments in English noble society followed those of the European mainstream. Most obviously, in England as on the continent a growing interest was taken by the elite in lineage and nobility. The fact that the coat of arms, a key ensign of identity, could, unlike knighthood itself, be passed down the generations was probably a factor in this process. The pride which every gentleman took in his family's coat of arms encouraged him to think in hereditary terms.

The extent to which heraldry took the place of knighthood as the principal mark of social distinction is evident from the heraldic preoccupations of some of the senior squirearchical families of the day. A good example is provided by the Dallingridge family, a line based in Sussex in the fourteenth century. Sprung from a family of foresters and originating near Dalling Ridge in Ashdown Forest, the Dallingridges were socially ambitious.[3] In or around 1311 John Dallingridge married Joan, daughter and co-heiress of the wealthy knight Sir Walter de la Lynde of Bolebrook in east Sussex. Through this lady he acquired extensive lands in Sussex, Lincolnshire and the West Country, yet he was never tempted to assume knighthood. What he did do was take over the de la Lynde arms. It is not clear whether he was of armigerous rank beforehand but, if he was, he discarded his old insignia. The de la Lynde arms now became the arms of Dallingridge. Symbolically the Dallingridges had assumed the de la Lynde identity and had appropriated their social distinction. It is with the de la Lynde arms on his jupon that John's son and successor Roger, a leading associate of the earl of Arundel, was to be shown on his brass in Fletching church.

Still more striking is the case of a fifteenth-century esquire, William Finderne of Childrey in Berkshire. Finderne was a lawyer. A junior member of a Derbyshire knightly family, he rose through service and won the hand of a Berkshire widow, Elizabeth, daughter and co-heiress of Thomas Chelrey.[4] Through her he entered into possession of lands in Berkshire and the Thames valley and settled down on his wife's main manor of Childrey. When he died in 1445, his wife honoured him with a magnificent memorial brass showing them both in heraldic attire. The two are dressed like playing-card characters, he in a tabard and she in a mantle. The prodigious display of heraldry on the brass appears to be entirely without precedent; this is the earliest extant memorial to show a husband and wife attired in this way. Yet Finderne was no grandly born aristocrat; he was only an esquire, a lawyer and an administrator. The point of the heraldry was to draw attention to his and his wife's bloodline. Transmuted into a matter of lineage and heraldry, late medieval chivalry became a codified discourse of nobility.

The Rise of the Gentry?

The late medieval period not only saw a shift of emphasis from knighthood to lineage and bloodline; it witnessed a related development: the emergence of a group separate from the nobility – the gentry. The gentry are a group of uniquely English construction. In most continental states contemporaries thought of the upper classes as a single undifferentiated *noblesse* containing families of varying means. In England the way in which people made sense of society was different. The 'lesser nobility' acquired a distinct identity as the 'gentry'. And within the gentry a carefully differentiated hierarchy emerged, mirroring that in the nobility above.

The emergence of the gentry was partly the result of a process of exclusion. In one sense the members of this group may be defined as those who had gradually forfeited the nobility which their ancestors had once shared with the lords. By the late fourteenth century, the wealthier of the lords were acquiring institutional definition as hereditary nobility identifiable with the parliamentary peerage. Once the nobility as a group had become associated with the peerage in this way, the gentry could be considered the losers. They were those who had been shut out: landowners now deemed only 'gentle', who competed for election to the lower house of parliament. Stephen Scrope, scion of a great magnate dynasty, was conscious of the new social difference when, referring to his stepfather, Sir John Fastolf, he said, 'I am com of blode and he but be gifte of jentilnes.'[5]

If exclusion played a part in the formation of the gentry, so too did processes of coalescence and recognition. The raw material of the gentry class was to be found in the undifferentiated mass of lesser landowners which stretched from the knightly and sub-knightly ranks down to the franklins and yeomanry. Hitherto ill defined, in the fifteenth century this group emerged as an elite of armigerous rank, demarcated internally into a hierarchy of knight, esquire and gentleman, mirroring the equivalent hierarchy in the peerage.[6] This process of self-definition was in part a defensive reaction to the growing assertiveness of the lower orders in the years of rising wages after the Black Death. The lesser landowner class – the small employers of the day – wanted to affirm their membership of the elite and so separate themselves from those below, whom they saw as belonging to the labouring class. Gentry formation formed part and parcel of the larger social process by which English society became divided into rulers and ruled.

To a remarkable degree, it is possible to trace this story in the changing conventions governing entitlement to the use of coats of arms. Before the third quarter of the fourteenth century the use of arms had, nominally at least, been restricted to those of knightly rank. Esquires were not recognised as an armigerous class in their own right. Thus in the Statute of Arms of 1292 it had been laid down that in tournaments esquires should bear the arms of the lords by whom they were retained. By the 1370s, however, esquires had won the right to bear coats of arms themselves. In Sir Robert Laton's roll of arms of *c.* 1370 the arms of esquires appeared alongside those of knights.[7] This was a novelty. From the time of the compilation of this roll it became almost routine to include the arms of knights and esquires alongside them. With this development, esquires may be said to have been fully accepted within the ranks of the armigerous.

To some extent, esquires were simply stepping into a social and military vacuum. With the steady decline in knightly numbers, by the fourteenth century there was a shortage of men appropriately qualified to fill the offices and commissions of local government. In many counties the Crown was finding it difficult to find men ready and willing to serve. As early as John's reign there are reports of meetings of the county court which had to be adjourned because no knights were present. Against this background, it was natural to allow those who were knightworthy but not knights themselves to act in their place. By the mid-fourteenth century this practice was happening quite regularly. Non-knights were serving as sheriffs and keepers of the peace, even being elected to parliament. And with administrative recognition came social recognition. Esquires were accepted as the equals of knights.

But there were also developments in the military sphere which promoted the rise of esquires. The kind of warfare practised by Edward III in the Hundred Years War involved rapid mobility. Edward found the secret of his success in the capacity for speedy movement of the forces he took with him on campaign. Edward's forces in France were essentially cavalry, comprising knights, esquires and mounted archers fighting alongside each other. These were armies of a very different kind to the slow-moving forces which Edward I and Edward II had deployed in Scotland, and there was little to distinguish the mounted esquire from the knights alongside whom he was serving. Both groups were horsed; both wore the same sort of armour; and both used the same sorts of weapons. War was no longer an activity which allowed the heavily armed knight to stand apart from the esquires because he was horsed and they were not.[8] The effect of the new style of fighting was to bring about a blurring of the distinction between knights and esquires. The key role of military experience in the forging of identities is indicated in the terminology generally favoured from the late fourteenth century to describe esquires. In the past a whole series of words had been used to describe these men – *armigeri, valletti, esquiers* – the precise choice depending on the language of the user and the context in which he was writing. By the end of the fourteenth century, however, one word had emerged in preference to the others – the Latin *armiger*, or armour-bearer – the word with the strongest military connotations. The experience of war had played a major role in shaping the structure and vocabulary of the emerging hierarchy of the social elite.

In the fifteenth century yet another group was to secure a place in the hierarchy – the gentlemen. Gentlemen formed the bottommost rung of gentry society. The term first made its appearance as a status designation in 1414 following the passing of the Statute of Additions, which required all defendants in original actions leading to outlawry to be identified by rank, and quickly became a widely used status appellation signifying entitlement to the use of arms. Gentlemen were an immensely diverse group, a biblical house of many mansions. By virtue of their position at the base of the elite, they encompassed men of varied backgrounds. They were urban as well as rural, professional as well as leisured. There is no simple way of delineating their character as a social estate.

Some of the new gentlemen had fought in war, although the link between military service and status was weaker at this level than higher up. As Nicholas Upton, canon of Salisbury and Wells and author of the tract *De Studio Militari*, was to observe in the 1440s, 'In these days we see openly how many poor men, labouring in the French wars, are become noble: some by prudence, others by valour, and others again by endurance . . . many of whom on their own authority have assumed arms to be borne by themselves and their heirs.'[9] In the mid-fifteenth-century phase of the French war men were still able to lever their way up the hierarchy by achievements in arms. Shakespeare captured something of the experience when, in the St Crispin's Day speech in *Henry V*, he makes the king say:

> 'For he today that sheds his blood with me
> Shall be my brother; be he ne'er so vile
> This day shall gentle his condition.'

There is evidence in the rolls of arms of soldiers of quite humble origin rising up through the ranks through valour. Thomas Maisterson, for example, a Cheshireman whose arms are included in the County

Roll of *c*. 1400, was one such, rising from obscurity to modest fame and prosperity on the strength of his service in France. Nicholas Upton himself designed arms for two soldiers who were ennobled for their bravery at the battle of Verneuil in 1424.[10] Even as the war in France drew to a close, the profession of arms was still regarded as having the power to ennoble a man.

With participation in war declining from the second quarter of the fifteenth century, however, far more of the new gentlefolk were of civilian origin. A fair number were agriculturalists who had benefited from the fluid conditions in the countryside in the wake of the Black Death by snapping up cheap land and picking up demesne leases at a discount. Quite often such proprietors would combine land acquisition with changes in land use, substituting animal husbandry for arable. The process of self-assertion among proprietors at this level can be seen with exceptional clarity in the case of the Hydes of Denchworth in Berkshire. In the late fourteenth century the Hydes, the leading freeholder family in the village, began a build-up of lands and titles which was to bring them ascendancy in Denchworth within a generation. John Hyde, who took his name from his family's original hide or property, acquired land piecemeal, eventually reaching the point where he was able to buy one of the manors in the village outright and create a manor out of his lands in another.[11] His son, likewise called John, was referred to as a gentleman in 1418 and his son in turn as an esquire in 1448.[12] Men of this sort had been referred to as franklins or sergeants in the graduated poll tax returns of 1379. Their successors in the next generation, newly confident of their position, were able to style themselves gentlemen. Nicholas Upton, ever observant, commented on the phenomenon. 'We see dayly,' he wrote, 'how housebond men of the cowntrey, throwghe there diligeance, ryse dayly hyer in state of civilitie, so that there yssue atteyn to nobilitie.'[13] The pretensions of these proprietors were brilliantly satirised by Chaucer in his portrait sketch of the Franklin in the General Prologue of the *Canterbury Tales*.

Yet another category of gentlemen were the urban professionals, men who were entitled to honourable recognition because of their particular skill or expertise. The dominant group here were lawyers, a profession whose numbers expanded rapidly in the fifteenth century. William Worcester, lamenting the mid-century decline of arms, complained that many knights' sons and esquires now 'lerne the practique of law or custom of lande, or of civil matier' instead of taking up arms, as they should.[14] Chief Justice Fortescue (d. 1476) agreed with him, writing that 'there is scarce a man learned in the law to be found in the realm who is not genteel or sprung of gentle lineage'.[15] Lawyers, however, were by no means the only professionals whose dignified employment entitled them to recognition as gentlemen. There were also so-called gentlemen bureaucrats, the pen-pushers who staffed the administrative departments of the Crown at Westminster. Before the fifteenth century this class had been composed principally of clerks in holy orders, who qualified for their posts by their literacy. With the spread of lay literacy, however, the bureaucracy was gradually laicised, and a white-collar class came into existence which, in common with lawyers, regarded its work as honourable.

A final category of gentlemen overlapped with that of the bureaucrats. This was the class of retainers and servants of the nobility, the men who prospered in magnate service. These were men of broadly similar character to the bureaucrats in that they acted as administrators – auditing accounts, running household offices and administering estates – certain offices in private administration, those of steward or receiver general, commonly being regarded as honourable. In the world of magnate service, however, it was not employment alone which brought honourable recognition; it was proximity to the lord himself, contact with a man of nobility and 'worship'. Something of the great man's distinction was held to rub off on those who moved in his circle and laboured in his service.

Gentility was an imprecise concept in late medieval society. It was not a measurable absolute, like membership of the House of Lords; it was a quality or condition which to some extent lay in the eye of the beholder. People were not always certain whether they were gentlemen themselves or whether those they observed were gentlemen. When appearing in court, to cover themselves they often employed aliases. In the 1480s John Tame of Fairford in Gloucestershire was described as 'husbandman, alias merchant, alias gentleman, alias woolman, alias yeoman'.[16] Income levels gave little help in establishing gentility. There was no set income threshold for gentility, as there was for knighthood. In the fifteenth century gentlemen might have incomes of five, ten or even fifteen pounds per annum; it was not until 1530 that the heralds settled for a qualification of ten pounds yearly from lands or possession of movable goods worth £300.[17] In the eyes of the heralds gentility was established principally by 'common fame' or 'reputable witness'. In 1460, when Clarenceux King of Arms granted a coat of arms to Thomas Launder of Somerset, he said that he had satisfied himself of his virtue by 'reputable witness'.[18] Other grants of arms made by heralds used much the same language. But how was the quality of common fame or good repute established? How could an aspirant to arms demonstrate that he was a gentleman? Such matters were by no means straightforward in a society as fluid and competitive as that of late medieval England.

Heralds and lawyers were both agreed that there were certain things which a gentleman ought not to do. Most of all, a gentleman should not soil his hands by engaging in manual labour. He should not be seen to work in 'vile and bestial service'. As John Blount, the translator of Nicholas Upton's treatise on heraldry, wrote, gentlemen 'ought not to medell with tyllyng or plowing of lands nor kepyng off bestes nor occupying of marchandise'.[19] To live as a gentleman involved occupational separation from the labouring class, leaving the hard physical work of tilling the land to others.

More generally, establishing gentility was a matter of 'doing' as much as of 'being'. It was a matter of performance, behaviour, constant affirmation and reaffirmation of position. It involved acting and dressing the part. A gentleman, for example, was expected to acquit himself honourably in conversation. When, in *Sir Gawain and the Green Knight*, Gawain arrived at Sir Bertilak's castle, there was high anticipation among his hosts that they would 'see displayed the seemliest manners and the faultless figures of virtuous discourse', for Gawain was a knight of good breeding; he would know 'how to hold good conversation'.[20] At the same time a gentleman should be well dressed, at the very least in possession of an elegant furred robe. When John Woodcock, a Yorkshire gentleman, was sentenced in the Court of King's Bench in 1424 his gentle condition was established by the fact that, although he held no land, he had a black gown furred with beaver and a silver belt. On another occasion in the King's Bench the possession of a collar by a king's servant was cited as evidence that a man of servant rank could be reputed a gentlemen. The granting of collars and robes was one reason why aspirant gentlemen were so eager to be taken on as retainers by magnates. The rich clothing which they were awarded constituted one of the obvious marks of gentility.[21]

To own or to take a lease on a country estate might also be taken as a mark of gentle condition. The Andrews, a minor Warwickshire freeholder family, assumed the airs and graces of gentry after Thomas Andrews, a grazier from Sawbridge near Coventry, took a lease on the manor of Charwelton in Northamptonshire and grew rich by grazing sheep there. In 1476 Thomas secured a grant of arms for himself on the evidence of a fictitious pedigree, and on his brass in Charwelton church, commissioned in the 1490s, styled himself 'merchant and gentleman'.[22] In the next century his grandson, another Thomas, acquired the lordship of the manor of Charwelton and on his own brass styled himself *armiger* – esquire. Lordship of a manor, the most prestigious form of landownership, set the seal on the acquisition of gentility; it associated gentle status with the exercise of magistracy and authority. Lordship found its most characteristic expression in the holding of a manorial court. The Pastons of Norfolk, a family ever alert to what made folk gentle, legitimised their status by the holding of manorial courts for their tenants. Manorial formation was inseparable from gentry formation; the two were aspects of a single process of social and political self-assertion.

More generally, manners, appearance and lifestyle might be markers of the gentle condition. A gentleman had to be seen to engage in the right sorts of leisure activity.[23] Hunting was a pursuit particularly closely associated with the gentry. According to Sir Thomas Malory, only gentlemen were supposed to know the esoteric terms 'that jantylmen have and use' in the chase, so a knowledge of hunting alone could enable 'all men of worship [to] discover a jantylman frome a yoman and a yoman frome a vylane'. In the fourteenth century the parliamentary class sought legislative support to protect their monopoly of gentlemanly sports. In Richard II's reign a statute was passed imposing a year's imprisonment on any artificer or labourer or lay person with less than forty shillings annual income who owned greyhounds or who used other implements to take 'deer, hare, rabbits or other gentles' game'. However, it was not only the traditional sports of the chase which were associated with gentility. Sedentary indoor activities might also be deemed honourable. Margaret Paston wrote to her husband, John, reporting that she had carefully checked with two of her more distinguished lady neighbours 'qwat sportys were husyd' in 'placys of wurschip' on the first Christmas following a death in the family. They informed her that, while no 'lowde dysportys', such as 'dysgysynggys nere harpyng' were appropriate, quieter pastimes such as 'pleyng at the tabyllys and schesse and cardys' were allowable.[24]

When gentility depended so much on personal performance and behaviour, it is not surprising that a flourishing literature grew up advising aspirant gentlemen and gentlewomen on how to conduct themselves in public. In the Middle Ages it was common for young gentlemen-to-be to be brought up in aristocratic households, the finishing schools of their day. For this reason much of the advice given in the literature took the form of instructing gentleman-apprentices in the household tasks expected of them – serving, carving, riding, dancing, singing – all class-related activities which marked the individual as a member of the aristocracy. A treatise called *Urbanitas*, which was probably used at the court of Edward IV, instructed its readers in such matters as speech, cleanliness, appearance, table manners and, all-importantly, how to ingratiate oneself with lords of high rank. One of the most popular treatises was the *Boke of Nurture*, of John Russell, usher to Humphrey, duke of Gloucester, Henry VI's uncle. This took the form of a set of instructions by a teacher to an unhappy young man of his acquaintance whom no one will employ because he was 'wantoun . . . and lewd' and lacking in the necessary social skills.[25] It guides him through all the duties likely to be required of him by a lord, particularly the tricky art of how to carve fish and fowl.

Courtesy books were widely read in the fifteenth century by those who sought to acquire the polish needed to ascend the social ladder. As one historian has put it, they were cherished for showing 'how to win friends and influence people'.[26] If their principal concern, however, was with teaching etiquette as a pathway to social advancement, they were also appreciated for showing how etiquette buttressed the established order. The twin concerns of the books hardly sat comfortably with one another. The tension between them, indeed, highlighted a central difficulty in late medieval attempts to explain and define gentility. This was the absence of any agreement on whether gentlemen were born or could be made. Was gentility to be seen largely as a matter of nurture, something that could be, with effort, acquired? Or was it rather a matter of birth, a quality determined by ancestry and blood? These arguments dragged on throughout the central and late medieval periods, gathering pace after 1350 or thereabouts. Heralds, poets and academics all weighed in with their views. The energy with which the arguments were conducted is a measure of the importance of the issues at stake. For what was involved here was a question that struck at the heart of the aristocracy's position in society: how was aristocratic privilege to be justified?

The Great Debate

Gentility was a word that tripped off many a late medieval nobleman's tongue, often in the same breath as nobility. Together, the two summed up the collection of qualities that constituted and justified the upper-class way of life. But what was the essence, the inner source of gentility? What were its intellectual foundations? The attributes of style, speech, dress and manners discussed in the courtesy books were mere externals. Was there, at the heart of gentility, an intrinsic worth which justified a claim to a superior way of life? Most contemporaries were agreed that there was, although its precise character was a matter of intense debate.

One widely held view was that the essence of gentility was found in birth – in lineage. The belief was held that a man's worth was inseparable from that of his kin. His very being as honourable had been transmitted to him through the blood of his ancestors, themselves honourable men. Honour was thus not merely an individual posses-sion; it was that of the collectivity, the lineage. The fifteenth-century Burgundian writer Olivier de la Marche argued that it was lineage – breeding – which lent the essential underpinning to gentility. 'The gentleman is he who of old springs from gentlemen and gentlewomen, and such men and their posterity by marriage are gentle.' Nobility, 'which is the beginning of gentility', he continued, could be acquired either by service to a prince or by profession of arms, but *ancient* nobility could come 'only from ancient riches; and happy is he, and the more esteemed, who commences his nobility in virtue than he who brings his to an end in vice'.[27]

That was one view. A rival tradition argued a different case: that alongside, or instead of, the claims of lineage should be set those of virtue. In the fourteenth century the Italian jurist Bartolus of

Sassoferrato, assessing the relative claims of lineage and virtue, held them in delicate equipoise. Nobility, he argued, could be divided into two kinds, what he called civil nobility and natural nobility. The former was conferred by a prince and involved recognition of the beneficiary's claim to ancient riches and fine manners, while the latter denoted those marked out by their virtue, specifically by their capacity to rule.[28] Bartolus's contemporary the jurist Beaumanoir, likewise arguing for the claims of both lineage and virtue, suggested a different relationship: lineage, he thought, was a consequence of virtue. In his view gentlefolk were the descendants of those who were sought out after the Fall as the wisest, strongest and most handsome to rule over people and defend them from their enemies.[29] Not all would have agreed with his biological explanation, but in arguing for the importance of virtue more generally Bartolus was following in the steps of a succession of writers going back through Raymond Lull to John of Salisbury in the twelfth century. They all emphasised the same point: that virtue had a role in defining gentility: lineage raised gentility above nobility, while virtue made it a source of honour.

Gnawing away at these arguments, however, was a problem which fatally undermined their integrity: the very obvious point that the claims of birth and virtue were hardly compatible. Virtue was an individual quality which a person might or might not possess, whereas birth in the sense of good blood was a hereditary attribute with which those without virtue might be endowed. It is true that the same language, the same vocabulary, was employed for honour of status as for virtue of character, but the two were in reality quite different. The point was driven home relentlessly from the twelfth century by a succession of clerical writers whose claim to authority rested on qualities other than lineage.[30] Nobility of the body, they argued, was a carnal thing. It was little better than a 'sack full of filth', derived from 'an unclean and shameful act of the parents'. It could not be honoured or respected because it had not been 'personally earned'. The essence of true nobility was to be found in virtue alone. Juvenal had argued for the importance of virtue in ancient Rome, and Boethius had taken the same line in the last years of the Roman Empire. Virtue could not belong to those whose only interest was hunting, hawking and fighting, for such men were the representatives of the 'carnal nobility'. It had to belong to the more learned, the educated, the 'true nobility'. Nobility as virtue was an argument which undermined the claims of heredity and led inescapably to recognition of the claims of an elite of the mind.

Chaucer reviewed these debates at points in the *Canterbury Tales*. In the *Wife of Bath's Tale* he wove a consideration of the nature of gentility into a larger discussion of the proper relationship in marriage of husband and wife. He did so in the context of reworking the familiar tale of the loathly lady. The Wife tells how a knight, convicted of rape, has his death sentence commuted into a quest to find the answer to a seemingly impossible question: what is it that women most desire? Just when the time allowed to the knight is close to expiry, he alights on a group of maidens near a wood. As he approaches them, however, they vanish, leaving only a wizened old hag, to whom out of desperation he puts his question. The answer the hag gives, elicited on condition that he agrees to give her whatever she wants, turns out to be the right one – womanly sovereignty in marriage – and when he returns to court the knight is granted his life. At this very moment, however, when he thinks his ordeal over, the debt is called in: the hag springs forward to remind him of his promise. 'Keep your promise,' she cries, 'and take me for your wife.' The knight, seeing no escape, bows to her will, and as the two retreat to bed the hag reminds him of his duties as a husband:

> 'But, for ye speken of swich gentillesse
> As is descended out of old richesse,
> That therefore sholden ye be gentil men,
> Swich arrogance is nat worth an hen.
> Looke who that is moost virtuous always,
> Pryvee and aprt, and moost entendeth ay
> To do the gentil deedes that he kan;
> Taake hym for the grettest gentil man.
> Crist wole we clayme of hym our gentillesse,
> Nat of oure eldres for hire old richesse.
> For thogh they yeve us al hir heritage,
> For which we clayme to been of heigh parage,
> Yet may they nat biquethe, for not thing,
> To noon of us hir virtuous lyvyng,
> That made hem gentil men ycalled be,
> And bad us folwen hem in swich degree.'[31]

Genility, it is clear, has more to do with manner of life than with lineage or ancient riches. Just to press home this point, she says,

> 'And he that wole han pris of his gentrye,
> For he was boren of a gentil hous,
> And hadde his elders noble and virtuous,
> And nel hymselven do no gentil dedis,
> Ne folwen his gentil auncestre that deed is,
> He nys nat gentil, be he duc or erl.'[32]

At the end of her homily she asks the knight to kiss her. Closing his eyes, he agrees to do so, and when he reopens them he finds that she is transformed into a beautiful maiden. By conceding mastery and exhibiting virtue, he gains his reward.

Although Chaucer based his tale on an existing poem, his remodelling of it was so extensive that the views expressed in it can be taken as his own. Gentility, in Chaucer's eyes, was a matter of individual virtue: it was an attribute accorded to those who performed gentle deeds. This was a view only to be expected of a man whose own claims to gentility were founded on virtue rather than birth. Born in the 1340s into London civic and mercantile society, Chaucer acquired what gentility he had from his career in administration and service. In his youth he had served as a page in the household of Elizabeth de Burgh, countess of Ulster, and from this position he moved to that of an esquire of the king's household. Chaucer stood at the intersection of contrasting social worlds. He was a Londoner and yet he had a seat in the country, in Kent. His roots lay in the city and yet he found his home and employment at the royal court. His career attested to the openness and fluidity of society in late fourteenth-century England. Experience and outlook both disposed him to associate gentility with virtue, good behaviour and reason.[33]

Indeed, Chaucer's view that the essence of gentility resided in virtue was the consensus on which most writers were settling by the late fourteenth and fifteenth centuries. Even the more conservative elements of the aristocracy were ready to concede a rough identification of gentility with virtue.[34] In a few quarters, however, the emerging consensus was not entirely accepted. The author of the *Boke of St Albans*, for example, stuck to a more traditional view. Offering a reworking of biblical history, the author recalled the story that Noah, cursing his son

Ham, who had mocked him, had said to his good son Japheth, 'I make thee a gentleman.' Accordingly, it was from Japheth's offspring that the gentlemen Abraham, Moses and Aaron were to descend, along with 'the kings of the right lyne of Mary, of whom that gentilman Jhesus was borne very God'.[35] In more conservative social circles there was still a feeling that good blood and breeding must contribute something to gentility. As Elizabeth's minister Lord Burghley was to say in the sixteenth century, 'gentility is ancient riches'.

The differences between the two points of view did not deter contemporary commentators from attempting to reconcile them; indeed, they actively encouraged such attempts. One particular feat of ingenuity involved an appeal to eugenics. The point of departure was provided by Aristotle's observation that the foals of swift horses are usually swifter than those of other horses. The Spanish writer Diego de Valera, applying this observation to humankind, proffered the suggestion that 'if a father is noble and is in a virtuous disposition at the time when his son is engendered, then the son will be also, as like follows like'.[36] In the thirteenth-century Arthurian cycle particular emphasis was placed on the powers of heredity in the Prose *Lancelot*. While the young Lancelot was said to have been spurred to great deeds by uncertainty about his birth, it was nonetheless the qualities inherited from his noble ancestors which enabled him to establish his reputation.[37] Much was made in the romance of the fact that Lancelot stood in a distinguished line of descent, stretching back on his father's side to David and Joseph of Arimathea and on his mother's to the kings of the Grail. For all the ingenuity shown, however, attempts to establish links between virtue and the process of human procreation in the end lacked conviction. In their way stood the insuperable obstacle of the biblical cases of the bad sons of Adam and Noah. Here was proof, if any were needed, that virtuous parents do not always bear virtuous children.

More promising was the argument of the instructive example. It was this argument which Dante had in mind when he wrote in the *Convivio*: 'the stock does not make the individual noble, but the individuals ennoble the stock'. A generation earlier Jean de Meung had said much the same thing: 'he who strives to come at the truth must agree that in gentility there is no good unless a man seeks to emulate the prowess of his noble ancestors. This should be the quest of everyone who calls himself gentle.'[38] The idea of lineage as the nurse and instructress of nobility, and hence of gentility, was to be an enduring one in the late Middle Ages. It explains the keen interest which some of the more history-conscious noble lineages took in promoting a semi-mythical ancestor as founder of the family line. Thus the Beauchamp earls of Warwick looked to the mythical Guy, a hero who performed valorous deeds before becoming a hermit, while the de Bohuns found an exemplar in the Swan Knight, whose badge they adopted.[39] The basic idea was that the achievements of the ancestor would serve as an example and inspiration to those who claimed descent from him. This notion of privilege founded on past achievement hints at what contemporaries considered to be the main difference between nobility and gentility. The two overlapped but were subtly different. Nobility, it was agreed, stood in close relation to lineage – it was a quality transmitted by blood. Gentility, on the other hand, was held to describe something deeper. It conveyed that manner of life and conduct which had stood the test of time over the generations. The difference was wittily captured by James II, who reportedly said in reply to a lady who importuned him to make her son a gentleman, 'Madam, I could make him a nobleman, but God Almighty could not make him a gentleman.'[40]

If the shift of emphasis to a nobility based on virtue implied a growing interest in reason and the peaceful arts as foundations for the noble life, in the fifteenth century prowess and achievement in arms still carried weight as legitimations of noble rank. In 1450, when Garter King of Arms made the grant of a coat to Edmund Mille, a prosperous Sussex gentleman, he said that Mille had 'followed the career of arms and has borne himself so valiantly and honourably' that he could be admitted to the company of old gentility. Such wording was fairly standard in fifteenth-century grants of arms.[41] The recipient might be, as Mille was, a civilian bureaucrat, a lawyer and a pen-pusher. Yet the language in which his claim to gentility was expressed referred to the world of chivalry, prowess and arms. In the same way, such a gentleman, while lacking any experience of war in the field, would routinely have himself shown on his tomb in armour, equipped with all the accoutrements of knighthood. Fifteenth-century society still visualised gentility in the traditional terms of chivalry and military achievement. Values, as A. B. Ferguson once wrote, changed more slowly than the society which conditioned them.[42]

IO

Chivalry and Violence

Did the cult of chivalry aggravate the problem of violence in upper-class society in medieval England or did it limit it? Questions of this sort are very difficult to resolve satisfactorily. The apparently ready resort to violence of knights is well attested in court records, which show knightly offenders indicted out of all proportion to their number.[1] At the same time, however, their chivalric ethic could act as a moderating force, providing a code of polite behaviour which prevented disputes from tipping over into violence. On the face of it, two opposing forces in chivalry were in conflict; it is not immediately clear which triumphed.

Chivalry and Aggression

One approach to the problem is to look at the evidence of the romances which formed the staple of knightly entertainment in the Middle Ages. These works afford a range of insights into the thought patterns of knights because they drew on the experience of everyday life, collective memory and personal aspiration. The picture they give is of knights vying with one another in prowess – with prowess being measured in achievements in arms. The knights of the romances lance their opponents in combat, jerk them from their saddles, split open their heads and trample them under their horses. In hand-to-hand combat, they trade blows, draw blood, give and receive buffetings, and lop off heads and limbs. Raw violence had been a feature of the *chansons de geste* of the eleventh and early twelfth centuries; in a more ritualised form it was to be a feature of the romances which took their place a century or so later.

Many examples of the sheer violence of knightly combat are afforded by the tales of Sir Lancelot in the *Vulgate* cycle. In a tournament at Pomeglai Lancelot is said to have drawn out

> his sword like an expert swordsman and delivered heavy blows to the right and left, felling knights and horses with blows of the sword blade and by the hilt. He grabbed men by their hoods of mail and by the edge of their shields; he pulled helmets from their heads; and he hit and shoved and pounded and struck with his limbs and his horse, for he was very skilled in doing all that a great knight should do.[2]

Later, in a tournament at Camelot, fighting against the Knights of the Round Table, Sir Lancelot again displayed his prowess:

> Lancelot put his hand on his good sword, striking left and right . . . He began killing knights and horses and striking down whatever he met in his way . . . Then were there great marvels of his prowess . . . for he split knights and horses and heads and arms and lances and shields; he did so much in so little time that those who had been pursuing others stopped to watch him and see the marvels performed.[3]

In the *Death of King Arthur*, which forms the conclusion of the *Vulgate* cycle, one of the high points in the narrative is a mighty combat between Sir Lancelot and Sir Gawain:

> Then a great battle began between the two; whoever could have seen the blows given and received would have realized that the two men were of great nobility. The fight continued for some time and eventually the two men took to their swords, and they struck each other so often that their coats of mail split. Their shields were so damaged and torn at top and bottom that you could have put your fist through the middle of them . . . Both men had many wounds, the least of which could have killed another man and yet despite their exhaustion, caused by blood loss, they fought till nearly Terce. Then they had to rest.[4]

When the fight resumed, Sir Gawain pressed Sir Lancelot with such force that the blood flowed from his body in more than thirteen places. Lancelot, however, rallied, gaining the edge on his opponent: 'Gawain was so exhausted that he could hardly hold his sword. Lancelot, still able to fight, rained blows on him, and drove him now forward and now back. However, he held out and endured it, covering himself with as much of his sword as he had left.'[5] When Lancelot saw that there was no fight left in his opponent, he granted him his life. Arthur congratulated him as the finest and most courteous knight he had met.

If the objection is raised that the Arthurian romances are so completely fictionalised as to be largely unrelated to real life, it is nonetheless striking that a broadly similar picture is given in works of chivalric history. History and romance closely overlapped in the Middle Ages; they sprang from the same stock and celebrated the same virtues. In his narrative of the Third Crusade the jongleur Ambroise pictures Richard the Lionheart laying about him in the manner of Lancelot:

> And then he charged into the troop
> Of hostile Saracens to pierce
> Them with an impetus so fierce
> That if a thunderbolt had driven
> Clear through them it could not have riven
> Them more. He cut and smote and smashed
> Through them, then turned about and slashed
> And sheared off arm and hand and head.
> Like animals they turned and fled.[6]

In that masterpiece of chivalric biography the *History of William Marshal*, the Marshal and his companions are shown trading and receiving blows in similar fashion amidst the rough and tumble of the tournament. In a clash near Nogent two knights

> came together at such speed
> that not one of them, for a moment, had an eye
> to protecting his property.
> They boldly hacked at each other:
> Just as a carpenter chops
> And carves wood with his axe,
> So they struck one another.[7]

In other works of chivalric biography the picture is much the same. In Barbour's *Bruce*, Robert Bruce's followers are said to swipe their opponents so boldly with their swords that the ground below them shook. Bruce himself is honoured for his most celebrated feat of arms – splitting the head of the English knight Sir Henry de Bohun at the opening of the battle of Bannockburn.[8] Later in the work he is said to have defended the Bannock brook so bravely that as the English fell the pile of their bodies in the water grew ever larger. In all these works the picture conveyed is the same: knights and those who recorded their deeds revelled in violence; they gloried in the splitting of heads and the trading of blows. The knightly ethic was founded on the lionisation of physical prowess.

It is hardly surprising that knightly literature should have been so dominated by violence. Knights were a military class and they found fulfilment in proving their expertise in arms. Moreover, the culture and ethic of violence was not confined to the campaign trail but spilled over into the experience of everyday knighthood at home. Violent, aggressive behaviour was a feature of the disputes that knights engaged in over land and status as much as it was of their conduct in arms. Inevitably, some of the worst offenders were knights who had been inured to violence by their long experience of soldiering.

A good example is provided by the case of Sir John Cressy of Dodford in Northamptonshire. Cressy was one of the veterans of the Lancastrian phase of the Hundred Years War. He was to spend almost all of his adult years upholding the cause of Henry V and his son in France.[9] It is possible that he had begun serving in Normandy as early as the age of thirteen. The first firmly recorded evidence of his military service, however, comes from his late teens, when he is found accompanying Thomas, Lord Roos, who had retained him.[10] By the 1430s he had established himself as an able and experienced captain. He was employed as the duke of Bedford's lieutenant at Rouen, and he took a valuable prisoner, Jean Faicault, whom he ransomed for 500 *salus*. In the late 1430s, after a spell of garrison duty at Caen, he returned home to assume some of the burdens of local office-holding. He then crossed to France again in March 1441, this time under the duke of York, to assist in the defence of Pontoise. Three years later he was appointed to captaincies at Lisieux, Orbec and Pont-l'Eveque, key towns in the defence of Normandy. He died in March 1445 during a diplomatic mission to Charles VII in Lorraine.

The patterns of behaviour which Cressy developed in the course of his fighting in France translated into aggressive behaviour in defence of his territorial interests back home. On the occasion of his brief return to England in 1438–9 he found himself indicted in the Court of Common Pleas on a number of suits. He responded angrily, allegedly beating up the official sent to summon him, calling him a 'rusticum', or yokel, and threatening, with dagger drawn, to kill him. For his unruly behaviour he was obliged to seek a pardon from the king. His behaviour had distinct echoes of that of an earlier ruffianly knight who lost his temper in court. In 1333 one Sir John Trymnel likewise had to seek forgiveness for the offence of drawing his dagger before one of the justices of the bench.[11]

Equally instructive is the case of the author of the *Morte Darthur*, the Warwickshire knight Sir Thomas Malory, a man whose career was regularly punctuated by bursts of violence.[12] As a young man, Malory had served in Gascony in the last years of English rule under his kinsman Sir Philip Chetwynd. On his return in 1443 he became embroiled in a series of disputes with leading landowners in Warwickshire. In January 1450 he is said to have lain in wait with over two dozen men near Combe Abbey to ambush the duke of Buckingham, a former patron of his. The following year he was the subject of an indictment for cattle-rustling and deer-poaching in a park jointly owned by the dukes of Buckingham and Norfolk at Caludon, near Coventry. In July 1451 he was imprisoned for these and other offences, but escaped and broke into Combe Abbey with a band of followers, stealing money and treasure. After his rearrest and trial, he was imprisoned again, on this occasion more securely, in the Marshalsea in London. In the 1460s, after the Yorkist takeover, he worked off his aggression by joining Edward IV's campaigns against Lancastrian diehards in Northumberland. Around 1468, however, he was in trouble again, apparently for joining in a plot to overthrow the king. Malory was imprisoned once more, probably in Newgate, London, where he passed his time finishing the *Morte Darthur*. He died in March 1471.

Malory's career is simply the most picturesque of many such that could be recounted. The message is much the same in them all: that those who lived by the sword in the field often lived by the sword at home. Violence formed part of the warp and weft of noble society.

The Heroic Tradition

The chronicler Walter of Guisborough tells a famous story about one of Edward I's magnates, John de Warenne, earl of Surrey. He says that when the earl was challenged by the king's justices to show by what warrant he held his lands, he produced a rusty old sword, declaring, 'Look my lords, this is my warrant: my ancestors came with William the Bastard, and conquered their lands with the sword; I will defend them with the sword against anyone who tries to seize them.'[13] The episode illustrates an issue of central importance to explaining the high level of violence in knightly society and the role of chivalry in producing it. Did the ready resort to violence by the knightly class originate in the chivalric ethic as such? Or was it instead a by-product of something older, the traditional entitlement of the nobleman to defend his rights by arms? It was to this ancient tradition of self-defence that Warenne appealed when he made his appearance before the king's justices.

The workings of this older heroic tradition can be traced in the epic literature of the Old English period. The values celebrated in these poems are those of traditional warrior societies: valour, prowess and loyalty. Heroes slay dragons, perform deeds of arms, go into battle alongside their companions and die fighting to the very last. In the pre-chivalric era they are not yet performing great deeds of heroism to win the favour of fair ladies. Nonetheless, a strong emphasis is placed on the nexus of bonds which would remain central to noble society, chief among them those of loyalty to the lord and faith to one's own lineage.

The importance of heroism in early English society is evident in the most celebrated poem of the era, *Beowulf*.[14] *Beowulf* tells a story of men and monsters. The eponymous hero, a prince of the Geats, is summoned by King Hrothgar to his kingdom to deliver his hall from the depredations of the monster Grendel, a creature of chaos and darkness. After slaying the monster and then its mother, the latter in a lair deep under a lake, Beowulf is rewarded with the kingship of his people before himself falling in battle against a dragon at the Eagles' Crag. The poem's theme is the nature of the heroic life, in particular the character and expectations of leadership in a heroic society. At the start we are presented with an image of strong Germanic kingship in the person of Scyld Scefing, the founder of the Danish nation's prosperity and the most powerful ruler of his day. Scyld is honoured for his success in forcing many subject peoples to hand over tribute to him. 'That was a great king,' says the poet. King Scyld's great-grandson Hrothgar is also honoured as an exemplar of kingship, at least in his youth. He is said to have become so rich and successful in war that kinsmen competed to serve him, and his *comitatus*, or retinue, swelled to the size of a formidable army. Among all the nations, maintains the poet, it is only through those actions which merit praise that a man may prosper. A man must show courage, strength, wisdom and resolve. Endowed with these virtues, he will be able to perform heroic deeds, which will bring him praise and glory.

In *Beowulf* the poet is concerned principally with the role of leadership in a heroic society. He is not concerned with heroism in war as such. In a later Old English poem, however, the emphasis on fighting is more direct. This is *The Battle of Maldon*, an elegiac narrative of Ealdorman Byrhtnoth's doomed defence of an Essex causeway against the Danes in 991. The poem tells how the Danes overwhelmed the English, Byrhtnoth himself falling in the assault and many of his men fleeing, his retainers, however, vowing to stay to avenge his death. The poet works in many vivid descriptions of the cut and thrust of battle:

> Then the fight was near,
> glory in battle: the time had come
> when those fated to die must fall there; ravens circled,
> the birds of prey eager for carrion; there was bedlam in the land.
> They let the file-hard spears from their hands then,
> made fly the fiercely sharpened ones, the darts.
> Bows were busy, shield absorbed spearhead.
> The onslaught of battle was terrible; warriors fell
> On either side, young men lay dead.[15]

At Maldon the English suffered a crushing defeat; the story of the battle, as later of the evacuation from Dunkirk, is one of fortitude in adversity. For that reason, however, the values admired by the poet stand out all the more clearly. They are the values of a society led by a heroic warrior elite: bravery, loyalty and prowess.

The values which strengthened and sustained the warrior class in battle were reinforced by the emphasis which medieval society placed on manliness. In contemporary thinking there was a strong association between manliness and the values of prowess and courage.[16] In Middle English poems, for example, fighters act 'manlich' or 'as a man' in situations where death is a strong possibility and battle is accepted in preference to flight. Thus in *Guy of Warwick* the hero, fighting the Northumberland dragon, is felled from his horse and has three of his ribs broken, but struggles on, delivers himself 'manliche' and finally wins out: summoning all his strength, he launches one last assault on the beast and chops it in two. In other poems an appeal by a commander to 'manship' or 'manly' behaviour is invoked when it is thought that one last effort by the troops will turn the tide. In *William of Palerne* (c. 1340–60), for example, the queen of Sicily implores her men not to surrender but to maintain their 'manchip manlie a while' till God sends them good tidings. In late medieval society manliness, although a quality admired in all males, was necessarily associated mostly with males of high status because they were the fighters – it was fighting which provided them with their livelihood. For this reason, in the upper-class lexicon of values manliness was sometimes coupled with its antonym cowardice. In didactic texts the two opposing values were contrasted. A manly man was said to be vigorous in upholding his reputation, unlike the coward, who would willingly lose it. Strong and energetic, the true man lets no slight pass without exacting due revenge. In this way the contemporary preoccupation with manliness can be said to have contributed to the spread of violence in noble and gentry society. Manliness had no logical connection with chivalry and chivalric values – it was essentially a gendered construction – yet it encouraged violent behaviour by associating the values of manhood with those of courage, valour and honour.

One further influence may have contributed to the phenomenon of violence in noble society, and that was the customary noble right to self-defence, the right which Warenne invoked when challenged by the king's justices. At the root of this idea was the notion of lordship as associated with property rights, which carried with them a bundle of privileges and perquisites. Property, power and authority were all closely linked in the Middle Ages. If a lord believed that his interests were under threat, he felt justified in acting in whatever fashion he saw fit to defend them. In this way the traditional right of self-defence helped to perpetuate and institutionalise enmity, encouraging the spread of private war. In England the tradition of noble self-defence found its fullest expression in the lordships of the Welsh Marches, where landowners exercised rights of judicial and administrative autonomy under the Crown. Outside the Marches, however, the idea was to linger on even though it had little or no foundation in law. It would probably be an exaggeration to describe the nobility's constant resort to arms as constituting feuding, since feuding, strictly defined, involves a larger group than the original victim and stretches over several generations. Nonetheless, when carried on for years or sometimes even for decades, the pattern of tit-for-tat retaliation came close to it.[17] There can be little doubt that the survival of traditional ideas of violent dispute settlement lent respectability to ways of prosecuting disputes which involved the use of force alongside legal process. Almost certainly, it helps to explain the ready resort to violence shown by the Sussex knight Sir Edward Dallingridge in his bitter dispute with John of Gaunt in the 1380s. Dallingridge, the lord of Bodiam, was affronted by what he regarded as Gaunt's over-aggressive lordship in his own corner of the county, and over a period of three to four years pursued a campaign of intimidation against Gaunt's officials, breaking up their courts, beating and maiming them and burning their court records in front of them. When he was hauled before the king's justices at East Grinstead, he gave no indication of remorse for his actions. On the contrary, he threw down his gauntlet, invoked the law of arms and proclaimed his belief in an older and more traditional law than the law of the realm.[18] He was just as emphatic that he was entitled to defend his rights by force as John de Warenne had been before Edward I's justices a century before.

In a sense, the nobleman's claim to self-defence constituted a form of judgement by ordeal. Resort to the arbitrament of arms represented a way of transferring to the Almighty the responsibility for deciding between the two parties to a dispute. The Almighty, men believed, could be relied on to indicate through the outcome of an armed contest which of the claimants he believed to have the better right. In contemporary opinion the deity was the supreme judge, the universal justifier. Since God moved in a mysterious way, it was natural that there would be times when he would reveal his will through the medium of violence. Taking the view they did of the cosmos, contemporaries found little difficulty in coming to terms with violence as a means of dispute settlement; it seemed to them part of the natural order. The Almighty always supported the just, and on occasion he might feel moved to do so by the judgement of arms. Violence used in a just cause could be a way of bringing peace to a realm. Kings, for example, commonly vindicated their claims against one another through the waging of war. When a king declared war on a rival in defence of his rights, as the English king did against the king of France, he would secure the blessings of peace as his reward. This was a view of the right use of force espoused by both lawyers and theologians. It was also a view of the workings of the universe which had little or nothing to do with chivalry.

Chivalry and Honour

What effect, if any, then, may chivalry be said to have had on the problem of knightly violence in medieval society?

It has been argued that chivalry contributed to the spread of disorder because it was rooted in the aristocratic honour code, which provoked violence in defence of self-esteem. The aristocracy's sense of honour was one of the most striking aspects of their social behaviour in the Middle Ages. Honour may be described as the value which a nobleman placed on himself and the expectation he had that that value would be recognised by others. It found expression principally in terms of action and display. Honourable conduct was held to lie in such gestures as generosity, hospitality and open-handedness, and in the lavish display of wealth, loyalty, sexuality and martial prowess. The maintenance of honour was thus largely dependent on securing the attention of others and on the winning of peer esteem. Honour acted as a stimulus to aggression because the honourable man felt the need constantly to affirm his honour and, in doing so, he was bound to find himself challenging the honour of others. As Julian Pitt-Rivers has put it, when all other means have failed, the ultimate vindication of honour lies in physical violence.[19]

In the twelfth century, as the nobility became more conscious of their position at the peak of society, so their interest in defining noble conduct and values became correspondingly stronger. Once an informal set of behavioural values was agreed – in other words, the code we call chivalry – the notion of honour was developed as a way of securing acceptance of those values from others on the nobility's own terms.

What the fusion of chivalry with aristocratic honour did was lend a new vehemence and intensity to the conduct of disputes in noble society. It led to a greatly sharpened appreciation of the outward markers of rank, dignity and blood, and, at the same time, it encouraged the use of violence in the deeds by which honour was earned. Honour as such was not constituted one of the qualities or attributes which made up the chivalric ethic. Rather, it was one of the mechanisms by which that ethic was controlled and enforced. Disputes over rights which in other circumstances might have been settled peaceably were now fought with a new ardour. Whether a man won or lost in a dispute might have a major impact on his honour, in the sense of his standing in the eyes of others. Indeed, it might well be of crucial importance to his position in the pecking order of local society. It was above all his preoccupation with his local standing that made Sir Edward Dallingridge pursue his quarrel with Gaunt with such determination.

It is in another dispute involving Gaunt that we can best appreciate the importance which the nobility attached to the preservation of honour. This was the quarrel between the duke and the great northern magnate Henry Percy, earl of Northumberland, which erupted in the summer of 1381. Gaunt and Percy had once been close allies – it was Gaunt's influence at court which had been principally responsible for Percy securing his peerage in 1377. As a result of an affront which Gaunt alleged Percy had borne him, however, the two became bitter enemies. The quarrel between them was to rock English court politics for nearly the whole of the 1380s.

The origins of the dispute lay in Gaunt's unhappiness with Percy's treatment of him in the Great Revolt of 1381. In June that year, when the rebel hordes had poured into London, they had demanded the arrest of the 'traitors' – those whom they held responsible for misleading the king and encompassing the decline of the realm. Gaunt's name had been high on their list. For a brief moment the rebels achieved their aims: at the meeting with Wat Tyler, the rebel leader, at Mile End on 14 June Richard II acquiesced in their demand for the arrest of the 'traitors', and writs were issued on rebel authorisation to achieve that end.[20] Gaunt was at this time on the Borders, negotiating with the Scots for renewal of a truce. Hearing of events in the south and in particular of the demands for his arrest, he immediately sought refuge with Northumberland at Alnwick. On arrival before the castle gates, however, he found himself rebuffed: according to the *Anonimalle* chronicle, the earl's representatives said they could not receive him 'for doubt of the king'.[21] Gaunt was not only furious, he felt humiliated. The richest and most powerful magnate in England, he was without shelter and anywhere to lay his head. Swallowing his pride, he retraced his steps, dismissed his retinue and sought refuge with his former adversaries in Scotland.

Once the revolt had subsided, Gaunt returned to England and plotted his revenge. He could not allow such an affront to his dignity to go unpunished. The king decreed that he and the earl should confront one another at a council meeting at Berkhamsted in October. According to Froissart, Gaunt maintained that the earl had offended his honour by barring him from Alnwick and giving credence to reports that he was a traitor. In Thomas Walsingham's account the earl replied to the duke's reproaches disrespectfully, hurling down his gauntlet and challenging him to a duel. The king then called for calm, ordering the earl to be arrested for *lèse majesté* and requiring him to appear before a session of parliament.[22] The tense exchange at the council meeting seems to have escalated the crisis between the two parties. Northumberland had brought a large retinue of armed supporters with him to London, and the Londoners hailed and honoured them. Gaunt too had brought a retinue south; these men, however, found the gates of the city barred against them. Around the capital violence and disorder were daily expected.

When parliament opened in mid-November, the king announced that he would take the dispute into his own hands. He allowed each of the protagonists to make a statement, Gaunt renewing his accusations against the earl, and the latter citing letters which he said had authorised him to deny Gaunt entry. The king then proceeded to judgment. He sentenced the two envoys who had denied the duke entry to Alnwick to imprisonment, saying that he did so 'at the duke's suit'. The next day he received Northumberland's submission. The earl was obliged to perform a ritual abasement, entreating the king's and the duke's pardons and the latter's good lordship, which, he said, he 'desired wholeheartedly'. At the request of the chancellor, who spoke on the king's behalf, the duke and the earl then exchanged the kiss of peace, the public expression of friendship between them.

Despite these elaborate courtesies, relations between the two lords remained testy. The accusation of disloyalty to a kinsman which Gaunt had preferred against Northumberland was not one which could easily be laid to rest. Accordingly, eight years later, on the king's initiative the two men were brought together a second time, on this occasion at a council meeting at Reading. Gaunt had just returned from his unsuccessful bid for the Castilian throne, and the main business of the meeting was to reconcile him to the rebel lords, the so-called Appellants, who had waged war against the king two years before in his absence. At the end of proceedings, after reconciliation had been reached with the Appellants, the opportunity was taken to achieve a deeper reconciliation between the duke and the earl – in the words of the Westminster chronicler, 'to show the others how they might live in peace, once bitterness had been set aside'.[23] Accordingly, at the king's request Gaunt agreed to drop the grudge against his rival and to accept him again as his friend. In this way the rift between the two men was finally healed. The issue separating them had been Gaunt's concern to vindicate his honour. On and off for a decade the life of the court had been disrupted, and at one point the capital had been brought to the brink of disorder. The importance of honour to the workings of aristocratic society could hardly have been made plainer.

Left unchecked, the prickly aristocratic honour code could easily become a disruptive force in noble society. Every dispute over a petty right could turn into a major quarrel, with far-reaching implications for the protagonists' public standing and reputation. In practice, however, the worst effects of the honour code were usually avoided. Chivalry internalised an elaborate code of restraint which countered the potential explosiveness of the most bitterly fought disputes between men of rank by laying equal emphasis on a set of values which moderated the aggression prompted by the quest for honour – values of courtesy, benevolence, magnanimity and compassion. If a nobleman's urge to vindicate his honour necessarily made chivalry aggressive, the parallel insistence that he conduct himself 'honourably' tended to make it a conciliatory force and a means to the end of peace.

It was this conciliatory side to chivalry which had supplied the all-important corrective to the aggressive instinct from the earliest stirrings of the chivalric ethic. Back in the late eleventh century one of the conventions of chivalric behaviour had been that knights respect each other's persons and spare each other's lives.[24] While knights might be violent and aggressive in their behaviour, buffeting and bludgeoning each other in the lists, they also appreciated the importance of self-preservation. In the package of values which went to make up the chivalric ethic, aggression was balanced by courtesy, and anger by *mansuetudo* or gentleness.

The gentler side of chivalry had been highlighted in the twelfth century in the most significant early advice book on noble behaviour, the *Liber Urbani* of Daniel of Beccles. Daniel's text, written in Henry II's reign, constantly emphasised the importance of restraint.[25] Indeed, it can be seen as a manual of restrained behaviour. Keep close watch over your tongue, Daniel advised. Say as little as possible; avoid giving offence to others; make sure that your words are cheerful, courteous and polished; do not lose your temper, for example when defeated in a game of chess; do not mock or threaten; do not react violently to threats; do not take precipitate revenge, and do not harbour resentments. Do not make a point of insisting on your rights, for if you do, you will have few friends. Love moderation if you wish to be courtly; and so on. In all the late medieval courtesy literature the basic rule was the same: do not do or say anything which might offend or humiliate others, for if you do you should expect retaliation. It is sometimes argued that this emphasis on courtesy and restraint came in only with Renaissance humanist culture. Almost certainly, however, this was not the case. Courtesy was a medieval idea, a key element in the chivalric ethic and the essential counterbalance to martial aggression.

The commitment to moderation enjoined in the advice books had its counterpart in military affairs in the body of rules and conventions regulating the conduct of war. The effect of these rules in producing a code of honourable behaviour is evident in the handling of sieges, in which the prosecution of hostilities was most formulaic. In the wars in the north in the 1290s and early 1300s the Scots showed themselves especially punctilious in observing the niceties of restrained behaviour: they were at pains to display their chivalric credentials. When a Scottish force was besieging Dunbar in 1296, for example, the Scots commander allowed the castellan's wife to surrender honourably, even though he and his men regarded her husband as a traitor for supporting the king of England. In the same year, at the siege of Edinburgh, when one of the English messengers defected to the Scots' side, taking royal despatches with him, the Scots castellan refused to allow the letters to be opened 'for honour's sake', and the unfortunate messenger was sent back to his master. More remarkably still, at the siege of Stirling in 1299 the Scots granted the beleaguered English garrison freedom of egress after a prolonged blockade which had reduced them to starvation, providing escorts to accompany them to Berwick.[26] The especially courteous behaviour of the Scots shows that observance of the rules of restraint was a feature of chivalric culture across national boundaries and between knights of all allegiances.

In chivalric war there might still be occasions when a besieging commander felt the need to present an implacable face to a garrison. Even then, however, once the initial show of anger had been made, the commander would typically extend the hand of mercy. In 1304, for example, when himself besieging Stirling, Edward I, annoyed at the tough Scottish resistance, briskly dismissed any talk of surrender terms, threatening the garrison with hanging and dismembering; yet in the end his anger subsided and he granted the garrison their lives.[27] Nearly half a century later in 1346 Edward III was to take much the same line at the siege of Calais. In the famous story of Froissart, when at the end of a ten months' siege the French began parleying, Edward insisted on unconditional surrender but later changed his mind at the intercession of Sir Walter Mauny and other knights, who argued for mercy on grounds of pragmatism and honour. Edward's one condition was that six of the burghers, acting as representatives for their peers, should throw themselves on his mercy, for him to do with as he pleased.[28] The submissions at the end of both of these sieges formed part of carefully orchestrated rituals of peace-making. Once suitable acts of obeisance had been exacted from the defenders, the sparing of their lives could allow a besieging commander the opportunity to display the prerogative of mercy. Clemency was not automatic or inevitable, but its attraction was that it enabled a commander – particularly a king – to show compassion and magnanimity, admired chivalric virtues.

The kinds of conciliatory gestures displayed at the end of wars and sieges were often shown at the conclusion of quarrels between members of the nobility. A war, after all, was simply a dispute between two chivalrous lords writ large. It was only natural, then, that the patterns of pacification and reconciliation enacted in the larger theatre should be replicated in the smaller one of the quarrel. A very clear instance of how two adversaries might resolve their differences and be reconciled is afforded by the final stages of the dispute between John of Gaunt and Sir Edward Dallingridge.[29]

In June 1384 Dallingridge, finally hauled before the king's justices at East Grinstead, faced the prospect of defeat on almost all the charges brought against him. His gesture of defiance in throwing down his gauntlet to offer wager by battle had availed him little. At the end of the hearing the jury found him guilty on all but two counts and he was committed to the custody of the sheriff in Lewes gaol. For all his success in the courtroom, however, John of Gaunt showed himself careful not to press his advantage too far. He appreciated the importance of maintaining good relations with the gentry, whose interests Dallingridge had championed and for whom he acted as spokesman. A few weeks after the hearing John accordingly turned a blind eye when Dallingridge was released after a token imprisonment and, more remarkably still, abandoned the judicial and franchisal rights to which Dallingridge had taken such strong exception. On each side the dispute had been conducted with gusto – in Dallingridge's case particularly so – yet in victory Gaunt made a display of magnanimity, because it was only through magnanimity that healing could be achieved and the divisions opened in local society be repaired. If the chivalric honour code was inherently aggressive – and aggression was certainly built into it – the qualities of courtesy, generosity and magnanimity, equally essential to its being, ensured that for much of the time that aggression was contained.

Ideal and Reality

There can be little doubt that chivalry had contradictory impulses at its core. On the one hand it sustained the ideal of the perfect knight – the knight who fought to maintain order, defend the faith and protect the weak. On the other, by conferring legitimacy on violence, it fed the oppressions of a predatory knighthood. The ideal and the reality of chivalry were in conflict. The nobler side of chivalry elevated knighthood, making it a compassionate instrument of princely rule; the ignoble side made possible a debased knighthood which challenged public order, disrupted civil society and engaged in the pursuit only of its own interests. The twin aspects of chivalry could not easily be disentangled. The legitimate and illegitimate violence of chivalry had their origins in the same set of circumstances. If the difficulties raised by the relationship between chivalry and aggression were in part overcome in practice by the mechanisms which contained that violence, they nonetheless attracted comment from contemporaries who reflected on chivalry in the abstract. Discussion of these questions was especially vigorous in the late fourteenth century.

One of the fullest considerations of this subject was offered by Chaucer in his *Tale of Melibee* in the *Canterbury Tales*. *Melibee* was the second of the tales which Chaucer chose to narrate himself and may be taken as broadly representing his own views. It is a treatise, thinly disguised under an allegorical narrative, advocating the settling of disputes by peaceful means.[30]

The tale opens with Melibee discovering that intruders have broken into his house, assaulted his wife Prudence and critically injured his daughter. Melibee tearfully summons his servants and retainers, hoping that they will endorse his plan to make his foes pay for their villainy. The physicians offer him the advice that he wants to hear, and they are supported by the hot-headed youths, who are all for taking action. Melibee reckons without his forceful wife Prudence, however, who counsels strongly against retaliation. She argues that her husband's kindred are insufficiently large or formidable to daunt his foes; she warns that vengeance is not his prerogative but a matter for the law; and she forecasts that 'vengeaunce-takyinge' will escalate into an ugly and expensive feud. In short, she says, the only correct course is to 'suffre and be pacient'. In the face of these arguments, Melibee falls back on the most potent weapon in his armoury, the need to vindicate his honour. He then says to his wife, 'Now se I wel that ye loven nat myn honor ne my worshipe. Ye knowen wel that myne adversaries han bigonnen this debaat and bryge by hire outrage . . . Wol ye thane that I go and meke me and obeye me hem, and crie hem mercy? For soothe, that were nat my worshipe.'[31]

Prudence, in reply, stresses that her sole concern is the safeguarding of his honour and worship; the difference between them centres on their respective notions of honour. Whereas for her husband honour is rooted in manhood and strength, for her it is rooted in the heart. She acknowledges that every man must maintain his name and repute; however, she adds, this is not to be done by hewing down delinquents. It is better achieved by a quieter course – by showing restraint and moderation. For then, 'men mowe have cause and mateere to preyse yow of pitee and of mercy'. In the end her husband capitulates to her arguments. Through her redefinition of honour, she paves the way for a settlement of the dispute by a show of repentance on the one side and forgiveness on the other.

Prudence's arguments were not original. Chaucer's tale was in fact a close translation of a French version of the thirteenth-century *Book of Consolation and Advice* of Albert of Brescia. Yet his treatment of the story formed only one part of a wider critique which he offered of the untamed values of honour and revenge. He attempted a different approach to the same end in the burlesque foolery of his *Sir Thopas*, another tale which he chose to narrate himself. Through the medium of comedy Chaucer makes fun of his knight's quixotic eagerness to fulfil what he considered the duty of spontaneous bravado. Thopas, though a peacock in the hall, is yet a hare in the field and so is never in any serious danger of being taken seriously. Outwardly courageous, he spends more time in aimless galloping than in engaging the enemy, whose threats shock and unnerve him.

Chaucer's critique of chivalric honour is situated within the larger debate about the knightly class in the late fourteenth century. Among writers of Chaucer's time there was much discussion of what were seen as the weaknesses of the knightly class and its failure to honour the chivalric ideal. A variety of views was expressed. Sir John Clanvow, one of Richard II's counsellors, thought that knights were too aggressive. In his tract *The Two Ways* he argued that they spent too much time wasting and destroying foreign lands, even if they also indulged themselves on the proceeds.[32] The moralistic John Gower, on the other hand, thought that knights were not aggressive enough, arguing in his *Vox Clamantis* that they no longer bore arms for justice and had abandoned honour for self-interest.[33] Thomas Walsingham, endorsing Gower's view, complained of the effeminacy of the royal household knights, charging them with being knights of Venus not of Mars, more at home in the bedchamber than on the field.[34] To the author of one of the poems in the Digby Manuscript there was a contrast between the false knighthood of his own day and the ideal of true knighthood. True knights kept the faith, defended the realm and protected the poor.[35]

What emerges from these works is that to contemporaries the relationship between chivalric honour and aggression was itself a matter of debate. Some contemporaries saw knightly aggression as inherent in the honour code, while others, like Gower, thought knights too decadent to be capable of much fighting; their main interest was in luxury.

The truth of the matter is that the chivalric quest for honour did not automatically translate into testosterone-driven aggression. Not only did chivalry contain a range of pacific values which limited aggression and rendered it compatible with civil society; among contemporaries there was actually a debate about how chivalric honour might be upheld without violence. The Arthurian romances, with their heavy emphasis on knightly combat, naturally highlighted the aggression of the chivalric ethic. That aggression, however, was almost certainly exaggerated for the sake of a good tale. It is clear that we cannot take the fictions of the romances as directly mirroring the values and norms of chivalric society. Knights who read the romances could tell the difference between a rattling good tale and everyday reality. Some of them may have liked to picture themselves in the mould of the heroically bloodthirsty knights of romance; in most cases, however, their everyday lives were altogether less eventful. In the mid-fifteenth century the Norfolk knight Sir Miles Stapleton owned a copy of John Metham's tale of Armoryus and Cleopes, a story of 'manhood and chyvalrye'. There is no evidence, however, that Stapleton modelled his own behaviour on what he read there; for the most part, he was actually a retiring and law-abiding country gentleman.

Until the mid-fifteenth century the knightly class was united by a body of shared experience which went with participation in chivalric war. Culturally this experience found expression in the aesthetic preferences of the knights, the literature they read and, more generally, in their style of life. To acknowledge the role which war played in shaping the mental outlook of the knightly class is not to suggest that the aggression which fuelled it was precisely reproduced in their lives. The arts of peace would never have flourished had that been the case.

II

Chivalry and Christian Society

In the small country church at Salford in Bedfordshire is a late thirteenth-century tomb slab to a member of the de Salford family which nicely captures the ambiguity in the relationship between the chivalric class and the Church. On first inspection the emblem carved in low relief on the surface appears to be a cross, source of redemption and symbol of the Christian faith. On closer inspection, however, it becomes clear that it is actually a sword. The circular piercings at the ends of the crossbar indicate such, and a shield is shown suspended from a strap below. Where we would expect a cross, hinting at the deceased's need for intercessory prayer, we are actually given a weapon, a mark of military rank. The touch of ambiguity is surely deliberate.

The Church's own ambiguous relationship with chivalry is hinted at in another source, the Bayeux Tapestry. In the famous action-packed battle scenes Bishop Odo of Bayeux, the Conqueror's half-brother, is shown in the thick of the fray waving his mace and 'cheering the boys on'. According to canon law, churchmen were forbidden to shed Christian blood, and for this reason the bishop is shown wielding a blunted instrument, not a sword. Yet in every other respect he is presented as firmly martial in appearance. He is kitted out in body armour and a helmet, just like Duke William's knights. He is a knight in all but name.

The Salford slab and the representation of Bishop Odo between them illustrate the difficulties in the relationship between chivalric society and the Church. Chivalry was a secular institution, yet churchmen were deeply implicated in it. Knights were engaged in a Christian vocation, yet they could be guilty of terrible atrocities. How far, if at all, were the tensions between chivalry and the Christian life resolved?

A Knighthood for Christ?

The intellectual problems raised by the relationship between chivalric war and the faith were evident in the pages of the Bible itself. Here there were inconsistencies on a grand scale. In the Old Testament the people of Israel are shown fighting in defence of the faith commanded and protected by their God. In the New Testament, however, Christ preaches a message of peace and of turning the other cheek. Priority should have been given to the teaching of the New Testament over any customs and attitudes which preceded Christ's coming. Yet in a post-lapsarian world, not dissimilar to that of ancient Israel in which monarchs found attractive models in kings such as David, the teaching of the Old Testament could not entirely be set aside. The Church had to accommodate itself to imperfect conditions in which the exercise of force might be necessary to uphold the authority of God's anointed. At the Last Supper Christ himself, according to Luke, had told the apostles to equip themselves with swords (Luke, 22: 36).

For most of the early Middle Ages the Church was openly critical of the warrior class and the waging of war. In an era when the Church was heavily influenced by the monastic tradition and by ideals of withdrawal from the world, it was only natural that this should be so. The idea of retreat to the cloister inevitably reinforced the contrast between the *militia Christi*, monks who fought with their prayers, and the *militia secularis*, battling warriors who brought violence and bloodshed to the world. The penitential books of the time took a literal reading of the sixth commandment, 'Thou shalt not kill.' Most prescribed a forty-day penance for the sin of killing in war. At the same time, however, there was a recognition by the Church that warfare might sometimes be necessary. Like the ancient Israelites, Christians inhabited a world where war might be unavoidable in the face of attack from without. For precisely this reason, the doctrine of the just war was formulated. In a development of ideas first articulated by St Augustine, it was maintained that war could be waged for a just cause, provided it was directed to the end of re-establishing peace and fought on a limited scale.[1]

In the late tenth and early eleventh centuries, however, the attitude of the Church to war and to the warrior class underwent radical reshaping. Knights and men-at-arms, once regarded as scourges of society, were now embraced as champions and upholders of the Christian faith. An important factor in bringing about this shift was the Church's need to enlist the support of the knightly class in resisting the assaults of marauding heathens on Europe's frontiers. In some parts of the continent priests wrote special prayers for the blessing of banners to be borne in war against the heathen. At the same time a new liturgy was developed for the blessing of the warrior's sword, one which in some ways anticipated the later liturgical rite for the making of a knight.[2]

There was a second reason for the shift in the Church's attitude to the warrior class, and this was the breakdown of public authority in Europe itself. As princely rule weakened and predatory violence increased, the clergy became concerned for the safety not only of their possessions but of the peasantry who were the source of their wealth. In a bid to restore peace and order, churchmen in southern France bypassed powerless or ineffective princely rulers, dealing directly with the knights themselves by means of such initiatives as the Peace and the Truce of God. From local measures of this sort it was but a short step to developing the idea of a Christian knighthood which would not only refrain from violence but actually champion the cause of justice. Knights, chastened and directed to endeavours which were spiritually fulfilling, could be made to serve the Church's own ends. From being enemies of Christ, they could be turned, through Christian instruction, into instruments for the achievement of the *Pax Dei*.

In this way and by this means, in the twelfth century a legitimate and fulfilling role was found for knights in the Christian common-wealth. The new conception found clearest expression in the doctrine of the three orders, the tripartite division of society into those who prayed, those who fought and those who worked. Knights – *pugnatores* – comprised the second estate, allotted the task, previously discharged by kings alone, of defending the peace. The violent warrior ethic, about which churchmen had earlier been ambivalent, was now Christianised and to an extent legitimised. The knights themselves became a social order ordained by God. Gerald, bishop of Cambrai, one of the most eloquent exponents of the new doctrine, quoted the words of St Paul: 'The apostle also calls them [the warriors] servants of God, saying, "They are God's agents of punishment, revengers to execute wrath . . . it is not for nothing that they hold the power of the sword."' [3]

This new Christianised ethic of violence was internalised by the knightly class and accepted as integral to its vocation. Prowess was from now on seen as a gift from God, to be used in accordance with God's will and to God's ends. Since the Almighty, the source of chivalric honour, had given men the means to win fame and glory, the knight, in return, was expected to lead the life of a good, devout layman. William Marshal, the most highly esteemed knight of his day, was said by his biographer to have ascribed all his achievements as a knight to God's gift. [4]

The Christian conception of knighthood found clear expression in a tract by a thirteenth-century Spanish writer, Raymond Lull, the *Libre del Ordre de Cavayleria*. This highly popular work was translated into English in the fifteenth century and published by Caxton as the *Ordre of Chyvalry*.[5] Lull, a household knight of the king of Aragon, experienced a religious conversion in 1263 and spent the last years of his life as a wandering hermit. The *Libre* is a product of his years of spiritual reflection and was clearly influenced by them. Lull opened his book with an account of the origins of chivalry, which he saw as constituted to restrain and defend the people after the Fall. He went on to detail the duties of the knight, which he regarded as being to defend the faith and to protect the weak, women and orphans. After a chapter describing the qualifications for knighthood, he turned to the ceremony of knighthood itself, which he interpreted as a wholly Christian ritual. Knighthoods were to be conferred on one of the main feast days of the year, Pentecost, Christmas or Easter. The knight-to-be was to spend the eve of his knighting in prayer and contemplation in church. In the morning he was to attend Mass, along with any others to be knighted, listening to a sermon in which the meaning of the Ten Commandments and the Seven Sacraments was expounded. Before the altar he was to receive the order and distinction of knighthood from one who was already a knight. The symbolism of the arms given to the knight was then explained: the sword signifying that he should defeat the enemies of the cross, its two edges representing chivalry and justice; the leg harness symbolising his duty to punish malefactors; the shield standing for the office of knighthood; the horse and saddle for nobility and courage; and so on. Lull was sensitive to the symbolism of every piece of the apparatus of chivalry. He saw chivalric rituals as closely associated with religious values, the connection between them emphasising the divine sanction for aristocratic supremacy. Knights and priests, in his view, constituted two parallel castes, cherishing and supporting each other as honourable estates.

The vision of a Christian knighthood was to surface again in a tract of the next century, the *Livre de Chevalerie* of Geoffrey de Charny. Geoffrey, the standard-bearer to King John the Good of France, was killed holding the banner of the oriflamme at Poitiers in 1356. For Geoffrey, the world of chivalry was deeply suffused with Christian sentiment. Chivalry was akin to a religious order, a discipline oriented towards man's highest goal, salvation. The suffering endured by a knight was meritorious, constituting a penance in itself. When a knight took up arms in a just cause, whether his own or his lord's, he would ensure the salvation of his soul. The perfect knight should be humble and pious. He should ascribe his achievements to the grace of God and the Virgin Mary, trusting not in his own strength as Samson did. He should seek a model for ideal knighthood in Judas Maccabeus, the Old Testament warrior, who was both *preux* (valiant) and *hardi* (bold) while yet entirely without pride. He who could be likened to such a knight would achieve the highest rewards in chivalry – honour in this world and salvation in the next.[6] In the light of his visionary conception of knighthood, it is not surprising that Geoffrey should be the first recorded owner of the Shroud of Turin.

The religious conception of chivalry, encouraged by the Church and articulated in these treatises, fed through into romance and poetry. Knights in the Arthurian romances were invariably portrayed as devout, assiduous in prayer and obedient to the will of God. They repeatedly state their abhorrence of the prospect of dying without confession. In the *Lancelot du Lac* Arthur himself, thinking that he is about to die, cries out, 'Oh God! Confession! The time has come!' In the *Queste del Saint Graal*, when Sir Galahad passes a chapel, 'he turns towards it, for he was troubled if a day passed when he did not hear Mass'. In the *Mort Artu* Sir Lancelot is said to hear Mass regularly, praying 'as a knight should', and confessing to an archbishop before his combat with Sir Gawain. Throughout the Arthurian cycle, the Knights of the Round

Table swear by their favourite saints and beat paths to wayside chapels where they can hear Mass.[7]

In the stories which make up the long thirteenth-century Vulgate cycle, however, the fictions of chivalric romance were taken much further than this. An exotic mythology was developed which saw chivalry originating in the circle and in the lifetime of Christ himself. At the centre of this web of ideas was the story of the quest for the Holy Grail, the cup used by Christ at the Last Supper. The Grail story made its first appearance in Chrétien de Troyes' unfinished romance *Perceval*. Here, Sir Perceval, dining in the abode of the Fisher King, is made the privileged witness of a wondrous procession, at the end of which a fair young maiden holds an elaborately wrought 'grail' or bowl. The Grail in Chrétien's work, although bearing a Mass wafer, is not yet a vessel imbued with particular religious significance. It is in Robert Boron's *Joseph of Arimethie* that it becomes the Holy Grail, the vessel of the Last Supper, the iconic vessel of later legend. Robert tells how Joseph of Arimathea acquired the cup from Pilate and was entrusted with its safekeeping by Christ himself, who appeared to him in a vision. Joseph, he says, gathered together his in-laws and other followers and made his way to the west, to the vale of Avalon, to await the coming of a scion of their lineage who would take over as guardian of the cup. In one version of the story, the *Perlesvaus*, that guardian was to be Sir Perceval, the Fisher King's nephew, a descendant of Joseph's brother-in-law and a Knight of the Round Table. In another, the *Queste del Saint Graal*, the honour is bestowed on Sir Galahad, Lancelot's son by Elaine and another of Joseph's lineage. Galahad, however, having seen the vessel, dies in ecstasy, and the Grail vanishes from the world.[8]

The Grail legends invested chivalry with a religious authority entirely independent of the mediatory power of the Church. This element of independence found expression particularly in the story cycles developed around the figures of Sir Lancelot and Sir Galahad. It is not simply the case that the bloodlines of the two knights are said to go back to Joseph of Arimathea; the roles assigned to the pair seem almost consciously to recall the functions of Christ himself. These are knights for whom and through whom God willingly performs miracles. Towards the end of the *Queste* Sir Galahad heals a man who had suffered lameness for ten years. In the *Lancelot du Lac*

Colour-washed drawing of a kneeling knight, added *c.* 1250 to a Westminster Psalter of the early thirteenth century.

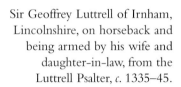

Sir Geoffrey Luttrell of Irnham, Lincolnshire, on horseback and being armed by his wife and daughter-in-law, from the Luttrell Psalter, *c.* 1335–45.

Odo, Bishop of Bayeux, on horseback and waving a club, in the thick of the Battle of Hastings, from the Bayeux Tapestry.

Tomb effigy attributed to
William Marshal, Earl of Pembroke (d. 12
in the Temple Church, London.

The chancel of St
d'Abernon Church, Sur
showing the vaulted roof,
remains of paintings on
east wall, and the brasses of
two d'Abernon knight
the floor in the foregrou
Probably third quarte
the thirteenth cent

The Round Table hanging
in the Hall of Winchester
Castle, made for Arthurian
court festivities in the
late thirteenth century. The
painted decoration dates fron
the reign of Henry VIII.

A rubbing of the brass of Sir Hugh Hastings (d. 1347) in Elsing Church, Norfolk, showing the figures of his companions in arms in the side buttresses of the canopy.

Encaustic tile showing a knight in action with a couched lance in Ottery St Mary Church, Devon, fourteenth century.

Cross-slab grave cover commemorating a member of the knightly de Salford family in Salford Church, Bedfordshire, early fourteenth century.

The 'English saints' window, showing Saints Edward the Confessor, George and Edmund, in the north aisle, Heydour Church, Lincolnshire, *c.* 1360.

Tattershall Castle, Lincolnshire, the keep, constructed of brick, by Ralph, Lord Cromwell, Treasurer of England under King Henry VI, *c.* 1430–50.

The keep of Dover Castle, Kent, built by King Henry II, *c.* 1170–88. Note the use of bands of stone of different colours.

Cooling Castle, Kent, built by John, Lord Cobham, in the early 1380s, outer wall of the inner courtyard, showing the use of patterned stonework.

The keep of Warkworth Castle, Northumberland, built by Henry Percy, earl of Northumberland, in the later fourteenth century. Its elaborate design makes it a masterpiece of domestic planning.

A drawing of the brass of Joan, Lady Cobham (d. 1434), the Cobham family heiress, showing her with her children, in the chancel floor, Cobham Church, Kent

Tomb of Reginald, Lord Cobham KG (d. 1361), in Lingfield Church, Surrey, showing him wearing the garter on his left leg and the arms of his companions in arms around the sides of the tomb chest.

Drawing of the brass of Robert Wyvill, Bishop of Salisbury (d. 1375), in lisbury Cathedral, showing the bishop looking out from the window of a castle and his champion in the gate below.

The chantry chapel of Richard Beauchamp, Earl of Warwick (d. 1439), on the south side of St Mary's Church, Warwick, showing the Earl's tomb monument in the middle.

Pen-and-ink drawing of the Battle of Shrewsbury, in which Henry IV defeated the Percies in 1403, from the Beauchamp Pageant, c. 1485–90.

Panel of the east window of East Harling Church, Norfolk, showing the kneeling figure of Sir William Chamberlain KG (d. 1462). Sir William is wearing the Yorkist collar of suns and roses.

Portrait relief of Sir Thomas Lovell KG, attributed to Pietro Torregiano, c. 1516–20, in the Museum of Westminster Abbey.

Lancelot's blood performs a miraculous cure when it restores the stricken Sir Agravain to health. In Malory's *Morte Darthur*, of the fifteenth century, Lancelot heals the grievously wounded Sir Urré by a laying-on of hands.[9]

The Church not surprisingly adopted an ambivalent attitude to the Grail stories, neither wholly endorsing nor wholly condemning them. What concerned the authorities was that, although the stories drew on a deep well of spirituality, they were yet mystical and anti-sacerdotal. There was no place in the Grail cycle for the Church, its institutions or its ministers. It is hermits and solitaries who are present as representative holy men, not bishops and archbishops or other members of the hierarchy. In the *Mort Artu*, when Lancelot turns aside to hear Mass, he does so before a hermit in a chapel. In the Quest stories, when Joseph of Arimathea receives his commission, he does so not from an ordained priest but from Christ himself. It is symptomatic of the ambivalent character of the legends that the story of Joseph's commission originated not in an orthodox source but in a fourth-century fabrication in the New Testament apocrypha.

What the Grail legends articulated was a quest not just for the Grail but for Eucharistic grace and communion in ecstasy with God. The Grail was a metaphor for something incapable of expression in mere words. As one scholar has put it, the legends expressed an ideal of knighthood not so much in the service of religion but as a religious service in itself.[10] In the twelfth century the Church was struggling to direct knighthood to spiritually rewarding ends which could assist in the cause of individual fulfilment and salvation. In the Grail legends, however, it saw chivalric yearning veering off into a world which mixed the mystical with the profane and the pious with the fantastic. The Grail stories are strange, exotic and unsettling, feeding on elements in Celtic myth as much as on Christian mysticism and asceticism. For all their apparent heterodoxy, however, they attest to a deeply idealistic streak in chivalry. Chivalry, if secular in origin and heroic in character, was nonetheless allied to a sense of Christian vocation. As the Lady of the Lake expressed it to Sir Lancelot in the Vulgate cycle, the good knight must subordinate worldly pride to the protection of the weak and the defence of the Church.[11]

In the everyday experience of knighthood, the Christian dimension to chivalry could find expression in more orthodox and institutionally focused ways. Raymond Lull had seen the ceremony of conferring knighthood as a ritual which drew attention to the knight's dedication of his service to God. In his treatise he explained the Christian symbolism of every stage of the knighting ceremony from the bath, which recalled baptism, to the girding with the belt, which symbolised chastity. By Lull's lifetime there is evidence that formal knightings were, indeed, sometimes carried out in churches, just as he had anticipated. Some of the best examples are provided by ceremonies which took place in England. In 1241 Queen Eleanor's kinsman Peter of Savoy was knighted with fifteen other young tyros in Westminster Abbey.[12] Fifty years later Edward I knighted four visiting esquires in the service of the count of Savoy in St Cuthbert's, Darlington, after they had spent the traditional overnight vigil in the church.[13] In 1306, in the grandest mass knighting of the age, Edward I dubbed his son Edward of Caernarvon and 297 other tyros in a series of ceremonies staged across Westminster Abbey and St Stephen's Chapel. The candidates for knighting spent the night in solemn vigil – the prince and some of his companions in the abbey, the rest somewhat uncomfortably crowded in the Temple church. Early the next morning the king girded his son with the belt of knighthood in St Stephen's Chapel, before raising the others to knightly rank in a ceremony before the high altar of the abbey itself, the candidates coming forward to receive the honour in pairs. The ceremonies were completed later in the day with the Feast of Swans in Westminster Hall, at which the king swore a solemn oath to subdue the Scots.[14]

The indications are that Edward I's reign witnessed the heyday of the ritual dubbing of knights in churches in England. References to such ceremonies are almost unknown after the king's death in 1307. In the mid-fourteenth century, however, Edward III's foundation of the Order of the Garter breathed new life into the idea of a link between chivalry and religion. Edward's conception of an elite knightly order dedicated to a Christian vocation broke new ground in that the knightly company was placed under the protection of a saint and linked institutionally with a chapel – St George's Chapel in Windsor Castle. According to the statutes, the companion knights were to assemble each year, on St George's Day, to celebrate Mass and to renew their vows of Christian service, and on their deaths their arms were to be placed above their stalls in the chapel choir. Together, St George's

Chapel and its fittings provided a vivid witness to the idea of the knight's dedication of his service to God and Crown. If the practice of ritual dubbings died out in the later Middle Ages, the ceremonies of the Garter ensured that the religious dimension to chivalry was to live on in another form for centuries to come.

'For England and St George'

Edward III's audacious appropriation of a Christian saint as patron of his new order illustrates another aspect of the association between chivalry and piety, the harnessing of the company of saints to the chivalric cause. English knighthood, by virtue of the king's master-stroke, acquired the blessings of celestial patronage.

In the late Middle Ages the saints were to come into their own as heavenly intermediaries between God and man. As the Church placed ever greater emphasis on the miracle of the Mass, so increasing the social distance between clergy and congregation, a void was opened which was filled by the saintly family – men and women of unblemished character, to whom the faithful could look to place their prayerful petitions before the Almighty. Particular saints became associated with particular causes or social groups – St Christopher with travel, St Zita with lost keys and St Roche with curing the plague. St George enjoyed a unique association with Christian knighthood.

Very little is known about the historical St George himself. Beyond the fact that he was a Roman army officer martyred for the faith at Lydda in the persecutions of the Emperor Diocletian, virtually nothing can be said about him.[15] In the course of the early Middle Ages his cult moved steadily westward, gathering popularity as it did so and acquiring an association with martial values. A major boost was given by the saint's miraculous appearance to the First Crusaders at the siege of Antioch in 1098. In the thirteenth century his following was boosted further by the circulation of James de Voragine's *Golden Legend*, apparently the first work to accord credibility to the story of the slaying of the dragon. By the fourteenth century, the cult was the object of devotion in places as far apart as Catalonia and Germany, Bohemia and Italy. It found expression in the veneration of images and in the representation of the saint's deeds in writing, painting and sculpture.[16]

In England the cult appears to have attracted only limited interest before the late thirteenth century.[17] There was a quickening of pace in the fifty years after the Conquest with the foundation of a community of canons dedicated to St George at Oxford, and the inclusion after about 1110 of the saint's appearance at Antioch in wall paintings at Hardham in Sussex. However, it is not until the mid-thirteenth century that firm evidence is found of a serious growth of interest at court. In the early 1250s Henry III commissioned a life of the saint from his steward Paulinus Piper, and shortly afterwards arranged for his image to be placed over the entrance to the great hall of his palace at Winchester. In the reign of Henry's successor, Edward I, the cult began to acquire more specifically military and chivalric connotations. According to an account book of the royal household, in the second Welsh war in 1282 the English infantry went into action wearing armbands displaying the red cross of St George. It is possible that Edward's interest in the saint had been aroused by his travels in Europe, where the cult was more firmly embedded.

In the early fourteenth century the saint's growing identification with chivalry is confirmed by a number of representations in manuscripts. In a book of hours in the Bodleian Library (c. 1325–30) he is represented as a knight alongside Edward II's cousin Thomas, earl of Lancaster, the two men shown standing and turned to each other, holding banners in their right hands and with shields strapped to their shoulders.[18] St George is identifiable by the arms attributed to him, a red cross on a white field.

Of roughly the same date is a representation of the saint in a stylistically related manuscript, a treatise on kingly rule presented by Walter Milemete, a royal clerk, to the young Edward III shortly after his accession in 1327.[19] As in the Bodleian manuscript, St George is shown in a paired composition, with the red cross on his surcoat, turning towards the dedicatee, to whom in this case he presents a lance and shield. A notable feature of the manuscript is the close similarity between the figures of the king and his saintly patron, the intention probably being to suggest that the former should emulate the chivalric values embodied in, and represented by, the latter.

It is against this background of growing royal interest in the cult of St George that Edward III made the saint patron of the Order of the Garter in the 1340s. Edward's determination to create a knightly

brotherhood which harnessed the resources of Christian knighthood
to the English monarchy meant that he had to find a saint who personi-
fied the values which the new company was to exemplify. St George
recommended himself both because of his heroic martyrdom and
because of the deeds of bravery retrospectively attributed to him.

The close interest which Edward took in the cult of St George
marked a major shift of emphasis in the saintly preferences of
the English monarchy. Since the mid-thirteenth century the saint
to whom English monarchs had shown themselves most deeply
committed had been St Edward the Confessor, the last legitimate
Anglo-Saxon king and second founder of Westminster Abbey. Henry
III had been a particular devotee of the Confessor, rebuilding the
abbey church in his honour and translating his remains to a magnificent new shrine behind the high altar. From the perspective of the
values associated with it, however, the Confessor's cult suffered from
a major disadvantage, and that was its association with peace – peace
in the sense of the absence of external conflict, and peace in the sense
of internal stability: it did not validate the aggressive martial ambitions
with which the English monarchy was increasingly associated. For this
reason, from the time of the foundation of the Garter the Confessor's
cult was to figure much less in English royal iconography, correspondingly more emphasis being placed on the chivalrous George. It was
St George who embodied in his person the values of chivalry and
martial endeavour, and it was St George who at the same time came
to be identified with England.

An insight into the dynamics of St George's ascent into the saintly
pantheon is provided by the 'English saints' window in Heydour church
in Lincolnshire.[20] This window, in the north aisle of the nave, consists
of three lights, St George occupying the central one, identifiable by
his red cross, holding a shield and lance, and the figures of St Edward
and St Edmund on each side of him, likewise identifiable by their
arms. What is interesting is the way in which St George, the foreign
intruder, is invested with an English identity by virtue of his association with the two traditional English saints while at the same time
having a transforming effect on them. Edward and Edmund are
normally shown dressed in rich civilian attire; here, however, they are
in armour. All three men are seen as soldiers of Christ, champions of
a chivalric knighthood dedicated to the service of God and king. The

window was commissioned around 1360 by Henry, Lord Scrope of Masham, an active soldier whose brother Geoffrey was prebendary of Heydour and patron of the living. Sir Henry had fought at Halidon Hill in the Scottish campaigns of the mid-1330s and at Sluys in 1340, and was later to serve in Ireland, France and Flanders. The perception of St George as an English warrior saint was one which would have come naturally to him and his peers, believing as they did in divine approval of English arms.

The cult of St George, however, was not only associated in people's eyes with those of 'English' saints; it was also seen as linked with that of the Queen of Heaven herself, the Virgin Mary. By the early fifteenth century St George was commonly referred to in religious literature as Our Lady's Knight. The popular perception of the saint was as the Virgin's loyal champion, the knight who represented his patroness in combat and defended her honour against all challengers. The idea of a linkage between the Virgin and St George had been represented in court art in the 1350s in the wall paintings which Edward III commissioned for St Stephen's Chapel, Westminster, in which St George was shown commending the king and the royal family to the Virgin and Child behind him. Just a few years later, on the Great Seal which Edward had commissioned after the Treaty of Brétigny, the king was shown on the obverse with the Virgin and Child on one side of him and the figure of St George on the other.[21]

The growing identification of St George with England was aided by a parallel process in which the Virgin herself was conceived in some sense as the special protectress of this hallowed realm, a land owned and cherished by her, in which she took a personal interest. In a sermon delivered in about 1350 mendicant preacher John Lathbury declared that 'it is commonly said that the land of England is the Virgin's dowry', and in a letter to the English bishops in 1400 Archbishop Arundel spoke in similar terms of England as 'Mary's dowry'. The notion of England enjoying the Virgin's protection constituted a challenge to the almost identical claim asserted at this time by the kings of France. Edward III, just as he had seized possession of the cult of St George, to which the French king and others laid claim, now staged a like takeover of the cult of the Virgin. This boldly presumptuous act was expressed heraldically in Edward's quartering of the lions of England with the lilies of France, the lily being seen as the Virgin's own flower. In this sense, as with Edward's claim to the kingly title, the Hundred Years War can be seen as a war over entitlement to a coat of arms.

The visionary linkage of the cult of St George with that of the Virgin was to reach its climax in the reign of Henry V (1413–22). The protection which the Virgin and St George extended to Henry and his subjects was repeatedly stressed in narrative accounts of the king's reign. According to the *Gesta Henrici Quinti*, in 1415, when the English crossed to Harfleur, the wind swung round in their direction at the behest of the Virgin, 'who, as is devoutly believed, had compassion on the people of Her dower of England'. On the eve of Agincourt, according to Thomas Elmham, the priests prayed to 'the Virgin, protectress of Her dower, and to St George and St Edward'. In the course of the battle itself, as Elmham relates, St George actually revealed himself to the English, urging them on and protecting them from their enemies.[22] In the wake of Henry's triumph at Agincourt, the idea of St George as England's special patron became an established part of English popular political thought.

What the growing appreciation of national sainthood indicates is a belief in England as a realm occupying a special place in the divine order. England was a land sanctified, a realm under the protection of celestial sponsors, foremost among them St George, the banner-bearer of Christ and patron of Christian knighthood. Although St George, as the protector of knighthood, bestowed his favour on knights everywhere, it was for his knights of England that he reserved his most fulsome blessings.

A Nation at Prayer

When he founded the priestly college of St George in Windsor Castle, Edward III was in one sense giving thanks to God for his victory at Crécy eighteen months before. Yet it would be wrong to suppose that he was merely looking to a glorious past; he was, at the same time, making preparation for the future. He saw his collegiate foundation as a kind of liturgical investment, a house of intercessory prayer which would contribute 'an increase in divine service', enhance the nation's favour with God and assist in the release of divine favours to come.

Victories, for Edward, were won not only by knightly prowess
or superior generalship in the field, but by securing the goodwill and
support of the Almighty. To maintain the nation's success in arms, it
was essential that England's stock of liturgical and intercessory provision be increased both by the enhancement of existing institutions
and the foundation of new ones. St George's and its supporting clergy
were to provide a model for a new type of religious community, the
form of priestly body known as the secular college. As the number
of these institutions grew in the late Middle Ages, so too did the
volume of petition and prayer rising to the Almighty. In the well-worn
metaphor of the day, the English ship of state was driven forward by
the prayers filling its sails.

The idea of soliciting prayers for the success of English arms was
not altogether new. For generations kings had been ordering bishops
to mobilise the prayers of the faithful on their behalf against the
nation's enemies. In 1297 Edward I had written to the archbishop of
Canterbury requesting prayers to invoke divine assistance against the
French king, whom he accused of trying to 'disherit' him of his rights
in Gascony. In 1338, when he crossed to the continent, Edward III
asked for prayers for a safe passage and for the success of his expedition on its arrival. In 1342, 1345 and 1346 the king cajoled the bishops
into organising prayers for the success of Duke Henry of Lancaster's
expeditions to Gascony.[23] The mobilisation of prayerful petition in this
manner was to be a regular feature of English military preparations
well into the fifteenth century. At every stage Henry V's campaigns
in France were mounted on 'wings of prayer', with parishes urged to
pray for the king's success in arms and to offer thanksgiving for his
victories. Orders for the mobilisation of intercession came at the rate
of once a year or more between 1415 and the capture of the Norman
capital, Rouen, in 1419. Henry's subjects at home were worked nearly
as hard in his support as his knights and foot soldiers were in the field.

What Edward was aiming to achieve by his foundation of a priestly
college at Windsor was the strengthening of these initiatives by the
provision of a specifically liturgical kind of celebration. The canons
of the new college were charged with honouring and petitioning the
Almighty not only in prayerful intercession but also through the regular
and seemly celebration of the liturgy. The liturgy, with the Eucharist at
its heart, was the central defining ritual of worship, affording the

faithful means of recommending themselves to the Almighty, soliciting his grace and favour, and begging the mediatory favour of his saints. Through appropriately decorous celebration a people could present themselves in the eyes of the Almighty as a righteous nation, and by an increase in the number and quality of Masses reap the benefit due to them as part of the living faithful. In England, by the fourteenth and fifteenth centuries that community of the faithful was coming increasingly to be identified with the nation at large. Accordingly, at a time of constant war with France it was believed that through investment in the liturgy the means could be found of invoking supernatural assistance for the nation's cause in war.

In the twelfth and thirteenth centuries a patron in Edward III's position would have constituted his foundation as a monastery, a house of monks bound by an established rule. Such an institution, however, by definition a place of solitude and retreat, would have been inappropriate in a busy castle bailey thronged with layfolk such as that at Windsor. Edward accordingly established his foundation as a college of secular canons – that is to say, a looser community made up of clerks who had not taken monastic vows. According to the founding ordinance, there were to be a warden and twelve canons, supported by thirteen priest vicars. This body of clerks was to pray in perpetuity for the good estate of the king and the brotherhood of the Knights of the Garter while they lived, and for the souls of the king and knights after their deaths. The model for the foundation was Louis IX's ordinance for the Sainte-Chapelle on the Île de la Cité at Paris. The provision for choristers and singing boys exactly matched that at the French royal college. Much earlier, at Westminster in the 1290s, the Chapel of St Stephen had acknowledged the inspiration of the French exemplar in its fine architecture. By this latest piece of imitative flattery, Edward III was making a bid to usurp French spiritual and liturgical leadership in Europe.

St George's, by virtue of its royal patronage, was bound to provide an influential model to prospective founders in the king's circle who wished to make their own provision for liturgical celebration and intercession.[24] Colleges exerted a particular appeal because, not being bound by rigid rules as monasteries were, they allowed founders to lay down whatever rules and regulations they liked. A small number of secular colleges had been established in the decades immediately before the founding of St George's. The two most important were Henry of Lancaster's house of the Newarke at Leicester in 1330 and Bishop John de Grandison's at Ottery St Mary in Devon seven years later. It was only in the wake of the founding of St George's, however, that the college as an institution moved into the forefront of larger-scale liturgical provision. It is striking that among the most active founders of secular colleges were members of the military aristocracy.

One foundation which owed an especial debt to Windsor was John, Lord Cobham's, college at Cobham in Kent – like Windsor an ambitious enterprise, with an establishment in its final form of a warden and no fewer than eleven priests. The influence of Windsor was especially evident in the college's architectural conception. The priests were accommodated in an irregularly shaped cloister to the south of the church, constructed as a set of timber-framed units around a garth, just like the Canons' Cloister at Windsor.[25] Lord Cobham's long experience of royal service under Edward III and Richard II would have familiarised him with the state-of-the-art plan at Windsor, and the style of the buildings suggests that his architect was none other than the leading court architect Henry Yevele.

In 1380 one of England's wealthiest magnates, Richard, earl of Arundel, founded a similarly conceived college at the church in Arundel in Sussex, suppressing a decayed monastery in the castle grounds in order to endow it. Like Lord Cobham, Earl Richard planned his foundation on an ambitious scale, providing for a community of a master and a dozen chaplains, and completely rebuilding the church to provide appropriately splendid surroundings for celebration of the liturgy. In the next thirty years there were to be a number of other large-scale foundations by the military aristocracy. Two of the most important were established by members of the royal family – Thomas of Woodstock's Pleshey, founded in 1394, and Edward, duke of York's Fotheringhay, in 1411 – in each case the castle landscape being redesigned to take in the church so that it acted as a focus for the display of magnate power. At Fotheringhay the church was to become the main burial place of the dukes of York. Other important colleges were founded by wealthy and important war captains, notably Bunbury in Cheshire, established by Sir Hugh Calveley, and Staindrop in County Durham, the creation of a Garter knight, Ralph, earl of Westmorland.

The tradition of founding colleges continued well into the fifteenth century. Ralph, Lord Cromwell, Henry VI's treasurer, founded a great college at Tattershall in Lincolnshire, associating it closely with his castle, which he rebuilt at the same time.

Collectively, these institutions brought about a massive increase in divine worship, reinforcing England's already high standing in the Almighty's favour and assuring her of the continued flow of his divine grace. In the reign of Henry V, moreover, further steps were taken to increase the stock of the nation's liturgical provision. Henry, a man of deeply felt piety, not content with the lavish provision already made by his predecessors, established a new wave of foundations to secure divine support for his kingship. Henry's patronage, unlike Edward's, went to the well-established regular orders. He conceived a scheme of three 'palace monasteries', all on the banks of the River Thames near his palace of Sheen in Surrey.[26] At Sheen itself he provided for a house of the Carthusian Order, a community which enjoyed a late flowering because of its spirituality and resistance to external influence. At Syon, on the opposite bank of the river, he established a house of Brigittine nuns, an English plantation of a Swedish order favoured by his friend Lord FitzHugh. A projected third house, of the French Celestine Order, failed to take root, perhaps because of the king's premature death in August 1422. The intention behind all three foundations was to strengthen liturgical celebration and observance in order to draw down divine favour. Henry, like Edward III before him, believed that by 'an increase in divine service' he could assist the success of English arms in war.

Henry's interest in strengthening liturgical provision extended to ensuring the seemly performance of services in his chapel. He believed that the ceremonies of the chapel royal both attracted divine mercy and set a model for the nobility's own observances. He took a keen interest in church music, either commissioning or composing a setting of the Gloria in the Old Hall Manuscript (c. 1418–22) and employing musicians of European-wide fame, among them John Dunstable and John Pyamour.[27] In a major initiative, in the wake of his victory at Agincourt he expanded the liturgy of the chapel by ordering invocations to St George, St Edward the Confessor and the Virgin. The encouragement that he gave to the worship of such saints as brought favour to England formed part of a more extensive programme of liturgical reform. In 1415 St George's feast day was promoted to a 'greater double' at his request, while the next year official backing was given to the cult of St John of Beverley, on whose feast day Agincourt had been fought. The aim of these additions to the liturgy was to promote the image of Henry as a *miles Christi*, fighting under the banner of national and military saints. Henry's vision of a strong national monarchy gained much from the propagandist efforts of an increasingly 'national' Church.

By Henry V's reign, the relationship between chivalry and religion had come a long way from those days in the eleventh century when an assertive Church had been bent on disciplining a violent and unruly knighthood. In the High Middle Ages, when the power of national monarchies had been weak, it had been the Church which had set the agenda for Christian knighthood. Four centuries later, the position was reversed: right across Europe national monarchies were establishing a solid ascendancy over local Churches. Nowhere in Europe was that ascendancy more secure or complete than in England. By the vigour of his rule Henry V had harnessed the resources of the Church to his ambition of vindicating his claim to the Crown of France. He achieved this, however, in the context of a larger programme for the salvation of kingdom and people. In England, at least for Henry's lifetime, the fusion of the Christian and chivalric ethics was complete.

The Clergy at War

The role played by the Church in providing intercessory support for England's war effort was matched by the involvement of many of the clergy themselves in day-to-day military administration. For most of the Middle Ages the clergy made up the greater part of the civil service which staffed the royal offices at Westminster – or wherever the king happened to be. This was not only because the clergy possessed the skills of literacy and numeracy needed to run the administrative departments; it was also because clerical staff provided the king with a convenient way of operating his government on the cheap. Since the clergy could be rewarded with Church benefices, the king did not need to pay them salaries from the royal purse. Many of the most senior clerks in royal service were promoted to deaneries or bishoprics on the king's nomination. Walter Langton, Edward I's ambitious and self-seeking treasurer, was appointed to the see of Lichfield, for example, and William Edington and William Wykeham, two of Edward III's chancellors, to the see of Winchester, the wealthiest in England.

In the reign of Edward I the department most directly concerned with the organisation of war was the wardrobe. Being smaller than the exchequer and closely attached to the royal household, the wardrobe offered the necessary flexibility to handle administrative arrangements in the more distant parts of the realm. The clerks of the wardrobe took responsibility for such tasks as paying troops, requisitioning equipment, arranging food supplies, checking horse valuations and, at the end of a campaign, drawing up accounts of expenditure. In the last years of Edward I's reign, when warfare was near-continuous, the keeper of the wardrobe was John Droxford, a long-serving royal clerk who regularly accompanied the king on campaigns and sometimes attended at the head of troops. In the opening campaigns of the Hundred Years War, the officials who filled Droxford's shoes were William Norwell, the keeper of the wardrobe, and two chamber clerks, Thomas Hatfield and William Kilsby. Between 1338 and 1340, when Edward was based in the Low Countries, these three were constantly at his side ensuring coordination between the king's household and the government at Westminster. Kilsby, like Droxford, was sometimes present at the head of troops. All three officials were to be well rewarded with benefices, Hatfield in 1345 being elevated to the wealthy see of Durham.

After the 1340s, as the king grew older and his health deteriorated, virtually all the big campaigns in France were led by lieutenants acting on his behalf. Where such an arrangement was created, those leading the expeditions took their own clerks with them as paymasters. In 1355 and 1356 the Black Prince, for example, took with him John Henxteworth, the controller of his household, while twenty years later John of Gaunt, on his *chevauchée* from Calais to Bordeaux, employed the services of his receiver general William Ermyn. Like their opposite numbers who served the king directly, these men were well rewarded for their work. William Ermyn accumulated canonries at York Minster and St Paul's in addition to a wealthy parochial living at Castle Ashby in Northamptonshire. The splendour of Ermyn's memorial brass in Castle Ashby church, showing him as a full-length figure in a cope, provides clear evidence of his wealth at his death.

The extensive involvement of these men in the administration of war sometimes spilled over into actual participation in the field. We have seen that several of the most senior royal wardrobe clerks supplied the king with retinues even if they did not command them in person. Other clerks, however, less heedful of canonical prescription, both supplied retinues and placed themselves, rather in the manner of Odo of Bayeux, at the head of them. In 1303–4 wardrobe clerk John Benstead served in Scotland at the head of a retinue of one knight and thirteen esquires.[28] In 1303 Edward I's cofferer Ralph Manton was on the march in Scotland when he met a grisly death in an ambush at Roslyn, near Edinburgh.[29] Men of episcopal rank sometimes donned armour to defend either their tenants or their dioceses. In 1346 the archbishop of York and the bishop of Carlisle took the lead in the force that defeated the Scots at the battle of Neville's Cross. Fifty years earlier, the notorious Anthony Bek, bishop of Durham, had been involved in Edward I's assault on the Scots at the battle of Falkirk. In the 1340s a no less martial occupant of the diocese of Durham, Thomas Hatfield, saw service against both the Scots and the French.[30] In 1383 the battling bishop of Norwich Henry Despenser, a veteran of the wars in Italy, took command of a force which challenged the French takeover of Flanders. In 1471 yet another warlike bishop of Durham, William Dudley, was to place himself at the head of 160 men to lend support to Edward IV on his return from exile.

These initiatives were wholly at variance with the precepts of canon law. It had long been canonical doctrine that the clergy should not be involved in any way in the shedding of blood. An explicit statement to this effect had been published at a council at Westminster in 1138: it was said to be 'ridiculous and inconvenient' that clerks should bear arms in war.[31] The prohibition on clerical participation in war was, however, applied flexibly. Certainly in England there was pressure from the Crown for its relaxation because of the need to involve the clergy in measures for local defence. The heyday of the clerical call to arms came in the late fourteenth and early fifteenth centuries, when the danger of invasion or attack was most severe. Between 1368 and 1418 over a dozen orders were sent to bishops instructing them to gather clergy to defend the realm and resist the malice of the king's enemies.[32] Clergy who held benefices were ordered to attend arrays properly armed and equipped, the precise equipment which they were required to carry varying according to their means. Bequests of arms and armour in clerical wills show that some at least of those involved took their responsibilities seriously. In 1407 Bishop Medford of Salisbury left what he referred to as 'my whole suit of armour' to his nephew.[33] In some parts of the country, where the danger of enemy attack was near-constant, the clergy could find themselves assuming a leading role in defence. In Sussex in 1377 Hamo de Offington, abbot of the appropriately named Battle Abbey, took the lead in the defence of Winchelsea against the French, repulsing the enemy after an affray lasting over three hours. In the same year the prior of Lewes, who was less well prepared for fighting, found himself taken prisoner.[34]

It was not so much in actual combat, however, that the clergy made its most significant contribution to English war efforts; rather, it was in the influencing of public opinion and the boosting of popular morale. Through the machinery of the Church the government was able to communicate its message to a much broader audience than that which could be reached through parliament.[35] As we have seen, from the 1290s the government regularly issued instructions to bishops ordering them to arrange prayers and masses for the success of English arms, English embassies, or some other goal.[36] In the first half of Edward III's reign writs to this effect were issued almost annually. When such letters were drafted the government usually went beyond the mere requesting of prayers; it seized the opportunity to explain, justify and promote its policies. In successive writs in the 1340s Edward III laid out his claim to the French throne, excused his delay in asserting his title and tore into the trickery and duplicity of his French opponent.[37] At times when the burden of taxation was particularly heavy Edward used letters to the clergy to beg the goodwill of his subjects. In 1338, in a letter to the clergy of the hard-pressed diocese of York, he apologised for the 'various burdens, tallages and imposts' which he had been 'compelled' to levy, assuring them that not avarice but military necessity had obliged his demands.[38] Sometimes Edward sought to underline his message by encouraging public ritual. In 1346, when he instructed Archbishop Stratford to read out a recently discovered French plan for the invasion of England, he told him to organise a public procession 'so that the people of the realm might be moved to esteem the king more fervently and pray for his expedition more devoutly'.[39] In the next reign, that of Richard II, the clergy were ordered to stage Masses and processions for the bishop of Norwich's 'crusade' of 1383, the earl of Arundel's expedition of 1387 and Richard's own expedition to Ireland in 1394. Up to the end of the Hundred Years War the crown made use of this system for promoting its wartime goals and seeking popular support for them.

An idea of just how deeply implicated the higher clergy were in the values of chivalric society is given by the extraordinary brass in Salisbury cathedral of Bishop Robert Wyvill, who died in 1375. Wyvill's main achievement in his forty-year reign as bishop had been his recovery for the see of the castle of Sherborne and the chase of Bere in Berkshire, which had been lost to the Crown in the twelfth century. This triumph was celebrated on his brass, which shows him looking out from a battlemented castle with his champion, holding a baton and shield, standing in front of the gate below. The champion was included because, if the issue had come to trial by battle, he would have fought in the lists on the bishop's behalf. Bishop Wyvill was the first holder of the see of Salisbury for 200 years not to be a scholar or theologian, and he saw nothing incongruous in employing military imagery on his brass. For him, as for Bishop Hatfield at Durham, episcopacy and chivalry could go unproblematically together.

The Church's involvement in chivalrous society accordingly had its roots in a view of war as justifiable if waged to uphold right or avenge injury. When knights were engaged in arms in a just cause, the use of violence was considered right and legitimate. In the early Middle Ages the Church had directed its endeavours to curbing the unruliness of those in the knightly class who were held to be bringing dishonour on their order. In the late Middle Ages, when strong national monarchies were emerging and the Church was validating national wars as just, there was a growing identification of clerical, and so religious, interests with those of the state. The English state itself took on a semi-religious guise, appropriating the idea of holy war and encouraging a view of the English as a chosen people fulfilling an appointed mission. By the fourteenth century England had become a land sanctified, with a chivalric class fighting in a divine cause under divine protection.

12

Chivalry and Crusading

In 1099, at the end of a gruelling three-year campaign, the First Crusaders captured Jerusalem, liberating the Holy Places, massacring the local populace and laying the foundations of the Latin settler kingdom. To the crusading Westerners, the sheer scale of their achievement seemed a sign of God's blessing on their enterprise.

From the first, the new kingdom lived in a state of siege. It was faced on its landward side by hostile neighbours, and manpower and money were in short supply. Although a massive programme of fortification was undertaken, at moments of crisis when the Muslims united against the Latin intruders, only military help from the West could guarantee survival. It was these vast support expeditions – *passagia*, as they were called – which we recognise as the crusades. Those who took part in them were granted remission of sins as their reward. After the fall of the crusader kingdom in 1291, the definition of crusading was extended to embrace wars on Europe's frontiers and against the Church's enemies within Europe.

Crusading and Medieval Society

In the eyes of the Church, the defence of the Holy Places in the east was the greatest and most ennobling task to which a Christian knight could commit himself. As late as the fourteenth century the crusading propagandist Philippe de Mézières could say, 'the first and principal glory of the dignity of true chivalry is to fight for the faith'.[1] In the 1140s Pope Eugenius III, when preaching the Second Crusade, had said, 'it will be seen as a great token of nobility and uprightness if those things which were acquired by the efforts of your fathers are vigorously defended by you, their sons'.[2] To the Church, part of the attraction of promoting crusading was that it offered the prospect of a reformed knighthood, a force for good in the world. As Guibert de Nogent wrote, 'God has instituted a Holy War, so that the order of knights . . . may seek God's grace in their wonted habit and in discharge of their own office, and need no longer . . . seek salvation by renouncing the world in the profession of the monk.'[3] Crusading, in other words, while providing a means to regain the Holy Places, also offered a solution to the long-standing problem of the unruly knight in Christian society. Crusading elevated the knightly estate, making it comparable in some way in Christian service with the priesthood. When preaching the First Crusade at Clermont, Pope Urban had contrasted the old unregenerate knight with the new knight who fought for a worthy cause: 'Now become soldiers of Christ, you who a little while ago were robbers. Now legally fight against barbarians, you who once fought against brothers and blood-relatives.'[4] Crusading focused the fighting spirit of the knightly class on a cause without compare, the supreme objective, the recapture of the Holy Places for Christendom.

The idea of crusading as an activity which could bring distinction to a knight was widely appreciated in the Middle Ages; it was to be a popular theme in contemporary writing. That there was a widespread acceptance of crusading as an expression of the Christian vocation can hardly be doubted. To recognise this, however, is not to suppose that all aspects of crusading appeals were received with equal enthusiasm by their intended audience. There is every likelihood that knightly listeners were selective in the way they responded to such appeals and sermons. One aspect of crusading propaganda to which they almost certainly paid little attention was the distinction made between the illegitimate violence of secular quarrels and the justified violence of holy war. In a society which lived by an aristocratic honour code and in which violence might sometimes have to be met by violence, such a distinction ultimately lacked conviction. To most of the knightly class, holy war did not so much constitute an alternative to secular war, as the clergy maintained; it represented a natural extension of it. It was another expression, albeit a much higher expression, of war in a just cause.

In the same way, crusading neither bypassed nor rejected the normal structures by which war in medieval society was organised; it drew on them, exploiting them on a larger scale and in the name of a nobler cause. Just as throughout the late Middle Ages lords raising men for a feudal or national war looked to their dependants to provide the core of their force, so too did lords raising men for a crusade. The lord's household was the essential building block in the assembling of contingents for the crusades just as it was in the assembling of armies for the French or Scottish wars. Matthew Paris records that the knights and men-at-arms Richard of Cornwall took with him on crusade in 1240 were members of his *familia* – his household – while Henry of Derby's account book of a century and a half later reveals that the force which the earl took with him to Prussia was composed of the retainers of his father, John of Gaunt.[5] In the same way, when leaders of crusading contingents found it necessary to expand their retinues beyond their household core, they did so in the same way as they would for any other expedition, by resort to short-term indentures. The indentures which the Lord Edward, the future Edward I, made for his crusade to the east in 1270 afford some of the earliest examples of the use of this method of recruitment to raise an armed retinue. Crusading at its most successful relied on exactly the same resources of lordship as underpinned warfare more generally. Crusading was in no sense an activity separate from the wider experience of war in society; on the contrary, it was very much part of it.

To Jerusalem

To all intents and purposes, the history of English involvement in crusading begins with Richard the Lionheart's participation in the Third Crusade of the 1190s. Before this time English participation had been relatively slight. A few English knights had gone east in the wake of the capture of Jerusalem in 1099, and rather more had responded to the preaching of the Second Crusade in the 1140s. A small number who could not go on crusade in person pledged their support for the movement by giving alms. By comparison with the degree of commitment to crusading found in contemporary France or western Germany, English support for the movement was decidedly meagre.

The principal reason for this lack of interest is not difficult to find. Knightly participation in crusading was largely dependent on the involvement of the knight's lord or king, and in England in the early years this top-level commitment was lacking. William Rufus, an unusually secular-minded man, had shown little or no interest in the First Crusade in the 1090s, and the Anglo-Norman contingent which took part in it had been led by his brother Robert. At the time of the Second Crusade in the 1140s the Anglo-Norman world had been embroiled in the bitter civil war between Stephen and Matilda, with the result that Stephen, a crusader's son, had little opportunity to participate. With Richard I's accession in 1189, however, the situation suddenly changed. Richard was to emerge as one of the most significant and heroic figures in the history of crusading.

The cause of the upsurge in activity which resulted in the Third Crusade was the capture of Jerusalem by Saladin in 1187. In July that year a settler army led by the king of Jerusalem had been destroyed by a Muslim force under Saladin at Hattin in Galilee. The military strength of the Latin state was virtually eliminated, and three months later Jerusalem itself was taken. News of Hattin and the consequent loss of the Holy Places sent shock waves across the west. Immediately, preparations were set in hand for the launching of a major new crusade to regain the Holy City and save what was left of the crusader state.

In England the initial steps in the preparation of an expedition had been taken by Henry II in the months before his death. At Geddington in Northamptonshire in 1188 he had launched an urgent appeal for money and equipment to match the equivalent plea he had made on the continent at Le Mans. On his son's accession the following year, the task of assembling the expedition was made the new government's main priority. Richard's plan was to link up with the French king at Vézelay, marching with him to the Mediterranean coast and embarking for the east at Marseilles, whither he despatched his fleet to meet him. Richard's preparations were extensive, but the total size of his force is hard to estimate. Richard of Devizes's guess, probably an accurate one, was that the king's fleet consisted of at least a hundred ships, each carrying thirty sailors and forty infantry, and fourteen large transports carrying twice that number. These figures point to a total force of between 8,000 and 9,000 men. In addition, Richard had a land army which may have numbered some 6,000 men, recruited from all over the Angevin world. The main part of the king of France's force, by contrast, has been put at no more than 2,000. Most probably, by the time all the contingents at Richard's disposal had assembled, his force may have totalled around 17,000 troops and seamen, an enormous army in the late twelfth century.[6]

Raising the money to provide for such a force posed a challenge which Richard's exchequer officials showed themselves more than capable of meeting. A large part of the cost was met by a 10 per cent levy on goods and property, known as the Saladin tithe, which Henry II had instituted in 1188. Estimates of how much money was raised by the tax vary, but Gervase of Canterbury's figure of £70,000 may not be far from the truth. Certainly the pipe rolls, the account rolls of the exchequer, record large sums of money being carried around for the king's use: 200 marks were carted to Bristol, presumably for shipping; 2,500 marks to Gloucester, perhaps for horseshoes from the Forest of Dean; and 5,000 marks to Southampton, again presumably for shipping. Large though the sums raised by the Saladin tithe were, much more money was needed to pay for an expedition to the Holy Land. Richard found this by organising an auction of almost everything to which he could lay claim. In the words of Roger of Howden, 'He put up for sale offices, lordships, earldoms, sheriffdoms, castles, towns, lands, everything.' Towns were obliged to buy new charters; forest rights were sold; empty bishoprics were awarded to the highest bidders. Richard is reported to have said that he would have sold London itself if he could have found a buyer. Overlooking nothing, he even made sure to take his cut of the property left by Jews massacred in the riots at York and elsewhere in 1190.

The war chest which Richard assembled gave him the means to meet virtually all of his initial expenses. It also enabled him to defray some of the expenses of those accompanying him. Crusading was a hugely expensive business, involving those engaged in it in much higher costs than did war nearer home. Money was needed not only to meet the usual expenses of armour, horses, weapons; it was also needed for shipping, clothing, tools, bribes, perhaps even for religious relics. Those who took on the leadership of contingents, moreover, were faced with much higher wage bills than would have been the case in a local war. Commanders could be in the field for up to two years, in hostile surroundings, without ready access to cash.

It was in recognition of the unique challenge of crusading that Richard decided to help meet some of his crusaders' start-up costs. Hitherto it had generally been the case that crusaders met all the cost of the long passage east themselves. A major element in this massive sum was the expense of hiring a ship. Richard, however, offered many of his men free passage on his own shipping. He also supplied many of them with food. The pipe rolls show royal officials engaged in bulk-buying of provisions – cheeses from Essex, beans from Cambridgeshire and Kent, and no fewer than 14,000 pigs' carcases from Lincolnshire, Essex and Hampshire. Richard's expedition was almost certainly among the best provisioned of its day. Richard also seems to have undertaken to supply horses to a large proportion of his force. On the evidence of the massive sums spent on purchasing horseshoes – no fewer than 60,000 of them were bought – it seems that he provided mounts not only for his own men but also for many in the service of other lords.[7] The gain to the king was a force not only well equipped but also well motivated to meet the challenges which it was to face in the east.

The majority of those who took the cross between 1188 and 1190 were fairly substantial magnates, knights and gentlemen. Gerald of Wales reports that in his country it was overwhelmingly nobles, knights and their retainers who responded to Archbishop Baldwin's preaching tour of 1188: the *crucesignati*, he says, were men 'highly skilled in the use of the spear and the arrow, most experienced in military matters'.[8] It was precisely men of this stamp and calibre whom Richard wanted to attract to ensure the effectiveness of his force. It is possible, on the evidence of the exchequer pipe rolls, to identify a good number of those who enlisted. Many were members of powerful families, such as the earl of Leicester and his son, the earl of Derby, Nigel de Mowbray, Bernard of St Valery, Richard de Clare, Gerard de Furnival, Hugh de Neville, Waleran de Forz and Warin FitzGerald. There were also a few senior royal officials like William FitzAldelin, the steward, and Ralph FitzGodfrey, the chamberlain, and household staff and royal agents such as Richard de Camville and Eustace de Burnes. There were former royal sheriffs, among them Drogo FitzRalph and Ranulf and Roger Glanvill, and friends of the king such as Andrew de Chavigny. There were regional confederacies, including a band of Yorkshiremen who mortgaged virtually all their lands to raise money while yet scraping together some charitable donations to ensure the good health of their souls. Alongside these big well-supported retinues were small knightly companies, like the following of just ten who set out with Sir Ivo de Vieuxpont from distant Westmorland.[9]

The Third Crusade was the first great *passagium* to the east which was able to draw on extensive participation by the English knightly class. While it is true that Richard's army drew recruits from all over the Angevin dominions, there can be no doubting the scale of English involvement. Judged simply by its success in converting crusading aspiration into military action, Richard's crusade must be seen as a major event in English crusading history. It was also to be important for a second reason: its impact on the English chivalric imagination. Before the venture, the knightly class had on the whole shown little interest in crusading; after it, crusading was to figure in the forefront of those activities which shaped the chivalric ideal.

Much of the credit for this change of perception rests with the king himself. Richard's achievements on the crusade made him one of the outstanding leaders of his age. After King Philip's precipitate return to France in July 1191, Richard was the single most important contingent leader operating in the east. Well before his arrival in the Holy Land, he had shown his mettle as a commander. On his crossing of the Mediterranean from Sicily, he had conquered Cyprus in the space of a few months, winning it from its ruler, the Emperor Isaac. On his arrival at the port of Acre in Palestine, he brought to a conclusion, in under four weeks, a siege which had been dragging on for nearly two years, amply justifying his reputation as a master of siege warfare. On campaign in the Holy Land, he showed himself to be more than a match for Saladin. On the march to Jerusalem he scored a major field victory over his rival at Arsuf (7 September 1191), allowing him to relieve the port of Jaffa. While he failed to take Jerusalem, he scored further triumphs over Saladin's forces at Ascalon and al-Hasi. When, after two years, he and Saladin had fought themselves to a standstill, he negotiated a peace which guaranteed free access to the Holy Places and stabilised the crusader kingdom for another century. The First Crusade excepted, the Third was the only one which came anywhere near achieving its objectives.

The renown of Richard's achievements, however, was the result not only of their intrinsic importance but also of his skill in promoting and publicising them. Richard appreciated the need to shape and manipulate opinion at home. He was a pioneer in the use of newsletters, sending them to his ministers in England following the fall of Acre in July 1191 and in the wake of his victory at Arsuf two months later. At the same time he ensured that the chroniclers who accompanied his army reported his deeds approvingly. His admirer the jongleur Ambroise could always be counted on to peddle stories flattering to his master. It was Ambroise who related enthusiastically how Richard stormed ashore at Jaffa in 1192, leg armour stripped off, to drive the enemy back.[10] Richard de Templo, whose text draws on Ambroise's, was if anything even more extravagant in his praise for the king. Writing of Richard's prowess at Jaffa, he asked, 'What of the king, one man surrounded by so many thousands? The fingers stiffen to write of it and the mind is amazed to think of it. Who has heard of anyone like him? I do not know how he remained invincible and invulnerable among all his enemies, perhaps by some divine protection. His body was like brass, unyielding to any sort of weapon.'[11]

Stories of Richard, passed on by word of mouth as well as in the chroniclers' record, gained in the telling. In due course a variety of fictional yarns were added to their number. According to one story, Richard engaged Saladin in a duel, emerging victorious from the fray, while according to another he wrestled with a raging lion, tearing its heart out. The duel with Saladin was to be depicted on a set of thirteenth-century Chertsey tiles.

By the sheer scale of his achievements and by his skill in drawing attention to them, Richard generated new enthusiasm in England for crusading. From this time on, crusading was seen not only, as it had been, as a meritorious activity which brought spiritual reward; it was considered a uniquely ennobling form of war which could bring honour and distinction to a whole family. It says something for Richard's success in enveloping himself in mystique that later knights sought to burnish their credentials by claiming ancestors who had accompanied him on crusade. Sir William Carrington, an unremarkable Cheshire knight, claimed that his ancestor Michael had acted as Richard's standard-bearer in the Holy Land, a claim entirely without foundation.[12] The Cobhams of Cobham in Kent were to maintain that Henry, son of Serlo de Cobham, the first traceable member of their line, had fought alongside Richard at Acre, using this association to explain the family's Saracen's head crest.[13] Laying claim to a connection with the Lionheart on crusade was a way in which gentry lineages of obscure origin could add to their fame and standing.

If Richard stimulated new interest in crusading, he also placed a heavy burden of emulation on those who followed him on the throne. Images of his most famous deeds looked out at monarchs and their courtiers from painted and sculpted decoration in castles and palaces. Poems and tales celebrating Richard's deeds echoed through halls in recitals following feasts and banquets. Richard's achievements aroused new expectations of English chivalric kingship. When another crusader, the Lord Edward, succeeded to the throne as Edward I, he was acclaimed by one contemporary: 'Behold, he shines like a new Richard.'[14] Participation in crusading was now held to rank among the responsibilities of kingship in a way that it never had before. Gone were the days when a king could simply ignore crusading, as Rufus had done in the 1090s.

Some of Richard's successors rose to the challenge of his legacy more enthusiastically than others. Richard's brother and immediate successor, John, showed little appetite at all for crusading. Ignoring the calls which led to the Fourth Crusade in 1202, he took the cross only at the very end of his reign, and then principally to secure papal support against his opponents. The attitude of John's successors, Henry III and Edward I, were altogether different. Henry was acutely conscious of the challenge to his dynasty's prestige posed by the crusading achievements of the French kings, in particular of his contemporary Louis IX. He accordingly donned the cross no fewer than three times – in 1216, shortly after his accession, and again in 1250 and 1271. Yet, despite repeated promises to do so, he never actually departed for the east, pleading one excuse after another. In Henry's reign the main crusading adventure comprised the small expedition led by his brother Richard of Cornwall and brother-in-law Simon de Montfort to the east in 1240.

It was accordingly left to Henry's son the future Edward I to redeem his father's promise a couple of years before his accession in 1272. By the late thirteenth century the crusader state was in its death throes, and the need for substantial military aid was urgent. Louis IX of France had taken the cross in 1267, and Edward, together with a group of English nobles, followed suit in June 1268. After abandoning the original plan to launch a diversionary attack on Tunis, Edward and his men overwintered in Sicily and made their way to the east, arriving in May 1271. With only 1,000 men at his disposal, scarcely 200 of them knights, Edward could achieve little. After some desultory campaigning, he was forced to give up, his brother Edmund leaving for home in May, and Edward himself in October.

Disappointing though the military outcome of the crusade may have been, the mere organisation of Edward's venture represented a considerable undertaking by the English state. The cost of the expedition came to well over £60,000, or nearly twice the annual income the Crown drew from its hereditary resources. Roughly half of this sum was met by the levying of a twentieth on the value of all lay and clerical movable property, following the precedent of the Saladin tithe of Richard's reign. The rest was found by a tax on the Jews and the receipt of income from such feudal incidents as wardships and escheats. Even so, while in the east Edward had no option but to resort to borrowing. By the summer of 1272 he had run up debts of 3,000 livres tournois to creditors in Acre and nearly 7,000 pounds tournois to Italian merchants. On his return he was obliged to seek papal consent to the levying of further taxation on the clergy to clear the burden of debt that he had incurred.

In its composition Edward's force had had many of the characteristics of a royal army. It was made up of his military household and the households of those magnates who had agreed to accompany him. Edward raised a large part of his force by means of written contracts with leading captains, drawn up in 1270. The financial details entered on the account rolls of the exchequer rehearsed broadly the same formulae: the contracting party was to remain in Edward's service for a year, bringing with him a stipulated number of knights, and in return was to receive an annual payment at a rate of a hundred marks per knight. Henry of Almain, Edward's cousin, received 1,500 marks, William de Valence 2,000, Edmund of Lancaster, Edward's brother, 10,000, and Adam de Jesmond, Payn de Chaworth and Robert Tiptoft 600 each.[15] A few of the actual contracts survive to this day. The agreement with Payn de Chaworth and Robert Tiptoft required them to accompany Edward with ten knights and to remain in his service for a year from the time of embarkation, receiving 1,200 marks in payment, from which they were to meet the cost of their horses. In the event of circumstances preventing them from serving, they were to provide substitutes. In all probability the contracting parties then entered into sub-contracts with their own dependants in order to provide the quotas which they had agreed with Edward.

In this interlocking structure of recruitment ties of kinship and locality were closely interwoven with those of lordship. A number of well-defined social circles can be identified in the contingents that agreed to serve with Edward.[16] One such was formed by the members of his own household, ranging from John de Osbeston and Richard de Saundon, his esquires, to Hugh FitzOtto, probably his steward, and Richard de la Rochelle, his former justiciar in Ireland. Another group centred on the retinue attached to Eleanor of Castile, who accompanied her husband. A third group may be identified with the retainers of Edmund of Lancaster and included Sir Richard de Wykes, his steward, Sir Laurence de St Maur, Sir Alan de Lascelles and the esquire Roger de Conyers.

Edward's expedition to the Holy Land occupies no more than a footnote in the broad sweep of crusading history and the history of Europe's relations with the Near East. In the more limited context of English military organisation, however, it occupies a position of some importance. In the arrangements which Edward made for the recruitment and payment of his crusaders may be detected broadly the kind of arrangements to be used for raising armies in the Hundred Years War. The making of written contracts with the leading captains, the captains' use of contracts in turn, the levying of public taxation to meet wage bills and the entering of the financial details on the exchequer account rolls – all these were to be features of English military organisation in the age of the three Edwards. Neither the essentially household structure of Edward's army nor the presence of a contractual element within it were entirely new; both had been features of Anglo-Norman armies. Yet the standardisation achieved in 1270 and, more particularly, the resort to public taxation to pay for the contract forces pointed the way to the future. In the crusade of 1270 were brought together all the elements which were to dominate English military organisation for the next 200 years.

Crusading in the Late Middle Ages

The Lord Edward's crusade in 1270 was one of the last *passagia* to the east to be undertaken by a major Western leader. Just nineteen years after Edward left Acre, the Muslims overran the few remaining coastal settlements and the crusader kingdom ceased to exist. This did not, however, mean the end of crusading; on the contrary, the habit of fighting for and under the cross was to continue for years to come. Yet late medieval crusading was very different in character from the general *passagia* which had dominated in the past. Late medieval crusading was diverse and decentralised, consisting of small expeditions with limited objectives, usually organised under non-royal leaders and chiefly deployed on Europe's flanks, not in the Holy Land. For a number of the most militarily active English nobility the period actually represented an Indian summer of crusading. Families such as the Scropes, the Beauchamps and de Bohuns built up substantial records of crusading service, which they cherished as sources of chivalric pride. Even if in military terms the results of all this activity were of little significance, there can be no doubting the importance which the nobility attached to crusading as an expression of the knightly ideal.

Perhaps the best-known crusading knight of the late Middle Ages is the fictional Knight of Chaucer's *Canterbury Tales*, who had taken part in most of the crusading *passagia* of his lifetime:

> Ful worthy was he in his lordes were,
> And therto hadde he ridden, no man ferre,
> As wel in cristendom as in hethenesse,
> And evere honoured for his worthynesse.
> At Alisaundre he was when it was wonne.
> Ful ofte tyme he hadde the bord bigonne
> Aboven all nacions in Pruce;
> In Lettow hadde he reysed and in Ruce,
> No Cristen man so ofte of his degree.
> In Gernade at the seege eek hadde he be
> Of Algezir, and riden in Belamrye.
> At Lyeys was he and at Satalye,
> Whan they were wonne; and in the Grete See
> At many a noble armee hadde he be.

The career which Chaucer imagined for his pilgrim knight represents an idealised version of the careers of many late fourteenth-century English crusaders. The theatres which Chaucer carefully mentions are all immediately recognisable. Alisaundre is Alexandria, taken – and briefly held – by King Peter of Cyprus in 1365. Pruce, Lettow and Ruce – respectively Prussia, Livonia and Russia – were all territories in the Baltic opened up by the Teutonic Knights in their struggle against the Slavs. Granada and Algeciras were Muslim enclaves in southern Spain, the latter taken by the Castilians in 1344. Lyeys and Satalye are Ayas and Antalya, cities in Asia Minor assaulted by the same King Peter. Although it is unlikely that Chaucer had any one knight's career in mind when describing that of his own, a number of real-life individuals had campaigning records which closely resembled that of Chaucer's pilgrim. Sir Richard Waldegrave of Suffolk had seen service in Prussia, Asia Minor and Alexandria, three of the theatres which Chaucer mentions.[17] The poet's aim, however, was less to reproduce in mirror form a particular career than to evoke a representative figure who could embody the highest chivalric ideals of the age.

Generally, in the late fourteenth century, crusading was undertaken most vigorously in those periods when a truce or full peace brought a cessation in the long-running Anglo-French struggle. It was widely recognised by advocates of crusading that the launching of a successful *passagium* was virtually impossible as long as the two main powers in the west were locked in conflict. Not only would there be an insufficient number of knights to take part; there would be little chance of securing the international cooperation which was essential if knights of different allegiances were to come together under a single banner. For this reason, in the 1370s and later the papacy became deeply involved in the negotiations between the two sides, in attempts to promote a permanent peace between them. In the fourteenth century there were only two periods when crusading by English and French knights together could realistically be undertaken. One was the decade of peace which followed ratification of the Treaty of Brétigny in 1360, and the other the long period of semi-peace which followed the Truce of Leulingham in 1389.

The main advocate of a renewal of crusading in the 1360s was the ever-enthusiastic king of Cyprus, Peter de Lusignan, titular king of Jerusalem. In 1361 Peter pulled off a coup in seizing the Turkish-held port of Antalya in Asia Minor. Encouraged by his success, in 1363 he embarked on a recruiting tour of the west, pressing the case for a crusade as an appropriate way of employing the soldiery left high and dry by the winding-down of the French war.[18] In neither London nor Paris, however, did he encounter the degree of support that he had hoped for, Edward III in particular proving lukewarm. Accordingly, what Peter had originally conceived as a joint Anglo-French *passagium* to the east boiled down, when launched, to no more than a surprise assault on the port city of Alexandria. The attack was initially successful and the city was taken; Peter, however, lacked the strength to secure his prize and was forced to withdraw after a week. In 1367 he launched a new round of attacks on Turkish fortresses on the coastlines of Cilicia and Syria, and at the end of the decade he was deeply implicated in papal initiatives to bring relief to Constantinople, which was by this time virtually encircled by the Turks. In 1369, however, his death at the hands of an assassin brought an end to crusading initiatives for some twenty years.

While Peter's expeditions turned out to be smaller than he had anticipated, they nonetheless attracted considerable interest in England. The statements of some of the deponents in the Scrope–Grosvenor controversy in 1386 shed light on the scale of English involvement.[19] The esquire Nicholas Sabraham was to recall that he had seen the Yorkshire knight Sir Stephen Scrope of Masham being knighted by none other than King Peter himself at the capture of Alexandria.[20] Sir Richard Waldegrave, the Suffolk knight whose career closely resembled that of Chaucer's knight, recalled seeing another member of the Scrope family, Sir William, in the earl of Hereford's company at the taking of Antalya, so providing evidence not only of his own involvement and Scrope's but also of Hereford's.[21] Sabraham, who recalled Stephen Scrope's knighting, also cited his own involvement at Constantinople, the 'Bras de St Jorge', Alexandria and the Black Sea port of Messembria, on the last occasion when serving with the count of Savoy.[22] Among other knights who can be shown to have fought in the 1360s are Sir William de la Pole of Castle Ashby in Northamptonshire, Sir Thomas Ufford, son of the earl of Suffolk, Sir Miles Stapleton and Sir John d'Argentein. Another earl – Thomas Beauchamp, earl of Warwick – is known to have enlisted for service in the Mediterranean, but probably ended up going to Prussia instead.[23] To all these knights involvement in crusading brought chivalric pride and perhaps spiritual satisfaction even if the military results of their efforts were insignificant.

In the 1390s, when the negotiation of the long truce between the

English and the French at Leulingham brought a fresh lull in hostilities, there was another renewal of interest in a crusade to the east. By this time the relentless Turkish advance was posing a threat to almost every Christian principality in south-east Europe. After their crossing of the Bosphorus in 1338, the Turks had established a bridgehead into Europe at Gallipoli, effectively encircling Constantinople and cutting the city off. During the 1360s and 1370s they embarked on a major push north into the Balkans. In 1361 they took Edirne and two years later Plovdiv, while in 1371 a victory at Maritsa gave them control of Bulgaria and Serbian Macedonia. They completed the conquest of Orthodox Serbia by eliminating the Serbian army at the battle of Kosovo in 1389. By 1394 they had largely taken over the Greek Peloponnese, reducing the Christian principalities there to a state of vassaldom.

The Turkish advance into Europe made Western leaders more receptive to the plans for a crusade put forward in the 1390s by the propagandist Philippe de Mézières. De Mézières, former chancellor of Cyprus and childhood tutor of Charles VI, conceived an ambitious, if visionary, scheme whereby, after peace was made between England and France, a grand *passagium* to the east would be organised under a new crusading fraternity, the Order of the Passion.[24] In the early 1390s de Mézières sent two of his 'evangelists', as he called them, on tours of the European courts to enlist recruits for the order and to generate support for a new crusade. Some eighty knights in all joined the order, among them in England John of Gaunt, Thomas of Woodstock and Edmund of Langley, the king's uncles; John Holand, his half-brother; and the earls of Rutland and Northumberland.[25] De Mézières went on to draw up rules for the order and even designed robes for its member knights. The mood at the English and French courts was broadly supportive of his initiatives, encouraging him in 1395 to address a letter to Richard II himself urging support for his schemes.[26] It is possible that the Wilton Diptych, the most elegant expression of the court art of the period, had a crusading context in that the iconography of the cross and the symbols of the Passion are reminiscent of those in the manuscripts of de Mézières' letter. When, early in 1393, a small Anglo-French force was sent to fight in Hungary, it seemed that the scene was set for a major new *passagium* to follow.

This larger expedition, so long in the making, finally gathered in 1396.

It was a force of very different complexion from the one which de Mézières had originally anticipated. He had envisaged a large multinational force in which the knighthood of France, England and other principalities would all be represented. The force as eventually assembled at Buda was almost entirely Franco-Burgundian in composition. It nonetheless represented a body of some size, numbering perhaps some 10,000 men. In the second week of September the crusaders advanced to Nicopolis in Bulgaria, where they were joined by Venetian and Genoese shipping and by a contingent of Hospitallers. Sultan Bayazid, who was besieging Constantinople, broke off his operations to meet them. In the resulting hotly fought battle the Turks crushed their opponents, who grossly underestimated the strength of the Sultan's heavy cavalry. The dream of expelling the Turks from Europe was over and the Balkans lay open to the sultan's advance.

One other theatre was to prove attractive to would-be crusaders, and this was the Baltic front. Here the Teutonic Knights, combating the pagan Lithuanians, welcomed adventurers from the west, attracting them with lures of feasting, hunting and military action. Campaigns were usually conducted in winter, when the rivers were frozen and thus passable, and took the form of mounted raids known as *reises*. Foreign knights would arrive, campaign and be feasted and feted all in a matter of months, before returning home to honour and acclaim. Many left witness to their presence in the form of armorials in the windows of Prussian castles and churches.

It is clear from the evidence of the Scrope–Grosvenor hearings that more than a few English knights made their way to the Baltic in the late fourteenth century. Members of the Scrope family were particularly active. William Scrope of Bolton and his cousins William, Geoffrey, Stephen and Henry, of the Masham branch, all recalled with pride their service in the Baltic. Various retainers or supporters of the Scropes regaled the judges with vivid memories of the region when giving evidence. Sir Thomas FitzHenry described how he saw young Geoffrey Scrope being buried in Prussia in the family's heraldic insignia. John Rither, an esquire who attended Sir Geoffrey's funeral, recalled seeing the arms of Scrope in a window in a church at Königsberg. In later cases in the Court of Chivalry further evidence was afforded of English involvement in the Baltic. In the case of Lovell v. Morley in the early fifteenth century William Grey, parson of Reydon, recalled how Sir Robert Morley's heart had been brought back for burial there, his body having been interred in Prussia.

Perhaps the most vivid insight into English crusading in the Baltic, however, is afforded by Henry of Derby's well-documented expedition to Prussia in 1390–1.[27] Henry embarked on his venture with some 300 men, about ten of them knights, the rest esquires and hangers-on. They made their way by sea to the Hanse port of Danzig, where they stayed for a few days in the house of the 'Lord de Burser', possibly the English lord John Bourchier. Here Henry was told that the marshal of the Teutonic Knights, Engellard Rabe, had already begun his *reise*, and Henry made ready to join him. Leaving Danzig on 14 August, he and his men made their way east through thick forest to Ragnit, on the far side of the Nieman, where they linked up with Rabe. The object of the campaign was to pursue the Lithuanians, who were mobilising with a strong force further east. Rabe decided to launch an immediate attack and, taking the enemy by surprise, inflicted a heavy defeat, capturing the Lithuanian commander and three of his dukes. After resting for a few days, they went on to attack the hilltop city of Vilnius, the Lithuanian capital, burning its outer suburbs. The army then split up, and Henry and his men returned to Königsberg. Henry spent the winter there and engaged in tourneying, hunting and feasting. His hosts honoured him with gifts of horses and hawks, deer, bears, a wild bull and apparently even an elk. Henry began his long journey home on 9 February 1391. He spent a few more weeks at Danzig, making a pilgrimage around the city's churches and enjoying the Easter festivities. Then on 31 March he embarked for England and arrived at Hull, after further stops, late the next month.

Henry of Derby's expedition to Prussia cost something in the order of £4,400, equivalent to some three times his annual income. The greater part of this sum was provided by his father, John of Gaunt, from the money paid to him by the Castilians after the surrender of his claim to their throne. Only a lord of Gaunt's ample means could afford to bankroll an expedition on this scale. From the perspective of the interests of the house of Lancaster, however, the money was well spent. Gaunt almost certainly had in mind promoting his son's prospects as a possible successor to the childless Richard II. A noteworthy feature of Derby's conduct of the expedition was his concern to keep opinion back home informed of his activities by regular despatch of newsletters.[28] The signs are that he was deliberately seeking to create a chivalric image for himself in the mould of the Lionheart two centuries earlier. If crusading formed part of the normal chivalric experience of an active fourteenth-century knight, it was not without a political dimension when undertaken by a junior member of the royal house.

Later in life, Henry of Derby – Henry IV, as he was to become – was to look back nostalgically on his time in Prussia. In 1407, in conversation with a German envoy, he was to recall his 'gadling days', as he called them, when alongside the marshal of the Teutonic Knights he and his men had spent four weeks trying to take Vilnius, fighting till their powder ran dry. Henry affirmed that he would be ready the next summer to undertake another expedition, for he was a 'child of Spruce', and there was no land beyond the sea in which he would rather serve.[29]

For all Henry's enthusiasm, by the early fifteenth century the days of crusading as an enterprise central to the experience of the English knightly class were passing. One by one, the main crusading theatres were closed off. In south-east Europe the prospects of a crusade were abruptly ended by the terrible defeat at Nicopolis, while in the Baltic expeditions were halted by the Lithuanians' triumph over the Teutonic Knights at Tannenburg in 1410. At the same time, within western Europe the social and institutional structures which had supported crusading and which had helped convert personal enthusiasm into military enterprise had begun to change. Crusading had always depended on a combination of international cooperation and acceptance of papal leadership. In the late fourteenth century securing these conditions was becoming ever more problematic. Confidence in the papacy was undermined first by its long residence at Avignon and then by the schism between two obediences, while international cooperation was rendered impossible by the long war between England and France. In England itself a further difficulty was posed by the growing belief that public taxation, so essential to pay for a crusade, could only be sanctioned for national, not international, war. Henry V may have nurtured the ambition on his deathbed of leading a joint Anglo-French force to liberate Jerusalem; the reality was that the war which he had unleashed in France and the means by which he had chosen to finance it rendered such an ideal unattainable. Warfare in the late Middle Ages took the form almost exclusively of national, not international, action.

It remains the case, however, that for some two centuries or more the English knightly class had been touched to some degree by the appeal of crusading. English engagement with the movement had never been as close or as intense as that of the French knightly class. The English had come relatively late to crusading. They had played little part in the First and Second Crusades, and their subsequent involvement owed much to the example and inspiration of the Lionheart. Yet for the two centuries from the 1190s crusading was to figure prominently in the collective experience of English knighthood. The majority of militarily active English knights would have acknowledged the importance of crusading in defining the Christian identity of knighthood, even if in most cases they were prevented by circumstances from going on crusade in person.

Beneath the smooth continuities of English crusading, however, significant shifts can be detected in the balance of motives which led knights to dedicate themselves to the enterprise. In the late twelfth and thirteenth centuries those who took the cross were motivated by two factors above all: commitment to a holy war in the quest for personal salvation and the knightly quest for adventure. A letter which William de Ferrars sent back to England in 1219 from the Fifth Crusade shows the characteristic mixing of the twin aspects: William expressed concern for the interests of his tenants and estates in England, while relating in visionary terms how God had brought his men success against the Muslims because 'the most High, who does not desert those trusting in Him, has worked for us miraculously and mercifully'.[30] William, while mindful of both family and territorial commitments, was yet articulating a sense of being engaged in a divinely ordained mission. Some two centuries later, when the goal of recovering Jerusalem had ceased to be realistic, this passionate sense of involvement in a spiritually satisfying cause was no longer so evident. Of greater importance to those tempted by crusading were such worldly considerations as the quest for honour and an appetite for the exotic. On those relatively rare occasions when crusading was singled out for mention on tomb epitaphs, it was chiefly to affirm the honour and prowess of the commemorated. When in 1468 at Drayton Beauchamp in Buckinghamshire Sir John Cheyne was said to have combated the

Turks and visited the Holy Sepulchre, it was in the context of a
lengthy epitaph which celebrated his extreme longevity, his slaying
of a giant, and the size and splendour of his household.[31] When, forty
years later on an epitaph in St Mary's, Swansea (c. 1510), Sir Hugh
Johnys was recorded as having fought under the Byzantine emperor
against the Turks and having received the honour of knighthood at
Jerusalem, it was again in the context of a lengthy tribute which
sought to honour and dignify him – in his case, by invoking his service
in France under the dukes of Norfolk and Somerset, to associate him
with men of superior status to himself.[32] By the end of the Middle
Ages it was sufficiently rare for a knight to participate in a crusade
for the fact to be singled out for mention in an epitaph. The context
of such a reference, however, was principally chivalric and honorific.
Crusading had become absorbed into the more general chivalric
tradition. Spiritual fervour had been displaced by the indulgent
enjoyment of one's youthful 'gadling days'.

Chivalry and Fortification

In *King Henry IV, Part II* Shakespeare dismissively refers to Warkworth Castle, the earl of Northumberland's northern stronghold, as 'that worm-eaten hold of ragged stone'. Worm-eaten and ragged may be the way a late sixteenth-century dramatist pictured a great medieval Border fortress; as descriptions of Warkworth in its heyday, however, the terms are seriously misleading. Northumberland's castle was as much a stately home as a fortress, its state-of-the-art keep laid out on a Greek cross plan containing apartments which combined the latest in residential comfort with architectural splendour of a high order.

The contrast between the Warkworth of Shakespeare's imagining and the real castle illustrates the gap which opened in the sixteenth century between the popular image of the medieval castle and what these structures had actually been like. To writers of the High Renaissance, medieval castles were little more than grim redoubts from which a defiant baron could keep royal authority at bay. This was a view which bordered on caricature. In reality, the castle was a complex structure which performed a whole variety of functions. In one sense it was a strongpoint – a garrison building and a place of last resort; in another, it was a social and administrative centre and a lordly residence; and in another again, a structure with the symbolic functions of attesting to magnate power and affirming the supremacy of the chivalric estate. Away from the dangerous border areas, the walls of English castles were hardly ever subjected to the assaults of enemy siege engines.

The Origins of English Castles

The type of fortification we call the castle was introduced into England by the Normans after 1066. It was essentially the private fortified residence of a lord, and as such it differed from the fortifications of the late Roman period, which were either communal, as in the case of city walls, or largely military, as with the army forts on Hadrian's Wall. The castle as a residential fortress was a product of the feudal Middle Ages.

The castle, in its developed form, had its origins in France in the late tenth and early eleventh centuries. The earliest such structures were found in the feudal states of Maine, Normandy and Anjou, which were then in process of formation. At Mayenne in north-west Maine, hidden inside the structures of a thirteenth-century fortress, are the remains of a castle-like tower house with attached hall – all masonry built. These remains have been dated to the first half of the tenth century and may well constitute the earliest recognisable extant castle buildings. At Loches, in Anjou, there survives the earliest fully formed example of a great tower, or *donjon*, incorporating hall, chamber and chapel, apparently dating from the second quarter of the eleventh century. The tower is over a hundred feet tall and is built of high-quality masonry with half-shafts on pilasters articulating the exterior.[1] At Langeais, just to the north-west of Loches, is a broader but squatter *donjon*, again datable to the second quarter of the eleventh century, and apparently built by Count Fulk of Anjou.[2] All these buildings are examples of embryonic castles bearing a high degree of similarity to the structures built later in England. Fortified dwellings with a somewhat looser resemblance to the later castle are found more widely across central and southern France. Those who raised them included bishops and other senior ecclesiastics as well as lay magnates. By the end of the eleventh century across France there was a sliding scale of fortifications, ranging from the more fully formed fortresses like Loches to simpler types with more of the character of manor houses. The castle was not a structure set sharply apart from other high-status dwellings; it was of broadly similar character, but more strongly defended.

The fortification of dwellings in the early Middle Ages seems to have arisen as a result of a number of factors. Most obviously, it was a response to the growing disorder and insecurity in France between the late ninth and eleventh centuries. As Charlemagne's empire broke up, and the ability of his successors as king-emperors to protect their vassals weakened, so those who had lived in the king's peace began to take their own measures to safeguard themselves and their property. One very practical option to which many of them resorted was the fortification of dwelling houses previously unfortified. Undefended high-status hall houses were now strengthened by the addition of *donjons*. In most European medieval and pre-modern societies the construction of fortifications was connected in some way to the spread of disorder.

At the same time there were broader social changes to which the building of castles was related. In the tenth and eleventh centuries there was a major shift in the balance of wealth and power in western Europe. As the old Carolingian political structures collapsed, so a new political order came into existence in which public authority was usurped by local strongmen, who established new units of rulership centring on their own persons. The emergence of the castle can be seen against the background of this intense social and political upheaval. The process of fortification was more than a simple response to the spread of violence and disorder; it was a means by which local strongmen gave architectural expression to their sense of position in the new hierarchy. It is no coincidence that it was around this time that the image of the three orders was taking hold. As Adalbero of Laon expressed it in about 1026, society was made up of three groups: those who prayed; those who fought; and those who laboured.[3] What appealed to knights about this conceptualisation was the legitimacy that it gave to their social role by associating them with a divinely ordained task, that of fighting. The castles which the knights created out of their previously unfortified dwellings can be seen as an expression of their sense of vocation and of the values of their order. The emergence of the castle formed part and parcel of the creation of the new chivalric order more generally.

On their arrival in England the Normans embarked on the construction of castles very similar to those they had known back in Normandy. In the Bayeux Tapestry they are shown throwing up a simple timber and earthwork structure at Hastings before their advance into Sussex. In the aftermath of victory, Duke William raised castles at London, Pevensey, Wallingford and other strategic points in the south-east. These new structures made a vivid impression on contemporaries. Anglo-Norman chroniclers suggest that nothing like them had ever before been seen in England. Orderic Vitalis said that it was because the English did not have castles that the Normans were able to take over the country so easily – there were no physical strongpoints to block their path.[4]

Even if castles in the Norman sense were a novelty, it is nonetheless clear that fortified dwellings of a more modest sort had existed in pre-Conquest England. According to an early eleventh-century legal text, 'Of People's Ranks and Laws', a man could be regarded as thegn-worthy (lordly) if he possessed five hides of land and resided in a house with a chapel, a kitchen, a bell-house and a *burhgeat* or defended gatehouse. A house of this lightly defended sort probably had little to distinguish it from one of the more modestly conceived castles of eleventh-century Normandy. Only a small number of these *burh* sites have been excavated. Those which have been examined in detail – at Goltho in Lincolnshire and Sulgrave in Northamptonshire – consisted in each case of a wooden hall and outbuildings, the two surrounded by a ditched and fenced enclosure of the ringwork kind. On the Sulgrave site there are masonry remains which may have been the foundations and lower stages of an entrance tower. The burhgeat, like the castle, gave its owner some of the trappings of elite status. It has been suggested that the gate tower served a semi-ceremonial purpose as the setting for public appearances by the lord.[5] Whether or not this was so, both castles and *burhgeats* belonged to a type of residence clearly distinguishable from the modest wooden dwellings of the churls and other free folk. What marked off the later castle from the *burhgeat*, and what led to a transformation of upper-class architecture in England, was the castle's possession of two features which the *burhgeat* lacked – the *donjon* and the motte, the latter the great mound of earth on which the *donjon* was raised. It was these two features above all which gave the new Norman castle a more menacing aspect than its English counterpart.

What were the functions of the new Norman castles? It is helpful to see these structures more as symbols of power and authority than as physical tools of an alien occupation. Once the surge of English rebellions of 1067–71 was over, there was little internal opposition to the Normans. Such rebellions against the king-duke as there were had their origins within the Norman elite. Thus the Conquest had the character essentially of a change of management, of the replacement of one ruling group by another, rather than of an act of ethnic suppression. The way in which the Normans chose to demonstrate their ascendancy in England was the way so often adopted over the centuries by incoming conquerors – by building, and building on a massive scale. Alongside the castles, they raised great new cathedrals, abbeys and parish churches, modelled on the fashionable new styles of Normandy. At Durham, the castle and the cathedral were placed together within a single enclosing wall, dominating a narrow peninsula within a bend of the River Wear. At Norwich the mighty *donjon*, also near a cathedral, was covered externally by an elaborate system of arcading which served no other purpose than to identify it as the king's new headquarters for East Anglia. In Norman England castles and cathedrals together were made the vehicles of an ambitious architectural imperialism, the means by which the new elite could show off its political and territorial mastery.

Many of the new castles were sited in places where they would command immediate attention. It can hardly be coincidental that, of the thirty-six castles known to have been built by William the Conqueror, no fewer than twenty-four were raised in or near urban centres. The Conqueror wanted to impress the Norman presence forcefully on the main social and economic centres of England. Sometimes positions were found for castles on the sites of existing high-status structures to perpetuate the idea of the exercise of some kind of lordly authority. At Stamford in Lincolnshire the Norman castle overlay the double-ditched enclosure of the residence of a pre-Conquest lord of the town. In other urban centres castles were placed in the corner of existing wall defences, so as to take advantage of extant fortifications and to command attention from a distance. This was the case at London, Leicester, Gloucester, Winchester and Wareham. In whatever positions they were built, castles were constructed on such a scale as to dominate the towns in which they were placed. At Norwich the mighty *donjon* is a brooding presence in the town even today, towering over the market place at its feet.

As the process of settler colonisation spread across England in the years after the Conquest, so the building of castles – usually baronial castles – was undertaken as much in open country as in the towns. The distribution of castles between one part of the country and another was for the most part determined by tenurial geography. Within particular localities or fiefdoms, considerations of relationship to the landscape appear to have been a major factor.[6] A number of early castles were built in dominant positions on the edge of natural promontories. At Beaumont Chase in Rutland, Birdsall in Yorkshire, Bincknoll and Castle Combe in Wiltshire the castles were all set high up and silhouetted so as to be visible for miles around. In low-lying Berkshire the king's palace at Old Windsor was transferred to the rocky promontory of New Windsor, to take advantage of a commanding position with wide views over the Thames valley. Other castles built by the Normans took advantage of hilltop positions previously occupied by the earthworks of Iron Age forts. The most famous of these is Old Sarum in Wiltshire, where the castle and the cathedral were placed together, as at Durham, until the abandonment of the city in the thirteenth century. In Cheshire the dramatically sited castle of Beeston is another which occupies a former hill fort. Beeston was built to serve the administrative needs of the Blundeville estates, but was raised high on its rocky eminence for largely scenic purposes. A number of other castles were sited at strategically important points on communications networks. In these cases it is again noticeable that the positions chosen had the attraction of drama as well as practicality. Skipton, for example, was placed in a key position at the head of the Ribble valley, with commanding views over the old Roman road through the Aire gap, which connected the two blocks of the Clifford family lands. The great border fortress of Norham occupied a dramatic position at an ancient fording point across the River Tweed into Scotland.

The location of castles was also influenced by a policy of what may be termed cultural appropriation. The Normans raised some of their most substantial strongholds on sites the antiquity of which lent legitimacy to their own exercise of power. The best-known example is provided by Colchester, where the great *donjon* was raised directly on the podium of a former Roman temple dedicated to the emperor/god Claudius. The decision to build a castle of such ambition on this site, which was entirely lacking in strategic significance, can only be understood in terms of the Normans' quest for cultural and historical legitimacy. Confirmation of such an idea is found in the otherwise inexplicable retention near the castle of a pre-Conquest chapel dedicated to St Helena, mother of the Emperor Constantine and associated with a creation myth linking Colchester to the Iron

Age king Cunobelin. At Colchester the Normans were seeking to link themselves with Roman antiquity and Britain's ancient mythic past. The Normans' interest in establishing links with Roman antiquity is also evident elsewhere. It is found even in the heart of London, where their *donjon* – the famous White Tower – was placed inside a ringwork formed in the angle of the old Roman city wall. The entrance to the *donjon* itself took the form of a big ashlar-built vestibule with wide steps which evoked the entrances to buildings of antiquity. For the Normans, castles often served functions which were symbolic as well as narrowly practical.

Castles, Symbolism and Lordship

Castles were raised in England in very considerable numbers right through the Middle Ages. It is difficult to estimate with any accuracy just how many there were because not all castle sites have been identified. Moreover, it has to be remembered that not all castles were active at the same time: just as new ones were being built, so old ones were going out of use. Nonetheless, a few speculations on numbers can be offered.[7]

On the evidence of earthworks and surviving fabrics, it is likely that there were around 1,000 castles in England and Wales in the period 1066–1200. This number probably rose to a peak of nearer 1,200 in the civil war of King Stephen's reign (1135–54). It is then likely to have declined in the reign of Stephen's successor Henry II, levelling out at perhaps 500 or below by about 1180–1220. In the late Middle Ages there are signs that the number rose again as socially ambitious proprietors sought licences from the king to crenellate their houses, so as to give them a castle-like appearance. Overall in England and Wales in the late Middle Ages there are likely to have been as many as 1,500 castles or castle-like properties. In a country which had no more than 200 baronies this suggests that castle-building was a frenetic activity undertaken by proprietors well below baronial standing.

As they spread across the countryside, castles – at least those of the richer landowners – became larger, grander and more elaborate. By the early twelfth century the modest wooden structures of the post-Conquest period were being rebuilt in stone, in many cases with big *donjons*, while the richer lords added square or semicircular flanking towers to the exposed perimeter walls of outer baileys. In the early thirteenth century great double-towered gatehouses were built, for example at Dover, rivalling the *donjons* in size. The expenditure lavished on rebuilding was often enormous, eating deep into castle-owners' wealth. It is possible to get some idea of the sums spent on the construction and repair of royal castles from the entries in the account rolls of the exchequer. Between 1154 and 1216 Henry II, Richard and John spent no less than £46,000 on castle-building, a sum disbursed across around 130 properties. Some £8,000 was spent at Dover, £4,000 at the Tower of London, £3,000 at Scarborough, £1,800 at Windsor and some £1,400 at Orford.[8] A century later the exchequer disbursed approximately £80,000 on the massive castle-building programme inaugurated by Edward I in north Wales.[9] Figures for the construction on improvement of castles by private lords are harder to come by, because few private accounts have come down to us. However, the unusually complete accounts of William, Lord Hastings record expenditure of as much as £1,088 on the construction of Kirby Muxloe Castle in Leicestershire by the time of the owner's death in 1483. According to William Worcester, the Norfolk knight Sir John Fastolf spent no less than £6,000 over thirty years on the building of Caister Castle, near Great Yarmouth. In the sixteenth century John Leland was to record the tradition that Richard, Lord Scrope spent £12,000 on the building of Bolton in Yorkshire in the 1370s.[10]

What caused landowners to lavish such enormous sums on the building and rebuilding of castles? When the activity was at its peak in the twelfth century, it was in part a response to insecurity. For well over a decade during Stephen's reign the country was torn apart by a civil war which turned largely on competition for control of the countryside. While order was restored under Henry II, Stephen's successor, there was to be further internal strife in the 1170s, when a substantial part of the baronage rebelled, and in the 1190s, when the future King John fomented trouble during Richard's absence abroad. The construction of castles can be seen in part as a reactive strategy by the baronage, by which, in their quest for security, they equipped themselves with strongpoints from which to control the country and hold challengers at bay. In times of instability possession of a castle gave the lord who held it the assurance of personal security and the opportunity to await the outcome of events. William of Malmesbury, commenting on the tactics of the barons in Stephen's reign, wrote, 'Some of the castellans kept themselves in the safety of their fortresses, waiting to see how things would turn out.'[11] From a complementary perspective, the massive sums which kings were to spend on castles in the twelfth and thirteenth centuries can be seen as an attempt by the Crown to beat baronial castellans at their own game. The building of castles represented a way of reasserting royal power through a combination of bravura display and dominance of the landscape. In the 1180s Henry II constructed Orford in Suffolk as a response to the threat posed by the rebel Hugh Bigod's castle nearby at Framlingham.

On the borders of the kingdom the multiplication of castles was in part a response to insecurity of a different sort – the threat from neighbours with whom relations were often uneasy. In the twelfth and thirteenth centuries the more unstable of the two English frontiers was that with Wales. Castles were built by the English Marcher lords both as defensive strongpoints and springboards for further advance into Wales. In Herefordshire and Shropshire castles were particularly thick on the ground, with 93 in the former county and 112 in the latter. In the late thirteenth century, however, after the subjugation of Snowdonia, the main focus of border concern switched to the north, where the start of the Scottish war led to the militarisation of the Border country. New castles were built at strategic sites like coastal Dunstanburgh, while previously unfortified manorial residences, such as that at Aydon, were fortified for the first time. In the late Middle Ages Northumberland had the largest number of castles – 233 – of any English county. A notable feature of the architecture there was the keep-like pele tower, which owed some of its popularity to the gentry's need for protection against the Scots.

There can be little doubt that awareness of danger played a major role in the proliferation of castles along the frontiers of the kingdom, particularly in those periods when English weakness made the borders permeable to raiders from outside. In these violent zones castles were raised for strictly practical purposes: to provide defensive strongpoints and to pose a strategic challenge to invaders. Considerations of this sort, however, can hardly explain the proliferation of castles in the English heartland. It has been calculated that there were at different times twenty-eight castles in Wiltshire, thirty-one in Warwickshire, thirty-three in Essex and no fewer than thirty-five in unlikely Northamptonshire.[12] There was no conceivable practical need for so many castles in such safe inland counties. England was, by the standards of medieval Europe, a relatively peaceful country. Between Stephen's reign and the Wars of the Roses it saw only very brief periods of unrest. Its monarchy, highly centralised and served by a network of officers in the shires, was able to impose effective public order. So why were so many castles built when there was apparently no need?

It is important to recall that castles were complex multifaceted institutions which served a whole variety of purposes. If in some cases they were built to serve as defensive strongpoints, in others their construction was rooted more in such factors as local jockeying for position and the desire of particular owners for symbolic affirmation of status. This mixing of motives, both practical and symbolic, is as evident in the castle-building activities of kings as of their subjects. Consider, for example, Henry II's construction of the fortress at Dover, a project on which he was to be engaged for a decade at the end of his reign.[13] Dover was a site of unique importance, occupying a frontier position at the narrowest crossing point between England and France. It might be supposed that Henry would have wanted to construct the most advanced, technologically sophisticated fortress in such a position – something of the kind that Richard the Lionheart was to raise at Chateau Gaillard in Normandy. Yet the great *donjon* which is the centrepiece of Henry's work is actually a very old-fashioned structure, a square keep of the type inaugurated in England over a century before at the Tower of London and Colchester. A consciously dated design, it exhibits all the defensive weaknesses of its type, notably square corner turrets, which were vulnerable to mining.

Henry must have had other considerations in mind than the purely military for a fortress on which he was to spend as much as £8,000. A clue to his thinking is afforded by the magnificent entrance staircase, which is wrapped round the south and east sides of the *donjon*. This takes the visitor up no fewer than three flights of steps to the king's audience chamber at the top, passing en route two tiny chapels, the upper of which is exquisitely vaulted and was evidently intended for the king's use. The message to the visitor is clear: Dover is the overwhelmingly impressive castle of an overwhelmingly powerful king. It seems that the *donjon* was intended to look particularly spectacular when viewed from the outside: a notable feature of the exterior, entirely without functional justification, is the horizontal banding in pale-coloured stone, which stands out boldly against the dark Kent rag. The castle's purpose was almost certainly to provide a major statement of royal power in a county where that power had scarcely been represented physically at all. All the most important castles in Kent were seigneurial, more specifically ecclesiastical. In 1170 Thomas Becket, Henry's bête noire, had been murdered at Canterbury only ten miles away, and his canonisation three years later created an anti-royal cult. The canonisation called for a royal riposte, and that riposte was the building of Dover.

The heavy emphasis on the display of power so obvious at Dover is no less evident in the castles of the higher nobility. In the 1140s, in Stephen's reign, the wealthy magnate William d'Aubigny built a magnificent new castle at Castle Rising in Norfolk. D'Aubigny's father had been a close associate of Henry I and had risen high in his service, while d'Aubigny himself had married Henry's widow. It can hardly be a coincidence that the architectural model for Castle Rising was the mighty *donjon* which Rufus and Henry I had raised at the county town of Norwich nearby. Both buildings are of a low square type, and both show the same interest in external decorative stonework. D'Aubigny's design for Castle Rising was a study in imitative flattery, a deliberate attempt to draw attention to his status by associating himself with a dominant royal power.

Tower-building as a form of architectural self-assertion appears to have had a particular appeal to the 'new men' of the mid-twelfth century. Aubrey de Vere, one of the most prominent of Henry I's new men, built a tower of vertiginous proportions as the centrepiece of his castle at Castle Hedingham in Essex. The Hedingham tower was to be among the most skyscraper-like of all twelfth-century keeps. It stands a hundred feet high to the top of the turrets, not far off Rochester's record-breaking 113 feet. Aubrey had made his way up the political ladder as Henry I's court chamberlain, and it is suggested that he embarked on the *donjon* after his promotion to the earldom of Oxford by Matilda in 1142. It was his way of proclaiming in the grandest possible terms that he had arrived; that he was the main power in that part of England.

Tower-building was also to be a favoured architectural pastime of the newly arrived men of the later Middle Ages. In the years after 1400 the *donjon* was to enjoy a spectacular revival after many years of relative disuse. The revival owed much at the outset to Henry V's construction of a tower house at Sheen (now Richmond) in Surrey. The dissemination of the tower type, however, was to be largely the work of the self-made.[14] In the 1440s the wealthy royal treasurer Ralph, Lord Cromwell, ambitious to make his mark, built a brick *donjon* as the focal point of his remodelled Tattershall Castle in Lincolnshire. Thirty years later, when William, Lord Hastings, Edward IV's chamberlain, wanted likewise to make a mark, he too raised a huge tower, in his case at Ashby de la Zouch in Leicestershire. Earlier in the century another parvenu, Sir William ap Thomas, founder of the Herbert line, had proclaimed his arrival with an eye-catching *donjon* at Raglan in south Wales. The choice of a tower by this group of ambitious careerists seems deliberate. It was a dominant architectural feature which could be made a medium for the display of magnate power. In almost every age the idea of building upwards has exerted an appeal over those who have sought to impress, and the Middle Ages were no exception. The *donjon* provided lordly owners with a way of drawing attention to their social position by embodying it prominently and imposingly in stone. Inside, a tower did something more: it made possible the creation of hierarchical effects in the arrangement of apartments. Since the rooms of highest status were always reserved for the top, the owner could emphasise his superiority by making the visitor ascend lots of stairs to reach him.

If castle-building had particular appeal to the flashy and the self-assertive, it should not be supposed that it was entirely confined to such men. On the contrary: it was an activity spread widely across the ranks of the nobility and upper gentry. Indeed it was undertaken most extensively by those to whom it had most natural appeal – the chivalric class, those whose profession was fighting. Through its architectural vocabulary the castle made concrete the values of chivalric lordship. Its repertory of towers and battlements evoked the traditions of knighthood, the lifestyle of the great and the stories of Arthurian legend.

It is not surprising therefore that one of the most ambitious castles of the late Middle Ages was built by a family especially proud of its chivalric credentials, the Beauchamps of Warwick. Warwick was almost entirely remodelled by two successive earls of the Beauchamp line between the 1340s and 1390s. Earl Thomas I, who died in 1369, appears to have rebuilt the great suite of apartments on the river front, including the hall, chamber, antechamber and inner chamber with storage rooms beneath, while he and his son together were responsible for the show front on the eastern side facing the town.[15] This last structure is one of the most spectacular castle frontages in England. It comprises a powerful central gatehouse and barbican linked by curtain walls to lofty corner towers, the twelve-sided Guy's Tower towards the town and the trilobed Caesar's Tower towards the river. Each tower contains stacked apartments for visitors or retainers.

Architecturally, Warwick Castle provides affirmation in stone of the values and achievements of the Beauchamp family. The Beauchamps had succeeded to the earldom in 1268. In almost every generation they fulfilled the obligations of their order by providing military service to the crown. Earl William, the first of his line, served Edward I in Wales and Scotland and his son, Guy, who died in 1315, fought with Edward II in Scotland. Earl Thomas I was involved in almost all of Edward III's wars, while his son, Thomas II, who succeeded in 1369, fought in Edward's later campaigns and in the early campaigns of Richard II. If Warwick's architecture of chivalry was in part a paean of praise to the family's achievements, it was also influenced by the power of myth. Among their family ancestors the Beauchamps numbered the legendary Guy, whose heroic feats of arms and experiences on crusade were celebrated in thirteenth-century romance.[16] The two eastern towers of the castle, Guy's and Caesar's, evoked the memory of heroes with whose companionship in war a Beauchamp might have felt at ease.

Another castle which bears the clear imprint of chivalry is Bodiam, in Sussex. Bodiam was built in the 1380s by the swashbuckling knight Sir Edward Dallingridge. It is a castle of exceptional elegance and compactness, square in plan, and symmetrically laid out with projecting towers at the corners and on the sides, and gateways to the north and south. The impression of strength is reinforced by the broad lake-sized moat, which makes the castle look bigger than it actually is. In the licence to crenellate granted to him in 1385 Dallingridge pleaded the need to provide for the defence of the south coast against major French attacks. The warlike appearance of the castle, however, for all its plausibility, is deceptive. The windows are so low and large as to be forceable; the wall walkway is too narrow to be effective; the arrow slits have insufficient internal splaying to be usable; and the moat could easily be drained.[17] Bodiam, impressive in its external aspect, could never have withstood a serious assault.

The key to understanding Bodiam is to be found in the life and personality of its builder. Sir Edward Dallingridge was the self-appointed leader of the Sussex gentry, a vigorous man with a keenly felt sense of honour. At the time Bodiam was being built, he could already claim some twenty years' experience of service in arms. He had fought on French soil in 1359–60, 1373 and 1378, and in 1385 he was to accompany Richard II to Scotland.[18] As events were to show, he was a man for whom the chivalric code determined his way of life. In 1384, when he was embroiled in his dispute with John of Gaunt, he appealed before the justices at East Grinstead to the law of arms, throwing down his gauntlet to plead wager by battle.[19] Dallingridge belonged to the exotic world of chivalric gesture, and it is precisely this quality which is captured in his castle. The use of French-style machicolations over the gates, the placing of staircase turrets on the towers to make them look grander, the use of antique-looking tracery in the chapel window – all these add to the chivalric flavour of the castle. In 1375, when his father died, Dallingridge had inherited an unfashionable old manor house at the other end of the village of Bodiam. A decade later he replaced it with this entirely new castle on a virgin site, where chivalric splendour could be properly displayed. Bodiam, like Warwick, bore witness in stone to the chivalric values of its builder.

Another fourteenth-century castle which delights in the use of gesture is Cooling, in Kent. Cooling was built a few years earlier than Bodiam, by John, Lord Cobham, a courtier lord and Kent landowner who moved in circles which overlapped with Dallingridge's. Cooling is substantially bigger than Bodiam, reflecting Lord Cobham's higher standing. It consists of two courtyards, not one – an inner court with corner towers and a gateway, and an enormous outer court with an entrance gate on the south side by the road. Cooling was essentially a lordship seat and status symbol, a witness to its owner's ambition. Down by the Thames, it was much too low-lying to be of serious military value. Lord Cobham, however, justified its construction in terms of its contribution to national defence. In a gesture of pure theatre, on the tower of the outer gate he placed a fictive charter with four lines of boast:

> Knouwyth that beeth and schal be
> That I am mad in help of the cuntre
> In knowying of whyche thing
> Thys is charter and wytnessyng.

The hollowness of the boast was to be shown in 1554 when, on the one occasion that the castle was besieged, it surrendered in less than a day. In Kent in the fourteenth century serious coastal defence was represented by a very different castle, Edward III's Queenborough, on the Isle of Sheppey. Queenborough was tall and well armed, and directly overlooked the River Swale. Cooling was a castle-type structure of a more symbolic sort, essentially a witness to power and status. It is noticeable that the theatrical touch found on the outside gate was picked up within. To the right of the inner gate, facing the visitor, is a piece of decorative flushwork standing out boldly against the pale ragstone of the wall. Ostensibly, its purpose was to draw attention to the formal residential apartments within, but in reality it was more concerned with demonstrating the owner's status. Cooling, like Bodiam, was all about self-promotion and the affirmation of lordly standing.[20] If castle-building in the late Middle Ages was not entirely a matter of smoke and mirrors, neither was it necessarily all that it appeared to be.

Crenellations with Everything?

Once the role played by fantasy and artifice in castle-building is appreciated, then it becomes possible to rethink what actually constituted a castle. If we accept that battlements were more a form of decoration than a means of defence, then the way is open to a broader, more all-encompassing definition of the term. No longer need a castle be regarded solely as the fortress residence of a lord; it can potentially be any house or dwelling built in a castellated style. Fortified or semi-fortified manor houses, episcopal residences, even the fortifications which surrounded towns, can all be considered castles.

It was in these broader terms that people in the Middle Ages almost always thought of castles. The heavily battlemented structures we choose to call castles were referred to interchangeably by contemporaries as *castra, castella* or simply *donjons*.[21] What is striking is that these terms were used not only to describe castles in the strict sense, but other types of fortress residence. The terms *castrum* or *castellum* appear to have been quite loosely applied. *Castellum*, for example, was by no means exclusively identified with the form of fortified residence introduced by the Normans. It was instead used to describe defensive residences or enclosures more generally. Such broad usage was encouraged by the widespread employment of the Latin *castellum* in authoritative biblical and classical texts.[22] It was believed that castles of the high medieval type had existed in the antique world long before the Normans introduced them to England. From the earliest days of castle-building in England, they were associated with the communal fortified buildings put up by the imperial Romans. Reuse by the Normans of Roman sites and of materials from Roman forts encouraged the idea of continuity with the Roman *imperium*. In the medieval period the castle was thus understood as a reconstruction and reclamation of what was seen essentially as an antique architectural form.

Carrying as it did such wide cultural and political connotations, castellated architecture became an almost universal architectural vocabulary. It is thus unlikely that any clear distinction was drawn between castles strictly defined and other forms of castellated dwelling. The castellated house type stood on a sliding scale of fortification from the heavily fortified castle at one end, to ornamental hunting lodges, town walls, cathedral precincts and bishops' palaces at the other. The terms used by contemporaries to describe these different types of building showed little regard for architectural form. The words castle, hall, manor and so on were all used without apparent logic. Wardour Castle in Wiltshire was called a castle when it was actually more of a hunting lodge, and Cooling a 'mansion in a manor' when many would have thought of it as a castle.[23] Penshurst, in Kent, was referred to as a 'place' when it was halfway between a manor house and a palace.[24] Ightham manor, also in Kent, was called a mote when many other manor houses with moats were not so called. The distinction, such as it was, between a castle and a manor house or a mote was a distinction without a difference. The main reason why, in later centuries, so many of these dwellings came to be called castles was simply that their later owners wanted to raise their status by calling them such.

The fascination, however, of later generations with the capacity of castles to attest to status is appropriate, given that status is what castellated architecture was always about. As we have seen, its employment originated in the eleventh-century idea of society as divided into three divinely ordained estates. Once the knights had secured recognition as the fighting class, it was only natural that they should adopt the fortified residence as their dwelling type because it drew attention to the chivalric values of their class. By the mid-twelfth century people appear to have conceived of a fortified dwelling house as a mark of status much as they saw the employment of heraldic insignia on a shield in such terms. In an age which accepted the Platonic view of outer as a reflection of inner, castellation gave outward and visible approval to the role of the second estate as a chivalric class.

In medieval society it was generally the case that whenever new cultural forms were developed by the aristocracy, they were quickly taken up by the knights below them. In the case of castellated architecture, however, the process of dissemination was neither as rapid nor as straightforward as it usually was. The lesser knightly class does not appear to have immediately taken to the new architectural style of its superiors. The main reason appears to have been that, while towers and crenellations carried connotations of status, so too did another residential form closely associated with aristocracy – the hall. Throughout the early Middle Ages it had been the oak-raftered hall which had constituted the main forum for the display of aristocratic wealth and power. In the tenth century the author of *Beowulf* had hailed Hrothgar's timber hall as 'the greatest of houses'. In the 1090s, when William Rufus wanted to raise the status of his palace at Westminster, he equipped it with a magnificent new hall; he did not think of crenellating the long palace roofline. For those who sought a medium for high-status residential display, the hall was a perfectly acceptable model to set beside the battlemented castle.

Thus, for several centuries, when lesser knights and gentry wanted to upgrade their residences, they did so by building bigger and better halls, not by castellating their walls. A good example of a hall-type dwelling which remained unfortified despite later development is the manor house excavated at Penhallam in Cornwall, which belonged to the de Cardinham family. The initially fairly small chamber-block dwelling underwent several stages of enlargement in the twelfth and thirteenth centuries. First, in the late twelfth century a stone first-floor hall was added to an existing ringwork. Then, about half a century later, a larger stone hall and a series of other chambers were built, effectively turning the house into a courtyard dwelling.[25] At no point in this process did Penhallam acquire the airs and graces of a castle.

It seems to have been only from the late thirteenth century that towers and crenellations became primary indicators of nobility. Part of their attraction may have been the owner's need to obtain a royal licence to crenellate, itself a mark of status.[26] By the mid-fourteenth century crenellations had become virtually de rigueur on knightly dwellings. Their spread across the architectural range, however, in no way encroached on the hall's position as a sign of status: the hall was for long to retain its importance as the primary place where the lord displayed his greatness before visitors. Crenellations on parapets supplemented the message of the hall: they lent added status to a house, both enhancing its grandeur and strengthening its identification with chivalry. One of the earliest manorial-type dwellings to make use of the new castellated style was Stokesay in Shropshire. Stokesay was acquired in Edward I's reign by Laurence de Ludlow, a wealthy wool merchant who, after years in trade, craved the respectability of a country landowner. In the 1290s he rebuilt the house, providing it with a big new hall range terminated, at the south end, by a crenellated tower modelled on those of the castles in north Wales. The complex shape of the tower – an octagon combined with two dodecagons – lent it the character of Denbigh Castle gatehouse. The Stokesay south tower affords an unusually early example of the use of crenellations to embellish a gentry manor house; it also affords an excellent instance of the employment of visual tricks to dazzle and impress the visitor. Crenellated architecture of a more modest kind was employed around the same time on manor houses at Little Wenham in Suffolk and, slightly later, Markenfield in Yorkshire. In the early fourteenth century the rapid spread of the pele tower in Northumberland may have owed as much, or more, to gentry status-consciousness as it did to the need for defence against the Scots.[27]

The widespread adoption of crenellations across the architectural spectrum from the late thirteenth century led to a merging of the earlier distinction between the castle and other forms of elite residence. It was largely as a result of this process that the confusion of descriptive terminology arose. The spread of crenellations, however, did more than just make country dwellings look castle-like. It also led to a merging of the hitherto quite different building styles of town and country. Over time, a uniform architectural language came into existence which led to a growing similarity between the buildings constructed by the rural and urban elites. The crenellated style of the gentry residence rubbed off on to the public architecture of towns, becoming as much a badge of identity for urban communities as it had been for knights and esquires. Towns prided themselves on the magnificence of their crenellated walls and gateways. At Canterbury Henry Yevele built a gatehouse over the western entrance to the town which was indistinguishable from the gateways he had earlier built at Cooling and Saltwood castles. At York, London and elsewhere battlements figured on the stepped gables of civic guildhalls. In the circumstances, it is hardly surprising that crenellated walls and gates should have figured on the seals which urban officials used to authenticate formal documents. Crenellations were a mark of status, and burgesses saw in them a way of affirming the dignity of their towns and cities.[28]

A similar process of assimilation may be observed in the architectural styles of townsmen when they went to live in the countryside. The manor houses which these men built when they acquired rural estates consciously appropriated the architectural styles of the gentry. As we have seen, Laurence de Ludlow's manor house at Stokesay aped the towered and crenellated dwellings of the aristocracy – in the case of its tower, the style of the Edwardian castles in Wales. Half a century later, the manor house built by wealthy Londoner Sir John Pulteney at Penshurst had as its centrepiece a hall the equal of any baron's in scale. Significantly, Pulteney was the first London merchant to receive the honour of knighthood. The process of assimilation between town and country was to go on to the very eve of the First World War. In the 1890s the Newcastle armaments manufacturer Sir William Armstrong rebuilt the ruined castle at Bamburgh on the Northumberland coast as a baronial stronghold, massive and rugged as befitted its setting. In the early 1900s Julius Drewe, a London tea trader, employed Lutyens to build Castle Drogo, near Drewsteignton in Devon, as a Norman castle, evoking an imagined history linking the Drewe family to the site. These self-made men were doing something not so very different from what the nouveau riche of the Middle Ages had done. They were fitting themselves out in the architectural trappings and lifestyle of the gentry to set the seal on their transition from town to country. For them, as for their predecessors, castle-building was effectively a branch of performance art. Being a country gentleman involved playing the part of the country gentleman.

Castles and Romance

One of the achievements of recent research on castle architecture has been to highlight the romantic possibilities of the castle. While there has long been an appreciation that castles served such non-military functions as the affirmation of status, it is only as a result of recent interest in their cultural context that it has become possible to see how these buildings filled more imaginative roles. It is now suggested that castles could have been objects of delight to visitors, focal points in ornamental landscapes and witnesses to family history and legend. To the extent that such meanings added to the symbolic value of the castle, it could be said that their effect was further to enhance the owner's status.

The point may be illustrated by reference to the twelfth-century castle of the d'Aubignys at Castle Rising in Norfolk.[29] Today, as we have seen, the most significant feature of this fortress is the great *donjon* built in the 1140s and modelled on that at Norwich. Around the keep, however, are mighty earthworks which hint at an extensive reworking of the landscape to create an appropriate setting for the building. It is highly significant in this connection that the *donjon* was not built on the highest point of the locality, as it would have been had defence been the uppermost consideration. Rather, it is placed low down, so that it would catch the eye of visitors as they approached over the crest of the nearby hill. The keep was only one element, admittedly the most important, in a landscape rich in seigneurial imagery. The others included a deer park, a chase and rabbit warren, a planned town and a dovecote. The deer park was the feature most closely related to the castle, occupying the high ground immediately to its south, and appears to have been conceived principally as a leisure amenity for the entertainment of high-status visitors. Large-scale hunting was undertaken in a separate area, the chase, which lay further to the south-west and took the form of a palisaded landscape with bounds stretching some sixteen miles. In roughly this same area was the rabbit warren, like the chase and deer park a mark of aristocratic status because rabbits were highly prized.

To the north of the site lay the town of Castle Rising, a planned settlement of the same date as the castle and probably integrated into the main visitor route. Outside the town lay a moated enclosure known as the Isle, situated alongside a channel cut from the River Babingley. This was probably an ornamental feature enjoyed by visitors as they took in the view of the castle. Gardens of this sort were incorporated in a number of twelfth-century castle grounds. It has recently been shown there was a fine one at Richmond Castle immediately below Scolland's Hall, the main domestic building in the fortified enclosure. Lord and ladies would gaze down at it from a projecting gallery at the end of the hall.[30]

To their lordly owners, castles were objects of pride just as much as cathedrals and abbeys were to their officiating clergy. Owners delighted in showing off their properties to distinguished guests or retainers. In 1247, when he was expecting a French visitor to Dover, Henry III instructed the constable, Bertram de Criol, to show the Frenchman round the castle eloquently (*faceto modo*), so that its nobility (*nobilitas*) should be fully apparent to him, and he should be aware of no defects in it.[31] The nobility of a castle, to contemporaries, was a function of such factors as its size, its physical setting and its sheer beauty. Beauty – *pulchra fortitudo* – was a quality especially evoked in contemporary descriptions of castles. In medieval aesthetic writing it was closely associated with the display of light and colour. Medieval castle interiors were invariably brightly decorated, their walls whitewashed, and details such as mouldings and bosses picked out in golds, reds and blues. While disappointingly little of this decoration has come down to us, the records of such work enrolled in the royal accounts give an idea of its richness. In the hall of Winchester Castle in 1233 Henry III had the capitals and bosses gilded, the side walls whitened and lined, and a big wheel of fortune painted in the east gable.[32] In the case of some of the grander castles, the use of colour extended to their external walls. At Llantilio in Monmouthshire it was its whitewashed outer walls which brought about a change of name to White Castle.[33] It is well known that it was the whitewashed exterior of the great keep of the Tower of London which gave the White Tower its name.

In the twelfth century the German poet Hartmann von Aue had spoken of the 'courtliness' of castles, their essential character as aristo-cratic living spaces. He was singling out a quality not so very different from the 'nobility' of which Henry III had spoken. Something of the character of the courtly castle is captured in the illustrations of the duke of Berry's castles in France in the *Très Riches Heures*. In the painting of Lusignan, for example, the brilliant white walls, the turreted skyline, the heavy machicolations, the fluttering pennons and the neat parkland setting all combine to imbue the castle with romance. Around 1400 the chronicler of chivalry Jean Froissart, ever alert to aesthetics, was to describe another of the duke's castles, Mehun-sur-Yevre, as 'the most beautiful house in the world'.[34] In England the Gawain poet had a castle of this courtly kind in mind when he penned his description of Bertilak's castle:

> The comeliest castle that ever a knight owned,
> It was pitched on a plain, with a park all around,
> Impregnably palisaded with pointed stakes . . .
> The wall went into the water wonderfully deep,
> And then to a huge height upwards it reared
> In hard hewn stone, up to the cornice;
> Built under the battlements in the best style, courses jutted
> And turrets protruded between, constructed
> With loopholes in plenty with locking shutters.
> No better barbican had ever been beheld by that knight.
> And inside he could see a splendid hall
> With towers and turrets on top, all tipped with crenellations . . .
> Many chalk-white chimneys the chevalier saw
> On the tops of towers twinkling whitely,
> So many painted pinnacles sprinkled everywhere.[35]

Medieval castles belonged to the world of high chivalric romance. They inspired wonder, awe and admiration. If their function was partly defensive, they also had a symbolic value, demonstrating the owner's standing and the fame and antiquity of his family. Castles could be bearers of history and legend. Where there was an Arthurian link to be exploited, then it was. In the mid-thirteenth century Richard, earl of Cornwall, Henry III's brother, acquired the site of Tintagel, building a clifftop castle there for no better reason than to associate himself with the world of Arthurian legend. If castles brought their owners defensive strength, they also brought much more: they were the epitome of the quintessential medieval talent for mixing form and beauty, romance and reality, power and symbolism. Castles were the architectural face of chivalry.

14

Chivalry and Women

According to the hostess in the fourteenth-century English poem *Sir Gawain and the Green Knight*, 'the choicest thing in chivalry' is knights doing deeds for their ladies.[1] Chivalry in the hostess's sense ritually elevated women, investing them with power over their menfolk and giving them the means to play games with suitors for their favour. At the same time, however, in a different way chivalry left women in an ambivalent position, reducing them to mere objects of male desire and making them appendages of men in a male-dominated society. Chivalry was a novelty in medieval aristocratic culture in that it provided a structuring framework for relations between the sexes. While principally an ethic conceptualising the values of knighthood, it also established new sexual mores. It laid emphasis on *eros* (love) in place of the platonic and intellectual *agape* of old. The relationship between chivalry and gender as mediated to us in the romance literature of the Middle Ages was one fraught with ambiguity.

Sexuality and Courtly Love

What we recognise today as courtly love was essentially the anguished longing of the male lover which was so powerfully explored by the lyric poets of the twelfth century. The mood of this new lyric poetry could hardly have been more different from the mood of the love poetry written in classical antiquity. The Greeks and more especially the Romans had treated love as a sickness, a fever, a source of pain. Love was not idealised, much less invested with the semi-religious aura to be found in the literature of the Middle Ages; at times it was treated as a tragic madness. The god of love was a jealous and despotic god, a deity who teased and tormented those in his thrall. The tender quality of twelfth-century poetry contrasted sharply with the often quizzical character of the work of antiquity. The mood of the twelfth century contrasted equally strongly with the earlier treatment of human relationships found in the epics and *chansons de geste*. The epics had chiefly celebrated manly values: they told of desperate struggles between men and monsters, of heroes locked in bitter conflict with the forces of darkness. While the *chansons* analysed male bonding, they said little or nothing about relations between the sexes. There was no place in them for affairs of the heart. Heroes like Roland spoke of women only in the crude vocabulary of the war camp. Women figured in a purely incidental capacity: they were present as devoted wives, loyal companions, helpers in times of need. In no poetic work were they central to the unfolding drama.

In the writings of the twelfth-century troubadours and lyric poets we find the first stirrings of a sensuous new mood. Love and the amorous desires of the heart were for the first time treated as central to the poetic vision. The humble knight of the lyrics is shown engaged in a quest, ostensibly a quest for adventure but actually one for the affections of a lady. He undertakes his quest alone, even though typically a member of a brotherhood, because love is an inward thing united only to its unique object. The story of the quest is ritualised. The lady who is the object of the knight's love is portrayed as cold, heartless, unfeeling and distant, indifferent to his anguish. In an inversion of the normal gender relationship, she is shown in a superior position, empowered to grant her favours or to withhold them as she sees fit. The knight, through displays of prowess, strives to prove himself worthy of the lady and to persuade her to accede to his desires. His sufferings are agonising and prolonged. The attainment of his purpose, the union of his heart with its desired object, is always just one stage further off. Marriage may or may not be achieved. Sexuality, always hinted at, is usually sublimated.

The new mood of eroticism found its earliest expression in the works of the troubadours of southern France in the early 1100s. Some of the troubadours were clerks well versed in the writings of classical antiquity, particularly the poetry of Ovid and Virgil. Others, however, were lettered lay aristocrats. One such aristocrat was a founding father of the new movement – William IX, count of Poitou and duke of

Aquitaine, who died in 1126. William, we are told, had the image of his mistress painted on his shield, saying that it was 'his will to bear her in battle, as she had borne him in bed'.[2] In William's work we find all the hallmarks of the new poetic genre – the amorous longing of the knight, the mood of intense introspection and the yearning of the suitor knight to perform homage to his beloved. In the works of another Frenchman, Bernart de Ventadorn (c. 1147–70), may be detected the first signs of the contradictions which were to appear in poetic understandings of courtly love. In Bernart's work love is considered social: it is the source of all worth and a model for human relations, yet at the same time it is antisocial, bringing folly and isolation to the lover. Equally, love is perceived as erotic because it provokes desire for physical union, and yet it is also deeply spiritual. In this web of contradictions writers of romances were to find much of the subject matter for their work in the years ahead.

Bernart de Ventadorn was one of the main conduits for the dissemination of the courtly genre of poetry because he was an acquaintance of Chrétien de Troyes, the most significant romance writer of the second half of the twelfth century. The two men are known to have exchanged poems, entertaining one another with rival ideas on the passionate versus the rational aspects of love.[3] Among those who gave encouragement to the poets and commissioned work from them the most significant figure was Marie de Champagne, Chrétien's main patron. Marie's mother Eleanor was the granddaughter of William IX of Aquitaine, daughter and heiress of William X, himself an important patron, and wife of Henry of Anjou, later Henry II of England and Normandy, sometime patron of Bernart de Ventadorn. Written against the background of this nexus of connections, Chrétien's masterpieces – *Cligès*, *Yvain* and *Erec and Enide* – may be seen as firmly grounded in the cultural fabric of southern and western France.

In England the most significant early figure to make love a central theme of her poetry was Marie de France. Marie was probably a Frenchwoman who lived for at least part of her adult life in England: the earliest manuscript with a complete text of her works is a book from Reading Abbey. Her *Lais* consist of twelve short poems concerned with passionate, romantic love. The theme of 'Yonec' is 'the grief and sorrow which [lovers] suffer for love', while 'Chaitivel' dwells on 'the suffering which [the lady's lovers] endured because of the love they had for you'. In 'Yonec' a young girl exclaims how her heart is taken by surprise as she falls in love and her lover is equally 'caught by surprise by love'. In an anticipation of the later use of language, Marie uses the language of death to express her characters' depths of passion. One lover says to his beloved, 'Lady, I am dying for you,' while another exclaims, 'You are my life and death.' [4]

A characteristic of Marie's work is the considerable prominence accorded in it to adultery. Eight of the twelve *Lais* involve adulterous relations, while a ninth centres on a rejected adulterous invitation. It is possible to see this interest as originating in the particular circumstances of twelfth-century aristocratic society. As primogeniture gradually took root, so a class of landless younger knights grew up whose only route to wealth lay in winning the hand of a lady possessed of both land and riches, yet the chances were that such a woman would already be married. In the twelfth century the Church had succeeded in making marriage a sacrament, the marriage, once made, being deemed indissoluble unless the relationship could be shown to fall within prohibited degrees. Marriages which proved unsatisfactory for whatever reason now had to be endured, with the partners finding sexual satisfaction elsewhere. It is against this background that the romantic theme of a young knight's longing became associated with that of a lady's secret liaison. The stories of Iseult's liaison with Tristan and of Guinevere's with Lancelot drew on real-life relationships between lovers. In recognition of the superior standing of the lady the poets sometimes described the knight's relationship with his beloved as one of vassalage. The knight was thus said to perform service to his lady, and the lady to receive his homage. In this way the relationship could be presented, after a fashion, in quasi-legal terms. An illicit liaison could be clothed in a veil of respectability, and the amorous longing of the knight given the character of a knight's allegiance to his lord.

It would be wrong to suggest, as C. S. Lewis did in *The Allegory of Love*, that adultery is the social relationship predominant in the romance genre as a whole.[5] While adultery is certainly a theme in some of the romances – indeed, centre stage in Marie's *Lais* – across the range it is absorbed into a more general celebration of love between aristocratic men and women. In many cases it is not actually the constraints on women which are explored; rather, it is the very freedom which they enjoy.[6] The reason for this is to be found in two highly significant but contradictory changes which occurred in the Church's attitude to marriage in the twelfth century. On the one hand, as we have seen, the Church made marriage a sacrament – an initiative which limited the couple's freedom by making the bond between them virtually indissoluble. On the other, and the essential counterbalance to this, the Church insisted that a marriage be freely entered into, so that matches to which the spouses were opposed would be less common. This crucial second change paved the way for marriages based on affective love rather than political or dynastic calculation.

The new emphasis placed by the papacy on the partners' consent reversed the teaching of previous centuries, which had emphasised the role of kindred and lords as stakeholders in marriage. The business of choosing a partner represented a crucial stage in the life of any individual, and particularly of an aristocrat, since marriage not only involved the making of an alliance between one family and another, it could have a major bearing on how a family's property would descend and be distributed. For this reason, in the early Middle Ages it had been a feature of both the Christian and Roman traditions that the interests of those with a stake in these matters be protected. Two main principles were promulgated: the first, that the consent of a person's parents or guardian was necessary for a match to be valid; and second, that marriage take the form of a public ceremony. It was this long-standing approach to the rules of marriage which was challenged by the revolutionary changes of the twelfth century.

From this time on, spouses were free to choose their partners without interference from their parents, and, equally important, matches contracted in secret were judged to be valid provided the consent of each partner was freely given. In England the notion that marriages among the well-born should be free had become by the thirteenth century a lawyers' commonplace. For those who enjoyed wardship rights, there was one disadvantage of this development: they could no longer oblige wards to marry suitors of their choice. To safeguard the interests of those in this position, it was established that they receive financial compensation. From the 1190s the pipe rolls of the exchequer are littered with payments from wards, particularly heiresses, buying the right to contract their own marriages.

As one historian has written, the Church's new theory of consent to marriage soon came to function as a lover's charter.[7] Many individuals whose matches would earlier have been forbidden were now perfectly free to come together as husband and wife. In Germany in 1193 Duke Henry of Brunswick married his beloved Agnes of Hohenstaufen in defiance of the wishes of the emperor, her brother, and of both their fathers. In England, nearly three centuries later, Edward IV confounded the political establishment with the announcement of his marriage to Elizabeth Woodville. This match was to be particularly controversial with far-reaching consequences for domestic and foreign policy. Edward, after he had become king in 1461, was the most eligible royal bachelor in Europe, and his ministers and advisers, Warwick in particular, were anxious for him to marry a lady of French or Burgundian royal descent. The match with Elizabeth upset every courtier's calculations. Before the twelfth century combined clerical and dynastic opposition would probably have stood in the king's way. Three centuries later, however, Edward's critics could do nothing to stop him. The Woodville match was canonically valid: there was no disputing that the consent of the two partners had been freely given.

Alongside such cases initiated by a well-born male may be set instances involving a reverse relationship: a well-born lady eloping with a man inferior in status to herself. In 1297 Joan of Acre, daughter of Edward I, angered her father by a secret liaison with Sir Ralph Monthermer, a knightly retainer of her late husband. Joan is said to have told Edward to his face that if a noble could marry a poor girl, then a noble lady could marry a poor knight.[8] Edward proved reluctant to recognise Monthermer in the title of earl; nonetheless the validity of the marriage stood.

In the fifteenth century there were to be massive and lengthy ructions within the Paston family of Norfolk when they were faced with a case of *mésalliance*. Margery, youngest daughter of John and Margaret Paston, had fallen in love with Richard Calle, the family bailiff. To the socially ambitious Pastons, Calle was totally unsuitable for he was common-born whereas they were gentry. The younger John Paston said, 'I will not have my sister selling candles and mustard in Framlingham fair.'[9] When Margery proved obdurate, the family closed their doors against her, and she and Richard had to seek shelter in a local nunnery. The bishop of Norwich, examining them, could find no impediment to their marriage for, like Edward IV and Woodville, they had freely consented. Early in 1470 the pair were married in the face of continued opposition from Margery's kin. The theme of liaison between a lady and a family servant must have been one played out in many an aristocratic *ménage* in the late Middle Ages.

The legal background to these stories is thus found in the all-important shift in the Church's policy on marriage. On the one hand, suitors were now able to choose their partners freely and without parental obstruction, while, on the other, their ability to repudiate them afterwards was seriously curtailed. These opposed but neatly balancing effects together explain the variety of relationships explored in chivalric romances. In some works it is adultery which provides the dominant theme of the poetic narrative; in others it is the capacity of regulated love to bring fulfilment in the form of marriage between a smitten couple. In terms of how the amorous liaison affected the knight's own conduct, however, there was little to choose between the two relationships. Both served to enthuse the knight, inspiring him to deeds of prowess for his lady and filling him with the ambition to prove himself worthy of her love. It is the working out of this psychological dynamic which provides the link between the world of courtly love and the chivalric culture of valour. Geoffrey de Charny captured the linkage in a perceptive comment: it is good for a man-at-arms to be in love; it teaches him to seek higher renown to honour his lady.[10]

The literature of Arthurian romance was to provide one of the main vehicles for the exploration of this relationship between erotic love and achievement in arms. The theme of erotic longing formed the central thread in the romantic stories of Sir Lancelot's liaison with Arthur's queen, Guinevere. In Chrétien's *Le Chevalier de la Charette*, which set the pattern for most later discussion of the topic, one of the set pieces is the tournament in which Sir Lancelot shows off his prowess before the crowd. Throughout the event Lancelot acts the part of the obedient lover, initially showing himself a coward at Guinevere's command while later, on her instruction, carrying all before him in her presence. After Chrétien, the tourneying scene in which the young lover performs deeds of prowess before his watching lady became almost a fixture of chivalric romance. It was to be one of the main means by which the hero was to show himself worthy of his lady's affection under her direct gaze and inspiration.

Arthurian literature acted in some sense as a school and source of instruction for chivalry. As we have seen, some of the grander late thirteenth-century tournaments were little more than staged re-enactments of episodes of Arthurian romance. The poet Sarrazin gives a vivid description of the play-acting at a tournament at Le Hem in Picardy in 1278. Jeanne, sister of the Lord de Longueval, took the part of Guinevere, while Robert, count of Artois, pretended to be Yvain, rescuing four maidens from the 'Knight of the White Tower', while another knight, Sir Kay, provided a comic commentary on events.[11] In England a few years later Edward I was to stage an Arthurian tournament in which the 'loathly Damsel' made a dramatic entry with a nose a foot long (her part being taken by an esquire in disguise). Tournaments which enacted episodes of Arthurian romance were to be a regular feature of chivalric court culture again in Edward III's early years.

The theme of life imitating art, however, did not find its only, or even its clearest, expression in the staging of tournaments. Actual deeds of fighting and errantry were undertaken by knights in the manner found in the romances. In 1318, according to the *Scalacronica*, Sir William Marmion ventured to Norham on Tweed with a golden helm given to him by his mistress, chancing all in an assault on the castle which nearly cost him his life.[12] On the Scots side, the chronicler Barbour tells the story of Sir John Weberton, who had sworn to guard Lanark Castle for a year, as a trial worthy of his lady – but died within the term, defending the place against Sir James Douglas.[13] In Jean le Bel's chronicle is the story of the English knights at Valenciennes in 1340 who each wore a patch over one eye until each had performed a deed worthy of his lady.[14] Le Bel's successor Froissart tells the tale of how, at Saint-Inglevert in 1390, the French knight Sir Reginald de Roye inflicted a devastating blow on an English knight 'because he was so smitten with love for a young lady that all his affairs prospered'.[15]

The clear lesson of these stories is that allegiance to a lady acted as a source of inspiration to knights, providing them with the incentive to perform ever more daring deeds of arms. The longed-for lady was the source and begetter of excellence in her lover, the spur to a spiritually ennobling passion in he who fell under her spell. According to Andreas Capellanus in the thirteenth century, to ennoble was part of her function: 'if she takes a man who is none too good, and makes him praiseworthy through her good character, she makes a good man better'.[16] Love, in Andreas's view, made all things good.

Paradoxically, however, for all the importance of the lady's role in the romances, her character and personality remain elusive. Rarely in romantic writing is she, as heroine, subjected to the kind of psychological probing accorded to the man. It is the man, the suitor, who is the main subject of the poet's interest. The lady remains an enigma: distant, shadowy and aloof. It is the suitor's anguish and longing which attract the poet's attention. In this respect, as in others, we are reminded of one of the main characteristics of chivalry: its values were solidly masculine. Chivalry was the cultural expression of the rough world of the fighting man.

Chivalry, Pageantry and Family

In the fantasy world of the romances it was the regular convention for men to dance in submissive attendance on their womenfolk, and the romances, as we have seen, had their roots in real-life social predicaments. Their essence lay in the exploration of relationships between aspirant knightly suitors and haughty aristocratic chatelaines. Yet in significant respects, for the sake of literary effect, the romance writers misrepresented the position of the women they portrayed. The notion of the noblewoman as director and inspirer of menfolk, although imitated in life, was in reality largely a fiction. In the strongly masculine world of chivalry women more usually occupied a position of subjection and subordination. Socially as well as physically they stood on the sidelines, spectators of events rather than participants in them.

In no social arena was this clearer than in that of the tournament. In the earliest such encounters, in the mid-twelfth century, there had been no place for women at all. Tournaments were violent rough-and-tumble affairs, miniature battles in which only the tougher sex were involved. Later, however, as colour and pageantry crept in, women made their appearance on the stands as supporters. Gradually, their role was ritualised, the knights seeing themselves as performing deeds in their honour. The reality, however, was that the woman's

position was always subordinate: that of an enthusiastic but passive
spectator in a theatre whose principal function was to provide knights
with training in arms.

The first mention of women at a tournament is found in a passage
in the *Life of William Marshal*, where the narrator says that the Marshal
arrived at a tournament to find the countess and her ladies already
present. At their request, he then entertained them with a song until
the action began.[17] The narrator was describing an event which had
occurred around 1180 or earlier. In most of northern France it seems
it was only in the first half of the thirteenth century that the presence
of women became at all routine, and in England it was probably later
still. There is no chronicle reference to women in attendance at an
English tournament until 1279, when their presence is recorded at a
round table at Kenilworth for 'a hundred knights and ladies'. Only in
Edward III's reign does the presence of women on the stands appear
to have become at all frequent. The patronage of Queen Philippa may
have done something to make the female presence more fashionable
and respectable. On three occasions her husband specifically ordered
the attendance of women in large numbers. On one of these he
summoned no fewer than 500 ladies of good lineage to attend jousts
in honour of the countess of Salisbury.

For the combatants, having women on the stands cheering them
on was a source of inspiration, just as in the Arthurian romances. In
the fourteenth century one of the most striking witnesses to female
inspiration was the wearing of ladies' tokens by rival combatants.
Such tokens were usually articles of clothing – sleeves, veils and head-
gear being the most popular objects of favour. The knightly ideal of
service to a mistress, which lay behind the wearing of tokens, was
also played out in ceremonies of prize-giving by women. According
to his biographer William Marshal was presented with the prize at a
tournament at Pleurs by 'une dame de pris'. In 1390 at the tournaments staged by Richard II at Smithfield ladies presented the prizes
each evening to the best jouster in each party. Sometimes there is a
record of kisses being exchanged between prize-givers and champions.
It is by no means clear whether women were involved in the actual
judging of the competitions as well as in the giving of awards to
champions. Although there are many references to women as judges,
it seems that the process involving women judges was little more than

a ritual; the reality was that experienced knights took the lead. Women, although ritually elevated, were actually subordinate in everything beyond the showier aspects of tourneying.

This picture of women – as absorbed into chivalric society yet involved in it on male terms – is highlighted by what we know of heraldry. Heraldry had been introduced in the first quarter of the twelfth century as a means of identifying knights in tournaments and battle. With the passage of time, however, and as the ownership of coats became hereditary, these stylised insignia acquired distinction as marks of lineage and rank. Coats of arms were jealously guarded as items of family property and were passed down in the male line over the generations. Given the high rate of extinction among males, it was bound to be the case that at some stage a coat would be inherited by a woman. At this point a woman born into a family of armigerous rank would herself be brought within the fold of armigerous society.

The earliest examples of women adopting paternal arms as their own come from relatively early in the history of heraldry. Around the mid-twelfth century Roesia, countess of Lincoln, sister of Gilbert de Clare, earl of Hertford, authenticated a document using the distinctive chevronny arms of de Clare. In the next generation her example was followed by her daughter Alice, who was married to Simon de Senlis, earl of Northampton. There are grounds for supposing that even at this early date coats of arms were quite widely used by women. In the twelfth century a number of similar-looking arms were used by families which were in some way related to one another.[18] The famous chevronny coat associated with the de Clares was also used by the FitzWalter lords of Dunmow. Equally, the checky coat of Waleran, count of Meulan, one of the earliest known, was used by a range of families connected with Waleran, notably the holders of the earldoms of Warwick, Leicester and Surrey. It seems clear that the ties of kinship which such family arms affirm came in a striking number of instances from descent through a woman. In the case of the Beaumonts there is a single connecting figure, Isabel de Vermandois (d. 1147), sister of Ralph, count of Vermandois, by her second marriage the wife of John, earl of Surrey, and by her first mother of Waleran of Meulan. Women were hardly less conscious of lineage than men and through use of heraldic charges acted as transmitters of family identity.

Women's appreciation of the role of heraldry in shaping identity can be detected in the choices they made for the manner of their representation on their tombs. By the later thirteenth century the first examples are found of female effigies decorated with either coats of arms or charges derived from coats of arms. On the effigy of Isabella de Brus, first wife of Sir John Fitzmarmaduke, at Easington in County Durham, there are popinjays, derived from her husband's arms, carved in low relief on the kirtle which covers her chest, while on the brass of Margaret, first wife of Sir Ralph de Camoys, *c*. 1310, at Trotton in Sussex, there are no fewer than nine shields on the lady's figure and another eight surrounding it. From the late fourteenth century there survive the first examples of monuments commemorating both husband and wife on which heraldic attire is employed. At Southacre in Norfolk on the brass of Sir John Harsick and his wife (1384) John himself is shown wearing a jupon charged with his arms and his wife a kirtle on which her husband's arms are impaled with her own. This brass is all the more valuable as a witness to female taste as it was probably commissioned by Lady Harsick after her husband's death. From the mid-fifteenth century comes the magnificent brass at Childrey in Berkshire of William Finderne, who died in 1445, and his wife Elizabeth, on which he is shown wearing a tabard bearing his arms, and she a kirtle and mantle, the former charged with her husband's arms and the latter with her own. This brass too was almost certainly commissioned after the husband's death by his widow. In the late fifteenth century brasses or relief effigies of women attired in heraldic dress, in the manner of playing-card characters, became quite common. The normal convention was that the husband's arms were shown on the kirtle and the lady's on the mantle.

The close interest which women took in heraldry is evident from the attention they gave to which arms should appear on the shields on their tombs. If the woman was an heiress, she could use the opportunities afforded by heraldry to represent the lines of descent which had come to rest in her person. In the 1480s Margaret, John Paston's widow and the Mautby family heiress, gave very clear instructions: 'Upon that stoon I wulle have iiii scochens sett at the iiii corners, whereof I wulle that the first scochen shalbe of my husbondes armes and myn departed [i.e. impaled], the ii^{de} of Mawtebys armes and Berneys of Redham departed, the iii^{de} of Mawtebys armes and the Lord Loveyn departed, the iv^{de} of Mawtebys and Sir Roger Beauchamp

departed.'[19] Margaret provided for no fewer than five families' arms
to be represented on the tomb. It was her own family's arms, however,
which she ensured would be given the greatest prominence: they were
to figure, impaled, on all four shields. The arms of her late husband,
by contrast, were to appear just once.

On the memorial of another fifteenth-century widow and heiress,
Joan, Lady Cobham, who died in 1434, at Cobham in Kent the array
of arms was still greater. Here six shields were provided, three on
each side, and six families' arms were displayed. Joan was an heiress
twice over. Through her mother she claimed descent from the prominent
Kent magnate John, Lord Cobham of Cobham, and through her
father, Sir John de la Pole of Chrishall in Essex, from the wealthy de
la Poles of Hull. Joan's sense of dynasty, of her position as the bearer
of family histories, is amply displayed on the armorial on her brass.
It provides an epitome of her parents' descent. Reading from the top,
the arms on the dexter side are those of Cobham; Peverel quartering
de la Pole and impaling Cobham, for Joan's father and mother; and
Braybrooke impaling Cobham, for one of Joan's marriages; and on
the sinister side, Cobham impaling Courtenay, for her grandparents;
Cobham quartering de la Pole; and Brooke, for Joan's son-in-law,
impaling Cobham. Yet, for all its preoccupation with history, the brass
looked to the future as well as to the past. The bottom sinister shield,
with the arms of Brooke, attested to the marital alliance which was
to carry the Cobham inheritance to the successor line, the Brookes
of Devon. The brass may be regarded as looking to the future in
other ways too. At Joan's feet are two groups of children, six boys
and four girls, representing her issue by three of her five husbands.
Only one of the brood was to survive to adulthood, however, a
daughter, yet another Joan, who was to marry Thomas Brooke of
Devon. Yet the fragility of the dynastic transition was glossed over:
Joan was presented as the fecund matriarch, the bearer of healthy
issue. The brass thus presented a reassuring fiction, a misleading
impression that there was continuity where in fact there was none
at all. Joan's own identity was submerged in that of the male lineage
to which she belonged. The brass emphasised her transitional role,
her position as a bearer of family histories and the means for their
preservation in the future.

Womanhood and Selfhood

The strong impression conveyed by the heraldry on female tomb monuments is that women had a rather limited sense of their selfhood. They are seen as standing at the intersection of a series of group identities, associating closely with their families – their own or their husbands' – and allowing their sense of selfhood to be subsumed in the dominant masculine values of the aristocratic society of their day.

Is there, then, any evidence of aristocratic women being able to construct an independent cultural space for themselves? Can we find any indication that they were able to shape their own destinies and fashion their own images? In practice just how much a woman could achieve was dependent partly on the stage she had reached in her life. When a woman married she lost her independent personhood in law, her property becoming that of her husband and her legal interests being held to be wholly subsumed in his. It was only when she became a widow that she recovered her position as a *femme sole*, regaining the right to sue in the courts and to acquire and dispose of property. It was thus in widowhood that a woman can be said legally to have emerged in her own right. Equally it was in widowhood that a woman became the possessor of substantial wealth of her own. A proportion of that wealth came from the dower lands to which she was entitled on the day that her husband died; much more, however, was to come after the fourteenth century from her jointure – that is to say, from the lands which she held in joint tenancy with her husband. In the last two centuries of the Middle Ages the use of jointures became increasingly common. Generally, the higher the wife's standing, the greater the proportion of the couple's lands held in jointure. To secure the hand of a really rich heiress, a man might have to promise a jointure of almost everything he possessed. It is the spread of the jointure across aristocratic society that made the fourteenth and fifteenth centuries the first great age of the dowager in England. Never before had aristocratic widows had such ample resources at their command, and never perhaps were they to do so again.

The wealth of the very richest widows made them the envy of those who sought to win their hands.[20] In 1454 Alice, widow of William de la Pole, duke of Suffolk, held estates in no fewer than twenty-two counties, which brought her an annual income of £1,300, comparable with that of an earl. Earlier in the same century Joan, Lady Abergavenny, daughter of the earl of Arundel, held an estate in the Midlands which brought her an income of almost £2,000. Perhaps the richest late medieval widow was Elizabeth de Burgh, Lady of Clare, youngest of the three sisters and co-heiresses of Gilbert de Clare, earl of Gloucester, who enjoyed an income before the Black Death of £3,000 per annum. Some of these well-to-do widows were also extremely long-lived. Marie de St Pol survived her husband Aymer de Valence, earl of Pembroke, for no fewer than fifty-three years, to die in 1377 in her late sixties or early seventies. Alice, duchess of Suffolk, survived her third husband, the murdered William de la Pole, by a quarter of a century, to die at the age of about seventy-one. The remarkable Margaret of Brotherton, duchess of Norfolk, outlived her siblings, her two husbands, her niece, her four children and even her eldest grandson, to die in 1399 aged about eighty. Most extraordinary of all was Katherine, daughter of Ralph Neville, earl of Westmorland. Widowed at the age of thirty, she married in rapid succession Thomas Strangeways, a servant of her late husband, John, Lord Beaumont, and finally, to universal disgust, in her mid-sixties, the young John Woodville. She died aged about eighty in 1483, having survived even her last husband.

With such reserves of wealth at their disposal, these women had the capacity to create distinctly female patterns of patronage. What we know of their tastes, however, suggests that in most respects these were scarcely distinguishable from those of high-ranking menfolk. Women readers, for example, were just as keen on romances as men with their chivalric appreciation of war. An insight into their appetite for romance is afforded by a list of the English royal book collection in the Tower of London in the 1320s and '30s. This collection consisted of some 160 volumes, of which no fewer than fifty-nine were romances.[21] The clerk in charge of the books records them as regularly being lent out. Among the borrowers were Queen Isabella, Edward II's widow, Margaret, countess of Cornwall, and Elizabeth de Burgh, the wealthy Lady of Clare. Queen Isabella, the notorious paramour of Roger Mortimer, seems to have been a particular devotee of the genre: she borrowed a romance history of the Normans, the romance of Renard the Fox and the cryptically titled 'romaunz de Meraugys et Sade'. A romance of which she was in possession at the time of her death, the story of Perceval and Gawain, may also have come from the royal collection. There is no indication that the tastes of these royal and aristocratic women were unusual. Well-born women are often found leaving books of romances in their wills. In 1412 a Lincolnshire widow, Elizabeth, Lady Darcy, left a copy of *Sir Lancelot of the Lake* and a book of romances called *Leschell de Reson* to her son Philip or, if he were not interested, to Sir Thomas Grey.[22] Broadly similar tastes are observable in women when they acted as patrons of writers. It is worth remembering that it was for a female patron, Constance, wife of Ralph FitzGilbert, that Geffrei Gaimar wrote his romance-tinged *Estoire des Engleis*.[23]

The tastes of widows – indeed, of women generally – in artistic and architectural patronage also seem to have closely resembled those of their menfolk. They were founders of chantries; they commissioned books of devotion; and they added to the fabrics of parish churches and monasteries. In many cases identification with their husbands' interests led to a strong commitment to building projects which their husbands had initiated. At Tewkesbury Abbey in Gloucestershire, for example, Eleanor, widow of the younger Hugh Despenser, completed the lavish rebuilding of the eastern arm of the abbey church, on which her husband had embarked in his years of power after 1318. Eleanor herself is possibly the naked donor figure represented at the foot of the easternmost of the series of windows which she played a part in commissioning.

If there is any evidence of cultural taste of a distinctly female kind, it is probably to be found in such women's private religious observances. Some rich noble widows took vows of chastity as part of preparing for the next world, which enabled them to lead semi-religious lives in their homes. Elizabeth de Burgh took such a vow in 1343, when she was allowed to enter the London Minoresses, while Lady Margaret Beaufort, Henry VII's mother, was granted permission by her last husband to live a life of chastity amounting to that of a vowess.[24] In the case of Cecily, widow of Richard, duke of York, and mother of Edward IV, a set of ordinances survives indicating how a whole household could be organised as a religious community.[25] Cecily rose at seven to hear matins and, after breakfasting, attended chapel with part of her household to assist in the Office of the Day and to hear Low Mass; from chapel she passed immediately to dinner, a public meal accompanied by pious readings, and after that to meetings with her staff. Her day ended with evensong, the Little Office and finally dinner. Upper-class widows like Duchess Cecily were frequently owners of considerable collections of devotional manuscripts. Cecily herself had a particular interest in works of mysticism. Earlier in the century Elizabeth, Lady FitzHugh, owned two psalters, two primers and a prayer book, which she left to members of her family, while Eleanor Hulle, a Somerset gentlewoman, possessed a great and a little breviary, a psalter and a Latin Bible.[26]

The religious interests of one late medieval widow are also attested to by a remarkable building scheme, the grandiose reconstruction of Heckington church in Lincolnshire, a rich decorated church in a county notable for such churches. The rebuilding was initiated by the lady of the manor, Isabella, widow of Sir John de Vesci and cousin of Edward II, acting in liaison with the incumbent, Richard de Potesgrave, a courtier clerk and chaplain of the king. Potesgrave was responsible for the rebuilding of the chancel, while Isabella undertook work on the nave. The big rebuilt church was notable for its elaborate scheme of sculpted decoration, one of the finest of its date in England. The subject matter of the scheme focused on the themes of penance for sins and salvation through the sacrament of Christ, popular in devotional works of the time. It is interesting that a number of the subjects depicted were critical of women.[27] Among the exterior corbel sculptures are several showing men and women fighting, a number alluding to women's vanity and one telling the story of Tutivullius and the gossips. Tutivullius was the devil who sat on the shoulders of women who chattered during sermons. The inclusion of these subjects points strongly to Isabella's taste and influence, suggesting an awareness on her part of the 'weaknesses' of her sex. Here was a lady conscious of the danger to her soul of the sins associated with women and perhaps keen to take on the task of alerting other women to them.

Besides widows, there was one other female group which had the capacity to create patterns of patronage in their own image, and that was heiresses. Like widows, with whose ranks they overlapped, heiresses were a numerous and influential group in late medieval England.

This was because of the high rate of male extinction in the aristocracy, which meant that a quarter of all noble families died out in the male line every twenty-five years. While a few families, like the Bassetts of Drayton in Staffordshire, came to an end with no close kin at all, the majority possessed female representatives who carried their inheritances in marriage to another family. Heiresses were the greatest prizes in the medieval marriage market. There was intense competition for their hands among males seeking to secure an inheritance for themselves and consequently they were a much-married and much-dowered group. Joan, Lady Cobham, was, like the Wife of Bath, married no fewer than five times. Her first husband was chosen for her by her grandfather when she was a minor, while the remaining four she chose herself. As her brass at Cobham shows, heiresses could play a major role in the nurturing and preservation of family memory. A generation later there was to be another, still greater, heiress who was to play a role in the preservation of specifically chivalric memory. This was Anne Neville, daughter of Richard Beauchamp, earl of Warwick, and sister and heiress of his son Henry, duke of Warwick, who died young. Anne's self-appointed task in the last years of her life was to cherish and protect the memory of her late father, one of the Lancastrian monarchy's greatest captains.

Anne's achievement was to commission the beautiful folio book known as the *Beauchamp Pageant*. This unique pictorial life of an English nobleman traces Earl Richard's career in a series of fifty-three pen-and-ink drawings, each accompanied by a text in English.[28] The emphasis is very much on the earl's 'noble actes' – his honours, accomplishments and chivalric exploits. It tells of his knighting by Henry IV, his prowess at the battle of Shrewsbury, his election to the Order of the Garter, his pilgrimage to the Holy Land, his long service in the French wars, his appointment as tutor to the young Henry VI and, finally, his death in 1439 at Rouen. On the evidence of its artistic style, the manuscript can be assigned to a date in the 1480s – or at the very latest the early 1490s – the naturalism of its drawing being paralleled in Flemish manuscript art of the period. A possible context for Anne's commissioning of the book can be found in the seizure of the crown by Richard III, which made her grandson, the king's son, briefly heir to the throne. It has been suggested that the volume was a book of instruction for the young boy, intended to edify and entertain him, and to set before him a model of noble and honourable conduct drawn from his ancestry. The idea of the *Pageant* as an *exemplum* would explain the process of careful selection observable in the work. Throughout, the emphasis is placed on the earl's heroic and knightly exploits and his service to the Crown; the less glorious moments of his career – his unfortunate absence from Agincourt and involvement in the prosecution of Joan of Arc – being omitted. The picture we are offered in the book is of a model of knightly conduct associated with the well-being of the realm.

The *Beauchamp Pageant* was by no means the only work commissioned after the earl's death to honour his memory. The most visible tribute is his magnificent tomb in the Beauchamp Chapel on the south side of St Mary's Church, Warwick. This was commissioned in the 1440s and ranks among the finest tomb monuments of the Middle Ages. The earl's effigy shows him in Milanese armour on a Purbeck marble chest with brass epitaph and a curving hearse above. His high estate is proclaimed by the choice of gilt bronze for his effigy, unique for a non-royal lay figure. The iconography of the chapel itself celebrates his reception into the kingdom of heaven. His gaze is fixed on the figure of the Virgin Mary on the roof above and his hands are drawn apart as if in wonder at the splendour of the vision unfolding around him. In the windows to one side a choir of angels serenades his ascent. Amid this scene of heavenly jubilation, however, the signs and symbols of this world are never far absent. On the effigy and chest strong emphasis is placed on lineage and dynasticism. Family badges abound – the swan at the earl's head and the bear at his feet, both for the Beauchamps, and the griffin, likewise at his feet, for the Despensers. In niches around the sides a procession of kinsfolk mourn the dead earl, all of them identified by their coats of arms. Tomb and chapel together provide a connecting point between past, present and future. Through the medium of this celebration of his life, those who succeeded the earl in the comital title laid claim to his political and cultural inheritance.

In theory, responsibility for both chapel and monument lay with the earl's executors, a group of men drawn from his most loyal retainers. A major influence in the background, however, would have been the earl's son-in-law and eventual successor, Richard Neville, 'the Kingmaker', Anne's husband. From the time of the Kingmaker's succession to his father-in-law's estates in the late 1440s the executors would have found Neville influence near-inescapable in all that they did. The strength of the Neville interest provides an immediate explanation for one very obvious characteristic of the tomb – the attempt to present the earl as a hero figure, a paragon of chivalry probably well beyond the reality. The purpose of such elevation could only have been to allow Richard Neville to appropriate the earl's posthumous repute to himself as his successor. One way of understanding Anne's commissioning of the *Pageant*, therefore, is to see it as a response to the challenge posed by the assertion of Neville interest in both chapel and tomb. Anne's relations with her Neville kin do not appear to have been particularly close, and it is quite possible that she found the Kingmaker's at times heavy-handed manipulation of her father's image presumptuous and off-putting. In addition to his likely involvement in the tomb, he was also instrumental in the grandiose re-establishment of Earl Richard's chantry foundation at Guy's Cliffe. If the chapel and the tomb together may be taken in some sense as representing the Kingmaker's response to the earl's achievement, the *Pageant*, a work of Anne's last years and dating from over a decade after the Kingmaker's death, may equally be seen as an expression of her own reflections on his career. The commissioning of the *Pageant* provides a clear instance of an elderly heiress shaping the way in which family and chivalric memory was to be transmitted into the future.

Just over a century earlier another elderly widow had been involved in the preservation of family and chivalric memory. This was Joan, Lady Cobham, who died in 1369, a distant relation of the much-married Lady Cobham mentioned above and widow of the Garter knight Reginald, Lord Cobham. Reginald, a distinguished comrade-in-arms of Edward III, had died in 1361, and she commissioned a monument to him in Lingfield church. The monument, which survives, is rich in chivalric reference. Reginald is shown in armour, with the Garter round his left leg, on a chest with an armorial around the sides which celebrates the ties he forged on the campaign trail. On the south side, facing the chancel, are the arms of the earls of March, Oxford and Northampton, all leading commanders and men with whom Reginald had fought in the wars of the 1340s and 1350s; on the north, alongside the arms of the commemorated and his wife, are the arms of two more lords with whom he had fought, William, Lord Roos, and Sir

Walter Pavely; and at the foot are those of his two main recruiting sub-contractors, Sir Stephen de Cossington and Sir Waresius de Valognes. The armorial constitutes an eloquent celebration of Cobham's career in arms from its earliest days in the 1330s through to the Black Prince's campaigns of the 1350s. That his widow should have commissioned the scheme demonstrates her close identification with his values, achievements and priorities. Chivalry, it seems, was as much a part of her cultural world as of his. In her will, made in 1369, Lady Joan reveals herself as a person of both piety and humility. She requested burial outside – not inside – the Church of St Mary Overy at Southwark, near where she lived. Conceivably, like Elizabeth de Burgh and other pious widows, she had taken a vow of chastity to live a modest life. Nonetheless, she appears to have seen no conflict between the respective claims of chivalry and personal religion. For her, the campaigns which her husband had fought were just and legitimate wars to uphold Edward III's rightful claims.

Women like Joan Cobham and Anne Beauchamp lived in a chivalric milieu dominated by male aristocratic values. Their position in this world was, for the most part, one of subordination to the interests of their menfolk. All the same, it was one in which they appear to have found personal fulfilment in the promotion of family and dynastic interests.

15

Memory and Fame

A chivalrous society was in a very real sense a community of memory. The valorous deeds performed by knights lived on in the recollection of friends, family and descendants. Chivalrous men recognised that deeds of the highest valour could be inspirational to generations to come and so their memory would be perpetuated. King Arthur was said to have ordered the adventures of the Knights of the Round Table to be written up in books and chronicles kept at Salisbury. In the statutes of many late medieval secular orders of knighthood it was ordained that the deeds of members be recorded by an officer of the order. In thirteenth-century Castile King Alfonso X prescribed in his law code that 'accounts of great deeds of arms should be read to knights while they eat', much as religious texts were read to monks in refectories.[1] Chivalric memory fed into the training, education and schooling of knights. It formed part of the web of structures by which chivalric culture was recorded in the present and transmitted to the future.

But how are we to understand the notion of chivalric memory in the Middle Ages? It is perhaps best seen as a form of family memory, part of the stock of myths and narratives passed down over the generations, which brought lustre to a family's name. Stories of the martial deeds of heroic ancestors were cherished by families for the honour they conferred, honour which would accumulate over the generations as the deeds performed by family members multiplied. There was a sense, however, in which chivalric memory also belonged to the chivalric class as a whole. As the hearings in the Scrope–Grosvenor case of 1386 showed, knowledge of the valorous deeds of knights was widely disseminated in chivalric society. Knights took pride in cherishing the recollection of each others' achievements. Churchmen who were related to or associated with knights shared in that wider sense of pride. If the families of knights may be considered the main conduits of chivalric memory, there was yet a role for the wider community of honour in ensuring that the fame of the bravest knights lived on.

Heraldry and Memory

From no later than the twelfth century a key role in the preservation of chivalric memory was played by the heralds, those witnesses to chivalric achievement, servants and supporters of knights, designers and interpreters of coats of arms. The emergence of heralds in the mid- to late twelfth century is closely associated with the appearance, around that time, of the tournament as an institution for the training and practice of knights. Tournaments brought together great assemblages of people – esquires, armourers, minstrels, jongleurs; and the earliest heralds were probably found among these hangers-on. Originally employed to publicise and proclaim tournaments, they quickly developed an expertise in recognising and recording knights' coats of arms. By the thirteenth century the more senior of them were acting in a registrar capacity, recalling and writing down coats of arms for the benefit of the knights who employed them.

This informal responsibility of recollection laid the foundation for one of the most important means by which chivalric memory was preserved, the compiling of rolls of arms. These colourful heraldic inventories, sometimes containing the blazons of many hundreds of knights, were drawn up in a number of contexts and connections. Some fall into the category of local rolls – rolls which brought together the arms of knights living in a particular locality. Others, the general rolls, were of a less specific nature, lacking any area- or event-related context and sometimes including the arms of foreign knights. Others again, significantly in the present context, were the so-called occasional rolls, which contain the blazons of knights assembled for a particular episode such as a siege or tournament. Good examples of these are the Falkirk Roll of 1298, associated with the battle of Falkirk, and the first and second Dunstable Rolls of 1309 and 1334, both associated with tournaments held at that town. On some occasions heralds who possessed skills of minstrelsy composed verse narratives to go with their rolls. In 1300 a poet-minstrel composed the 'Song of Caerlaverock', which celebrated the encirclement by the English of Caerlaverock Castle in southern Scotland. In the first part of this work the author describes the blazons of the leading knights on the expedition, enlivening his descriptions by reference to chivalric myth, while in the second he relates the details of the English assault and the feats of individual knights. It is possible that the author was the herald of Sir Robert Clifford, the knight who was granted the castle after the siege, who was later to become marshal of England.[2]

In the course of the thirteenth century the role of heraldry in preserving memory was greatly extended as it was adopted as a signifier of patronage and ownership. Coats of arms were deployed in a variety of settings – on household objects and furniture, in stained-glass windows, on the walls of churches and refectories, over the gatehouses of castles, in the nooks and crannies of tombs – wherever they could be made to serve the purposes of identification and display. The great fourteenth-century nave of York Minster had one of the most extensive displays of heraldry in England. High in the clerestory windows and between the arches of the main arcade were the arms of the rich northern families who had contributed to the cost of the building. In aristocratic manor houses heraldry was displayed on the ornaments and fittings of private chapels. Coats of arms were a feature of altar vessels, service books, vestments and furnishings. Henry, Lord Scrope, bequeathed no fewer than sixty-five copes bearing his arms to Yorkshire churches. The books of hours of the Luttrells, Nevilles, Pulleins and other families had their owners' arms on their opening folios. The antiphonal used by Sir Thomas Chaworth of Wiverton, who died in 1459, had his and his wife's arms scattered liberally throughout the text. At Etchingham church in Sussex Sir William de Etchingham had his arms placed high up over the tower on the weathervane. They are still there today.

The great attraction of heraldry to the medieval knightly class was its ability to articulate in bold visual form their military and cultural concerns.[3] For an active fighting knight, his coat of arms was both a means to individual and retinue recognition in the field and an expression of his family's identity, honour and sense of lineage. In the chivalric context heraldry, memory and identity were all closely associated. In 1314

Sir Edmund Deincourt, fearing the loss of his family surname and arms on the succession of a daughter, diverted the succession to his estates to a male kinsman provided that kinsman assume both the family name and arms.[4] In an age of high visual recognition individual coats of arms could convey messages of ownership, kinship and tenurial connection, while whole collections of arms together could proclaim the solidarity and ascendancy of the armigerous elite. In grand architectural settings heraldry could sometimes take on a timeless quality. The display of arms in a manor house or church might attest to a connection between a family and a place stretching back time out of mind. This was the case in the church at Chalgrave in Bedfordshire, where the painted arms of the local lords, the Lorings, and their associates adorn the nave walls to this day.

Coats of arms were especially effective in conveying messages relating to companionship in war. One highly distinctive relationship to which they could bear witness was that of brotherhood-in-arms, the tie between knights which brought them together as partners or blood brothers. On the tomb of Sir Hugh Calveley (d. 1394) at Bunbury in Cheshire, the arms of Calveley alternate round the sides with those of his companion Sir Robert Knolles. Calveley and Knolles had fought together in the wars in France and Spain from their earliest days as esquires in Brittany through to their involvement in the *chevauchées* of the 1370s. Calveley was to name Knolles as his chief executor with responsibility for the foundation of his chantry college. The relationship between the two knights was one which amounted to brotherhood even if it was not given actual legal standing as such. Knolles was a man fascinated by heraldry and commissioned heraldic schemes for the windows of two churches which he rebuilt in Norfolk.[5]

More remarkable still as a witness to knightly brotherhood is a tomb slab now in the Archaeological Museum at Istanbul. This commemorates two English knights, Sir John Clanvow and Sir William Neville, and was originally in the Dominican church at Galata, where they were buried. The slab measures two metres by one, and shows the knights' shields tilted towards one another, each bearing the impaled arms of them both, and each surmounted by the knight's crest. Since impaling was the way in which the arms of a husband and wife were represented on a shield, the relationship between the two must have been one akin to that of marriage, in other words brotherhood-in-arms. Clanvow and Neville were both chamber knights of Richard II and were on a journey to the east in 1391 when they died. The relationship between them was probably even more intimate than that between Calveley and Knolles honoured at Bunbury.[6]

A broader range of relationships was memorialised on some other tomb monuments of the period. A whole career in arms was celebrated in the armorial on the tomb of Reginald, Lord Cobham, who died in 1361, at Lingfield, Surrey. Cobham was one of Edward III's most outstanding commanders, serving in the campaigns in Scotland and the Low Countries in the 1330s, on the Crécy–Calais campaign in 1346–7 and on the Black Prince's *chevauchées* in Aquitaine in the 1350s.[7] On the south side of the tomb are the arms of some of the leading magnates whom he accompanied – Roger Mortimer, earl of March; William de Bohun, earl of Northampton; John de Vere, earl of Oxford; and Bartholomew, Lord Burghersh – on the north those of two up-and-coming knights with whom he campaigned – William, Lord Roos and Sir Walter Pavely, the latter, like Cobham, a Knight of the Garter – and at the foot those of two local knights who acted as his recruiting serjeants – Sir Stephen de Cossington and Sir Waresius de Valognes. Taken as a whole, the armorial constitutes one of the grandest heraldic celebrations of the Edwardian phase of the Hundred Years War.

The years around Crécy produced other grandiloquent chivalric celebrations in heraldic form. Probably the best known is the armorial in the east window of Gloucester Abbey, now Gloucester Cathedral. At the foot of this massive glass screen are three groups of shields, those on the left representing Richard, earl of Arundel; Thomas, Lord Berkeley; Thomas, earl of Warwick, and William de Bohun, earl of Northampton; those on the right Laurence Hastings, earl of Pembroke; Richard, Lord Talbot; Sir Maurice de Berkeley; and Thomas, Lord Bradeston; and those in the centre Edward, the Black Prince; Henry, duke of Lancaster, and the king himself. What the owners of these arms had in common was their involvement in the Crécy–Calais campaign, and the date of the window, about 1350, strongly suggests that it was a celebration of the twin victories. Two of the men represented in the window were almost certainly brothers-in-arms – Thomas, Lord Bradeston, and Sir Maurice de Berkeley of Uley, both Gloucestershire knights with a long and distinguished record of service together. It is possible, although it cannot be proved, that the window was Bradeston's tribute to his friend, who had died of dysentery at the siege of Calais.[8]

There are other armorials which attest to English pride in achievement in war in these years. A good example is that on the tomb of Sir John Sutton (d. 1356) at Sutton-on-Hull, Yorkshire, on which the arms of Fitzwilliam, Greystoke, Darcy, Cantilupe, Ros, Percy and Lucy are those of the deceased's fighting companions. The antiquary Dugdale recorded an armorial on the tomb, now lost, of Ralph, Lord Basset of Drayton, Knight of the Garter (d. 1390), in Lichfield cathedral, which included the arms of military companions as well as those of the deceased's kinsmen.[9] The mighty victories of Edward III's reign – those of Sluys, Crécy, Calais and Poitiers – generated feelings of martial pride which found their characteristic visual expression in armorial celebration. The rows of arms in glass and painted stone both honoured knightly achievement in arms and ensured its continued remembrance.

There seems to be no parallel to this outpouring of heraldic celebration in the second phase of the Hundred Years War, which was to open in the early fifteenth century. The great victory at Agincourt in 1415 and the conquest and settlement of Normandy which followed produced very few celebratory armorials, mainly because the Lancastrian war effort, at least in its later years, did not draw as extensively on the support of the English military class as Edward III's campaigns had. The armies of the fifteenth century were generally small and in the period from 1430 drawn for the most part from the English settler community in Normandy. By the second quarter of the century the waging of war had ceased to be part of the collective experience of the English knightly and armigerous class, and the relative absence of military celebration from armorials reflects that fact.

The subject most widely represented on armorials after 1400 was not campaigning history, but family history, real or imagined stories of family lineage and descent. The displays of arms on tomb chests, sometimes paralleled in armorials in stained-glass windows close by, told narratives of the antiquity of families and the accumulation of honour to which long ancestry bore witness. On the brass of Sir Thomas Chaworth, who died in 1459, once in Launde Abbey, Leicestershire but now lost, there was a display of the arms of no fewer than eleven families on nine shields, tracing the Chaworths' connections and descent,

and providing a visual counterpart to the genealogical details set out
in the long epitaph.[10] On the brass of Joan, Lady Cobham at Cobham,
already mentioned, there was an equally rich armorial identifying the
lines of descent which had come to be represented in her person.[11]

Sometimes these displays were apt to conceal or distort as much
as they laid bare. There were occasions when heraldry was used to
gloss over awkward moments in a family's history, when a new identity
was assumed or a transition to another family negotiated. In a window
once in St Chad's, now in St Mary's, Shrewsbury, the donor, Sir John
de Charlton, took the opportunity to associate himself with his wife's
family, the Poles of Powis, which was of superior blood to his own,
by having himself shown bearing her arms.[12] At Ewelme in Oxfordshire
Alice, daughter of Thomas Chaucer, strove to make her family look
grander than it actually was by assembling around the sides of her
father's tomb the arms of all the rich aristocratic families with which
he had been associated, omitting the humbler ones in which she – and
he – had no interest. In cases like these the none too subtle omissions
and ill-concealed sleights of hand show just how important lineage
was to the armigerous class. A no less selective approach is found in
the construction of epitaphs. The lengthy text on the brass of Sir
Thomas Green, who died in 1462, at Green's Norton in Northamptonshire
reads like one of the genealogical books of the Old Testament. It tells
us that Sir Thomas was the son of Sir Thomas, who married the
daughter of Lord Ferrers of Chartley, and that he in turn was the son
of another Sir Thomas, who married Lord Talbot's daughter . . . and
so on through the generations, carefully linking the Greens with local
baronial families of note. Except in the case of a few crusaders' monuments, by the fifteenth century pedigree had almost completely
eclipsed the honouring of military achievement on armorials and tomb
epitaphs. It was a microcosm of the larger change in chivalry from
the celebration of prowess to the celebration of blood, lineage and
social connections.

Tombs, Churches and Memory

In August 1408 the officials of the Court of Chivalry held a hearing in
Elsing church in Norfolk. The visit had been arranged at the request

of Sir Edward Hastings, who was defending his entitlement to the arms *or a manche gules* against Reginald, Lord Grey of Ruthin.[13] Up to this point the court had been holding its sessions at Norwich cathedral priory, Hastings having connections with the city. On 4 August, however, the court and its officials adjourned to the hall of Elsing parsonage, some twelve miles away. There on 6 August Sir Edward declared that in Elsing church 'there were evidences necessary to him, namely tombs and arms and images in several of the windows, which could not be carried to the courtroom without doing them harm'. At his request the court then adjourned and reconvened later in the day in the church. In the centre of the chancel Sir Edward drew the judges' attention to the brass of his great-grandfather Sir Hugh. He pointed out that the knight was shown holding a shield with the arms *or a manche gules* (with a label), to which he laid claim.

The transcript of the court's hearings contains a lengthy description of the brass, which survives, albeit mutilated, in Elsing church to this day. It is a rare contemporary description of a medieval monument. Sir Hugh was said to be shown dressed in a mail suit, with vambraces and rerebraces of plate, the visor of his bascinet raised, and his arms on his surcoat, shield and sword hilt.[14] Two angels, one on each side, were said to be supporting a pillow on which he rested his head. Details were given of four shields, two bearing the arms of Foliot, Sir Hugh's wife's family, and two bearing the arms of Hastings. Above the knight's figure there was said to be a tabernacle – a canopy – in the sides of which were figures, well and honourably worked, all identifiable by their arms. On the south side there were four such: working from the top, the king, the earl of Warwick, Hugh, Lord Despenser, and Lord Grey of Ruthin; and on the opposite side another four: Henry, duke of Lancaster, Laurence Hastings, earl of Pembroke, Ralph, Lord Stafford and a knight whom the record could not identify but who is known to have been Sir Aymer St Amand. The description concluded by noting the marginal epitaph (now lost) and the wealth of religious imagery in the canopy – Sir Hugh's soul being lifted heavenwards by two angels, the representation of St George triumphing over the dragon in the central oculus and the two-stage representation of the coronation of the Virgin at the summit.

Like Reginald, Lord Cobham's monument at Lingfield, the brass was a witness to the power of chivalric memory. It honoured Sir

Hugh's key role in Edward III's wars in Scotland and France. The figures represented in the 'tabernacle' were those of Sir Hugh's companions in arms.[15] Sir Hugh had fought under Laurence Hastings, earl of Pembroke, his half-brother, in Brittany in the early 1340s and in Aquitaine in 1345 on an expedition led by Henry of Lancaster; Warwick and Stafford were both commanders under whom he served at the siege of Calais in 1346–7; while Sir Aymer St Amand was a fellow Norfolk knight alongside whom he served in the same opera-tion. Sir Hugh Hastings was one of the ablest and best-connected retinue commanders of his day. He died on 22 July 1347 a month before the end of the siege of Calais, probably a victim of the dysentery which swept through the English camp. Had he lived, he might well have been numbered among the Founder Knights of the Order of the Garter. The brass was almost certainly commissioned by one who was an actual founder member – Henry, duke of Lancaster, the most senior of the co-executors. The inclusion of St George points strongly to the involvement of a patron familiar with the ideas which were to coalesce in a brotherhood under that saint's protection.[16]

The memory of Sir Hugh's achievements in arms, perpetuated by his brass, was to assure him a firm place in the Hastings family's remembrance of its past. There are tantalising hints that a knowledge of this same knight's deeds was also to live on in the collective memory of a family related to him by blood. This was the Camoys family of Trotton in Sussex, successive generations of which rebuilt and lavishly decorated Trotton church in the fourteenth century. The Camoys's artistic commissions at Trotton show a remarkable interest in chivalric imagery, which points to an intense pride in the chivalric and military traditions of their wider kin.[17] At the beginning of the 1380s Sir Thomas Camoys (later Lord Camoys) commissioned a dramatic series of wall paintings shortly after his succession to the family estates. Other than on the west wall, the subject matter of the scheme was entirely secular and chivalric. The paintings on the north wall consist of four big figures of knights, identifiable as Camoyses from the arms on their jupons, wearing tournament-style helms sporting the Camoys crest, set in a stark red landscape of stylised trees and bushes. One figure, set slightly apart from the others, holds a dog on a leash, apparently standing over dead game. Some twenty years after the completion of these paintings Lord Camoys commissioned a second set, again on a family theme, on the south wall. These take the form of a donor scene, Camoys himself kneeling before a prie-dieu and behind him his son Sir Richard and the latter's wife Joan (née Poynings). The Camoys crest and arms are again both shown. A little lower down, to the east of the door, is yet another heraldic scheme, today too faded to be reconstructed.

Camoys appears to have commissioned these paintings at least in part in response to the murky circumstances of his accession. A member of a collateral line of the family resident in Norfolk, he succeeded to the Sussex estates on the death without issue of his uncle, another Sir Thomas, with whom his relations had been uneasy. It is not impossible that Camoys was himself of illegitimate birth. In 1372, when the inquests on his uncle's lands were held, the jurors, after detailing the terms of the settlement, said that they did not know who his heir was. Whether or not Camoys was of the full blood, it is hardly surprising that he should have wanted to affirm his position by commissioning paintings in the church on a genealogical theme: he was in search of dynastic reassurance.

Almost certainly, however, there was a second factor which weighed with him, and that was the legacy of his Norfolk origins. On his mother's side he was related to Sir Hugh Hastings. His mother, Margaret, was one of the two sisters and co-heiresses of the one-time lord of Elsing Sir Richard Foliot, the other sister and co-heiress, Margery, marrying Sir Hugh. It was by virtue of this marriage that Hastings had gained possession of the manor of Elsing. As we have seen, according to the record of the Court of Chivalry the arms of Foliot had been depicted on Sir Hugh's brass. Thomas Camoys's decision to commission a chivalric display at Trotton may well have been inspired by an appreciation of the potential for such display in a church suggested by the Hastingses' earlier work at Elsing. Almost certainly he had seen Sir Hugh Hastings's brass at Elsing as a young man. The Camoyses were anyway a line with a strong sense of heraldry. Thomas's father, Sir John, had made a grant of a crest to another Norfolk knight, Sir John Harsick, which Harsick's son was proudly to display on his brass at Southacre in 1384.[18]

As the evidence from Elsing and Trotton shows, the churches of the gentry were replete with artefacts and imagery showing the ancestral power of the lords who held sway over them. Tombs, brasses, donor panels, dedicatory inscriptions, funerary armour, the ubiquitous heraldic displays – all these played a role in attesting to and authenticating a family's antiquity, proclaiming its version of its history and safeguarding its chivalric identity against the vexations of time.

The process by which a family set about creating such a visual witness to its past was intimately connected, as the Elsing case shows, with rituals of remembrance. Remembrance in the Middle Ages was not, as it is understood today, a matter largely concerned with recognising that those who were gone were gone. Rather, it was concerned with ensuring a continuing place for those who were gone in the memory and hearts of those still alive. Remembrance was, above all, about overcoming the finality of death through the establishment of ties binding the dead to the living. The process was set in motion at the funeral ceremony of the deceased, and subsequently perpetuated through the various re-enactments of it which followed, typically after an interval of one month and annually thereafter on the anniversary of the funeral.

The funerals of the aristocracy in the Middle Ages were typically very grand and ceremonious affairs. Their two main aims – the two related – were to demonstrate the honour and immortality of the deceased's family and to emphasise the religious dimension to Christian knighthood. Knights sometimes went into considerable detail in their wills to specify the trappings which were to accompany their obsequies. In 1347 John de Warenne, earl of Surrey, said that at his funeral at St Pancras Priory, Lewes he required 'four of my great horses to be armed with my arms, two for war and two for peace [to go] before my body on the day of my burial; those of war to be barded and to remain, and to be given to, the church of St Pancras with my [heraldic] arms in which those who shall ride them shall be clad'.[19]

Processions of richly decked chargers ridden by men dressed in the arms of the deceased were a striking feature of aristocratic funerals in the fourteenth century. In 1394 Sir Brian Stapleton, Knight of the Garter, willed that at his funeral at Healaugh Priory there should be 'a man armed with my arms, with my helm on his head, and that he be well mounted and a man of good looks of whatever condition he be'. In 1355 another northern lord, Ralph, Lord Neville of Raby, asked for his body to be borne into Durham cathedral on a chariot drawn by seven horses, and his coffin, before burial, to be carried down the nave on the shoulders of eight soldiers, four of whom were to display his peacetime arms and four his arms of war. Thirty years later Ralph's son Sir John was to ask for two men on mounts, wearing his armour, to carry between them a banner bearing the Neville arms with the chariot following them, bearing his body, likewise decked in the same arms.[20] By the end of the Hundred Years War the military character of funerals was to be reduced somewhat, as the nobility's direct experience of war weakened. By way of compensation, however, their heraldic character became still stronger. In 1463 the reinterment of the earl of Salisbury and his younger son at Bisham Abbey, a rich pageant-filled affair, was accompanied by the drawing up of an elaborate roll of arms which celebrated the Neville lineage. By the Tudor period heralds were regularly involved in the organising and recording of aristocratic funerals. It was under their influence that the practice developed of leaving behind the trappings of funerals – banners and helms – for display in the church. In Cobham church in Kent two such helms from Cobham family funerals are still to be seen today.

Once the funerary obsequies were over and the coffin lowered into the ground, the deceased's place of burial was marked by a large black cloth until such time as a tomb monument could be raised over it. There was a general expectation that the monument – whatever form it might take – should be in place within about a year of the deceased's passing. A longer time would be allowed when a very large monument, such as Earl Richard Beauchamp's at St Mary's, Warwick, was being commissioned, but were much more than a year or two to elapse, the deceased's family would risk bringing shame and dishonour on itself.

From the thirteenth century the practice developed of having an effigy in the likeness of the deceased placed on the tomb. Previously knights had been commemorated by simple cross-slab grave covers adorned with the symbol of their occupation – the sword. This kind of commemoration was still used in some parts of England, particularly the north, as late as the fifteenth century. Cross slabs would sometimes be identified by a marginal epitaph, but more often by the painting of the deceased's coat of arms alongside the sword. The origins of effigial commemoration are to be found in the revival of figure sculpture on the continent in the twelfth century. Under the impact of a revived humanism the practice developed of carving figures on church facades recognisably lifelike in character instead of the mask-like mortals of the past. The earliest such figures were commissioned in those parts of Europe most touched by the new sensibility – principally northern France and western Germany. It was accordingly in those areas that the first tomb effigies were commissioned. The new mode of sculpture was imported into England in the late twelfth century by the senior clergy, the pioneers of the commemorative avant-garde, and the first knightly effigies were commissioned in the early thirteenth. Knightly effigies in the West Country bear a strong resemblance to the armed figures on the west front of Wells cathedral, an indication that sculptors thought of tomb effigies as facade figures laid flat on their backs. The same teams of carvers were probably employed on both.

The finest early knightly monument effigies exhibit a raw, youthful energy. They show the deceased recumbent yet alert and ready to fight. A superbly carved knight at Dorchester Abbey in Oxfordshire shows the commemorated in the act of drawing his sword from its sheath. The dress code on the figures was determined by the theory of the three estates. Knights, since they were the group whose divinely ordained duty was to fight, were shown attired for war. At Walkern in Hertfordshire a knight of the Lanvallei family was shown wearing a massive tournament-style pot helm with eye slits, his face almost completely hidden. The sculptors of these effigies very likely had actual pieces of armour in their workshops to work from. The grim realism of the Walkern effigy is such that its presence in a church today looks incongruous. Yet at the time no incongruity would have been felt because knighthood was seen as a calling dedicated to God.

The main means by which the military status of the commemorated was shown on these effigies was through the careful representation of armour. By the regular updating of their models sculptors kept pace with the changing styles for four centuries, from the early thirteenth century to the mid-seventeenth. Their quality of observation was so precise that the history of armour in the Middle Ages can be written almost exclusively from a study of these effigies. Up to roughly Edward I's time knights were shown in a fairly standard harness, consisting of a mail hauberk, the foundation of bodily defence since before the Conquest, a linen surcoat thrown over the hauberk and a shield held in the left hand. From the early fourteenth century a number of reinforcements were added to these basic defences. The brass of Sir William Fitzralph, of about 1335, at Pebmarsh in Essex shows the knight with metal plates over the front of his legs and the sides of his arms, and extra plates or leather reinforcements protecting the elbow joints and shoulders. By the mid-fourteenth century the linen surcoat, already shortened by the 1340s, had been superseded by a new garment, the tight-fitting jupon, while the rest of the body was encased in plate. In the first quarter of the fifteenth century changes to the harness focused on the elaboration and strengthening of the plate armour. The mail aventail (or collar) round the neck was replaced by the metal gorget; additional defences were provided for the shoulders and arms; and extra plates were attached to the skirt. When knights in their testaments asked to be shown 'honestly according to [their] estate', what they meant was that they wanted to be shown in the most up-to-date armour. The sculptors and engravers of the day went to great lengths to achieve this. Examples of effigies showing knights in precisely observed armour are to be found at Stoke d'Abernon in Surrey, Lowick in Northamptonshire and St George's Chapel, Windsor Castle.

If accurate representation of armour was a measure of the effigy's importance as a witness to status, a very different aspect, the position of the commemorated's hands, made clear its other function, that of acting as a focus for intercession. By the early fifteenth century it was the near-universal practice for effigies to be shown with their hands pressed together in prayer. At one level this pose can be seen as an expression of the deceased knight's pious devotion, a mark of his Christian commitment; at another, however, it can be seen as an indication of his need for intercession, his dependence on both priest and passers-by for prayer. Medieval tomb effigies performed the vital role in contemporary strategies for salvation of acting as mnemonic prompts, as spurs to the offering of prayers for the soul of the commemorated. Since it was the general belief of the time that most souls after death went directly neither to heaven nor to hell but to a place in between called purgatory, whence they could be moved by the prayers of the living faithful to heaven, most knights in their wills took care to ensure a steady supply of prayer. The text often employed for the opening line of tomb epitaphs – 'Orate pro anima' (Pray for me) – was a reminder to priest and passer-by of the urgency of the commemorated's need for their assistance.

In grander commemorative schemes the tomb and altar might well stand at the centre of a rich intercessory discourse stretching across several media – stone, woodwork and glass. During the Court of Chivalry's visit to Elsing in 1408 Sir Edward Hastings was able to draw attention not only to Sir Hugh's brass but also to the rich display of heraldic glass in the windows.[21] In the east window, he pointed out, there were the kneeling figures of his great-grandfather and his wife: 'In the window above the altar in the chancel [there is] the figure of a knight carrying the arms of Hastings and the figure of a lady vested in the arms of Foliot, the two kneeling and supporting in their hands a church, and a helm with a crest bearing the same arms between them.' What Sir Edward was describing here was a donor panel of the sort to become familiar in the fifteenth century, in which the figures of the donors were shown with a representation of the church which they had paid for. Along the sides of the same window and along the top, Sir Edward continued, there was further evidence which backed his case – a gallery of no fewer than sixteen shields, all bearing either the same arms or the arms of Hastings and Valence. At the foot of the window there was a short inscription which read, 'Pray to your Sone made Marye, In whos wirshipp yis Chirch have rowght. Hugh the Hastynges, and Maiorie my Wyf, Lady foryete us noght.' Sir Edward described other, smaller windows in the church – the six shields in the side windows of the chancel bearing the arms of Hastings and Foliot, and the row of shields with the same arms in the nave windows, nine on the south side and five on the north. The armorial which he highlighted, parts of which survived to the eighteenth century, was one of the grandest and most comprehensive of its day. It formed part of a multimedia display by means of which Sir Hugh not only marked the church out as his creation but also involved priest and parishioners alike in offering up prayers for his soul.

Richer still in its imagery and textual discourse was the scheme commissioned to assist the soul of a later and still greater knight, Richard Beauchamp, earl of Warwick, who died in 1439. Beauchamp had asked to be buried in St Mary's, Warwick, and after his death a chantry chapel was constructed on the south side of the church by his executors to house his tomb, the chapel and tomb being conceived together as an artistic unity. The overall theme of the decoration is the earl's reception into the kingdom of heaven, the earl's upward ascent being serenaded in the windows by a chorus of angels running along the traceried lights at the top, while below, on his tomb, the earl's hands are drawn apart in awe at the drama of the unfolding vision. The earl's effigy, although a witness to worldly status, is conceived as an image of Christian knighthood. He is shown as the perfect paladin, the visionary knight, a servant of both God and king.

In a chantry foundation of the kind established for Beauchamp's benefit the secular priorities of knighthood were set in the larger context of the need to secure maximum intercessory benefit for the deceased's soul. The twin aspects of these foundations, the secular and the religious, might be thought to sit in somewhat uneasy relation with each other, indeed to be mutually opposed. Yet in reality contemporaries saw little or no conflict between the two, for in their eyes religion was essentially family religion. For knights prayerful commemoration went hand in hand with the cherishing of ancestry and the nurturing of a sense of the past. The process might be assisted by the commissioning of retrospective monuments.[22] In 1420, when Sir Arnald Savage endowed prayers in Bobbing church in Kent for his soul and those of his parents, he commissioned two big canopied brasses, one for each of the parties commemorated. A generation earlier in 1376, when Sir Marmaduke Constable founded a chantry chapel at Flamborough in Yorkshire, he provided for no fewer than three brasses, one each for his grandfather, mother and himself. The establishment of chantries and anniversary Masses, while directed principally at the salvation of the soul, contributed to the preserving of family and chivalric memory. For the knightly class remembrance was family remembrance. Through chantry chapel foundations family identity was strengthened and the chivalric sense of lineage with it.

Literature and Memory

Memory in the early and central Middle Ages was often associated with physical objects. Objects in churches such as tombs, banners and items of funerary armour carried with them associations which helped preserve memory. Increasingly, however, with the spread of literacy, the witness of objects was supplemented by that of the written text. In churches short epitaphs identifying the person or persons commemorated were placed on the sides of tombs and tomb slabs. In windows appeals for intercessory prayer were inserted at the foot of donor panels. On the sides of fittings such as fonts and screens inscriptions were placed asking for prayers for those who had donated these objects. Textual discourse was ubiquitous in churches. Gradually, however, as literacy became more widely disseminated, the interest of the laity in writing took more secular forms. Knights and noblemen began commissioning family histories, authorising chivalric biographies and compiling cartularies, or collections of title deeds. History in a written form was taking on a life of its own.

Some of these early exercises in written transmission were fairly basic in character. Typically they were the work of small religious houses with which the families commissioning them were associated as patrons. For the most part they were composed of two main elements, the history of the house in which they were compiled and the genealogy and armorial bearings of the patron's family. It was historical writings of this sort which often informed the recollection of the deponents in the Scrope–Grosvenor suit of 1386. The abbot of Bridlington, for example, sent two canons along to the hearings with a book of chronicles to substantiate his support for Lord Scrope's claim to the disputed arms. These chronicles, it was said, traced the history of the Scrope family back to a certain Hugh Scrope in the time of King Stephen, whose son Richard had granted property to the priory, and made reference to certain Scropes who had come over with William the Conqueror.[23] The heads of other religious houses gave evidence in the hearings on the basis of chronicles in their possession. The prior of Watton produced a chronicle allegedly written at the time of the Conquest which contained a list of the lords who had come over from Normandy and numbered members of the Scrope family among them.[24] The clergy who compiled these chronicles appear to have been as well versed in the details of lineage and descent as the knights themselves. In many cases their recollection was aided by the presence in their churches of tombs and banners commemorating the people they wrote about. A text from the north Midlands, the 'Pedigree of the Founders of Worksop Priory', written by one Pigote around 1470, refers to the layout of the tombs in Worksop priory church, noting precisely where each of the priory's patrons was buried and proceeding from this information to give brief biographical details of each of them in turn.[25] The clergy were as deeply implicated in preserving chivalric memory as the chivalric class themselves.

There was a close relation between family chronicles and cartularies of title deeds. The compilation of cartularies had been pioneered in the early Middle Ages by the monasteries, which had felt the need for such documentary evidence to assist in the defence of their property at law. By the thirteenth century the practice of compiling cartularies had spread to the laity, in particular to proprietors of knightly rank who had put their estates together largely by purchase. Such collections of documents played a key role in the formation of gentry identity in these years. In the peaceful thirteenth century the fortunes of many knightly families were founded to a greater extent on property acquisition than on the winning of military renown. What links these volumes so closely to the family chronicles is their common interest in genealogy. On their opening folios cartularies typically included a version of the family's descent. These table-like documents, usually brief and to the point, were always carefully constructed and, like tomb armorials, often hid as much as they revealed. Since cartularies were concerned with the descent of an estate, and few estates descended uninterrupted in the male line, the descents did not usually record a lineage as such; they recorded descents with jumps and fresh starts. Often marriage rather than lineage was what mattered in the acquisition and dispersal of estates, and cartulary genealogies reflected that fact. Thus in the cartulary of the Pierreponts of Holme Pierrepont in Nottinghamshire the early history of the Pierrepont family is almost completely ignored because the Pierreponts had acquired the manor of Holme, to which they added their surname, in the late thirteenth century, by marriage to the heiress Annora de Manvers.[26] Accordingly, in tracing the ownership of the Holme estate before the thirteenth century, it was the Manvers line which mattered, not that of Pierrepont. A family's recollection of its past was closely related to its sense of place. Lineage could be manipulated to suit a family's view of its social and geographical position in the world.

A cartulary which neatly illustrates the interconnectedness of the themes of family, land and place is that of the Pedwardine family of

Burton Pedwardine in Lincolnshire.[27] The Pedwardines, a family of
Herefordshire origin, had gained possession of the Burton estate near
Sleaford in the early fourteenth century through Sir Roger de
Pedwardine's marriage to Alice, daughter and co-heiress of Sir Henry
de Longchamp. Before the Longchamps' time the manor had been
held by the Crounes. The cartulary was put together at the end of
the fourteenth century by Robert Pedwardine, and it was added to
later, Robert's sons' birthdays being entered in the reign of Henry VI.
The collection brings together deeds relating to the family's lands in
Lincolnshire, Northamptonshire, Westmorland and Hampshire, all
arranged in alphabetical order of place. Prefacing the collection is the
customary genealogy. This is more detailed and informative than most.
It occupies a full spread and traces the descent of the Burton estate
from the twelfth century to the early fifteenth, giving details of heads
of the family, their dates of death where known, their spouses and
their places of burial. It says, for example, of Sir Henry de Croune
that he died on Tuesday after the feast of the Nativity of the Blessed
Virgin Mary in 1274, and that his body was interred in Swineshead
Abbey and his heart in the Lady Chapel of Burton Pedwardine church.
It says of Alice de Longchamp that she married Sir Roger de
Pedwardine, and that she died on 15 May 1330 and was buried on the
north side of the Lady Chapel of the same church. An especially
noteworthy aspect of the genealogy is the evidence of the family's
growing identification with Burton Pedwardine parish church. The
entry for Sir Roger II, for example, records that he entirely rebuilt the
fabric except for the south aisle. As in the case of the Pierreponts at
Holme, the Pedwardines' sense of identity was closely bound up with
the geographical setting of their lordship. The importance which they
attached to that setting is reflected in the attention accorded to it in
the cartulary. Their attachment to the other signifier of identity, the
family coat of arms, also stands out: the arms of all three families
who held the estate were displayed in the margins against the entries
relating to them.

Cartularies were compiled by landed families of both very ample
means and very few. Some of the grandest such volumes were put
together for families of the highest magnate rank. The cartularies
compiled by the Beauchamps and the Mortimers, both fourteenth-
century productions, are massive volumes. In the archives and muniment

chests of the nobility, however, there would probably be, alongside them, other types of record which preserved family and dynastic memory. If there was any one matter to which the nobility attached even greater importance than the transmission of their estates, it was the memory of ancestral achievement in arms. Ensuring this more chivalric sort of recollection entailed the keeping not only of cartularies but chronicles, genealogies, poems and, in some cases, an assortment of family heirlooms.

The family which appears to have taken the greatest interest in preserving recollection of its chivalric achievement was that of the Beauchamp earls of Warwick. The Beauchamps were one of the oldest and most distinguished families in the peerage. They had held the ancient comital title of Warwick since the thirteenth century and they prided themselves on their long tradition of crusading and service to the Crown in war. Well before the celebrated Richard Beauchamp took to the field under Henry V they had enlisted in all the main English campaigns in Scotland and France. The cultivation of chivalric distinction formed an essential part of their self-fashioning.

A noteworthy aspect of the Beauchamps' interest in their past was the importance which they attached to ancestral legend. In the thirteenth century an earlier earl of Warwick, of the Beaumont line, had commissioned a romance, *Guy of Warwick*, about a legendary forebear who had performed deeds of prowess in the Holy Land.[28] Versions of the *Guy* legend enjoyed wide popularity in the late Middle Ages, and by the fourteenth century the Beauchamps were claiming the eponymous hero as a real ancestor who could legitimise their ambitions. Generations of the Beauchamp family grew up in Warwick Castle surrounded by objects associated with Guy. There were fabrics, tapestries and bed hangings all 'wrought with the Armes and Story of Guy of Warwick', while in the hall were the sword, harness and ragged staves said to have belonged to him. In the mid-fourteenth century the cult was given a boost by Earl Thomas I, who encouraged the idea of Guy as a giant and commissioned an enormous statue of him for the chapel at Guy's Cliffe, where he had lived as a hermit. For generations the name Guy was one bestowed on sons in the Beauchamp line. In the 1420s two new lives of the legendary hero were written, a French prose version commissioned by Earl Richard and a verse life commissioned from the poet Lydgate by Margaret, the earl's daughter.[29]

It is against this background of the nurturing of chivalric reputation that the interest of the later Beauchamps in their family history needs to be seen. The Beauchamps were a lineage with an unusually sharp eye to the past. In the 1480s the last of the line, the elderly Anne Beauchamp, Earl Richard's youngest daughter and the Kingmaker's widow, commissioned two remarkable works celebrating the family's history. One was the so-called Rous Roll, a pictorial account of the earls and countesses of Warwick with their coats of arms, compiled by John Rous, a family retainer; and the other the *Beauchamp Pageant*, an illustrated life of Earl Richard himself.[30] The coverage of the earl's life in the *Pageant* is remarkably full and wide-ranging. Where the concerns of the more modest Rous Roll are essentially local, the *Pageant's* interests extend to events right across England, France and further afield. The implication must be that the illustrator-author of the work drew on an account or accounts of the earl's life compiled in his lifetime, among them probably a narrative written by one Master Brewster, a clerical retainer employed by Earl Richard, whose notes were later used by William Worcester. Very possibly too the illustrator-author had access to an account of the earl's *pas d'armes* at Guines in 1415, an event in which the earl distinguished himself and to which the illustrator-author gave ample coverage in his work. Both the *Pageant* and the range of sources which lie behind it attest to the keen interest which the Beauchamps took in their history. That we think so well of them today is due in no small part to their own efforts to ensure that we do. They appreciated that while a knight could win fame for himself by performing brave deeds, that fame could pass away. If a reputation were to live on, it had to be nurtured and cherished. It had to find permanent witness in writing or art.

Much the same point can be made in respect of the reputations of some of the knights who had made their names in the earlier stages of the Hundred Years War. Then, as later, great reputations were not the spontaneous outcome of great deeds of arms; they were the result of careful nurturing and manipulation by those who controlled the flow of information. We can take, for example, the reputations of two knights who fought under the Black Prince in France, Sir John Chandos and Sir James Audley.[31] Chandos and Audley were among the most celebrated knights of their day. Knighton described Chandos as 'the most talked about knight of the age', while for Walsingham he was 'the most famous of knights'. Audley owed his fame to his achievements at the battle of Poitiers, where according to Geoffrey le Baker he was the bravest warrior on the field. What is interesting is the sheer consistency with which in contemporary sources the two men are spoken of together. In the newsletters which the prince and his captains sent back to England in 1355–6 the two were invariably presented as almost inseparable. In the *Life of the Black Prince*, written in the 1380s, they were treated almost as one. The author of this latter work presents them as inseparable even in death, telling us that when Chandos died, so too 'as often happens, the other follows'. There seems to have been a clear attempt to present the two as brothers-in-arms – not merely as famous knights each in his own right, but as the Roland and Oliver of their day. So successful was the literary tactic that it is in precisely those terms that we see them today; the spin-doctoring worked. If there was a tendency in chivalric literature to present knights as born and not made, it is equally the case that knightly reputations could be made when not naturally born.

Chivalry generated a rich repertory of contemporary witness: tombstones and tomb effigies, funerary armour, objects associated with legendary heroes, armorials on walls and in windows, rolls of arms, biographies and family chronicles. Chivalry was found in the landscape, in churches, in baronial halls, even in abbey refectories. Contemporaries made little distinction between text and symbol in the recording and authentication of chivalry. The memory of chivalry lived on in the culture which it created, and that culture was at once visual, physical and literary. Its overriding concern was to achieve everlasting fame for the knight. As Sir John Clanvow wrote in the 1380s, 'a thing that worldly men desire greatly is that their fame might last long after them upon earth'.

16

Chivalric Literature, 1250–1485

By the late Middle Ages the world of chivalry was being described, recorded and evoked in a rich variety of literary forms – chronicles, romances, chivalric biographies and manuals of courtesy. Each of these genres presented chivalric knighthood as an ideal form of behaviour on which individual knights might base their own lives. The close attention which writers gave to crafting the knightly ideal as a code for imitation is found in both fictional and historical works, genres which today would be considered quite separate. Poets and writers of history alike sought to offer their readers models of knightly conduct perfectly fulfilled. The wide circulation which romance and knightly literature enjoyed in the late Middle Ages attests to its continuing importance in shaping and sustaining the chivalric ideal – and doing so still in an age when not all knights were active soldiers.

Readers and Reading in the Late Middle Ages

The strong literary dimension to late medieval chivalric culture is well illustrated by what is known of gentry reading matter in this period. By the mid-fifteenth century many well-to-do gentlemen were assembling what they called grete bokes, collections or miscellanies in which a variety of texts were brought together. One of the best examples, the grete boke of Sir John Paston, a courtier knight of Edward IV, compiled in the late 1460s, contains material relating to jousting, warfare, statecraft and the staging of chivalric ceremonial. Its lengthy opening section consists of a collection of knightly challenges and *pas d'armes* of the previous half-century, beginning with Richard Beauchamp's exploits at Guines in 1415, going on through the triumphs of Sir John Astley, and ending with Anthony Woodville's encounter with the Bastard of Burgundy at Smithfield in 1467. The middle section includes an English translation of Vegetius' treatise on war, some ordinances of war (those of Henry V and the earl of Salisbury) and a copy of a surrender summons used by Salisbury at the siege of Le Mans. The concluding section contains political and historical materials, notably extracts from Higden's *Polychronicon* and a text of the *Secreta Secretorum* in its English translation by Lydgate and Burgh – the so-called *Governance of Kings and Princes*.[1]

Paston's grete boke was heavily indebted, particularly in its opening section, to that of the knight whose most celebrated challenges and achievements were contained in it: Sir John Astley, a Knight of the Garter and household knight of Edward IV. Astley's own miscellany, put together in or after 1461, was one of the most compendious chivalric manuals of its day. Among its contents were the oath and ceremonies of the Knights of the Bath, a translation of Vegetius' treatise on war, Stephen Scrope's translation of Christine de Pisan's *Epistle of Othea*, a poem about Henry VI's coronation, an English version of the governance book the *Secreta Secretorum* and verses by John Lydgate.[2] Astley's grete boke, like Paston's, was both a descriptive text and a how-to volume, a guide to chivalry which served both as a reference book and a manual of instruction.

Chivalric material was admittedly not so prominent in some of the other grete bokes of the period, but it still figured, taking its place alongside other interesting material, notably texts on politics, history and courtesy. Like Astley's and Paston's, William Brandon's collection of the 1470s included Vegetius' treatise on war and the English *Secreta Secretorum*, mixing these with John Russell's book of nurture and two chronicles, Robert of Gloucester's rhymed *Chronicle* and a version of the Middle English *Brut*.[3] From the early sixteenth century, a composite book compiled by Humphrey Newton of Pownall in Cheshire contains a romance with echoes of *Sir Gawain and the Green Knight* which Newton may have composed himself, excerpts from the Middle English *Brut* chronicle, a king list, a pedigree of the earls of Chester, some Latin tracts, two English courtesy books and material on genealogy and lineage.[4] A collection which John Talbot, earl of Shrewsbury, presented to Queen Margaret of Anjou in 1445 contained the statutes of the Order of the Garter, various *chansons de geste* and chronicles, and treatises on government and warfare.[5] Yet another collection brought together still more familiar items: extracts from Vegetius' treatise, the English *Secreta Secretorum*, a version of the romance *Guy of Warwick*, a tract on virtues and vices and, more enigmatically, a 'boke of Saynt Isodre'.[6] In many other miscellanies much the same assortments of material are again brought together – tracts on chivalry, extracts from chronicles, heraldic and genealogical matter, books of nurture and occasionally lives of saints.

It is significant that material on chivalry should have been juxtaposed in these volumes with material on such a variety of other subjects. Texts take on additional meanings from those alongside them. If chivalric content appears in a volume in which there is also content on politics, governance and nurture, then it is likely that it was read with an appreciation of this other matter in mind. Much the same can be said if a book exclusively concerned with chivalry had a place in a library which also featured books on other, albeit related, subjects. Sir John Paston's grete boke, like Astley's, was almost entirely concerned with matters of chivalry and heraldry, yet it formed part of a library which also included a book of statutes, volumes on other legal matters and a range of devotional literature. It can plausibly be argued, therefore, that its owner saw some sort of connection between the subjects of all these volumes.

Sir John Paston, like other gentry book owners, came from a family whose members were active in local government and in the administration of justice. The concerns of people like him were for the most part mundane, centring on the acquisition and protection of property, the enhancement of family repute and the management of local business on the bench and in the county court. Whether the lives of these knights were varied or humdrum, busy or inactive, it seems unlikely that matters chivalric were ever far from their minds. Chivalry had a bearing on a whole variety of matters central to gentry identity – heraldry, courtesy and nurture, jousting and the practice of war. It provided the gentry with an ethical system to their taste and an organising framework for personal relations. As these miscellanies of texts show, it was also seen as having a bearing on seemingly unrelated aspects of their experience. In the late Middle Ages chivalric assumptions were crucial to the upholding of personal and family honour, the conduct of relations between fellow gentlemen, the handling of litigation and the burdens of government. The practice and lore of chivalry underpinned the whole political order. It is no wonder that books and tracts on chivalry are found in so many gentry book collections of the time.

Arthurian Romance

The huge appetite for chivalric literature in aristocratic circles led to an outpouring of Arthurian writing in the later Middle Ages. The earliest texts of this sort to achieve a wide circulation – Wace's *Brut*, for example – were written in French or Anglo-Norman. From the end of the thirteenth century English adaptations were being made of these, some in prose, others in rhymed couplets and various stanzaic patterns. By the early fourteenth century the flow of Arthurian literature was rapidly turning into a flood. Some twenty-three separate Arthurian romances have come down to us from the period 1300–1500, many of them in multiple copies. These represent a full quarter of the hundred and more English rhymed romances written during these two centuries.[7] A minority of the works belong to the distinct alliterative tradition, the most important being the *Morte Arthure*, one of the masterpieces of the so-called alliterative revival. Works in the alliterative mode, unlike the other poems, bear little or no trace of French influence. With only a few exceptions, the authors of this group of works withheld their identity. It is suggested, on the evidence of his familiarity with the laws of war, that the author of the *Morte Arthure* was a clerk with diplomatic experience.[8] Most of the other poems were probably the work of men of moderately humble background. The absence of dedicatory epistles suggests that they were rarely if ever written at the behest of illustrious patrons. Almost certainly they were non-commissioned, but written in anticipation of finding a ready market among the gentry and urban elites. The evidence of circulation suggests that their authors were rarely disappointed.

In several respects the romances developed a distinctly insular strain which distinguished them from the corresponding literature of France and other parts of Europe. One notable characteristic is their appetite for violent and sensational incident. Where physical combat and fisticuffs are lacking or low-key in a French original, or where some favourite trial of arms is missing, the English redactor will make good the deficit. In *Sir Launfal*, for example, a version of the delicate Arthurian *lai* of *Lanval* by Marie de France, a tournament and a giant-fight are gratuitously added, radically altering the balance of the original. When compared with the tastes of their French counterparts, the English poets are relatively unsophisticated. Their instinct was always to enliven the narrative with lots of buffetings, punch-ups and rough and tumble. In an age when the English were often doing well in war with the French, this was doubtless just the kind of incident that audiences wanted to read.

The strong emphasis on masculine vigour chimes with another characteristic of the romances: their comparative lack of interest in the more refined aspects of love. Where a French poet would instinctively include a risqué love encounter to enliven his work, his English redactor would usually opt for something less sensuous. In English romances women are trivialised, even marginalised, indeed in some cases dismissed altogether. The poetic emphasis is much more on highlighting and valorising the bonds between and among men than on exploration of the delicate relations between the sexes, for which the romance genre is distinguished. It is striking, for example, that in English poems of the period adultery is far less prominent a theme than in the French originals. In Malory's *Morte Darthur* what causes the downfall of the Round Table is less the adulterous affair between Sir Lancelot and Guinevere as such than the heinous ambitions of the slippery Sir Mordred. In Malory's version of the story Guinevere's manipulativeness is turned not on Lancelot but on Mordred, whom she first tricks and then renders powerless by her retreat to the safety of the Tower.[9] The place traditionally occupied by adultery in French narratives of the end of the Round Table is occupied in their English counterparts by deeds of treachery and arms.

The English romances can also be distinguished from their French counterparts in the prominence they accord to Sir Gawain as a figure through whom to explore the dilemmas of knighthood. In English romance the gallant Sir Gawain features almost as prominently as King Arthur himself. In no fewer than seven of the romances he stands as the unchallenged hero. In Geoffrey of Monmouth's original version of the Arthurian story, in his *History of the Kings of Britain*, Gawain had been pictured as an energetic, headstrong, valorous young knight.

These characteristics were seized on and developed by Chrétien de Troyes, whose works established him as the model of masculinity, a hero dedicated to fighting. It was because of his uncomplicated manly qualities that Gawain was to exert such a powerful appeal to English writers: to them he was the archetype of the fighting knight, the essential foil to knightly heroes motivated by consuming erotic or mystical drives. Lacking any clear vision or destiny, he could be made a knight for all seasons.[10]

Gawain entered into his starring role in three major poems of the late fourteenth century – the stanzaic *Morte Arthur*, the alliterative *Morte Arthure* and, above all, the exquisite *Sir Gawain and the Green Knight*. In all three works he is accorded a position of honour. He is presented as brave, valiant and chivalrous, someone around whom things happen; he is invested with the status of a hero. In the poems in which he meets his death it is his loyalty which is stressed. He is pictured as the good 'son', the submissive accepter of Arthur's authority. In the *Morte Arthure* his slayer, the evil Mordred, even goes so far as to pay tribute to him, lauding him as 'matchless on earth, the most courteous knight, hardiest in strength, most affable in hall, most gentle in conduct'.[11] Gawain's character is subtly developed in the closing stanzas of the poem. He is made to command our respect not only for his prowess but for his courtesy and restraint, his composure in moments of crisis; and this deeper chivalric distinction adds something to his standing as an exemplar of knighthood. It is difficult not to see in the Gawain of the English romances something of the chivalric ideal to which English knighthood aspired in the age of the Hundred Years War.[12]

In *Sir Gawain and the Green Knight*, one of the masterpieces of the late fourteenth-century alliterative flowering, Gawain, the simple unquestioning fighting knight, is made a vehicle for the exploration of the conflicts and dilemmas inherent in the knightly ideal itself.[13] *Sir Gawain* is a relatively short and concentrated work of some 2,500 lines written in stanzas of varying length, each concluding with five short lines of rhymed verse. It survived in a single manuscript alongside three other poems – *Pearl*, *Patience* and *Purity* – all apparently of the same authorship. Although the identity of the common author is unknown, it seems likely, on the evidence of his dialect, that he came from the north-west Midlands. Quite possibly he developed ties with the court as a result of Richard II's cultivation of his Cheshire power base in the 1380s and 1390s.

The story of the poem skilfully weaves two main themes, the challenge or beheading game and the temptation test. At King Arthur's Christmas court the Green Knight rides in and issues a challenge: anyone present can strike him a blow provided that he, the recipient, can return the blow in a year's time. Gawain takes up the challenge and strikes off the knight's head, but the latter, picking it up, tells him to meet him a year hence at the Green Chapel. As the appointed day approaches, Gawain rides forth and on Christmas Eve comes to Bertilak's castle, where the next theme is picked up with his temptation by his hostess. Gawain strikes a deal with Bertilak that at the end of each day, after Bertilak has gone hunting while Gawain has stayed behind, each will pass on to the other the day's winnings. Gawain dutifully keeps faith with his host by rendering to him the kisses which he receives from the lady on her daily visits. However, he accepts from her, without passing on to Bertilak, a magic girdle which will protect him from violent death. When the encounter with the knight at the Green Chapel finally arrives, the knight survives the blows which Gawain strikes at him and reveals himself as none other than Bertilak. Gawain realises that he has been drawn into a plot to tempt him into a betrayal of his honour and the honour of the Knights of the Round Table. He returns to Arthur's court wearing the girdle sinister-wise as a badge of shame, to indicate his sense of personal and cultural failure.

In this penetrating work the poet, instead of offering us, as we might expect, a grand finale – the medieval equivalent of a shoot-out at the corral – chooses a deliberately low-key ending. The attraction of this strategy is that he allows himself the opportunity to reflect on the dilemmas which Gawain has faced on his quest. Was Gawain right to place a greater value on saving his life than on keeping faith with his host? Was the keeping of his promise more important than any other consideration? How should he have behaved each time the lady visited him at his bedside? With great care and subtlety the poet reworks the elements traditional in the Gawain story to subject the compromises at the heart of medieval chivalry to interrogation and analysis. The issue raised is the eternal one of conflict between an idealised code and the limitations of the humans who live by it. Gawain on his return sees himself as having fatally undermined his integrity by the compromises he has made. The reader, recognising the difficulties that he faced, might say that in the circumstances he acquitted himself with some honour and no little distinction.

In no later work would the dilemmas facing a knight be explored with as much insight as in *Sir Gawain and the Green Knight*. Indeed, in the fifteenth century it seemed as if the Arthurian cycle was exhausting its capacity for creative enterprise. The sequels to the Gawain story produced by the poetasters of the fifteenth century were, for the most part, as unoriginal as they were lacking in artistry. At the very end of the Middle Ages, however, one more great work was produced, a work on an epic scale, a summing-up of the whole Arthurian cycle – Sir Thomas Malory's *Morte Darthur*.

Malory undertook his ambitious redaction of the Arthurian stories in eight long romances, each telling a single story.[14] He began with Arthur's birth and the establishment of the Round Table, continued with Arthur's war against the Romans, the stories of Lancelot and Gareth, Tristan and Iseult, and the Quest for the Holy Grail, and concluded with the tragic unravelling of Arthur's world – the doomed affair of Lancelot and Guinevere, Arthur's death in battle and the final break-up of the Order of the Round Table. Malory saw his intended audience, in his own words, as 'Jentyl men and Jantyl wymmen': that is, people of his own rank and background. It appears that he wrote for his own satisfaction, not at the behest of a powerful patron. On internal evidence completion of the work can be dated to the late 1460s, when Malory was detained in Newgate prison on suspicion of plotting against Edward IV. In 1485, the year of Bosworth, a text of the work was produced by Caxton, whose didactic aim was to instruct his readers in 'noble actes of chyvale', and the work quickly became a bestseller. It was reprinted, with some changes and additions, in 1498 and 1529 by Wynkyn de Worde, Caxton's successor. Three more editions were to follow in the century or so before the Civil War, in 1557, 1585 and 1634. After a fall from grace in the Enlightenment it enjoyed a revival in the early nineteenth century and since then has never been out of print.

For nearly four and a half centuries the only known text of Malory's work was that produced by Caxton. Then in 1934, in one of the great literary discoveries of the twentieth century, a manuscript copy was found in a safe in the warden's bedroom at Winchester College. For the first time it became possible to approach Malory's work with some directness, circumventing Caxton's extensive editorial interventions. The Winchester manuscript, it was clear, was not Malory's original – that, almost certainly, is lost beyond recall. Nonetheless it brought the reader closer to the working of Malory's own mind than ever before. To compare the Winchester text with Caxton's was to be taught a number of illuminating lessons. Caxton's edition of the *Morte Darthur* had given the reader a text which brought the various narrative units together as chapters in a book. The Winchester manuscript showed that this impression of seamless unity was the result of editorial tidying-up. The Winchester Malory not only lacks the book and chapter divisions found in the Caxton edition; it is also marred by inconsistencies and awkwardnesses, most of which Caxton, when preparing his text for publication, took care to smooth out. It was now clear that the view of Malory which readers had enjoyed before 1934 was skewed by Caxton's editing. In the light of the discrepancies between the two texts, it is reasonable to ask how far Malory conceived of his stories as comprising a single, all-encompassing history. The suggestion has been made that he may have written the work as a collection of almost independent parts with little or no structural connection between them. Against this hypothesis, however, should be set the fact that Malory's text contains an elaborate system of embellished initials which establishes its own structural divisions to assist the reader. Thus it appears that Caxton simply replaced this scheme with a more user-friendly one with roots in continental practice.[15] To appreciate the changes which Caxton made is not to suggest that Malory's original work was entirely without unity. On the contrary, Malory conceived of it, in his words, as a 'hoole book'. He saw it as amounting to much more than the sum of its parts.

Malory, like most medieval writers, did not picture himself in modern terms as an original author. In the manner of the day, he was essentially a redactor and translator. He tells us in the *Morte Darthur* that he 'reduced' his source texts into English. By this he meant that through a process of editing, translating and abbreviating he turned a disparate body of French material into a narrative acceptable to an English audience. In the often substantial adaptations which he made to his French sources we are able to detect something of what he considered distinctive about English taste in the late fifteenth century.

One of the most notable features of Malory's work is the importance he attached to the person of Sir Lancelot. Lancelot had featured relatively little in English romances before the late fourteenth century. While he had enjoyed a high profile in the stanzaic *Morte Arthure* of around 1400, it was only in Malory's work that he was brought to the fore as an exemplar of perfect knighthood. Indeed, in Malory's narrative he dominates at the expense of Arthur himself. In Book 2, which tells of Arthur's war with Rome, Malory ruthlessly edited his sources so as to emphasise Lancelot's key role; it is thus Lancelot, not Arthur, who emerges as the most valiant fighting knight. By the end of Book 3, 'The Noble Tale of Sir Launcelot Du Lac', a book necessarily devoted to his deeds, his pre-eminence among the Knights of the Round Table is assured: 'At that time,' says Malory, 'Sir Lancelot had the greatest name of any knight in the whole world.' In Book 5, the story of Sir Tristram, the theme most strongly emphasised in the long opening section is the friendship between Lancelot and Tristram. 'Of all the knights, he [Lancelot] bears the flower,' says Tristram. At the very end of the saga, as the Round Table breaks up, it is by Lancelot, and not the dying Arthur, that the speech of lamentation, which forms the epilogue, is spoken.

Malory saw in Sir Lancelot the model for a practical, rather than a visionary, knighthood. In his estimation a revived and reformed knighthood would find its true vocation in service to a chivalrous king. Thus in Book 2 he made both Lancelot and Gawain retinue leaders in the army under Arthur's command. In the French romances, in which he found his sources, the two knights had been cast in the role of knights errant. In Malory's work the notion of the questing knight of French romance was in the process of being superseded by a knighthood committed to serving the common weal.

Malory's singling out of Lancelot connects with another shift of emphasis in his work: his portrayal of chivalry as an essentially non-religious institution. Malory regarded the Knights of the Round Table as a purely secular fellowship, bound in loyalty to Arthur and sworn to duties set out in an oath taken each Pentecost. By the terms of their commitment the knights were to 'flee treason and give mercy to those who ask mercy, to give succour to ladies, gentlewomen and widows, to support right, and never to undertake war in a wrongful quarrel'. Close parallels are to be observed between the Pentecostal Oath and the oaths sworn by a number of the tourneying societies operating on the continent at this time. The key idea informing them all is that of championing justice, upholding right and protecting the poor, a set of ideals likewise prominent in Malory's source, the French prose *Lancelot*. It follows that in Malory's version of the Arthurian story the knights experience adventures with a moral, rather than a strictly religious, content. In Malory the rescue of damsels and the overthrow of wicked knights figure more prominently than the enchantments and marvels which characterised his French originals. Malory cuts back the strong magical element of the French romances in favour of earthier, more realistic detail, even if an overall impression of the marvellous is still retained. Malory's distinctive slant is also apparent in his approach to the presentation of the Grail legend. He shows little or no interest in the doctrine of grace emphasised so strongly in the *Queste del Saint Graal*, condensing the latter's long theological arguments and adding few details of his own. Malory also sharply reduced the officiating Catholic presence, so that religious officials hardly figure in his narrative at all.

One last distinctive feature of Malory's work is his virtual dismissal of traditional notions of courtly love. For Malory, courtly love, whether married or not, is more an obstacle to a knight's true vocation than a spur to it. As Iseult points out in Book 5, when Sir Tristram refuses to go without her to Arthur's court: 'What shall be said of you among all knights? . . . 'Tis a pity he was ever a knight, or had the love of a lady.' To Malory the knightly vocation itself is the single most important source of the knight's drive and the fount of his prowess. Knighthood, in his view, could only survive if valour alone constituted the knightly ideal. At the end of his work Malory accordingly reversed the normal order of events in order to give added emphasis to the destructive consequences of Guinevere's adulterous liaisons. Instead of positioning the Roman war near the end and making it the prime cause of Arthur's downfall and death, he placed it near the beginning, leaving the story of Guinevere's adultery and Mordred's consequent treachery as the dramatic climax.[16] For Malory, the downfall of knighthood began when knights put personal feelings before their obligations to their order.

Malory's knighthood was, therefore, a very down-to-earth affair, a vocation from which there was no respite. This was a view which accorded well with the realities of late medieval chivalry, in which knights combined the performance of brave deeds with a record of service to the Crown. It is possible that a good deal of the inspiration for Malory's ideas was to be found in the revived chivalry of the late fifteenth century.[17] In both England and the continental polities there was growing interest in the use of chivalry as a way of strengthening royal power.[18] Underlying and informing this interest was a parallel revival in the writing of romances on an Arthurian theme. In France in the 1460s the duc de Nemours commissioned a volume of texts based on the French Arthurian cycle, and volumes of a similar kind were produced in Burgundy and Italy. In England the revival of chivalry associated with the reign of Edward IV centred particularly on the holding of tournaments.[19] These were staged regularly in the 1460s, at precisely the time Malory was writing the Morte Darthur, among them the celebrated jousts at Smithfield between Anthony Woodville and the Grand Bastard of Burgundy. Tournaments had hardly been staged at all in the thirty years or so before Edward's accession. It is hardly surprising, then, that their revival should have had an impact on Malory's chivalric imagination. Malory sometimes inserted tournaments into his narrative where they had not figured in the French sources. At the end of the Morte Darthur, just before the terrible final drama unfolds, he inserted the 'Grand Tournament' as a last apotheosis of the Round Table. To Malory the chivalry of King Arthur was no lost ideal, a vision beyond recovery; it was a living reality, a model for chivalric renewal in his own day.

But how realistic was Malory's vision? The embarrassing contrast between the lofty ideal at which he hinted and the tortured paradoxes of his own life cannot go unremarked. Malory, the author of the Morte Darthur, was also the Malory who emerges from contemporary records as a ruffian, a thief, a rapist, a would-be murderer and oft-imprisoned felon.[20] He wrote against the background of a bitter dynastic civil war in which he was himself at times involved and of which he was to some extent the victim. Many of Malory's contemporaries would have been only too aware of the yawning gap between the idealised world of Arthurian knighthood and the debased chivalry of their own time. The contradiction gnawing away at the integrity of contemporary chivalry was evident in every one of the stories which made up

Malory's great cycle – chivalry, while in one sense a force for moderation and restraint, was in another a force which legitimated violence. In Malory's account the knights who acted courteously at one moment were the same knights who freely administered buffetings the next. Chivalry had inherited the culture of violence from the old Germanic aristocratic war ethic. Although it contained within itself mechanisms for limiting the scale of disruption, the approval given to violence was nonetheless damaging to the social fabric. Arthur's own world, after all, had collapsed amid internecine strife, family conflict and civil war.

Malory hinted at a possible resolution of the problem in a reformed chivalry which found fulfilment in service to a prince. In the *Morte Darthur* the Round Table can probably be read as a metaphor for the body politic. Yet if, for Malory, knighthood could redeem itself by acting less independently, it might still suffer the scars of the violence and disruption woven into its fabric. When in the *Morte Darthur* internecine fighting led to the break-up of the Round Table, it led also to the break-up of Arthur's great empire. What Malory failed to anticipate was the redefinition of knighthood in terms of the performance of non-military service to the prince. This is the key idea which was advanced in his own day by humanist writers such as John Tiptoft, earl of Worcester.[21] Malory, on the cusp between the Middle Ages and the Renaissance, was in many ways a figure who looked to the past rather than one who anticipated the future.

Chivalric History

By the late fourteenth century the growth of literary patronage among the nobility and gentry was encouraging a new kind of chivalric literature written in the form of history. Before this time the writing of history had been undertaken chiefly by monastic chroniclers and annalists, whose approach to interpreting the past was to see it as the unfolding of God's design for mankind. These authors tended to be fiercely patriotic in outlook and might well have recorded the details of military affairs to please their patrons. However, they did not bring a perspective to events which was distinctly chivalric. Around the mid-fourteenth century this situation began to change. A new type of chivalric chronicle appeared, which sought to present a purely secular view of events and owed nothing to the old theological framework. To this was added, in the third quarter of the century, a flowering of chivalric biography, a genre which had been anticipated in the 1220s or '30s in the *Life* of William Marshal but which had failed then to take root. To some extent, the demand for this new literature originated in the desire of patrons to read flattering accounts of campaigns in which they themselves had taken part. Equally, however, it was informed by a strong moral and didactic purpose: it was designed to instruct as much as to entertain.

This new literature had its immediate origins in the rich chivalric culture of Hainault, the county wedged between France and Flanders. William, count of Hainault in the early 1300s, was a keen patron of tourneying and errantry, and both he and his brother John had links with England: Philippa, William's daughter, was to marry Edward III. There was only one distant precedent for the particular type of writing which was to appear now. In the thirteenth century Geoffrey de Villehardouin, the marshal of Champagne, had penned a remarkable prose narrative of the taking of Constantinople on the Fourth Crusade. For well over a century, however, this work had stood alone. Chivalric chronicles and biographies such as those of Jordan Fantosme and Ambroise had almost always been written in verse. The late medieval French prose chronicle was the creation of two important writers whose background lay in Hainault – Jean le Bel and Jean Froissart. Both owed much to the favour and encouragement of John of Hainault, the count's brother, who had actually taken Jean le Bel with him on a visit to England in 1328 and allowed him to accompany him on the campaign against the Scots that summer. The decision which the two writers made to publish in French, not Latin, was in part a response to their mainly secular audience. It was also a way of asserting the essential difference between their work and the traditional chronicle, Latin being the language of divine revelation.

The pioneer of the new genre was Jean le Bel, a clerk and from 1313 a canon of St Lambert's Cathedral, Liège. Le Bel was born into the wealthy mercantile elite of that city, his father being a former burgomaster and his brother an alderman. Le Bel enjoyed the good life: he dressed splendidly, kept a big retinue, and loved hunting and hawking. He also moved in chivalric circles: he actually participated in jousting and enjoyed the company of the titled aristocracy. Like Froissart after him, he was something of a snob.

Le Bel began compiling his chronicle in 1352 at the request of John of Hainault. When after a decade he laid down his pen he had completed an account of the period from the late thirteenth century down to 1361.[22] His main subject was the French wars of Edward III. He said that he wanted to record 'the notable perilous adventures and battles, feats of arms and prowess' since Edward's accession. He was keen to honour and perpetuate the memory of such chivalric heroes as the king himself, John of Hainault, the Black Prince and Duke Henry of Lancaster. It was his ambition to replace with authentic history the old verse accounts, which he considered to be full of lies and fabrications. Despite his concern for accuracy, however, he was heavily influenced by the romance tradition. His narrative is studded with valorous knights and brave men doing brave deeds. Edward III is his principal hero, the 'valiant, gentle king'. His court is said to have been comparable to King Arthur's, and we are told that men could not praise him too much. John of Hainault, his patron, is his other main hero. John is said to have helped Queen Isabella and the other English exiles in 1326 because 'all good knights must comfort ladies and damsels in distress'. In England John was the idol of all the 'countesses, ladies and damsels'. Jean le Bel gave his attention to those knights most deserving of honour, and he seems to have found more of these in England and Hainault than in France.

Jean le Bel's work fundamentally informs the earlier part of the chronicle written by his literary heir and successor Jean Froissart. Froissart was perhaps the most distinguished chivalric chronicler of the late Middle Ages and a man whose works held up to the nobility a mirror of all the values they held most dear.[23] Froissart, like le Bel, was born (c. 1337) into a wealthy burgess family and, again like le Bel, entered holy orders, becoming a canon of Chimay. In the course of his long life – he lived to the early 1400s – he travelled extensively. In 1360 he left Hainault for England, probably at the invitation of Queen Philippa, staying for some five or more years in the queen's household. In 1365 he visited Scotland, gathering material for his romance, *Meliador*. In 1367 he was in Bordeaux when Richard II was born and the following year accompanied Lionel of Clarence to Italy. After Queen Philippa's death in 1369 he transferred his residence to the Low

Countries, from there visiting Foix and Béarn in south-west France in 1388, and England again in 1394. On this last occasion he presented King Richard II with a book of poems on the subject of love. Froissart, like le Bel, enjoyed hobnobbing with the rich and powerful. It is typical of him to say, as he did when writing of his second visit to England, that his old friend Sir Richard Stury 'was delighted to see' him and gave him 'a hearty welcome'.[24]

Froissart's chronicle, the main French narrative of the Hundred Years War to 1400, survives in three main redactions, each written at a different stage of his career. The first redaction follows Jean le Bel down to 1361, continuing independently for the next eight years, and is strongly pro-English. The second, written some time after 1376, when he was resident in Brabant, is less dependent on le Bel and is more evenly balanced between the English and French. The third, written in the final years of his life, is wholly original, incorporates a lot of oral evidence gathered in the course of his travels and is much embroidered.

The secret of Froissart's success lay in the brilliance and fluency of his writing style. He was a gifted storyteller and enlivened his narratives with a wealth of colourful incident. It is Froissart, for example, who tells the famous story of the blind king of Bohemia at Crécy. The king, as Froissart relates, instructed his followers, 'blind as I am, take me to the centre of the engagement that I may strike one blow with my sword'. In Froissart every battle is reduced to a sequence of hand-to-hand encounters between knights in which the protagonists display their bravery and prowess in arms. History, for Froissart, was essentially didactic. As he said in his prologue, the object of his work was to ensure that 'the honourable enterprises, noble adventures, and deeds of arms, performed in the wars between England and France, may be properly related, and held in perpetual remembrance – to the end that brave men, taking example from them, may be encouraged in their own well-doing'. Froissart freely confessed that choosing material was difficult, for so many good knights had taken part in the war. There were some knights, however, who particularly distinguished themselves: notably Edward III himself, the Black Prince, Duke Henry of Lancaster, Reginald, Lord Cobham, Sir Walter Mauny, Sir John Chandos and Sir Fulk Harley. It was these men above all, he said, who were to be 'esteemed heroes of the highest renown'.

It is no surprise that Froissart's work enjoyed wide popularity with princely and aristocratic audiences right across Europe. Copies of his chronicle circulated wherever there were readers eager to admire the brave deeds of brave men. Numerous sumptuous editions of his work were produced, many of them richly illustrated. In England interest in Froissart's work seems to have been at its greatest in the years of chivalric revival under the Yorkists after 1461. In the early 1470s, while they were in exile in Flanders, Edward IV and his chamberlain William, Lord Hastings both commissioned de luxe copies for their personal use. The English outpost of Calais proved a useful hunting ground for those seeking copies of Froissart's works. Sir Thomas Thwaites, who served in the Calais garrison from 1468, accumulated five volumes of Froissart's *Chroniques*, in addition to Xenophon's *Cyropédie* and a six-volume set of French chronicles.[25] Earlier in the century a number of copies had come to England as a result of the dispersal of French book collections after Henry V's conquests. A copy of Book I, thought to have been commissioned for a French patron, was acquired after Agincourt by Sir John Arundell, in whose family it was to be passed down.[26] A number of copies now in continental collections appear from their decoration to have been commissioned for English patrons.

One of the curiosities of English literary history, however, is that for all the appeal of chivalric history, Froissart's work did little or nothing to encourage a native writing tradition of the same kind. Only one chivalric chronicle of English origin has come down to us from this period – the *Scalacronica* of Sir Thomas Gray, begun while its author was in prison in Scotland from 1356. This is a remarkable work, well informed about events in both Scotland and France, but it stands alone. England produced no writers of the sort represented by Jean le Bel or Jean Froissart in Hainault and the Low Countries. One possible reason for this oddity is the decline after 1400 of French as a vernacular in England, French being the language of prose chivalric writing. Another and more important reason, however, may well be the relative weakness of chivalry as an urban phenomenon in England. Jean le Bel and Jean Froissart were both products of an urban society – one, moreover, which cherished the values of chivalry almost as much as the aristocracy themselves. In England before the fifteenth century the urban elites seem to have adopted an attitude of almost complete detachment from chivalry and chivalric ceremony, being content largely with their own forms of cultural expression.[27] Thus the conditions for the emergence of a le Bel or a Froissart simply did not exist. Those authors capable of writing as these chroniclers did had no interest in chivalry and accordingly little incentive to pick up their pens.

There was another type of chivalric writing, however, which had the potential to appeal to English writers, and that was chivalric biography. Biographies were usually written by heralds, and heralds were based in aristocratic households. In the half-centuries before and after 1400 the biographies were written of a number of knights of distinction. The subjects were of all nationalities and allegiances, among them Jean de Boucicault in France, the Black Prince in England, Don Pero Niño in Castile and Jacques de Lalaing in Burgundy. The genre was European-wide in its appeal.

The essence of chivalric biography was to present the person as knight and not the knight as person. There was no serious attempt in these works to produce a rounded picture of the subject. Materials were selected for inclusion only insofar as they contributed to an impression of the protagonist as an embodiment of knightly virtue. All other material was rejected. In the case of Chandos Herald's *Life of the Black Prince*, nothing at all was said about the prince's role as a politician or administrator.[28] Someone as high-ranking as the prince would have had a considerable range of official responsibilities – among them supervising the government of his lordships, handling relations with foreign powers, raising and equipping his armies, and serving on kingly councils – all duties which could not easily be delegated to others. Yet these responsibilities made no appearance in the *Life*. They were not central to the chivalric ethic and contributed nothing to the shaping of a chivalric reputation. The author therefore deemed them irrelevant to the celebration of knighthood.

In many ways chivalric biographies have much in common with romances. Both genres were concerned with teaching by example. In both, the narrative centres on the achievements of a great hero figure. In both, the telling of the story is enriched by such devices as invented speeches. In both again, a high importance is attached to achieving a strong moralising literary effect. In Chandos Herald's *Life of the Black Prince*, for example, its subject is treated much as he might have been in a romance. Like a romance figure he is seen as a hero fully formed from the outset: 'This noble prince of whom I speak never, from the day of his birth, thought of anything but loyalty, noble deeds, valour and goodness, and was endowed with prowess.'[29] His many chivalric virtues were innate; he had no need to learn them. The author presents him as a model of martial prowess from the moment of his knighting in August 1346. At Crécy he is already the equal of the heroes of epic and romance: 'Such deeds of arms were done there that Roland and Oliver and Ogier the Dane, who was so courteous, might have met their match . . . The noble prince won fame there, for he was eager to do well, and he was but eighteen years old.'[30]

As the poem proceeds, the prince moves on to ever greater achievements, but these are seen merely as revealing qualities which had been present since birth; they are not considered stages in the development of character or skill. Thus chivalric biography bears little relation to biography as it is understood today. A poem like the *Life of the Black Prince* is best compared with romances such as Malory's tales of Sir Gareth and Sir Tristram, in which the hero, like the prince, is formed by nature not by instruction.

The *Life of the Black Prince* was the work of a writer thoroughly familiar with the conventions of French historical writing. Chivalric biographies, like chivalric chronicles, had their origins in France. As the writer's official title suggests, he was a herald in the service of Sir John Chandos, a distinguished English captain who served in the French wars from 1337 to 1370. Froissart refers to 'Chandos li hiraus' in his chronicle and was indebted to him for information about the prince's Najera campaign of 1367.[31] It has been suggested that he may be the same person as a certain Guyon mentioned in a charter of 1370, but the suggestion is unprovable. All that can be said for certain is that on the evidence of his dialect he came from the southern Low Countries. Perhaps, like Froissart himself, he was a native of Hainault, that nest of fourteenth-century chivalric culture.

The *Life* appears to be the only extant example of a verse biography of an English knight of the Hundred Years War. To recognise its uniqueness, however, is not to suggest that other verse biographies of valorous knights were not written. Indeed, it seems quite likely that they were. The cultural conditions of late medieval England were highly propitious for the production of biographies of this sort. Knightly biographies were written and circulated by professional heralds, and heralds enjoyed an honourable position in English chivalric society. There were heralds resident in most magnate households, and by the fifteenth century their responsibilities were extending to the policing as well as the granting of arms. Quite possibly, knightly biographies are to be included among what has been called the lost literature of medieval England. It is hard to see how the *Beauchamp Pageant* could have been created without the existence of some written account of Earl Richard's life, on which the artist or designer could have drawn.[32]

Reading and Politics

Reading in the late Middle Ages, as in any other period, was an activity which played a key role in the shaping of attitudes and beliefs. Typically it was not the private, isolating activity which it is today; it was more a social activity, involving groups. In some cases there would be an audience listening. In the period before general upper-class literacy the lord and his family might well listen to a lively romance read aloud after dinner. Later, in the fourteenth and fifteenth centuries, as literacy spread, readers might be linked by the exchange of texts. It was common for books and tracts to be passed around. Indeed, it seems to have been rare for books to stay for long in the hands of one owner. The Pastons, for example, used a London inn, the George in Lombard Street, for the exchange of such items. On the occasion of their visits to London they would leave books at the inn for others to collect, in turn picking up volumes which others had left for them. Book reading influenced people not only as individuals but as members of like-minded groups.[33] It promoted the growth and consolidation of a broad political awareness.

That chivalric literature should have been widely read in late medieval England is therefore a factor of considerable importance in understanding its political culture. In the miscellanies which constituted the gentry's staple reading, chivalric texts and romances sat cheek by jowl, as we have seen, with tracts on politics, history, governance and philosophy. This suggests that, when readers thought in abstract terms about matters of politics and public affairs, chivalric assumptions were never far from their minds. For those of the nobility and gentry whose thinking was influenced by literature, politics and chivalry went naturally together. It was on the back of these powerful literary foundations that the chivalric revival of Yorkist England was to be built.

17

The Wars of the Roses and Yorkist Chivalry

In the mid- to late fifteenth century warfare against England's enemies abroad was replaced by war at home. Barely a decade after the humiliating ending of the long conflict with France, a bitter domestic struggle erupted between two dynasties over the right of succession to the Crown. Arguments about chivalry and chivalric renewal figured prominently in both conflicts. The collapse of the English empire in France prompted agonised reflection on the right conduct of chivalric war, while in the wake of the Yorkist triumph in 1461 new ideas emerged about how chivalry could be redefined on ancient classical lines to serve the national interest. Against this background of crisis in war and government, chivalry was reshaped and made to serve radical new ends.

'War Inward' and 'War Outward'

When Henry V reopened the conflict with France in 1415, he did so with the avowed intent of reviving the chivalric kingship associated with Edward III. His three connected aims were to restore the prestige of the English Crown, heal the wounds afflicting the body politic and, above all, make aggressive war the means to achieve a just peace with his enemies. His spectacular victory at Agincourt in October 1415 demonstrated the legitimacy of his cause, setting the seal on Lancastrian kingship, establishing his right to the French Crown and affording proof of divine support for English arms.

In 1417, confident of his enjoyment of divine backing, Henry embarked on the systematic conquest of Normandy, to which he laid claim as part of the old Angevin empire. By 1419 he had occupied the greater part of the duchy, making Rouen his capital, and in the following year, with Burgundian aid, he imposed a peace settlement on the French which assured him the succession to the French Crown. While his premature death in August 1422 was to rob him of the chance to become king himself, when Charles VI died only two months later, his infant son Henry VI succeeded to the dual monarchy of England and France.

The momentum of Henry V's conquest was maintained in the early years of his son's reign despite the loss of Henry's messianic drive. In 1424 John, duke of Bedford, the deceased king's brother and regent in France, inflicted a severe defeat on the French at Verneuil in southern Normandy, consolidating English control of the duchy and further weakening French morale. The following year the earls of Salisbury and Suffolk took Le Mans and Mayenne, opening the way to the Loire valley. In 1429, however, the seemingly inexorable English drive south was halted at Orléans, where the French under Joan of Arc broke the English siege and inflicted defeat on a force coming to the besiegers' aid. Although the setback put paid to hopes of further territorial advance, in Normandy itself the English position remained secure. If the English found it difficult to break out of the duchy, equally Charles VII and the French found it difficult to break in. It was only in the autumn of 1435, following the collapse of the Anglo-Burgundian alliance at the Congress of Arras, that the position of the English in France began to fall apart. Paris, for all its importance, had to be abandoned because it was indefensible without Burgundian backing while, further west, difficulties in raising manpower and money made it impossible to launch a counter-offensive. The death of Bedford himself in September 1435 dealt a physical and symbolic blow to the English cause, removing not only a highly competent commander but also a personal link with King Henry V.

By the end of the 1430s the crisis facing the English administration in France was raising major questions for Henry VI and his government at home. The exchequer was running short of money and it was becoming ever more difficult to raise men. A gulf was emerging between the garrison class in Normandy and the gentry community at home, among whom war weariness was setting in. The view of the duke of Suffolk and his fellow ministers was that a negotiated peace with the French offered the best prospect of stabilising the situation, provided that satisfactory terms could be agreed. A very different view, however, was espoused by the war party associated with Humphrey, duke of Gloucester, another of the king's uncles, who believed that victory could still be secured by vigorous prosecution of the war. The question of how, and on what scale, the war in France should be fought was thus one of the key issues dividing Henry VI's government from its increasingly voluble critics.

A keen advocate of a more aggressive foreign policy was the Norfolk knight Sir John Fastolf, a distinguished war captain and from the 1420s major-domo of the household of the duke of Bedford in France. Fastolf had enjoyed a career in arms which stretched back nearly a quarter of a century to 1412, when he had first enlisted under Thomas, duke of Clarence.[1] He had served in Henry V's victorious army at Agincourt in 1415, and between 1417 and 1421 had been heavily involved in the conquest of Normandy, taking part in the sieges of Caen and Rouen. Appointed lieutenant of Normandy in 1422, he was charged with clearing the area to the south-west of Paris, and in 1424 had fought alongside Bedford at Verneuil. In the same year he was made a knight banneret and two years later a Knight of the Garter. He suffered a blow to his reputation in 1429 when, following his retreat from the battle of Patay, he was charged with cowardice and suspended from the Garter. Before long, however, he was to redeem himself with successful captaincies at Honfleur (1424–34), Verneuil (1429) and Caen (1430–7), and a field command with Lord Willoughby in 1431. He proved as resourceful in the field as he was strong-willed and determined. At Rouvray in 1429 he won the so-called battle of the herrings, using barrels of herring fish as a stockade to fend off the advancing French. After his retirement in 1439 he devoted himself to reflecting on his experience of war, and he set down some of his thoughts in writing. When he offered advice on strategy to Henry VI's council, he did so with authority and insight.

Fastolf first laid out his views on strategy in a memorandum which he submitted to Henry's French council in 1435. The background to this document was the breaking of the English alliance by the Burgundians at Arras. Fastolf was uncompromising. He urged the despatch of two armies from England, one to make 'sharp and cruelle war' in the east, from Picardy down to Burgundy itself, the other to do likewise in the western theatre around Chartres and Anjou. The unleashing of these armies over three campaigning seasons, he argued, would reduce these areas to 'an extreme famyn', creating a cordon sanitaire of devastation around Normandy. At the same time he urged effective sea-keeping in the Channel to protect English commerce and support the English armies in France. He set down his thoughts again thirteen years later in a paper for the duke of Somerset, just after the latter had taken up command in Normandy. He urged the duke to appoint loyal captains, victual and garrison the frontier towns, ensure that all victuals were paid for and keep men in reserve for a field army; at the same time he returned to his theme of the importance of sea-keeping, arguing that the Channel should be swept and the Channel ports properly safe-guarded. For Fastolf, the goal of upholding the English position in France was still realisable provided that the war was properly managed.[2]

Fastolf's thoughts on the waging of war found expression not only in his conciliar memoranda but in the writings of his amanuensis and man of affairs, William Worcester. At once classicist, antiquary, histo-rian, biographer and business manager, Worcester was a man who defies easy categorisation.[3] He entered Fastolf's service in 1438 and remained with him till his master's death in 1459. Worcester served his employer principally in a business capacity, running his estates, but was more than a conventional administrative official. He stood at the heart of Fastolf's intellectual circle. He was a member of a community, based in the knight's household, which was dedicated to upholding the vision of an austere, disciplined chivalry. In his *Boke of Noblesse*, written in about 1452 and revised at least twice later, he articulated this vision in a tract which drew extensively on his master's ideas.[4]

Worcester embarked on the *Boke* to exhort the English to avenge their defeats in Normandy and recover their empire in France. He lamented the disgrace and humiliation which the nation had suffered following 'the right great outrageous and most grievous loss' of the territories won by Henry V. He viewed failure in moral terms, public activity in his view being but an extension of private. People had grown soft and decadent, neglecting the common good: 'sensualite of the bodi now a daeis hathe most reigned over us to oure destruc-tion we not having consideracion to the generalle profit'. Placing his argument in an historical context, he said Englishmen should recall the 'acts in arms' which their nation had performed from its legendary origins in the 'noble ancient blood of Troy' through to the triumphs of Edward III and Henry V. Drawing on the works of Vegetius and Cato, he endorsed the spartan regime of the ancient Romans, whose vigour he contrasted with the decadence and decay of his own time. He provided instructive examples to demonstrate that the Romans had achieved their triumphs through strong discipline, daily exercise of arms and heeding the advice of counsellors who urged courage and prudence in war. Like Christine de Pisan in France, he conceived of war as a struggle of virtue against fortune, exhorting his fellow Englishmen to emulate the Romans who, having lost to Carthage, redoubled their efforts to overcome their enemy. He believed that the knighthood of England, properly schooled, should perform public service for the common good. Chivalry for him was an ethical code rooted in virtue – in 'true nobility', not in the empty tokens of lineage. The true knight should be a protector of the community, disciplined and lion-like, rising above considerations of self-interest to champion the cause of justice.

For all his preoccupation with the moral aspects of warfare, Worcester did not neglect the practical details of military planning so essential to an army's success in the field. He learned from Fastolf the importance of discipline in the ranks, regular payment of wages, adequate supply of victuals and respect for the property of civilians. While writing the Boke he assembled a collection of military documents – receipts, wage bills, requests for remuneration – which show his concern with the nuts and bolts of organisation.[5] In his discussion of the expulsion of the English from Normandy he stressed particularly the problems caused by inadequate supplies, which had forced the soldiery to plunder the local populace, so turning them against the occupiers.

Worcester's outlook and preoccupations were shared by another member of Fastolf's household, the latter's stepson Stephen Scrope. Scrope, scion of a distinguished northern family proud of its military traditions, made translations of two substantial works from French, The Dicts and Sayings of the Philosophers, a compendium of ancient lore, and Christine de Pisan's Epistle of Othea.[6] Christine's text, a treatise on knightly virtues couched in the form of a letter of advice, picked up a number of the themes touched on by Worcester in his Boke.

Othea, the Greek goddess of prudence and wisdom, urges her protégé Hector to attain true knighthood through the practice of virtue, arguing her case by discussion of the seven planetary gods and the qualities associated with them – valour, the attribute of Mars, good judgement, that of Saturn, and so on.[7] For Scrope, the attraction of Christine's mythographic text was that it drew attention to the moral and ethical dimension to chivalry, rooting it in an intellectual tradition that stretched back to antiquity. In the other work he translated, *The Dictes and Sayings of the Philosophers*, Scrope was particularly attracted by the emphasis which the sages, in the sayings attributed to them, placed on common sense and experience as supports for the claims of prudence.[8] There can be little doubt that Scrope saw the two works of translation as complementing one another. In his eyes they made possible a practical philosophy which could serve as a code of everyday knightly behaviour. For their ultimate begetter, Scrope's patron and sponsor Fastolf, they provided the intellectual justification for a chivalry rooted in moral responsibility.

The literary activities of the Fastolf circle provide a vivid insight into the beliefs and assumptions of those who in the 1440s still cherished the memory of Henry V's conquests and whose ambition was to see the king's vision realised. If theirs was an essentially conservative outlook, rooted in a hankering after lost glories, it was yet forward-looking in that it turned to the past to provide models for behaviour in the present and future. Drawing their inspiration from classical antiquity, these men articulated a vision of a virtuous chivalry, an austere, disciplined fighting class committed to national war and renewal. Their confidence in the power of a reformed chivalry was connected to a strong appreciation of England's historic destiny. Worcester set his call to arms in the context of English descent from the Trojans, while Scrope made implied comparisons between the Trojan wars and the English campaigns in Normandy. In the opinion of both men England could realise its destiny provided English knighthood committed itself to serving the common good. The goal of a reformed knighthood, in their view, should be not the selfish pursuit of gain but service to king and people. Chivalry, the cult of errantry, was thus turned into a patriotic ethic, the means to attain national glory.

By the 1450s the man to whom Fastolf and his circle increasingly looked to advance their ideas was one of the princes of the blood and a man with long experience of the French war, Richard, duke of York. York was a lord whose high birth had virtually guaranteed a leading place in the counsels of the realm.[9] He was sole heir to two great magnate inheritances, those of York and Mortimer. His father, Richard of Cambridge, was second son and eventual heir of Edmund, duke of York, and his mother, Anne, heiress of the Mortimer earls of March, from one of the great landowning families of the Welsh borders. York's wide estates, scattered across England, Wales and Ireland, yielded him a net income of some £4,000 a year, to which receipts averaging £600 a year from the exchequer could be added. With an income that befitted his rank he was able to maintain a large retinue, giving him access to a range of opinion which otherwise would have had no outlet as the court gradually closed in on itself, excluding criticism. In the 1450s Fastolf served as one of his officers and counsellors.

From his earliest adulthood York had been groomed to play a role of appropriate importance in the maintenance of the Lancastrian empire in France. In 1430 he had had his first taste of active service on Henry VI's 'coronation expedition', leading a small but well-equipped retinue. Six years later he was awarded the prestigious appointment of lieutenant of France, in succession to Bedford. In this key position he lent his support to Lord Talbot in resisting a major French assault on Normandy. In 1441, after a brief spell in England, he was sent to France again, to assist Talbot in raising the French siege of Pontoise, on the Seine. He returned to England a second time in 1445, confident that he would be reappointed as lieutenant. Instead, however, he saw the office go to the duke of Somerset, while he himself was nominated to serve in Ireland. It is easy to see his appointment to the Irish backwater as indicating official disapproval, yet there is actually no other evidence that the duke was being marginalised at this time. What does emerge from the sources, however, is that he was looked to in some quarters as the man best qualified to take on the defence of the remaining English possessions in France. In 1445 a translation was made for him of Claudian's *De Consulato Stiliconis*, an account of how the Roman consul Stilicho was invited to come to the salvation of a crumbling empire torn by the rivalries around a child emperor.[10] The translation was made at Stoke by Clare friary, a house with strong Yorkist connections, perhaps by Osbert Bokenham. York was invited to 'marke stilicoes life'. It is not difficult to imagine that he would have seen in the virtuous consul Stilicho, the embodiment of honesty and prudence, a symbol of his own position in an empire likewise approaching its doom.

For all the challenges that he faced in the 1440s, however, it was only in 1450 that the duke emerged as an open critic of Henry VI's government. In the summer of 1450 the last English strongholds in Normandy, Falaise and Cherbourg, fell to the French. Towards the end of the year James Gresham wrote to John Paston, 'we have not now a foote of lond' left in the duchy.'' The humiliating collapse in France led to the outbreak of major disturbances in southern England. In July rebels under the leadership of Jack Cade took over the capital, murdering Lord Saye and other royal counsellors and calling for the arrest of the 'traitors'. It was against this background of swelling crisis that in September York returned from Ireland, protesting his loyalty to the king but calling for counsellors' heads to roll.

It is not altogether clear what led the duke to abandon his long-standing ties with Henry VI's court and throw himself behind the opposition. The duke can hardly have been angered by Henry VI's peace policy and the decision to surrender Maine, for he voiced no criticism of the policy at the time; indeed, he had been involved in it in person, assisting in the arrangements for compensating local English landholders. Nor can he be said to have suffered badly from the government's failure to honour its debts to him. Financially he had fared no worse than any other of Henry VI's major creditors; given the state of the royal finances, he might actually be said to have fared rather well. On the evidence of his public pronounce-ments it seems the main reason for his disaffection was a grievance of a personal nature: his sense that his successor as lieutenant in Normandy, Edmund, duke of Somerset, had dishonoured him. The cause of the quarrel which was to spark off the dynastic conflict known as the Wars of the Roses was thus a point of chivalry – a point of chivalry arising from a war in France which was itself concerned with chivalry.

Edmund of Somerset, one of the king's Beaufort cousins, had been appointed lieutenant in Normandy in December 1447, a year before the unleashing of the French assault on the duchy. Although earlier in his career he had shown himself a commander of at least moderate competence, in this command he proved both feeble and defeatist. In the face of the massive French advance he lost his nerve, offering minimal resistance and surrendering Rouen and other key cities without a fight. Technically the surrender of a town without a show of resistance to the attacker was a treasonable offence, through injury to the king's majesty, so Somerset could have faced charges under the laws of war for his default. However, it was in regard to the effects of the collapse on his own position that York took his stand.[12] At the time of the collapse York held the office of captain of Rouen, and his retainers and lieutenants occupied defensive positions there. When the city was surrendered, York, by virtue of being in nominal command, suffered dishonour. Thus, when the next year he brought his public accusations against Somerset, it was in relation to the capitulation that he laid the most serious charges. The premature surrender of Rouen, the duke alleged, 'was a verray cause of the perdicion of Normandie'. Still worse, by the terms of the treaty of composition, towns were surrendered which were not even subject to siege. The military failure in Normandy had compromised the duke's personal honour. Accordingly, Somerset should be held to account so that Richard's own chivalric reputation might be vindicated.

Beyond the matter of Somerset's default, there was a broader sense in which the English collapse could be seen as the result of a failure of English knighthood. Henry VI himself had failed as a knight. Henry, who as king and so God's anointed bore ultimate responsibility for conduct of the war, had failed in that most vital aspect of his office, defending the realm from its enemies. To contemporaries, kingship and knighthood complemented each other in upholding justice and good government. Henry V had been the epitome of knighthood, valorous and disciplined but also magnanimous. The poet Lydgate had celebrated him as:

> Of knythod loodesterr,
> Wis and riht manly, pleynly to termyne,
> Riht fortunate, prrvid in pes and werr,
> Gretly expert in marcial discipline,
> Able to stoned among the Worthi Nyne.[13]

Henry's pathetic and inadequate successor, so unlike his father, stood no chance of inclusion among the Nine Worthies. Defective equally in prowess and prudence, he failed in both aspects of chivalric kingship, defending the realm and championing good justice. When his subjects criticised him for the inadequacy of his kingship, they were pointing not only to his dependence on poor counsel but also to his failure to discharge the traditional obligations of knighthood.

Chivalry Reinterpreted

In March 1461, after the Yorkist triumph at the battle of Mortimer's Cross, the hapless Henry VI was deposed and Edward, son of the now deceased duke of York, was crowned king as Edward IV. On Palm Sunday the new monarch consolidated his hold on power with another victory over his opponents at Towton in Yorkshire, the bloodiest battle of the Wars of the Roses.

In the opening years of his reign the new king was heavily dependent on the support of Warwick the Kingmaker and his Neville relations. It was the Nevilles who provided him with the essential backing he needed in the north, where Lancastrian sympathies remained strong. The thrust of Edward's policy as king was to construct his rule around the ascendancy of the royal household: that is, to make the household the centre of government and to draw all local centres of power into it. Edward agreed with the authors of the advice literature that if a king could rule his household, then he could rule the realm. Within a few years of his accession he had succeeded in bringing a new stability to England. In 1464, however, his achievement was called into question by his clandestine marriage to Elizabeth Woodville, widow of Sir John Grey, a deceased Lancastrian.

Elizabeth brought with her to court a large brood of relatives, no fewer than eleven siblings and two sons by her marriage to Grey. The Woodvilles attracted widespread criticism by virtue of their number and the startling rapidity of their advance. Within a couple of years of their coming to court, the king had arranged as many as seven marriages for them; further, the queen's father had been raised to an earldom, and her eldest brother granted a peerage and awarded custody of the Isle of Wight. The Woodvilles were deeply unpopular and there seems to have been some truth in the charge that they were arrogant and overbearing. One member of the family, however, stands out for his ability and the attractiveness of his personality. This was Anthony Woodville, Lord Scales, later Earl Rivers, one of the queen's brothers. Anthony was a noted jouster and an accomplished writer and translator. He is a key figure for understanding both the role of chivalry in Yorkist England and the redefinition of chivalric values in the late fifteenth century.

Woodville, though a keen student of letters, was principally a soldier and man of war. He was a familiar figure on the chivalric scene, jousting with the Grand Bastard of Burgundy at Smithfield in 1467. Having fought on the Lancastrian side in the opening engagements of the Wars of the Roses, he decided to throw in his lot with the Yorkists after his sister married Edward IV.[14] In 1470, when Warwick and Clarence launched their rebellion against the king, he was active in the campaigns against them, repelling Warwick in the Channel and taking part in the final battle against him at Barnet. In 1482 he was one of Gloucester's leading lieutenants in his campaign against the Scots to take Berwick.

Woodville's kinship with the king could easily have guaranteed him a position of high importance in the politics of Yorkist England; instead, however, he chose to follow the simpler life of the knight errant – fighting, travelling and jousting. It is possible to see in him something of Malory's Sir Lancelot or Sir Gawain. In 1471, following Edward IV's triumph over Warwick, he left England to go on a crusade against the Moors in Portugal. Two years later he went on pilgrimage to Santiago de Compostela, and three years after that he embarked on a pilgrimage to Rome and other holy places in Italy. As so often with medieval knights, his enthusiasm for deeds of arms was matched by a deep penitential piety which sought outlet in spiritual combat. His friend Caxton testified to his deep piety and his abhorrence of what he called 'thabhominable and dampnable synnes which communely be now a dayes'. Quite possibly Woodville's piety played a role in his decision to turn a group of didactic moralising works into English for the benefit of his fellow courtiers. It is these works which make him a significant figure in the history of Yorkist chivalry.

Woodville's programme of translations affords a fascinating insight into his priorities and the values by which he set store. One of the first

texts he took on was *The Dictes and Sayings of the Philosophers*, the work
which Stephen Scrope had translated a generation before.[15] The attraction of this collection of philosophical commonplaces was that it
provided models of virtuous living: it was, as he said, a 'glorious fair
myrrour to all good Christen peple to behold and understonde'. Based
on sayings attributed to biblical, classical and legendary figures, it
showed how wisdom could be made to serve the needs of daily living.
Woodville's translation of the text was the first work which Caxton
selected for publication in England.

Some time after 1473, when he was entrusted with the upbringing
of the king's son, the future Edward V, Woodville translated his second
work, Christine de Pisan's *Livre du Corps de Policie*.[16] This was a text
which appealed because it brought together writings from ancient
Rome which stressed virtue and self-discipline as the foundations of
imperial greatness. Woodville agreed with Christine that virtue was
the only true basis for ruling a realm. Christine had cited approvingly
Valerius Maximus' observation that merit counted for more than
nobility of birth. Woodville, endorsing this, followed her in arguing
that military and intellectual discipline were synonymous: in
Woodville's words, 'it is no doubte the exercise of arms and of wisdom
togeder helped them [the Romans] gretly in their conquests'. At the
beginning of her text Christine had spoken of knights and nobles as
the arms and hands of the body politic. To illustrate this she had
enunciated a series of principles supported by examples from ancient
Rome: knights should love the profession of arms; they should be
brave and constant in courage; they should encourage each other and
urge their companions to do well; they should be truthful and faithful
to their word; and they should cherish honour above all worldly things.
Provided they held to and cherished these ideals, they would be
rewarded with success in war. This belief corresponded to Woodville's
own view of how a nation could attain greatness. Woodville endorsed
the cyclical view of history implicit in Christine's writings. Decline
for him occurred when the masculine values of a society were eroded.
In the case of Rome's decline, 'while befor tym were manly and
worchippful in arms wexed softe and delicate as women. And so by
delycasye and ydelness they wer conquered.'

Christine based her work on French translations of Latin classics
in the library assembled by King Charles V, who reigned between 1364

and 1380. Woodville's decision to make her work accessible to English readers reflects his own sense of the importance of those classics. Like Fastolf and his circle a generation earlier, he found inspiration in ancient Rome. He saw in the Romans of old a model of austere self-discipline and common purpose which could serve as the basis for reform and renewal in his own day. What he wanted to achieve through his work was a social order based on reason and merit in which the governing classes would be trained for their various tasks: the knights for war, the lawyers for pleading, and so on. In a state so organised, the nobility would act as retained servants of the Crown, not as independent feudatories.

This idea of a nobility dedicated to state service was articulated in another work by a Yorkist nobleman, the translation of Buonaccorso da Montemagno's *Contraversia de Nobilitate* undertaken by John Tiptoft, earl of Worcester. Tiptoft, who served from 1462 as Edward IV's constable, was one of the most enthusiastic lay humanists of his day.[17] He was also a keen Italophile. In his early years he had travelled in Italy, studying law at the university of Padua, and in 1460 he had delivered an oration before the Pope which is said to have moved the pontiff to tears by its beauty. He was a key figure in the dissemination of new humanist political ideas in England.

In the *Declamacion of Noblesse*, to give the work its English title, the conflict between old and new ideas of chivalry was expressed in the form of a debate in the Roman senate.[18] Two suitors for the hand of a prospective bride are made to argue their cases by setting forth their respective views on nobility. Cornelius, the first suitor, argues for the traditional view, that the essence of nobility lies in ancestry, wealth and lineage: 'I have in champagne, fertile feldes, ryche possessions and fayr villages, which be allee to receive not only a grete howshold, but a grete hoost.' His rival Guyus Flammineus, a representative of the new breed of nobleman epitomised by Woodville and Tiptoft themselves, argues that, on the contrary, nobility has nothing to do with possessions or inheritance; instead, its essence is to be found in virtue and cunning, applied in the service of the state. Even a poor man could become noble provided he applied himself to advancing the common good. The best way to attain nobility, Flammineus says, is to devote oneself to the study of philosophy. For his own part, there was 'no day [that he] spent in idleness and no night without study or learning . . . to the service of the public weal of this city'.

In Flammineus' speech we have an elegant summary of the case which *littérateurs* such as Chaucer had long argued, that the essence of nobility was to be found in virtue not lineage.[19] Tiptoft was here lending his own imprimatur to the humanist view of the ruling class as an elite defined not by blood but by virtue and dedication to the service of the state. If he and Woodville took their exemplars principally from Roman antiquity, it is nonetheless worth remembering that there was an English ruler to whom they looked for inspiration, the austere warrior king Henry V. Henry's model of a strong martial state served by a disciplined nobility and wedded to an imperial vision was probably never far from the minds of those in the service of the Yorkist kings. The task which these men set themselves was essentially that of rekindling Henrician glory, but doing so by nurturing the virtues which had sustained an even greater empire than Henry's, the empire of Rome.

The Sun of York

From the moment of his accession in 1461 the Yorkist Edward IV placed the renewal of chivalry at the heart of his vision of a new monarchy. His kingship – indeed, his very name – aroused high expectations among his subjects. It was anticipated that he would emulate the achievement of his namesakes, Edward III and Edward, the Black Prince, in conquering broad swathes of territory in France. Edward himself was well aware of the burden of popular anticipation. In his household ordinances, the so-called Black Book, he lavished praise on the third Edward as the model king. He wanted his court to be a centre of chivalric companionship and honour, just as Edward's had been.

It was only natural, given his interests and background, that the new king should have been eager to stage tournaments as court spectacles on the model of Edward III's. In the long unglamorous years of Henry VI's majority tournaments had been infrequent events, and those which had been staged had been modest affairs. When Edward came to the throne not only did tournaments become more frequent, they also became grander, showier and more impressive. Much of the impetus for the revival of tourneying came from the chivalry-conscious Woodvilles, in particular the king's father-in-law, Richard Woodville, Earl Rivers, a keen participant in the lists. Woodville had married Jacquetta of Luxembourg, widow of the duke of Bedford, and through her had gained familiarity with the ceremony of the Burgundian court, which made great play with tourneying. The Yorkist revival of tourneying can be seen, in one sense, as part of a process of Burgundianisation. The Burgundian duke, Charles the Bold, the most romantic and flamboyant ruler of the age, was Edward's brother-in-law.

Tournaments appear to have been held almost every year in Edward's first reign, from 1462 onwards.[20] Edward regarded them as the ultimate knightly pastime, as his teasing of the renegade Henry Beaufort, duke of Somerset, in 1463 showed. The strongly Lancastrian-leaning duke had been defying the king from the castles of Dunstanburgh and Bamburgh in Northumberland, and Edward tried to win him over by inviting him to participate in jousts at Westminster. The duke obliged the king, albeit unwillingly as an observer noted, and without any distinction. Two years later, following the coronation of Edward's queen, a spectacular tournament was staged in London, organised by the master of the horse, for which no fewer than 200 lances were ordered. Lord Stanley was adjudged the winner and awarded a ring with a ruby as his prize. Two years after this occurred the most celebrated chivalric event of the age, the great contest at Smithfield between Anthony Woodville and Anthony, the Grand Bastard of Burgundy. Although one of the encounters was marred by an incident in which the Bastard's horse was killed under him, the jousting was generally acclaimed a success. To avoid giving offence to either of the participants, the outcome was declared a draw.

Some of the most active and distinguished knights of Edward's time were naturally enough honoured with election to the Order of the Garter. The order played nearly as significant a part in Edward's chivalric vision as it had in that of his namesake a century before. Under the feeble Henry VI the order had languished as a beacon of chivalry and distinction. Henry had regarded it as an essentially religious institution, with largely religious rituals; Edward viewed it very differently, as an expression of chivalric companionship. The highly exceptional circumstances attending the king's accession gave him the opportunity to reshape the order in his image. In 1461–2 no fewer than thirteen new knights were elected, probably the largest number at any one time in the order's history. Those to whom the Garter was awarded were generally relatives of the king, senior court noblemen and royal retainers with appropriately chivalric credentials; occasionally important foreign princes would be honoured. The elections to the order in Edward's first year followed broadly this pattern but accorded particular priority to chivalric credentials. Two of the new knights were the king's own brothers, George, duke of Clarence and Richard, duke of Gloucester. Five were peers: John Tiptoft, earl of Worcester; William, Lord Hastings; John Neville, Lord Montagu; William, Lord Herbert; and John, Lord Scrope of Bolton in Yorkshire. Three were no more than knights: Sir William Chamberlain, Sir John Astley and Sir Robert Harcourt.[21] The well-documented careers of two of these knights shed light on the sorts of men whom the new king saw fit to reward.

Sir William Chamberlain, whose tomb at East Harling in Norfolk is replete with Garter imagery, was a veteran of the closing stages of the war in France. He had served as Lord Talbot's deputy in the defence of Meaux in 1439 and fought at least once under York's command. The exalted reputation which he enjoyed owed much to his daring in a raid conducted when governor of Creil. According to Holinshed, 'he behaved himself so bravely, that with 500 Englishmen only, he issued out of the town, discomfited his enemies, slew 200 of them, and took a great number prisoner'. Through his marriage to Anne, daughter of Sir Robert Harling of East Harling, he stood at the heart of Garter society. Anne was granddaughter of the Lancastrian Garter knight Sir John Radcliffe, and as a ward had been raised by that other Garter luminary, Sir John Fastolf. Her third and last husband was to be yet another Garter knight, John, Lord Scrope of Bolton. The extent of this overlapping network of ties illustrates the strength of the bonds which held the company of valorous knights together.[22]

Sir John Astley was a knight of still greater fame and distinction. His chivalric tastes are attested to by his commonplace book, already noted, which contains a rich collection of military and heraldic treatises.[23] Astley first attracted attention in 1438 when, jousting with a Frenchman, Pierre de Massy, he accidentally drove his sword through his opponent's head, instantly killing him. Although there was criticism that the death might have been unchivalric, he had certainly demonstrated his prowess. Four years later, in a joust at Smithfield, he took on an Aragonese esquire, Philip Boyle, in another widely reported contest from which he emerged the victor. Henry VI, among the spectators, stopped the fight when Astley had Boyle at his mercy, knighting him on the spot and awarding him an annuity of forty pounds. In 1463, when he was conducting operations against a Franco-Scottish force on the Border, Astley had the misfortune to be captured and taken prisoner to France. He was to languish in a French gaol for nearly four years, not regaining his freedom until the payment of a substantial ransom in 1467. Shortly after his return he acted as counsel to Anthony Woodville in his combat with the Grand Bastard of Burgundy. In his last public act he was one of the canopy bearers at Edward IV's lying-in-state at Westminster in 1483. He died three years later.

Edward's sponsorship of knights such as Astley demonstrates the importance that he attached to chivalric credentials as qualifications for election to the Garter. His appreciation of the role played by the order in courtly and national life showed itself in many other ways. He took an especial interest in the ceremonies and rituals of the order as expressions of the cultural life of his court. It cannot be established precisely how many Garter feasts he attended, because the records are incomplete; however, he is known to have been present on at least two occasions in the 1460s and more regularly in his second reign. The chapter and feast which he attended at Windsor in April 1476 seem to have been particularly ceremonious affairs.[24] According to the account of Bluemantle herald, the king rode from his lodgings in the upper ward to the chapel for matins and then, after breakfast with the dean, returned to the chapel for High Mass, the queen joining him with her ladies. The king was present again in chapel in the afternoon for evensong; then in the evening he dined magnificently in the great chamber with the bishop of Salisbury, chancellor of the order, seated on his right, the dukes of Clarence and Suffolk on his left and the knight companions of the order at a side table. On the following day, Monday, the king and the knights proceeded yet again to the chapel, where after each of the knights had taken his stall the king presented the dean with a magnificent set of vestments, and he and the knights together made their offerings on the altar.

As the richness of the liturgical ritual shows, Edward, for all his absorption in secular chivalry, was by no means oblivious to the religious dimension to knighthood. Indeed, what he is best known for today is perhaps not so much his revival of the order as his magnificent transformation of St George's Chapel itself. Beginning in 1475, the king embarked on the complete rebuilding of the chapel, which had originally been built by Henry III in the 1240s. At the same time he showed his favour to the clergy whose duty it was to officiate in the building by securing for them a generous new grant of lands. One part of his purpose, he said, was to ensure that 'Almighty God was served daily in the said chapel'. But another, equally important, aim was to create a monument to the greater glory of the house of York, a fitting mausoleum in which he himself would be laid to rest amid the ceremonial richness of a revived knighthood.

The king's intention to rebuild the chapel had been signalled in 1473 by his appointment of Richard Beauchamp, bishop of Salisbury, shortly to become chancellor of the order, as master of the 'new works'. The bishop was given authorisation to impress stonecutters, carpenters and other workmen, and to acquire stone, timber, glass and all other necessaries. The task of clearing away the old buildings and levelling the site was begun in 1475, and thereafter work proceeded apace. Money to finance the rebuilding came partly from the profits of baronial estates in the king's hands during minorities and partly from exchequer drafts. By the time of the king's death in 1483 the choir and choir aisles had been raised to their full height and roofed over, and the knight companions had probably moved in. A notable aspect of the chapel's design was that it provided for a wooden and not, as might be expected in such a high-status building, a stone ceiling; only later was the present elaborate stone vault inserted. In the architectural projects commissioned by kings and princes, timber roofs were generally associated with secular rather than ecclesiastical uses, and it may have been secular connotations which the king was seeking to evoke here. Edward might have wanted his chapel to have the aspect of a great knightly assembly hall, a meeting place of chivalry, as much as of a place of worship. If he was thinking along these lines, then by dint of associating himself so strongly with secular military

values he was again showing his contempt for his unmilitary predecessor. It was within the walls of this stately, albeit half-finished, chapel
that his body was laid to rest on his premature death in 1483. He had
already created for himself a two-storey chantry chapel on the north
side of the high altar. In centuries to come, from its upper storey his
successors would be able to look down on what was, by the time of
its completion, the grandest royal chapel in Christendom.[25]

Chivalry Revived?

By his strengthening of the Order of the Garter and his ambitious
rebuilding of St George's, Edward went a long way to restore the
chivalric credentials of the English monarchy. Secure in his possession
of the crown after his return in 1471, he could present himself as the
new Arthur and his court as the new Camelot. But how far did he
succeed in promoting the revival of chivalry in England more generally? And to what extent did the values and aspirations of the Yorkist
elite percolate down to the knights and lesser gentry in the shires? On
these matters the evidence allows only a very equivocal answer.

In the mid-fourteenth century Edward III's promotion of chivalry,
on which Edward IV's was modelled, had formed part of a much
broader programme for the renewal of England's knighthood.
Edward III's absorption in chivalric values stemmed almost entirely
from his ambition to strengthen English knighthood as an instrument
of war against the French, and everything that he did to renew chivalry
was undertaken with this aim in view. When he engaged in promotion
of the cult of St George as patron of chivalry, it was to encourage
the idea of a knighthood dedicated to the service of king and realm.

When Edward IV promoted the revival of chivalry, it was, at least
on the surface, with essentially the same aim. He showed just as much
concern as his predecessor to associate himself with the valorous kings
of national history and legend. The great outpouring of prophetic
and genealogical literature which had greeted the king's accession in
1461 had traced his ancestry back through the Mortimers to the third
Edward, so connecting him with the tradition of chivalric kingship.[26]
In parliament in 1472 a speaker on his behalf was to argue that England
had been at her most prosperous when her kings had made 'war

outward' on their enemies, notably the French.[27] Edward's subjects were eagerly expectant that he would revive the tradition of triumphant warrior kingship. On the eve of Edward's expedition to France in 1475 William Worcester rededicated his *Boke of Noblesse* to him in the hope of encouraging him to reconquer the former English possessions across the Channel.

In the case of Edward IV, however, a yawning gap was always to open between promise and performance. The king's subjects might look to him to achieve national renewal in war, and he might well – as he did – encourage them to harbour such expectations, but when it came to turning popular enthusiasm into reality, he almost invariably fell short. In 1475, for example, when the opportunity came for him to achieve victory in battle against the French, his nerve failed him. That summer he had embarked on an invasion of France in alliance with his brother-in-law Charles, duke of Burgundy, taking with him a large and well-equipped army numbering perhaps as many as 11,000 men. The Crowland chronicler wrote, 'all applauded the king's intentions and bestowed the highest praise on his plans'.[28] Faced with the prospect of fighting a difficult campaign abroad, however, the king's resolve weakened. His adversary, Louis XI of France, was massing a sizeable army against him, and Edward became worried that Charles, whose army was bogged down besieging Neuss in the Rhineland, might fail to deliver the military support he had promised. Using his ally's threatened default as an excuse, he decided to enter into negotiations with Louis. At Picquigny on 29 August he and the French king agreed a treaty whereby Edward would evacuate his army in return for 75,000 crowns in cash and the promise of an annual French pension of 25,000 gold crowns. As the Crowland chronicler observed, after unbelievable expense and energy the expedition never even properly got started.[29]

What limited Edward's achievements as king was his failure to locate the revival of chivalry in any larger vision of national renewal through 'war outward'. His measures made little provision for engaging with the hopes and aspirations of the wider nation. Yorkist chivalry, unlike Edward III's or Henry V's, remained largely a court-based movement. This crucial limitation helps to account for the lack of any substantial increase in the number of knights in England in the king's reign. When Edward I and Edward III had promoted chivalric renewal, their measures had been rewarded with a significant increase in the number of knights for war. This happy outcome was not to be repeated in the Yorkist period. Reliable numbers are hard to come by, but it has been estimated that from a low of just under 200 knights in 1459, numbers increased to 237 in 1465 before falling again to about 220 in 1470.[30] Even if Edward had been more committed in his promotion of knightly revival, however, he would probably have achieved only modest results because knighthood was entering a sharp decline at this time. Blood quality and the possession of a coat of arms were taking precedence over knighthood as ensigns of personal dignity, and those who could support knighthood no longer saw much point in coming forward to take up the rank. It is doubtful if Edward and his counsellors could have arrested the long-term decline of knighthood even if they had wanted to.

For all the king's efforts to promote a grand chivalric renaissance, then, there is little evidence of knighthood reviving outside the court. Is it possible, however, to say whether another aim was achieved, that of bringing about a redefinition of knighthood? Might the humanist translators or redactors working at the Yorkist court have achieved their desired end of promoting a new knighthood, trained and dedicated to royal service? That Edward had in mind an enhanced role for the knightly class in the work of central and local government can hardly be doubted. We have already seen that his policy for the revival of royal power after 1461 centred on the assertion of monarchical government through an invigorated royal household. By the 1470s the knights of that household were being appointed to office in the shires, particularly the Home Counties, and to positions in charge of royal estates and castles. Edward's approach to the employment of household knights in government, however, appears to have been almost entirely pragmatic and intuitive. There is no indication that he was consciously responding to the advice of the treatises and translations circulating at his court and perhaps intended for his eyes. Edward's interest in reading, in fact, appears to have been limited. Of the manuscripts which he owned only two have personal *ex libris*, while the others are either large illuminated volumes showing little sign of individual selection or are dedication copies.[31] Edward was not a man of intellectual tastes; nor was he one inclined to treat textbooks as blueprints for government. If important steps were taken in his reign towards developing a new monarchy, as may have been the case, they are likely to have owed little to the ideas of intellectuals.

Edward's measures to promote the revival of chivalry, however, were not entirely without consequence. Indirectly, they lent encouragement to the idea of a new chivalry, a chivalry harnessed not to knight errantry but to the service of the state. This conception had its origins in the years well before Edward's accession in the writings of the circle which flourished around Sir John Fastolf. In William Worcester's *Boke of Noblesse* and in the translations made by Stephen Scrope the idea was developed of a chivalry, rooted in the values of ancient Rome and nurtured on manly virtue, which could serve the needs of king and kingdom. The idea was refined and developed at Edward's court in the translations of French and Italian texts made by Anthony Woodville and John Tiptoft. Where this new concept of chivalry differed from more traditional ideas was in the belief that true nobility was found in 'virtus' – in courage, wisdom and learning – and not, as in the past, in lineage. Tiptoft and Woodville gave active expression to such conceptions in their literary works and in their lives of public service to the Yorkist monarchy. The idea that nobility was rooted in virtue had been rehearsed by poets and treatise writers for many years, since at least the time of the twelfth-century renaissance. It was only in the mid-fifteenth century, however, that it was taken up as the basis for a programme for the renewal of the realm. In the revival and dissemination of Roman political nostrums by Yorkist courtiers were laid the foundations of the humanist chivalry which was to flourish in Tudor England.

18

The Decline of Chivalry

Chivalry and War

When did the age of chivalry come to an end? In what sense indeed may the age of chivalry be said to have come to an end? A wide variety of answers have been offered to these questions. On the one side are those who place the end of chivalry relatively late, notably Edmund Burke, writing in the eighteenth century, who claimed that the death of chivalry was a by-product of the French Revolution: 'The age of chivalry,' he wrote, 'is gone; that of sophisters, economists, and calculators has succeeded.' Mark Girouard, more recently, has placed the end of chivalry later still. Reflecting on the romanticised chivalry of the nineteenth century, he maintains that the experience of the First World War sounded its death knell. Many of the troops 'died there [in the trenches]; and there chivalry died with them . . . the war was a shatterer of illusions'.[1]

On the other side are those who situate the demise of chivalry much earlier. In the opinion of most medievalists chivalry went into decline when medieval civilisation itself did. Richard Barber proposes an end-date of around the turn of the fifteenth and sixteenth centuries. 'By the end of the fifteenth century,' he writes, 'there was little enough real substance in chivalry for moralists to regard it seriously.'[2] Sydney Anglo, arguing a similar case, opts for some time in the early sixteenth century: 'changes in the art of war', he writes, spelled, 'the practical decline of chivalry', while the notion of a Christian knighthood 'vanished with the Reformation'.[3] David Knowles, writing as a historian of monasticism, goes for a date early in Henry VIII's reign.

Seeking to explain the mighty land grab of the Dissolution, he argues quite simply that, by that time, 'the code of chivalry had gone'.[4]

A yet different answer again has been proposed by Mervyn James, a student of sixteenth-century social history. James argues for a date somewhere between these two extremes. For him chivalry, the idealised self-image of a lineage society, flourished for as long as a lineage-based society did. In northern England, he argues, chivalry was still an active force up to the Northern Rebellion against Queen Elizabeth in 1569.[5]

The markedly differing views as to when chivalry ended echo the broad differences of opinion on how chivalry itself is to be defined and understood. Chivalry is a much-contested phenomenon. For some it represents a code of war, a legal construct, a set of conventions for minimising the horrors of hostilities. For others it is more an aristocratic value system, a collection of ideal qualities: honour, courage, loyalty. For others again it is essentially a literary phenomenon, the creation of romance writers who like to tell of the brave deeds performed by knights for their ladies. How we define chivalry, therefore, has a major bearing on when and why we believe it went into decline.

Perhaps the most fruitful approach is to focus on the code of military behaviour at the heart of chivalry, for everything else was dependent on this. The essence of medieval chivalry was to be found in the set of humane values governing the conduct of war based on the principle of self-preservation among knights. Judged by this test, chivalry may be said to have gone into decline rather sooner than is sometimes supposed. The first signs of a falling away in mutual respect between knights in war are found in the late thirteenth and fourteenth centuries, not in the fifteenth, the period most often associated with decline. In other words, the erosion of chivalric values began in the very period considered by many to have been its heyday.

If we look at the conduct of the English in the wars they fought in France in the fourteenth century then it is evident that the seeds of decline were sown as early as the 1340s. At Crécy, the first great land battle of the Hundred Years War, very few prisoners were taken.[6] The battle, by the end, had turned into a bloodbath. On the estimate of the clerk Michael de Northburgh, itself probably based on a herald's headcount, no fewer than 1,542 French knights and men-at-arms were killed. Many of the chroniclers, relying on hearsay, put the figure higher still, at somewhere between 2,000 and 4,000 men. At any rate, not one major French nobleman or knight was brought back captive to England. The French king, Philip VI, appears to have been responsible for the fatal decision which led to this outcome. Fearing a scramble for prisoners to ransom, which might hinder his victory, he ordered the oriflamme to be unfurled, thereby signifying that it would be illegal for anyone, on pain of death, to spare a prisoner. Edward III, observing this, unfurled his own banner, and so sent the same message to his own troops.[7] As a result of the two signals, no quarter was expected, and none was given. In the words of the chronicler Adam Murimuth, the English slaughtered every person they took.

In this respect Crécy was not in the least exceptional among the battles of the first half of the fourteenth century. There was similar bloodshed at the end of some of Edward III's battles with the Scots. In the encounters at Dupplin Moor in 1332, Halidon Hill in 1333 and Neville's Cross in 1346 far more enemy combatants were killed than taken prisoner. At Neville's Cross perhaps as many as 3,000 Scots met their deaths, whereas fewer than a hundred seem to have been taken prisoner. Following the battle of Halidon Hill, according to a Scottish source, Edward ordered all of the Scots prisoners to be put to the sword, although some were in fact spared by 'good men' on the English side. While the estimates of 30,000 dead at Halidon Hill recorded by some chroniclers are an exaggeration, there can be little doubt that Scottish fatalities were high. The position was much the same in the lesser battles of the Hundred Years War in France. At Mauron in Brittany, according to the English commander Sir Walter Bentley, fourteen French lords, 140 knights and 500 esquires were killed, whereas only nine lords and 160 knights and esquires were captured. Among the large-scale encounters of the fourteenth century, it was only at Poitiers that a substantial crop of prisoners was taken: it seems that some 2,000 French knights and men-at-arms were brought back to England. A number of the smaller encounters also yielded sizeable harvests of prisoners. For the most part, however, it was ever more likely from the 1340s that a soldier on the losing side who failed to make good his escape would be put to the sword.

Evidence of growing brutality in domestic war is apparent well before the fourteenth century. The inhumane treatment of opponents was a notable feature of the civil war between Henry III and Simon de Montfort in the 1260s. In the final engagement of the struggle, at

Evesham in 1265, the royalists' assault on the Montfortians turned the battle site into a killing field. On Green Hill, where de Montfort fell, his son Henry, Sir Hugh Despenser, Sir Peter de Montfort, Sir Guy de Balliol, Sir William de Mandeville, Sir Ralph Basset, Sir Thomas de Astley, Sir William de Birmingham, Sir Richard Trussell and at least twenty other knights all met their deaths.[8] The body of de Montfort himself was mutilated, his hands, feet and head cut off, and his testicles hung either side of his nose and then stuffed into his mouth. Ultimately the severed head was sent, a gory symbol of triumph, to the wife of his enemy Sir Roger Mortimer of Wigmore. It is hard to say how many Montfortians were killed in all. The figure of 10,000 given by chronicler Richard of Durham is probably another exaggeration, yet there can be little doubt that the total was unprecedented. At the hard-fought battle of Lincoln in 1217, at which William Marshal had defeated the French, only two or three men of note had been killed. Equally, at Lewes in the year before Evesham, the scene of the Montfortians' triumph over the royalists, only some half a dozen knights had been slain. The terrible savagery which marred Evesham was unparalleled in England. Robert of Gloucester spoke of 'the murder of Evesham, for battle was it none'.

Heavy loss of life was to occur in later civil war battles. In 1403, at the battle of Shrewsbury, Henry IV's clash with the Percys, the level of knightly casualties was again high. The chronicler Walsingham says that on the royalist side more than ten knights and many esquires were killed, among them Sir Walter Blount and the earl of Stafford, while on the rebel side 'most of the knights and esquires of Cheshire fell'.[9] The rebels had targeted the king – a policy of decapitation. Walsingham says that they, 'thinking Henry was worth ten thousand of his men, looked for him, mowing down those who stood in their way, but when the earl of Dunbar saw their purpose, he led the king away'. Aiming to slay the king, which took the place of the earlier practice of merely capturing and controlling him, followed from the rebels' renunciation of allegiance to Henry on the grounds that he was a usurper and his rule therefore illegitimate. The royalists, however, aware of the rebel strategy, employed decoys for Henry. Several of these unfortunates were cut down in the melee.

In the Wars of the Roses, half a century later, there were to be more terrible bloodbaths. The horrific encounter at Towton on Palm

Sunday 1461 has the unenviable reputation of being probably the bloodiest battle in English history. On the evidence of heralds' lists, it has been estimated that somewhere between 20,000 and 28,000 men died. The bishop of Exeter, Warwick the Kingmaker's brother, spoke of bodies scattered over an area measuring at least six miles by four. As at Crécy, the bloody outcome was in part the consequence of orders issued by the commanders on the two sides. Edward IV, fresh from his seizure of the Crown and determined to end Lancastrian resistance to his title, ordered his men to give no quarter, and the Lancastrians responded in kind.[11] In the ensuing struggle the Lancastrians, overwhelmed by the Yorkists' advance, found themselves pushed down into the valley of the Cock, where, blocked by the river, they tumbled over one another, drowning or dying of suffocation. The nobility fared just as badly as the infantry. At least eleven Lancastrian lords were killed, among them the earls of Devon and Northumberland, and Lords Clifford, Neville, Willoughby and Scales.[12]

A new level of brutality was attained a decade later in the battle that ended Henry VI's restoration to the throne, the hard-fought encounter at Barnet in 1471. In this engagement Edward took on his former ally Warwick, who had switched his support to Henry VI and the Lancastrians. The battle was fought in thick fog and involved much hand-to-hand fighting. It ended in a crushing victory for Edward, Warwick being slain while attempting to escape. Overall figures for fatalities are elusive; nonetheless, it is clear that, relative to the numbers involved, losses were very considerable. On the Yorkist side Lords Say and Cromwell, Sir Humphrey Bourchier and Sir William Blount were all killed, and on their opponents', besides Warwick, his brother Lord Montagu and many of their knights.[13] One factor which contributed to the carnage was the sheer chaos. In the poor visibility the opposing forces became misaligned and confused; indeed, the Lancastrian earl of Oxford ended up attacking his own side. A new element, however, added significantly to the losses: this was the much harsher line which Edward took on the treatment of enemy infantry.

According to the French chronicler Philippe de Commynes, the king abandoned his earlier policy of sparing the infantry and slaying the noblemen; he now ordered that all enemy combatants were to be killed. In Commynes' words, this was because of the 'deep hatred he felt for the people of England for the great favour they had borne towards the earl of Warwick'.[14] Up to this time the rules of engagement in domestic conflicts had differed significantly from those governing wars abroad. In foreign wars the practice had been to kill the infantry while sparing the nobles because the latter could be ransomed. In domestic struggles, however, it had been customary to kill nobles because they represented rival claimants to power, while sparing the infantry on the grounds that they were fellow Englishmen. Edward's new policy overturned this convention, removing protection for the lower orders and introducing a new level of brutality to the conduct of domestic conflict. It was an unhappy moment in the history of warfare.

So why did the conventions of chivalry suffer such terrible erosion in the late Middle Ages? Why did the willingness to respect fellow combatants, a product of the civilised values of the twelfth century, wear so thin in the age of the Hundred Years War and the Wars of the Roses? There is no evidence that knights suddenly lost their appetite for rounding up the noblest and wealthiest of their opponents for ransom. The prospect of bagging a good ransom acted as a major incentive to military recruitment in the struggles of the Hundred Years War. At Poitiers, as we have seen, the Black Prince's victory over the French yielded a substantial crop of prisoners for ransom. What in that case made Poitiers exceptional? And why in other campaigns did the practical application of chivalric conventions apparently become so selective?

Much that may appear obscure in the conduct of late medieval warfare is to be explained by reference to the underlying principles of the laws of war. In regard to domestic strife these rules, as formulated in the fourteenth century, were very simple: those who opposed the king were rebels and were accordingly to be treated as such. The writings of the legists distinguished three main types of conflict: *guerre mortelle*, which was the most ruthless kind of war in which no mercy was shown; *bellum hostile* (in legal Latin), open public war between rival sovereigns; and *guerre couverte*, or private war between feudal magnates.[15] Civil or domestic conflict, the waging of war by dissidents against their king, fell into the first of these categories. This simple but important truth goes a long way to explaining the ruthlessness of warfare between king and subjects. Once the ruler or commander had unfurled his banner, it followed that no quarter would be given, no prisoners taken and no ransoms exacted. Man was free to kill man.

The two sides stood in mortal enmity. Peace could only be achieved by the unconditional submission of one side to the other.

Before the formalisation of these distinctions in the late Middle Ages kings had not always inflicted on those who opposed them the full punishment to which law or custom entitled them. In the interests of securing peace they had generally granted such people their lives, contenting themselves with the temporary confiscation of their lands. In England it was only from the time of the Montfortian wars in the 1260s that kings began to adopt a much tougher approach. What lay behind the new clarity brought to the legists' work was a significant shift in the king's favour in the balance of wealth and power between ruler and magnates. In the late eleventh and twelfth centuries, when dissident barons had rebelled, their retinues had been of near-equal size to the king's, and forgiveness and reconciliation had been the price the king had to pay to secure submission. In the fourteenth and fifteenth centuries, as kings waxed rich on the fruits of confiscations and national taxation, they could outnumber and outgun their opponents, and impose on them much harsher terms of settlement. At the same time their ability to enforce legal penalties had likewise grown stronger. From the late thirteenth century they had in their service a professional lay judiciary committed to upholding and enforcing the rights of the Crown. As Lancaster and the other dissidents who failed in rebellion against Edward II were to find, these judges saw it as their duty to exact the full rigours of the law on traitors. It is developments of this sort in the strengthening of royal power which provide the background to Edward IV's unforgiving policy at Barnet.

In the Wars of the Roses of the fifteenth century there was one other factor which added to the mayhem: the tit-for-tat killing which developed among the nobility as the struggle dragged on. The death of a knight or nobleman in one battle provoked in response a revenge killing by his kinsmen in the next. The beginnings of this unhappy sequence can be observed in the opening phase of the wars between 1455 and 1461. At the first battle of St Albans in May 1455 Somerset, Northumberland and Clifford were all killed by Yorkist soldiers. Five years later, at Wakefield, York and one of his sons were killed by an army commanded by the sons of those same three men. Three months later still the Yorkists were able to gain their revenge in turn when they killed the younger Northumberland at Towton. And so it went on. The urge for

revenge prompted by the need to vindicate family honour contributed
to growing bloodshed every time the wars ignited. Commynes
commented on the phenomenon: 'the lords in England killed their
enemies; then later the children of their victims gained their revenge
when times changed and favoured them and they killed the others'.[16]
He added, 'the wars lasted for so long that by the end all the members
of the houses of Warwick and Somerset had had their heads cut off or
were killed in battle'.[17] The propensity of the English for murdering
one another brought them notoriety in mainland Europe, an appetite
for bloodshed that seemed to go hand in hand with their instinct for
deposing and killing their kings. Yet, as Commynes also noted, despite
all this the countryside was left relatively unscathed: no non-combatants
were attacked, nor any towns or villages burned. At least something of
the old spirit of chivalric restraint was retained.

When we turn from domestic wars to wars abroad, the position
becomes more complicated. The laws covering the waging of international conflict provided a body of safeguards for both combatants
and non-combatants. In a key provision, knights were forbidden to
claim the lives of knightly adversaries other than in situations of dire
necessity. Should a knight find himself overcome in battle, he was
required to surrender himself to his captor, in this way indicating his
acceptance of an honourable relationship which involved him in
financial obligations to his captor. Underlying this doctrine was the
assumption that it was in everyone's interests to avoid butchery and
bloodshed.

When the legal position was so clear, how is the greater bloodshed
of late medieval warfare to be explained? It is tempting to seek an
explanation in the familiar story of the changing technology of war.
In many older histories the decline of chivalry was explained largely
in terms of the rise of artillery, especially artillery in the field. While
it is true that the introduction of cannon had a significant bearing on
warfare in the later fifteenth century, particularly on the continent, it
is doubtful if guns, or guns alone, were responsible for the rising toll
of noble casualties. Not only did the widespread use of cannon by
the English and French armies post-date the trend to greater casualties
by several decades, the functioning of these weapons was often unreliable, and before the 1450s the number of combatants they claimed
was small.[18] It was only in the last two battles of the Anglo-French

war, those at Formigny and Castillon, where their use by the French had the desired effect of provoking ill-judged English attacks, that they had any significant effect on the outcome.

More significant in bringing about an increase in noble casualties was another innovation – the celebrated longbow. This instrument, as developed by English archers in the fourteenth century, had one great advantage over its rival, the crossbow: it allowed a much more rapid rate of fire.[19] An experienced archer could release between ten and twenty arrow shafts a minute for every two or three bolts from a crossbow. At a range of 200 yards the effect could be devastating. A man hit by an arrow shaft in any part of his body was effectively *hors de combat*. The longbow gained in effectiveness from association with an important military change in this period, the introduction of the mounted archer.[20] In the 1330s and 1340s there was a marked shift in the composition of English armies from slow-moving infantry bowmen to lightly armed mounted archers. These men could take part in the swift-moving *chevauchées* across France, while having the capacity to dismount at a battle site and engage the enemy. By the mid-fourteenth century mounted archers often matched their infantry counterparts in number and in some cases outnumbered them. The two groups together could produce an arrow storm capable of tearing apart and destroying an advancing enemy formation. At Agincourt in 1415 Henry V ordered his men to advance and then release their volley as the enemy cavalry approached to within 200 yards. The result was devastating. The French advance was halted, and when the next column came forward they too fell victim to the same tactic, collapsing in heaps on top of their predecessors.

Volleys of arrows did not supplant the hand-to-hand combat between knights of earlier times; in most cases they were simply the terrifying precursor to such encounters. Once the archers had disrupted the enemy, knights would move in to engage them with swords and daggers, laying about them till victory was won. The use of archery, however, made warfare in the age of the Hundred Years War significantly different from that of earlier times in one vital respect: it made life far more dangerous for knights and men-at-arms. The inevitable result of arrow fire was to increase the number of knightly casualties. Even well-equipped and well-armoured knights fell victim to the devastating volleys. Arrow fire was undiscriminating; it was no respecter of person or rank. Whoever got in the way was struck down. In France the victims were French knights and the knights of allied lords or principalities. In England, in battles like Shrewsbury where heavy archery fire was employed, the victims were those who had been witnesses to its effects in France. At Shrewsbury, Walsingham says, men fell like leaves in cold weather after frost.[21] If chivalry as a code of humane conduct bit the dust in the late Middle Ages, it was due in large measure to the lethal work of the longbow.

Even so, the number of knightly casualties was not of the same order in all the battles of the Hundred Years War in which archery was employed. At Crécy and Agincourt there were far higher casualties among knights than there were at Poitiers, where the longbow was no less in evidence. Clearly there was some other factor at work which had a bearing on levels of mortality. There can be little doubt that that factor was the battle orders given by the opposing kings as commanders. At Crécy in 1346 both Philip and Edward, by unfurling their banners, invoked *guerre mortelle*, the most ruthless and uninhibited form of armed combat known in the Middle Ages. According to Geoffrey le Baker, the French king took this drastic step for fear that a quest for ransoms might produce indiscipline.[22] Almost certainly, however, the king had in mind legal considerations too. In Philip's eyes his English counterpart, as duke of Aquitaine, was a rebellious vassal and liable therefore to be treated as such. At Poitiers, on the other hand, a battle fought between the French king and the Black Prince, a condition of *bellum hostile* applied: the two opposing commanders fought as independent and unrelated rulers. What legal status a commander accorded to a battle had a major bearing on how savagely it was fought. In a sense, whether or not a battle was fought on chivalrous terms depended entirely on the initial decisions taken by the two commanders.

The significance of legal decision-making points the way to a larger truth. By the late Middle Ages, when kings made crucial decisions of this kind they knew they could carry them out because of the greater control they exercised over their troops than that enjoyed by their predecessors. The introduction of pay and the tightening of discipline in the ranks spelled the death knell of the errantry of old. By the late fourteenth century the individual interests of knights were being subordinated to collective action and commands in the cause of achieving nationally agreed goals. Against this background, individual knights could no longer go their own way questing for personal honour and renown. It was a sign of the changing times that at Agincourt Henry V could give an order for the slaying of prisoners because of the rumour of a renewed French attack. Those who had taken the prisoners faced potentially ruinous loss of income, yet the order was carried out. The greater good of the many took precedence over pursuit of individual knightly self-interest.

From the Old World to the New

It is ironic that, around the time when kings were establishing greater control over their armies, those armies should have taken to the field in smaller numbers and less regularly than at any time since the mid-thirteenth century. Well before the winding down of the French wars there was a retreat from the high levels of military participation seen in the reigns of Edward I and Edward III. Chivalry was undermined not only by the decline of knight errantry but also by the weakening of collective military experience in the knightly and squirearchical class.

The contracting of military horizons followed in large part from the very different way in which the French war was organised in the fifteenth century. In place of the irregular hit-and-run *chevauchée* raids of the previous century, from 1417 Henry V envisaged a war of conquest. His aim was to secure the complete takeover and occupation by the English of Normandy and the adjoining areas of northern France. Initially he took with him a fairly substantial army. At its peak in 1421 his force in the duchy numbered some 13,000 men, of whom perhaps 3,000 were men-at-arms, a host at least as large as those of the fourteenth century. For many of those involved, however, the conquest of Normandy marked the limit of their commitment. When Henry died in 1422 most of the nobility involved returned to England, and a gulf opened between the army of occupation in Normandy and the gentry back home, who were increasingly detached from the war and so decreasingly militarised. From the 1420s the war in France was carried on for the most part by a force of hardened veterans whose lives were spent almost entirely on French soil. Henry had anticipated the colonisation and settlement of Normandy by a feudal fighting class holding fiefs in return for military service, the disposal of which to any but another Englishman was prohibited. It was this militarised settler community which provided the core of the new veteran force. By the 1430s its members were acquiring their own identity and developing career patterns which diverged sharply from those of the native English gentry. Although expeditions were sent from England from time to time to provide reinforcements, these were too small and too irregular to revive the old pattern of military participation across the whole knightly class. War weariness began to take its toll in England. Among those gentry who had no direct interest in the *pays de conquête* in France the traditions of family military service gradually died out. In 1475, when Edward IV had the opportunity to revive past glories, he lost his nerve before he achieved anything substantial. By the 1480s the only experience most country gentry had of war was of civil war. But Towton and Barnet were no substitute for Crécy and Agincourt. The age of chivalry as militant knighthood had passed.

The transformation of knighthood into a civil and political vocation was thus in large part the by-product of a more general demilitarising of society. Knights who could no longer seek or achieve honour in arms found fulfilment instead in magistracy and the leadership of their local communities. What was involved in this adjustment to their position was, viewed in the broader perspective, perhaps more a shift of emphasis than a total change of role. The knights and nobility as a class had for a long time taken pride in serving the Crown in local administration. They had sat on juries since the twelfth century, and they had been active in county office-holding since the early thirteenth. Those who had fought in war were for the most part the same body of men who had served as sheriffs and justices and represented their shires in parliament. The active knightly class had long combined the military and civilian aspects of the knightly vocation. What happened in the fifteenth century was simply a much bigger shift to the civilian side. This was assisted by the spread of those humanist ideas which, as we have seen, stressed service in royal government as an expression of virtue and a source of ennoblement. By the end of the fifteenth century service to the Crown was providing a focus for the emotions which in earlier times had gone into war. From the Crown's perspective, the performance of civilian administrative service was henceforth to count as a factor in promotion as much as military and diplomatic service had in the past.

The contrasting styles of the old and new nobility can be illustrated by looking at the careers of two men who were active politically within a generation of each other but were of different backgrounds and made their mark in sharply different ways. The representative of the old style is a well-known figure, Richard Neville, earl of Warwick, the Kingmaker, and that of the new, Sir Thomas Lovell, a servant of King Henry VII.

To his contemporaries, Warwick the Kingmaker, at least until the twists and turns of his last years, was the representative of all that was best in nobility. To the author of some English verses penned in 1460 he was 'that noble knight and floure of manhode', while to a writer a decade later he was the 'lodestar' of knighthood. To many in a position to know he seemed the very paragon of English chivalry. Only later, after his desertion of Edward IV for Henry VI, did he incur the opprobrium which has been associated with his name to modern times.

What did Warwick do to attract these tributes and compliments?[23] In the first place he was conspicuously courteous: he behaved precisely as the contemporary aristocratic code required he should. The Burgundian writer Jean de Waurin, someone thoroughly familiar with that code, noted that Warwick received him well – that is, he received him in the right way. It strengthened his reputation for courtesy that he paid due respect to the dead. In 1463 he had the bodies of his father and younger brother, both killed at Wakefield, reinterred at the family mausoleum of Bisham Abbey in Berkshire. In the second place Warwick was very generous. Both English and continental observers commented on the size of his household and on the scale of his largesse. The feast which he gave in 1465 for the enthronement of his brother George as archbishop of York ranked as one of the most lavish of the age. In the summer of 1467, according to Waurin, when the French ambassadors whom the earl had escorted to England were snubbed by Edward IV, the earl 'maintained his honour by entertaining them in the grand manner'.

Most of all, however, what people admired in Warwick was his buccaneering spirit and his prowess. He was the Sir Francis Drake of Yorkist England. While he was hardly a gifted commander on land, at sea he was superb, where he was always performing deeds of derring-do. On 29 May 1458 he attacked a flotilla of Castilian vessels, scattering them in all directions. In July 1459 he triumphed in an engagement with five Genoese and Spanish ships, while ten months later he had a running battle with French ships from Dunkirk to Boulogne. At the time of Henry VI's restoration in 1470 he took the lead in a force which engaged a fleet of Flemings and Dutchmen from La Rochelle, capturing forty of their ships. Whatever his limitations as a politician, there can be little doubt that Warwick fulfilled traditional expectations of a nobleman in providing leadership in war.

Sir Thomas Lovell was a man of a quite different stamp.[24] He was not a member of the higher nobility; he was of gentry origin, rising through the ranks by virtue of hard work and self-assertion. His family were minor landowners in East Anglia, his father Ralph being a cadet of the Lovells of Barton Bendish in Norfolk. Sir Thomas himself was a lawyer by training, studying at Lincoln's Inn in the 1460s and 1470s and building an attorney's practice in East Anglia at the same time. Politically, he came into his own in the reigns of Henry VII and Henry VIII, developing a close association with the former and serving him in a variety of capacities. In central government his main responsibilities were judicial and financial. He held the offices of treasurer of the chamber from 1485 and treasurer of the household from 1503, while also being a councillor in the Court of Star Chamber. At a local level he held a portfolio of offices, among them the stewardships of the honour of Wallingford, of Enfield Chase in the duchy of Lancaster, and the manors of Wakefield and Hitchin in the duchy of York. He also held the farms of various forfeited local lordships and estates. It is interesting that many of these appointments were in parts of the country where he possessed no inherited lands or significant influence. In 1504, for example, he was appointed steward of Walsall in Staffordshire, far from his East Anglian base, the first outsider ever to hold the post.

Lovell owed his position of power entirely to royal patronage and favour. His rapid rise thus affords a good example of the success of the centralising policies of the new Tudor monarchy. At the same time, by the authority of a royal licence he built up a massive retinue, which gave his lordship at least the look of that of a magnate of the old school. In 1508 he had no fewer than 1,365 men in his pay. In contrast to the medieval nobility, however, he did not draw his recruits principally from his estates and household. He drew them from any locality where he held sway – which in his case meant principally from anywhere that he held office under the Crown. His retinue was a witness to the power of royal favour, not an outward and visible sign of the strength of inherited lordship.

Lovell was never actually raised to the peerage – Henry VII did not reward his servants with titles – so was there anything distinctly chivalric about Lovell's lordship and lifestyle? Was he anything more than a lawyer-bureaucrat raised up by an outsider-king who had little or no support among the nobility? A positive answer can probably be given in each case. For all his background as a bureaucrat – or perhaps because of it – Lovell valued the outward trappings of chivalry. He was knighted at the battle of Stoke in 1487, made a banneret – a superior knight – at Blackheath in 1497 and appointed a Knight of the Garter three years later. When he died in 1524 he was given a grand heraldic funeral based on that which the Kingmaker had provided for his father at Bisham in 1463. His domestic lifestyle was opulent. He accumulated houses much as Henry VIII collected palaces. At his death he owned three great residences: Holywell in Shoreditch, Elsings in Enfield, and East Harling in Norfolk. In the first two of these properties the main rooms were decorated with tapestries depicting St George and the Nine Worthies. In the circumstances it was only to be expected that he should have been an active and enthusiastic Knight of the Garter. Unlike many knights, whose attendance at ceremonies was at best intermittent, he attended eleven out of twelve consecutive Garter chapters between 1508 and 1523, and he is known to have attended at least three feasts.[25] His enthusiasm for the Garter was shared by another of Henry VII's counsellors, his fellow Garter knight Sir Reginald Bray, who left a bequest for the completion of St George's Chapel. Carvings of the Garter and of Bray's own badge of the hemp-bray adorn the stone fan-vaults of the nave aisles, which he paid for.

It is appropriate that we have for Lovell, a new man in a new age, a portrait likeness in a new form: a bronze medallion in low relief. This was executed in about 1518 by an Italian artist, probably Pietro Torregiani, the craftsman who was awarded the commission for the monument of Henry VII and Queen Elizabeth in Westminster Abbey. Lovell is shown, forceful and worldly-wise, in profile in the attire of the courtier, wearing an Italian-style hat, with the Garter, which he so esteemed, looped round the perimeter.[26] Looking for all the world like an Italian prince or duke, he presents the very image of the Renaissance courtier. In this roundel, which probably adorned the gate tower of one of his houses, we are afforded a vivid insight into a world which culturally and politically was taking on some of the characteristics of Medician Italy.

Lovell's career, with its heavy emphasis on royal service, sums up the shifting dynamics of power in early Tudor England. Unlike some of the successful climbers of the late Middle Ages, Lovell owed nothing to association with a great magnate. His advance was entirely the result of his ability and his indispensability to the king. In that respect he exemplifies a good many of Henry VII's courtiers. What was important for such men was face-to-face contact with the monarch. That this should have stemmed in the circumstances of the time from Henry's unlikely accession to the throne as an outsider is beside the point. Its significance is that it signalled the arrival of a new world, a world in which the traditional structures of magnate power counted for far less than they had and in which the task of mediating favour was exercised by men around the king who were great precisely because they were around the king. Lovell assembled his retinue not because he had vast inherited resources to draw on but because he had royal patronage to appropriate. The sources of a man's power in Tudor England came not from below but from above – less from the goodwill of a loyal tenantry than from his standing in the favour of the monarch.

Chivalry had originated in the late eleventh century in a pluralist and decentralised world in which the bonds of knights to each other counted for as much as those binding them to someone above. Of the ties which bound them to a superior the one which counted for most was that to an immediate lord, a great magnate, not that to a distant king. In chivalric culture there was little room for concepts of royal sovereignty or unconditional obedience. Chivalric society constituted a largely self-sufficient community of honour. In the fifteenth and sixteenth centuries this traditional world began to evolve into something quite different. The decline in military participation, the redefinition of chivalry in terms of peacetime service to the monarch and the strengthening of royal control over armies – or such armies as were now summoned – all these played a part in bringing about the change. The arrival in 1485 of a king who owed little or nothing to magnate influence and who remorselessly centralised power in his own hands simply represented one stage in this process.

The idea – brought to fulfilment around the turn of the fifteenth and sixteenth centuries – of the monarch acting as the ultimate source of chivalric impulse and fount of honour had been in gestation for some time. Back in the fourteenth century Edward III had sown the idea of the 'nationalisation' of chivalry when he had established the Order of the Garter. The heralds, whose duties were codified by the future Richard III when he was constable of the realm, had been granting arms on royal authority since at least the 1470s. In the sixteenth century and most of all in Henry VIII's reign the pace of change was to quicken. It was in these years that the heralds began assuming responsibility not only for the granting of arms but for the visitation and inspection of those already claiming and using arms. The self-authenticating honour-based society of the Middle Ages, which had for so long provided the foundation of chivalry, was rapidly becoming a thing of the past. In its place was now put a more hierarchic set of values which stressed service to the king as the source of all honour and saw grants of arms as expressions of the king's position as chivalric leader of the realm.[27] The honorific self-sufficiency that had underpinned medieval chivalric society had gone.

Conclusion

Each year on the Monday of Ascot Week – the best-attended race meeting in Europe – a ceremony is staged in the precincts of Windsor Castle which in outline dates back over six centuries. This is the annual gathering of the Order of the Garter, with the service in St George's Chapel as its centrepiece – the modern-day counterpart of the annual chapter meeting and Mass decreed by Edward III in the 1340s. The pageantry is rich and colourful. After the serving of lunch in the state apartments in the Upper Ward a procession is formed, headed by the heralds in their richly braided playing-card tabards, and including the princes of the blood and the companion knights and officers of the order attired in long blue mantles with the Garter on the left shoulder. On the arrival of the sovereign, the procession moves slowly across the Upper Ward to the Engine Court gates, where it is met by the governor of the castle and the governor of the military knights, and then down through the Norman Gate, the Middle and Lower Wards and the gateway of the Horseshoe Cloister to the west door of St George's Chapel, where it is met by the dean and canons. On the arrival of the sovereign herself at the door, a fanfare is sounded and the procession moves solemnly up the nave to the choir to the accompaniment of a stirring voluntary. The sovereign, her consort and the knights take their places in their choir stalls. If a new knight of the order is to be installed, the congregation remains standing while the sovereign calls for him to be taken to his seat. Towards the end of the service, the Register of the order, the dean of Windsor, leads the prayers of thanksgiving for the foundation of the most noble order. When the service is over, the procession reforms and makes its way back to the west door led by the governor and the military knights.

This annual ceremony at Windsor, watched each year by thousands of visitors, bears visual witness to the seamlessness and continuity of English history. Over 650 years from its foundation, the Order of the Garter still attests to the English monarchy's roots in a culture which wedded ideals of service to the Crown to the Christian vocation of knighthood. The regular celebration of Garter Day, rich in pomp and pageantry, provides a symbolic link with the age of chivalry and the culture of the mounted knight.

If Garter Day brings alive something of the theatricality of medieval chivalry, the habits of thought and action which gave meaning to such ceremonies have long since gone, casualties of the passage of time. Chivalry was constantly evolving even in its medieval heyday: the chivalry of 1500 was different from the chivalry of 1300, which in its turn was different from the chivalry of 1100. By the sixteenth century the affinity between the chivalric institutions of the early Renaissance and those of four centuries before had diminished almost to vanishing point. What was left by the age of the Tudors was less the substance than the form of the old knightly ideal. The growth of state power in the late Middle Ages had irreversibly undermined the solidarities which had once sustained an international knightly brotherhood, eroding independent sources of honour and encouraging the growth of a new civilianised concept of service. Chivalry in the sense of an holistic code which provided an essential reference point for knightly behaviour had become a thing of the past.

What is remarkable, however, is not so much that chivalry died but just how long it took to die. As a framework for aristocratic behaviour it flourished in court circles until well into Elizabeth's reign. In the 1580s, in the thick of the Anglo-Spanish wars in the Netherlands, chivalric custom could still be invoked when differences between opposing commanders had to be resolved. In the course of the autumn and winter of 1586 Peregrine Bertie, Lord Willoughby d'Eresby, the English governor of Bergen-op-Zoom, was locked in a bitter dispute with Frizzio Vittorio, his Spanish opposite number, about the ransoming of prisoners and the usages of war. In a furious exchange of letters the two men hurled insults at each other about conditions in the other's armies, Frizzio boasting of the gold he had for paying his men, and Lord Willoughby retorting that the Spanish only found gold useful for suborning traitors. In the end Frizzio challenged his opponent to settle their differences in a duel. Willoughby accepted the challenge, specifying the arms that he would use and taunting Frizzio with ignorance of the customs of chivalry.[1] Whether or not the rivals ever did meet in an armed challenge is unfortunately not known.

The honourable tradition of chivalry which found expression in an agreed code of military conduct was nurtured in Elizabeth's England, as it had been in medieval times, in the tilt yard and tourneying ground. Tournaments, for which romantic-sounding summonses were issued, were held regularly in both Elizabeth's reign and that of her successor James I. These were, for the most part, large-scale well-attended affairs, widely publicised and rich in theatricality. At a spectacular tilt in 1565 four knightly challengers rode into the yard, each accompanied by 'an Amazon apparelled in a long gown, with long sleeves of crimson satin'. In April 1581, in an entertainment for a party of visiting French envoys, four knights calling themselves the Four Foster Children of Desire staged an elaborate mock attack on the queen, who was esconced in the Castle of Perfect Beauty, from which she successfully kept them at bay.[2] Tilting plays an important part in Sir Philip Sidney's poem *Arcadia*, which reaches its climax in a tournament between the Knights of Iberia and the Knights of Corinth, in which Elizabeth and Sidney are thinly disguised as Helen of Corinth and the knight Philisides.[3] In the early 1600s one of Bess of Hardwick's younger sons, Sir Charles Cavendish, erected an extraordinary mock-medieval castle at Bolsover in Derbyshire specifically for the staging of tilts. At its highest point was the so-called Little Castle, a Norman-style keep of fantastic rooms and painted ceilings, and below this a vast bailey laid out for tilting.[4] Whether chivalric entertainments were ever staged at Bolsover is hard to say. Sir Charles was over sixty when the Little Castle was built. In his time he had been a skilled swordsman and horseman, and he enjoyed a wealth of connections with tourneyers in the Jacobean aristocracy. However, the finishing touches were only put to the castle after his death, and by that time the heyday of Elizabethan chivalry was well past. Bolsover as a castle of chivalry was the product of a particular set of historical circumstances.

In reality the late flowering of chivalry in Elizabeth's reign was more in the nature of revival than survival. Early in the reign tourneying in England had been close to its death throes. An announcement of a tournament at Hampton Court in 1570 referred to tourneying 'of late fallen a sleepe'.[5] The great upsurge in interest owed much to the Accession Day tilts inaugurated by Sir Henry Lee of Ditchley in the 1560s, in which the queen's knights jousted before her each year on the anniversary of her accession. The tilts appear to have started in a modest way, the work of a small body of enthusiasts, among them Peregrine Bertie, Lord Willoughby. By the 1580s, however, they had grown into major spectacles, with knights appearing under Arthurian pseudonyms such as Sir Segremore, Sir Guy and Sir Lancelot. Sometimes elaborate speeches were delivered, some of them written by Lee himself, and poems were written afterwards in celebration. Spenser's *Faerie Queene*, published in 1590, had its roots in this exotic culture, its theme of devotion to a virgin ruler and its elaborate apparatus of chivalry charged with allegory, philosophy and poetic sentiment matching the mood of Lee's tilts.

The chivalric world of Elizabethan England was a world in which knightly pageantry was deployed to serve an urgent national need. For the greater part of Elizabeth's reign England was a state under siege. A reformed Protestant kingdom, it was threatened with invasion by its powerful Catholic neighbours, and the queen herself, the guarantor of the Protestant ascendancy, stood in danger of overthrow and assassination. The Accession Day tilts and the pageantry which accompanied them were designed to generate loyalty to the queen, investing her with romance and turning her into a focus of national unity. The tilts linked the new Elizabethan regime to the medieval past, yet to an aspect of the past which was free from religious associations. Elizabethan chivalry was Protestant chivalry: that most chivalric of knights, Lord Willoughby, was an ardent Protestant.[6] Tilting and tourneying were made the vehicles of allegory and allegorical persuasion. As in the late Middle Ages, so now in Elizabeth's reign, chivalry was harnessed to serve the needs and purposes of English royal policy.

Tournaments were staged all the way through the reigns of James I and Charles I, their popularity sustained by the close links they had with the court masques of the time. The long chivalric tradition to which they gave lingering witness, however, finally came to an end in the Civil War of the 1640s, a casualty of the political crisis which engulfed the Cavalier class at court which was their mainstay. Chivalry survived into the nineteenth century in a slimmed-down form as a code of gentlemanly behaviour among soldiers. The phrase 'an officer and a gentleman' captures its essence. So what was to be the legacy of chivalry to the modern world? Is there anything of substance which it has bequeathed to us today?

Its most valuable legacy is perhaps the assertion of the principle that those captured in war should be treated with compassion. This principle was admittedly one applied selectively in the Middle Ages, limited to the knights and the chivalrous class. Knights spared each other's lives while choosing to take those of combatants socially inferior to themselves. In the pre-chivalric age, however, they had been unmerciful even to each other. The legacy of this more humane system was to live on in the idea of a body of rules limiting the brutality of conflict. The Church, oddly, contributed remarkably little to the formulation of this doctrine, being concerned mainly with defining the circumstances in which a just war could be fought. The rules of chivalric war were for the most part of secular creation, rooted in the experience and self-interest of the knights themselves. In the age of late medieval chivalric decline, when the former knights errant were transformed into the officers and stipendiaries of national armies, the code lived on in the form of a set of conventions governing the conduct of officers towards other officers. In this way it became the point of departure for the modern Geneva Convention on the treatment of prisoners, its distinction between knights and non-knights replicated in the convention's distinction between the treatment of captive officers and that of 'other ranks'.

There is a second respect in which chivalry can be said to have made an important contribution to modern values. This is the role it played in nurturing and developing a sense of the individual. Chivalry, almost by definition, was concerned with the individual knight: it celebrated the knight's prowess, his deeds of errantry. In the early Middle Ages men had generally thought in terms of collective identities, of the solidarities which held people together in groups. At all levels of society it was group identity which mattered most: lineage or war band for the aristocracy, family, parish, guild or tithing group for the middling and lower ranks. In the late Middle Ages collective ties were to remain important in holding the fabric of society together. Alongside them, however, the chivalric emphasis on errantry suggested a new model of identity, that of the individual. To be a knight errant was to shake off the bonds of society and to venture forth alone in search of brave deeds to perform or Christian territories to defend. Chivalric identity was a form of public identity to the extent that it was heavily dependent on the opinion of others. Nonetheless, the pursuit of errantry paved the way for the idea of individual self-fulfilment, a notion central to the development of the Western idea of personal values. Even when, from the late fourteenth century, chivalry was harnessed to the needs of the state and knights became stipendiaries of kingly rulers, the idea was not completely lost. It lived on as an ideal in the minds of the officer class. Without chivalry it would be difficult to think, as we do today, of an individual going his own way or 'doing his own thing'.

There is one final respect in which the legacy of chivalry may be said to be still with us. This is the way in which chivalry laid the foundations of the modern cult of celebrity. To seek fame, honour and glory, as the medieval knight did, was to seek celebrity and to crave the plaudits of an adoring public. Quite possibly, in the most able and successful of all medieval English knights, William Marshal, we have a candidate for the first English celebrity. The young Marshal, the most brilliant knight of his day, owed his success and rapid ascent almost exclusively to his fame as a tourneyer. In the circumstances of his early years there was little to suggest the greatness to come. He was a younger son and he lacked inherited wealth. By the end of his life in 1219, however, he had become regent of England. The foundation of his extraordinary success, the magnet which drew so many others to him, was quite simply his fame as the most glamorous, charismatic and exciting knight of his day. Similar observations can be made of some of the great knights of the Hundred Years War – Sir John Chandos, Sir James Audley and Sir Hugh Calveley among them. These men too enjoyed celebrity status in their day. Chandos was described by the chronicler Knighton as 'the most talked-about knight of his age'.[7] Like the Marshal, these men were admired, respected and held up as role models, and their prowess was celebrated by the chroniclers. They had star quality.

Before the age of chivalry there had been nothing quite like this quest for fame and pride in the achievement of fame. The soldiers who had led the war bands of the early Middle Ages are largely unknown to us by name. Very likely they too attracted the admiration of their fellows for their bravery and heroism, but they did not attract the aura of celebrity. This glitzier trait was a product of the idealisation of chivalric errantry; it involved a recognition of the knight as a proud, egocentric figure, someone wrapped up in himself and his quest for self-fulfilment. The emergence of this quality was inseparable from the birth and elaboration of chivalry. The practice of tourneying, an institution at the heart of chivalry, created a setting in which knights could perform their acts of derring-do before an admiring audience. It was the knights who performed best, the knights who caught the eyes of the ladies and of the heralds who recorded the deeds of valour in their chronicles and rolls of arms, who became the proto-celebrities of their day.

The age of questing knighthood may have long since passed away. It involved a celebration of assertive warrior values with which we today, cherishing our own very different priorities, feel uneasy. Chivalry more broadly, however, represented a stage in the development of Western society. At its heart were ideas and ideals which have done much to shape the way in which we see the world today.

Bibliography and List of Abbreviations

Works which are abbreviated in the notes are detailed here in full under both the abbreviation and the editor or author's name.

Unpublished Manuscripts

British Library, London, Additional MS 32101
British Library, London, Royal MS 15 E vi
Lambeth Palace Library, Register of Archbishop Arundel, i
Lincolnshire Archives Centre, 10–ANC / 322
Oxford, Bodleian Library, MS Dugdale 15
Stonyhurst College MS 1
The National Archives, Kew, C66

Printed Works

R. W. Ackerman, 'English Rimed and Prose Romances', in R. S. Loomis (ed.), *Arthurian Literature in the Middle Ages* (Oxford, 1959)

N. W. Alcock and C. T. P. Woodfield, 'Social Pretensions in Architecture and Ancestry: Hall House, Sawbridge, Warwickshire, and the Andrewe Family', *Antiquaries Journal*, 76 (1996)

C. T. Allmand, 'The *De Re Militari* of Vegetius', *History Today*, 54 (June, 2004)

C. T. Allmand, 'Two Fifteenth-Century English Versions of Vegetius' *De Re Militari*', in M. Strickland (ed.), *Armies, Chivalry and Warfare in Medieval Britain and France* (Stamford, 1998)

C. T. Allmand, 'War and the Non-Combatant in the Middle Ages', in Maurice Keen (ed.), *Medieval Warfare. A History* (Oxford, 1999)

Ambroise, *The Crusade of Richard Lion-Heart*, ed. J. M. Hubert and J. L. La Monte (New York, 1941)

Annales Monastici: H. R. Luard, *Annales Monastici* (5 vols, Rolls Series, 1864–9)

Anonimalle: V. H. Galbraith (ed.), *Anonimalle Chronicle, 1333–1381* (Manchester, 1927)

C. A. J. Armstrong, 'The Piety of Cecily, Duchess of York: a Study in Late Medieval Culture', in his *England, France and Burgundy in the Fifteenth Century* (London, 1983)

J. W. Armstrong, 'The Development of the Office of Arms in England, c. 1413–1485', in K. Stevenson (ed.), *The Herald in Late Medieval Europe* (Woodbridge, 2009)

A. Ayton, 'Armies and Military Communities in Fourteenth-Century England', in P. Coss and C. Tyerman (eds), *Soldiers, Nobles and Gentlemen. Essays in Honour of Maurice Keen* (Woodbridge, 2009)

A. Ayton, *Knights and Warhorses. Military Service and the English Aristocracy under Edward III* (Woodbridge, 1994)

A. Ayton, 'Knights, Esquires and Military Service: the Evidence of the Armorial Cases before the Court of Chivalry', in A. Ayton and J. L. Price (eds), *The Medieval Military Revolution* (London, 1995)

A. Ayton, 'War and the English Gentry under Edward III', *History Today*, 42 (March, 1992)

A. Ayton and P. Preston, *The Battle of Crécy, 1346* (Woodbridge, 2005)

Richard Barber, *Edward, Prince of Wales and Aquitaine* (London, 1978)

Richard Barber, *The Knight and Chivalry* (2nd edn, Woodbridge, 1995)

Richard Barber, 'Malory's *Le Morte Darthur* and Court Culture under Edward IV', in J. P. Carley and F. Riddy (eds), *Arthurian Literature, XII* (Woodbridge, 1993)

J. Barbour, *The Bruce*, ed. W.M. Mackenzie (London, 1909)

F. Barlow, *William Rufus* (London, 1983)

J. Barnie, *Wart in Medieval Society. Social Values and the Hundred Years War, 1337–99* (London, 1974)

C. M. Barron, 'Chivalry, Pageantry and Merchant Culture in Medieval London', in P. Coss and M. Keen (eds), *Heraldry, Pageantry and Social Display in Medieval England* (Woodbridge, 2002)

W. R. J. Barron (ed.), *The Arthur of the English* (Cardiff, 1969)

W. R. J. Barron, *English Medieval Romance* (Harlow, 1987)

G. W. S. Barrow, *Robert Bruce* (London, 1965)

R. Bartlett, 'Symbolic Meanings of Hair in the Middle Ages', *Transactions of the Royal Historical Society*, 6th series, 4 (1994)

R. Bartlett, *England under the Norman and Angevin Kings, 1075–1225* (Oxford, 2000)

C. Batt and R. Field, 'The Romance Tradition', in W. R. J. Barron (ed.), *The Arthur of the English* (Cardiff, 1999)

The Battle of Maldon AD 991, ed. D. Scragg (Oxford, 1991)

Beauchamp Pageant: A. Sinclair (ed.), *The Beauchamp Pageant* (Donington, 2003)

J. Bellamy, *The Law of Treason in England in the Later Middle Ages* (Cambridge, 1970)

G. F. Beltz, *Memorials of the Order of the Garter* (London, 1841)

Michael J. Bennett, *Community, Class and Careerism. Cheshire and Lancashire Society in the Age of Sir Gawain and the Green Knight* (Cambridge, 1983)

M. Biddle and others, *King Arthur's Round Table. An Archaeological Investigation* (Woodbridge, 2000)

M. Biddle, 'Why is the Bishop of Winchester Prelate of the Order of the Garter?', *Winchester Cathedral Record*, 60 (1991)

P. Binski, *The Painted Chamber at Westminster* (Society of Antiquaries of London Occasional Paper, new series, 9, 1986)

M. Blaess, 'L'Abbaye de Bordesley et les Livres de Guy de Beauchamp', *Romania*, 78 (1957)

C. Blair and J. Goodall, 'An Effigy at Wilsthorpe: A Correction to Pevsner's *Lincolnshire*', *Church Monuments*, 17 (2002)

A. Blamires, 'Chaucer's Revaluation of Chivalric Honour', *Medievalia*, 5 (1979)

F. Blomefield, *Topographical History of the County of Norfolk* (11 vols, London, 1805–10)

A. W. Boardman, *The Battle of Towton* (Stroud, 1994)

A. W. Boardman, 'The Historical Background to the Battle and the Documentary Evidence', in *Blood Red Roses. The Archaeology of a Mass Grave from the Battle of Towton*, AD 1461, ed. V. Fiorato and others (Oxford, 2000)

Boke of Noblesse: William Worcester, *The Boke of Noblesse*, ed. J. G. Nichols (London: Roxburghe Club, 1860)

J. Boffey, 'Books and Readers in Calais: Some Notes', in L. Visser-Fuchs (ed.), *Tant d'Emprises: So Many Undertakings. Essays in Honour of Anne F. Sutton* (*The Ricardian*, XIII, 2003)

Book of Chivalry: R. W. Kaeuper and E. Kennedy (eds), *The Book of Chivalry of Geoffroi de Charny: Text, Context and Translation* (Philadelphia, 1996)

D. Bornstein, *Mirrors of Courtesy* (Hamden, Connecticut, 1975)

J. Bradbury, *The Medieval Archer* (Woodbridge, 1985)

J. Bradbury, 'Geoffrey V of Anjou, Count and Knight', in C. Harper-Bill and R. Harvey (eds), *The Ideals and Practice of Medieval Knighthood, III* (Woodbridge, 1990)

P. Brieger, *English Art, 1216–1307* (Oxford, 1957)

R. A. Brown, *English Castles* (2nd edn, London, 1970)

R. A. Brown, 'Royal Castle-Building in England, 1154–1216', in his *Castles, Conquest and Charters. Collected Papers* (Woodbridge, 1989)

R. A. Brown, H. M. Colvin, A. J. Taylor, *The History of the King's Works* (2 vols, London, 1963)

Clive Burgess, 'St George's College, Windsor: Context and Consequence', in Nigel Saul (ed.), *St George's Chapel, Windsor, in the Fourteenth Century* (Woodbridge, 2005)

Calendar of Close Rolls 1413–19 (London, 1929)

Calendar of Patent Rolls 1350–4; 1377–81; 1361–4; 1391–6 (London, 1895, 1905, 1912)

M. Camille, *Mirror in Parchment. The Luttrell Psalter and the Making of Medieval England* (London, 1998)

D. A. Carpenter, *The Battles of Lewes and Evesham, 1264/5* (Keele, 1987)

J. I. Catto, 'Religious Change under Henry V', in G. L. Harriss (ed.), *Henry V. The Practice of Kingship* (Oxford, 1985)

W. Caxton, *The Book of the Ordre of Chyvalry*, ed. A. T. P. Byles (Early English Text Society, 168, 1926)

Pierre Chaplais, *Diplomatic Documents, I, 1101–1272* (London, 1964)

Chivalry in the Renaissance: S. Anglo (ed.), *Chivalry in the Renaissance* (Woodbridge, 1990)

Christine de Pizan's Letter: J. Chance (ed.), *Christine de Pizan's Letter of Othea to Hector* (Newburyport, Mass., 1990)

Chronica Maiora: D. Preest and J. G. Clark (eds), *The Chronica Maiora of Thomas Walsingham* (Woodbridge, 2005)

Chronicle of Pierre de Langtoft: T. Wright (ed.), *Chronicle of Pierre de Langtoft* (2 vols, Rolls Series, 1886)

'Chronicle of Richard of Hexham', in R. Howlett (ed.), *Chronicles of the Reigns of Stephen, Henry II and Richard I* (3 vols, Rolls Series, 1880–6)

Chronicle of Walter of Guisborough: H. Rothwell (ed.), *The Chronicle of Walter of Guisborough* (Camden Society, 3rd series, 89, 1957)

Chronicon de Lanercost: J. Stevenson (ed.), *Chronicon de Lanercost* (Edinburgh, 1839)

Chronicon Galfridi le Baker: E. M. Thompson (ed.), *Chronicon Galfridi le Baker de Swynebroke* (Oxford, 1889)

Chronique: Jean le Bel, *Chronique*, ed. J. Viard and E. Deprez (2 vols, Paris, 1904–5)

Chroniques de Jean Froissart: S. Luce, G. Raynaud, L. Mirot, A. Mirot (eds), *Chroniques de Jean Froissart* (Société de l'Histoire de France, 15 vols, 1869–1975)

M. Clarke, *Fourteenth Century Studies*, ed. L. S. Sutherland and M. McKisack (Oxford, 1968)

W. N. Clarke, *Parochial Topography of the Hundred of Wanting* (Oxford, 1824)

Cligès: Chrétien de Troyes, *Cligès*, ed. B. Raffel (New Haven and London, 1997)

Commynes, *Memoirs*: P. de Commynes, *Memoirs. The Reign of Louis XI, 1461–83*, ed. M. Jones (Harmondsworth, 1972)

P. Contamine, *War in the Middle Ages* (Oxford, 1984)

Peter Coss, *The Knight in Medieval England, 1000–1400* (Stroud, 1993)

Peter Coss, 'Knighthood, Heraldry and Social Exclusion in Edwardian England', in P. Coss and M. Keen (eds), *Heraldry, Pageantry and Social Display in Medieval England* (Woodbridge, 2002)

Peter Coss, *The Lady in Medieval England, 1000–1500* (Stroud, 1998)

Peter Coss, *The Origins of the English Gentry* (Cambridge, 2003)

Charles Coulson, 'Structural Symbolism in Medieval Castle Architecture', *Journal of the British Archaeological Association*, 132 (1979)

Charles Coulson, 'Some Analysis of the Castle of Bodiam, East Sussex', in C. Harper-Bill and R. Harvey (eds), *The Ideals and Practice of Medieval Knighthood, IV* (Woodbridge, 1992)

Charles Coulson, 'Peaceable Power in English Castles', in M. Chibnall (ed.), *Anglo-Norman Studies, 23* (Woodbridge, 2000)

Charles Coulson, *Castles in Medieval Society. Fortresses in England, France and Ireland in the Central Middle Ages* (Oxford, 2003)

S. Crane, *Insular Romance. Politics, Faith and Culture in Anglo-Norman and Middle English Literature* (Berkeley, 1986)

O. Creighton, *Castles and Landscapes* (London, 2002)

O. Creighton and R. Higham, *Medieval Town Walls. An Archaeology and Social History of Urban Defence* (Stroud, 2005)

J. C. Crick, *The Historia Regum Britanniae of Geoffrey of Monmouth, IV. Dissemination and Reception in the Later Middle Ages* (Woodbridge, 1991)

David Crouch, *The Image of the Aristocracy in Britain, 1000–1300* (London, 1992)

David Crouch, *Tournament* (London, 2005)

David Crouch, *William Marshal. Court, Career and Chivalry in the Angevin Empire, 1147–1219* (Harlow, 1990)

Crowland Continuations: N. Pronay and J. Cox (eds), *The Crowland Chronicle Continuations, 1459–1486* (London, 1986)

De Nugis Curialium: Walter Map, *De Nugis Curialium*, ed. M. R. James (2nd edn, Oxford, 1983)

The Death of King Arthur, ed. J. Cable (Harmondsworth, 1971)

D. Defoe, *The Compleat English Gentleman* (London, 1890)

Noel Denholm-Young, 'The Tournament in the Thirteenth Century', in R. W. Hunt, W. A. Pantin, R. W. Southern (eds), *Studies in Medieval History Presented to F. M. Powicke* (Oxford, 1948)

Noel Denholm-Young, *History and Heraldry, 1254–1310* (Oxford, 1965)

Noel Denholm-Young, 'Feudal Society in the Thirteenth Century: the Knights', in his *Collected Papers on Medieval Subjects* (Cardiff, 1969)

Rodney Dennys, *The Heraldic Imagination* (London, 1975)

Dialogus de Scaccario: C. Johnson (ed.), *Dialogue de Scaccario* (2nd edn, Oxford, 1983)

Dictes and Sayings: C. F. Buhler (ed.), *The Dictes and Sayings of the Philosophers* (Early English Text Society, 211, 1941)

F. R. H. Du Boulay, 'Henry of Derby's Expeditions to Prussia, 1390–1 and 1392', in F. R. H. Du Boulay and C. M. Barron (eds.), *The Reign of Richard II* (London, 1971)

W. Dugdale, *The Antiquities of Warwickshire* (2nd edn, 2 vols, London, 1730)

S. Dull, A. Luttrell, M. Keen, 'Faithful unto Death: The Tomb Slab of Sir William Neville and Sir John Clanvowe, Constantinople, 1391', *Antiquaries Journal*, 71 (1991)

Diana Dunn, 'Margaret of Anjou, Chivalry and the Order of the Garter', in C. Richmond and E. Scarff (eds), *St George's Chapel, Windsor, in the Late Middle Ages* (Windsor, 2001)

R. Eales, 'Royal Power and Castles in Norman England', in C. Harper-Bill and R. Harvey (eds), *The Ideals and Practice of Medieval Knighthood, III* (Woodbridge, 1990)

Ecclesiastical History of Orderic Vitalis: Marjorie Chibnall (ed.), *The Ecclesiastical History of Orderic Vitalis* (6 vols, Oxford, 1968–80)

A. Emery, 'Late-Medieval Houses as an Expression of Social Status', *Historical Research*, 78 (2005)

A. Emery, *Greater Medieval Houses of England and Wales, III. Southern England* (Cambridge, 2006)

Epistle of Othea: C. F. Buhler (ed.), *The Epistle of Othea* (Early English Text Society, 264, 1970)

Expeditions to Prussia: L. Toulmin-Smith (ed.), *Expeditions to Prussia and the Holy Land made by Henry, Earl of Derby* (Camden Society, new series, 52, 1894)

Katherine Faulkner, 'The Transformation of Knighthood in Early Thirteenth-Century England', *English Historical Review*, 111 (1996)

Arthur B. Ferguson, *The Indian Summer of English Chivalry* (Durham, NC, 1960)

E. Fernie, *The Architecture of Norman England* (Oxford, 2000)

R. Field, 'Romance in England', in D. Wallace (ed.), *Cambridge History of Medieval English Literature* (Cambridge, 1999)

Christopher Fletcher, *Richard II. Manhood, Youth and Politics, 1377–99* (Oxford, 2008)

E. Flugel, 'Eine Mittelenglische Claudian-Ubersetzung (1445)', *Anglia*, 28 (1905)

J. Fortescue, *De Laudibus Legum Anglie*, ed. S. B. Chrimes (Cambridge, 1949)

J. Frankis, 'Taste and Patronage in Late Medieval England as reflected in Versions of *Guy of Warwick*', *Medium Aevum*, 66 (1997)

J. Frappier, 'Le Graal et la chevalerie', *Romania*, 75 (1954)

J. Frappier, 'The Vulgate Cycle', in R. S. Loomis (ed.), *Arthurian Literature in the Middle Ages* (Oxford, 1959)

J. Froissart, *Chronicles of England, France, Spain*, ed. T. Johnes (2 vols, London, 1862)

N. Fryde, *The Tyranny and Fall of Edward II, 1321–1326* (Cambridge, 1979)

Gaimar, *Estoire des Engleis*: I. Short (ed.), Geffrei Gaimar, *Estoire des Engleis, History of the English* (Oxford, 2009)

Geoffrey of Monmouth, *History of the Kings of Britain*, ed. L. Thorpe (Harmondsworth, 1966)

Gesta Henrici Quinti: F. Taylor and J. S. Roskell (eds.), *Gesta Henrici Quinti* (Oxford, 1975)

Gesta Regum: William of Malmesbury, *Gesta Regum Anglorum*, ed. R. A. B. Mynors, R. M. Thomson and M. Winterbottom (2 vols, Oxford, 1998)

Gesta Stephani: K. R. Potter and R. H. C. Davis (eds.), *Gesta Stephani* (Oxford, 1976)

John Gillingham, 'The Context and Purposes of Geoffrey of Monmouth's *History of the Kings of Britain*', in M. Chibnall (ed.), *Anglo-Norman Studies, XIII* (Woodbridge, 1991), reprinted in his *The English in the Twelfth Century* (Woodbridge, 2000)

John Gillingham, 'Conquering the Barbarians: War and Chivalry in Twelfth-Century Britain', *Haskins Society Journal*, 4 (1992), reprinted in his *The English in the Twelfth Century* (Woodbridge, 2000)

John Gillingham, 'Some Legends of Richard the Lionheart: their Development and Influence', in his *Richard Coeur de Lion. Kingship, Chivalry and War in the Twelfth Century* (London, 1994)

John Gillingham, 'Richard I and the Science of War in the Middle Ages', in his *Richard Coeur de Lion. Kingship, Chivalry and War in the Twelfth Century* (London, 1994)

John Gillingham, 'War and Chivalry in the *History of William the Marshal*', in his *Richard Coeur de Lion. Kingship, Chivalry and War in the Twelfth Century* (London, 1994)

John Gillingham, '1066 and the Introduction of Chivalry into England', in G. Garnett and J. Hudson (eds.), *Law and Government in Medieval England and Normandy* (Cambridge, 1994), reprinted in his *The English in the Twelfth Century* (Woodbridge, 2000)

John Gillingham, 'Kingship, Chivalry and Love. Political and Cultural Values in the earliest History written in French: Geoffrey Gaimar's *Estoire des Engleis*', in C.W. Hollister (ed.), *Anglo-Norman Political Culture and the Twelfth-Century Renaissance* (Woodbridge, 1997), reprinted in his *The English in the Twelfth Century* (Woodbridge, 2000)

John Gillingham, *Richard I* (New Haven and London, 1999)

John Gillingham, 'From *Civilitas* to Civility: Codes of Manners in Medieval and Early Modern England', *Transactions of the Royal Historical Society*, 6th series, 12 (2002)

John Gillingham, 'Enforcing Old Law in New Ways: Professional Lawyers and Treason in Early Fourteenth-Century England and France', in P. Andersen, M. Munster-Swendsen, H. Voght (eds), *Law and Power in the Middle Ages* (Copenhagen, 2008)

Mark Girouard, *The Return to Camelot. Chivalry and the English Gentleman* (New Haven and London, 1981)

Mark Girouard, *Robert Smythson and the Elizabethan Country House* (2nd edn, New Haven and London, 1983)

C. Given-Wilson, *Chronicles. The Writing of History in Medieval England* (London, 2004)

C. Given-Wilson and F. Bériac, 'Edward III's Prisoners of War: the Battle of Poitiers and its Context', *English Historical Review*, 116 (2001)

J. Good, *The Cult of St George in Medieval England* (Woodbridge, 2009)

J. A. Goodall, 'Richmond Castle, Yorkshire', *Country Life*, 15 May 2003.

A. Goodman, 'The Military Subcontracts of Sir Hugh Hastings, 1380', *English Historical Review*, 95 (1980)

A. Goodman, *The Wars of the Roses. Military Activity and English Society, 1452–97* (London, 1981)

Gothic: Art for England: R. Marks and P. Williamson (eds), *Gothic: Art for England, 1400–1547* (London, 2003)

A. Gransden, *Historical Writing in England c. 550 to c. 1307* (London, 1974)

J. A. Green, *The Government of England under Henry I* (Cambridge, 1986)

S. J. Gunn, 'Chivalry and the Politics of the Early Tudor Court' in S. Anglo (ed.), *Chivalry in the Renaissance* (Woodbridge, 1990)

S. J. Gunn, 'Sir Thomas Lovell (*c.* 1449–1524): a New Man in a New Monarchy?', in J. L. Watts (ed.), *The End of the Middle Ages?* (Stroud, 1998)

T. Hahn, 'Gawain and Popular Chivalric Romance in Britain', in R. L. Krueger (ed.), *Cambridge Companion to Medieval Romance* (Cambridge, 2000)

G. L. Harriss, *Shaping the Nation. England, 1360–1461* (Oxford, 2005)

E. J. Hathaway (ed.), *Fouke Le Fitz Waryn* (Anglo-Norman Text Society, 1975)

Peter Heath, *Church and Realm, 1272–1461* (London, 1988)

P. Hebgin-Barnes, 'A Triumphant Image: Henry Scrope's Window in Heydour Church', *Medieval Life*, 4 (1996)

E.-D. Hehl, 'War, Peace and the Christian Order', in D. Luscombe and J. Riley-Smith (eds), *New Cambridge Medieval History*, 4, c. 1024–1198 (Cambridge, 2004)

Henry, Archdeacon of Huntingdon, *Historia Anglorum*, ed. D. Greenway (Oxford, 1996)

H. J. Hewitt, *The Organisation of War under Edward III* (Manchester, 1966)

High Book of the Grail: N. Bryant (ed.), *The High Book of the Grail* (Cambridge, 1978)

R. H. Hilton, *A Medieval Society. The West Midlands at the End of the Thirteenth Century* (London, 1966)

Historia Anglicana: T. Walsingham, *Historia Anglicana*, ed. H. T. Riley (2 vols, Rolls Series, 1863–4)

Historia Anglorum: Henry, Archdeacon of Huntingdon, *Historia Anglorum*, ed. D. Greenway (Oxford, 1996)

Historia Rerum: William of Newburgh, *Historia Rerum Anglicarum* in R. Howlett (ed.), *Chronicles of the Reigns of Stephen, Henry II and Richard I* (4 vols, Rolls Series, 1884–90), ii, p. 422

Historia Novella: William of Malmesbury, *Historia Novella*, ed. E. King and K. R. Potter (Oxford, 1998)

Historie de Guillaume le Conquerant: Guillaume de Poitiers, *Historie de Guillaume le Conquerant*, ed. R. Foreville (Paris, 1952)

History of Parliament: J. S. Roskell, L. Clark, C. Rawcliffe (eds), *History of Parliament. The House of Commons, 1386–1421* (4 vols, Stroud, 1992)

History of William Marshal: A. J. Holden, S. Gregory, D. Crouch (eds), *History of William Marshal* (Anglo-Norman Text Society, Occasional Series, 4–6, 2002–6), i

Norman Housley, *The Later Crusades. From Lyons to Alcazar, 1274–1580* (Oxford, 1992)

Hue de Rotelande, *Ipomedon*, ed. A. J. Holden (Paris, 1979)

Hue de Rotelande, *Protheselaus*, ed. A. J. Holden (3 vols, Anglo-Norman Text Society, 1991–3)

Jonathan Hughes, *Pastors and Visionaries. Religion and Secular Life in Late Medieval Yorkshire* (Woodbridge, 1988)

Jonathan Hughes, 'Stephen Scrope and the Circle of Sir John Fastolf: Moral and Intellectual Outlooks', in C. Harper-Bill and R. Harvey (eds), *Medieval Knighthood, IV* (Woodbridge, 1992)

Jonathan Hughes, *Arthurian Myths and Alchemy. The Kingship of Edward IV* (Stroud, 2002)

M. James, 'The Concept of Order and the Northern Rising, 1569' and 'English Politics and the Concept of Honour, 1485–1642', both in his *Society, Politics and Culture. Studies in Early Modern England* (Cambridge, 1986)

P. M. Johnston, 'Stoke d'Abernon Church', *Surrey Archaeological Collections*, 20 (1907)

M. C. E. Jones, 'Sir John Hardreshull, King's Lieutenant in Brittany, 1343–5', *Nottingham Medieval Studies*, 31 (1987)

M. K. Jones, 'Somerset, York and the Wars of the Roses', *English Historical Review*, 104 (1989)

M. K. Jones, 'The Battle of Verneuil (17 August 1424): Towards a History of Courage', *War in History*, 9 (2002)

W. R. Jones, 'The English Church and Royal Propaganda during the Hundred Years War', *Journal of British Studies*, 19 (1979)

Jordan Fantosme's Chronicle: R. C. Johnston (ed.), *Jordan Fantosme's Chronicle* (Oxford, 1981)

Richard W. Kaeuper, *Chivalry and Violence in Medieval Europe* (Oxford, 1999)

Richard W. Kaeuper, 'The Societal Role of Chivalry in Romance: Northwestern Europe', in R. L. Krueger (ed.), *Cambridge Companion to Medieval Romance* (Cambridge, 2000)

Richard W. Kaeuper, *Holy Warriors. The Religious Ideology of Chivalry* (Philadelphia, 2009)

Howard Kaminsky, 'The Noble Feud in the Later Middle Ages', *Past and Present*, 177 (2002)

Maurice Keen, *The Laws of War in the Late Middle Ages* (London, 1965)

Maurice Keen, 'Chaucer's Knight, the English Aristocracy and the Crusade', in V. J. Scattergood and J. W. Sherborne (eds), *English Court Culture in the Later Middle Ages* (London, 1983), reprinted in his *Nobles, Knights and Men-at-Arms in the Middle Ages* (London, 1996)

Maurice Keen, *Chivalry* (New Haven and London, 1984)

Maurice Keen, 'Richard II's Ordinances of War of 1385', in R. E. Archer and S. Walker (eds), *Rulers and Ruled in Late Medieval England* (London, 1995)

Maurice Keen, 'War, Peace and Chivalry', in his *Nobles, Knights and Men-at-Arms in the Middle Ages* (London, 1996)

Maurice Keen, 'English Military Experience and the Court of Chivalry: the Case of Grey v. Hastings', in his *Nobles, Knights and Men-at-Arms in the Middle Ages* (London, 1996)

Maurice Keen, *Origins of the English Gentleman* (Stroud, 2002)

Maurice Keen, 'Chivalry and English Kingships in the Later Middle Ages', in C. Given-Wilson, A. Kettle, L. Scales (eds.), *War, Government and Aristocracy in the British Isles, c. 1150–1500. Essays in Honour of Michael Prestwich* (Woodbridge, 2008)

Elspeth Kennedy, 'The Quest for Identity and the Importance of Lineage in Thirteenth-Century French Prose Romance', in C. Harper-Bill and R. Harvey (eds), *The Ideals and Practice of Medieval Knighthood, II* (Woodbridge, 1988)

Peter Kidson, 'The Architecture of St George's Chapel', in Nigel Saul and Tim Tatton-Brown (eds), *St George's Chapel, Windsor: History and Heritage* (Wimborne Minster, 2010)

R. L. Kilgour, *The Decline of Chivalry as Shown in the French Literature of the Late Middle Ages* (Cambridge, Mass., 1937)

King Arthur's Death: B. Stone (ed.), *King Arthur's Death. Alliterative* Morte Arthure *and* Stanzaic Le Morte Arthur (Harmondsworth, 1988)

A. King, 'A Helm with a Crest of Gold: the Order of Chivalry in Thomas Gray's *Scalacronica*', in N. E. Saul (ed.), *Fourteenth Century England, I* (Woodbridge, 2000)

A. King, 'Fortresses and Fashion Statements: Gentry Castles in Fourteenth-Century Northumberland', *Journal of Medieval History*, 33 (2007)

D. J. King, 'Anne Harling Reconsidered', in J. Boffey and V. Davis (eds), *Recording Medieval Lives* (Donington, 2009)

D. J. C. King, *Castellarium Anglicanum* (2 vols, New York, 1983)

J. K. Knight, *The Three Castles* (Cardiff, 1999)

Knighton: G. Martin (ed.), *Knighton's Chronicle, 1337–1396* (Oxford, 1995)

David Knowles, *The Religious Orders in England, III. The Tudor Age* (Cambridge, 1959)

O. de Laborderie, J. R. Maddicott, D. A. Carpenter, 'The Last Hours of Simon de Montfort: A New Account', *English Historical Review*, 115 (2000)

W. Lack and P. Whittemore, 'Portfolio of Small Plates', *Transactions of the Monumental Brass Society*, 15 (1992–6)

Lancelot du Lac: E. Kennedy (ed.), *Lancelot du Lac: the non-cyclic Old French Prose Romance* (Oxford, 1980)

Lancelot Part V, ed. W. W. Kibler, in *Lancelot-Grail: The Old French Arthurian Vulgate and Post-Vulgate in Translation, III*, ed. N. J. Lacy (5 vols, New York, 1993–6)

LCBP: R. Barber (ed.), *Life and Campaigns of the Black Prince* (Woodbridge, 1979)

Letter to Richard II: P. de Mézières, *Letter to King Richard II*, ed. G. W. Coopland (Liverpool, 1975)

Letters and Papers: J. Stevenson (ed.), *Letters and Papers Illustrative of the Wars of the English in France* (2 vols, Rolls Series, 1861–4)

R. Liddiard, 'Castle Rising, Norfolk: A Landscape of Lordship?', in C. Harper-Bill (ed.), *Anglo-Norman Studies*, 22 (Woodbridge, 1999)

R. Liddiard, *Castles in Context: Power, Symbolism and Landscape, 1066–1500* (Macclesfield, 2005)

P. Lindley, *Tomb Destruction and Scholarship. Medieval Monuments in Early Modern England* (Donington, 2007)

Literae Cantuarienses: J. B. Sheppard (ed.), *Literae Cantuarienses*, iii (Rolls Series, 1889)

S. D. Lloyd, *English Society and the Crusade, 1216–1307* (Oxford, 1988)

R. S. Loomis, 'Edward I, Arthurian Enthusiast', *Speculum*, 28 (1953)

R. S. Loomis (ed.), *Arthurian Literature in the Middle Ages* (Oxford, 1959)

A. Luttrell, 'English Levantine Crusaders, 1363–7', *Renaissance Studies*, 2 (1988)

Lydgate, The Minor Poems: H. N. MacCracken (ed.), John Lydgate, The Minor Poems (2 vols, Early English Text Society, 192, 1934)

P. Maddern, 'Gentility', in R. Radulescu and A. Truelove (eds), Gentry Culture in Late Medieval England (Manchester, 2005)

Major Latin Works of Gower: E. W. Stockton (ed.), The Major Latin Works of John Gower (Seattle, 1962)

E. Mason, 'Legends of the Beauchamps' Ancestors: the Use of Baronial Propaganda in Medieval England', Journal of Medieval History, 10 (1984)

E. Mason, 'Fact and Fiction in the English Crusading Tradition: the Earls of Warwick in the Twelfth Century', Journal of Medieval History, 14 (1988)

W. Matthews, The Tragedy of Arthur (Berkeley, California, 1960)

K. B. McFarlane, The Nobility of Later Medieval England (Oxford, 1973)

K. B. McFarlane, 'William Worcester: a Preliminary Survey', in his England in the Fifteenth Century (London, 1981)

A. K. McHardy, 'The English Clergy and the Hundred Years War', in W. J. Shiels (ed.), The Church and War (Studies in Church History, 20, 1983)

B. McNab, 'Obligations of the Clergy in English Society', in W. C. Jordan, B. McNab, T. F. Ruiz (eds), Order and Innovation in the Middle Ages (Princeton, 1976)

C. M. Meale, '"The Hoole Book": Editing and the Creation of Meaning in Malory's Text', in E. Archibald and A. S. G. Edwards (eds), A Companion to Malory (Woodbridge, 1996)

Memorials of Henry V: C. A. Cole (ed.), Memorials of Henry V (Rolls Series, 1858)

Middle English Translation of Christine de Pisan: D. Bornstein (ed.), The Middle English Translation of Christine de Pisan's Livre du Corps de Policie (Heidelburg, 1977)

R. J. Mitchell, John Tiptoft, 1427–1470 (London, 1938)

C. Moor, Knights of Edward I (5 vols, Harleian Society, 80–84, 1929–32)

D. A. L. Morgan, 'The Individual Style of the English Gentleman', in M. Jones (ed.), Gentry and Lesser Nobility in Late Medieval Europe (Gloucester, 1986)

D. A. L. Morgan, 'From a Death to a View: Louis Robessart, Johan Huizinga, and the Political Significance of Chivalry', in S. Anglo (ed.), Chivalry in the Renaissance (Woodbridge, 1990)

D. A. L. Morgan, 'The Political After-Life of Edward III: the Apotheosis of a Warmonger', English Historical Review, 112 (1997)

D. A. L. Morgan, 'The Banner-bearer of Christ and Our Lady's Knight: How God became an Englishman Revisited', in N. E. Saul (ed.), St George's Chapel, Windsor, in the Fourteenth Century (Woodbridge, 2005)

Philip Morgan, War and Society in Medieval Cheshire, 1277–1403 (Manchester, 1987)

Philip Morgan, 'Making the English Gentry', in P. R. Coss and S. D. Lloyd (eds), *Thirteenth Century England* (Woodbridge, 1995)

Colin Morris, '*Equestris Ordo*: Chivalry as a Vocation in the Twelfth Century', in D. Baker (ed.), *Religious Motivation. Biographical and Sociological Problems for the Church Historian* (Studies in Church History, 15, 1978)

Mark Morris, 'Edward I and the Knights of the Round Table' in P. Brand and S. Cunningham (eds), *Foundations of Medieval Scholarship. Records Edited in Honour of David Crook* (York, 2008)

R. K. Morris, 'The Architecture of the Earls of Warwick in the Fourteenth Century', in W. M. Ormrod (ed.), *England in the Fourteenth Century* (Woodbridge, 1986)

R. K. Morris, 'The Architecture of Arthurian Enthusiasm: Castle Symbolism in the Reigns of Edward I and his Successors', in M. Strickland (ed.), *Armies, Chivalry and Warfare in Medieval Britain and France* (Stamford, 1998)

J. Munby, R. Barber and R. Brown, *Edward III's Round Table at Windsor* (Woodbridge, 2007)

Murimuth: Adam Murimuth, *Continuatio Chronicarum*, ed. E. M. Thompson (Rolls Series, 1889)

A. Murray, *Reason and Society in the Middle Ages* (Oxford, 1977)

C. Nall, 'Perceptions of Financial Mismanagement and the English Diagnosis of Defeat', in L. Clark (ed.), *The Fifteenth Century, VII. Conflicts, Consequences and the Crown in the Late Middle Ages* (Woodbridge, 2007)

J. Nichols, *The History and Antiquities of the County of Leicester* (4 vols. In 8, London, 1795–1811)

J. Nichols, *The Progresses and Public Processions of Queen Elizabeth* (3 vols, London, 1823)

ODNB: *Oxford Dictionary of National Biography*, ed. H. C. G. Matthew and B. Harrison (63 vols, Oxford, 2004)

W. M. Ormrod, 'Knights of Venus', *Medium Aevum*, 73 (2004)

J. J. N. Palmer, *England, France and Christendom, 1377–1399* (London, 1972)

Paris, *Chronica Majora*: Matthew Paris, *Chronica Majora*, ed. H. R. Luard (5 vols, Rolls Series, 1864–9)

Paston Letters and Papers: N. Davis (ed.), *Paston Letters and Papers of the Fifteenth Century* (2 vols, Oxford, 1971, 1976)

L. Patterson, *Chaucer and the Subject of History* (Madison, Wisconsin, 1991)

Julian Pitt-Rivers, 'Honour and Social Status', in *Honour and Shame. The Values of a Mediterranean Society*, ed. J. G. Peristiany (London, 1965)

Colin Platt, *Medieval England. A Social History and Archaeology from the Conquest to 1600* (London, 1978)

Colin Platt, 'Understanding Licences to Crenellate', *Castle Studies Group Journal*, 21 (2007–8)

Political Poems and Songs: T. Wright (ed.), *Political Poems and Songs relating to English History* (2 vols, Rolls Series, 1859)

Political Songs: P. R. Coss (ed.), *Thomas Wright's Political Songs of England from the Reign of John to that of Edward II* (Camden Society, 1839, 2nd edn, 1996)

A. J. Pollard, *Warwick the Kingmaker. Politics, Power and Fame* (London, 2007)

E. Porter, 'Chaucer's Knight, the Alliterative *Morte Arthure*, and Medieval Laws of War: a Reconsideration', *Nottingham Medieval Studies*, 27 (1983)

E. Power, 'The Wool Trade in the Fifteenth Century', in E. Power and M. Postan (eds), *Studies in English Trade in the Fifteenth Century* (London, 1933)

M. Powicke, *Military Obligation in Medieval England* (Oxford, 1962)

J. O. Prestwich, 'The Military Household of the Norman Kings', *English Historical Review*, 96 (1981)

J. O. Prestwich, *The Place of War in English History, 1066–1214* (Woodbridge, 2004)

J. O. Prestwich, 'War and Finance in the Anglo-Norman State', *Transactions of the Royal Historical Society*, 5th series, 4 (1954)

Michael Prestwich, *Armies and Warfare in the Middle Ages. The English Experience* (New Haven and London, 1996)

Michael Prestwich, *Edward I* (London, 1988)

Michael Prestwich, *War, Politics and Finance under Edward I* (London, 1972)

'Private Indentures': M. Jones and S. Walker (eds), 'Private Indentures for Life Service in Peace and War, 1274–1476', in *Camden Miscellany, XXXII* (Camden 5th series, 3, 1994)

R. L. Radulescu, *The Gentry Context for Malory's* Morte Darthur (Woodbridge, 2003)

Radulphi de Diceto Opera: W. Stubbs (ed.), *Radulphi de Diceto Opera Historica* (2 vols, Rolls Series, 1876)

C. A. Ralegh-Radford, 'The Church of St Mary, Stoke d'Abernon, Surrey', *Archaeological Journal*, 118 (1963)

Recueil des historiens des croisades: historiens orientaux (Paris, 1887)

S. Riches, *St George. Hero, Martyr and Myth* (Stroud, 2000)

Felicity Riddy, *Sir Thomas Malory* (Leiden, 1987)

J. Riley-Smith, *What Were the Crusades?* (London, 1977)

Riverside Chaucer: L. D. Benson (ed.), *The Riverside Chaucer* (3rd edn, Oxford, 1988)

W. R. B. Robinson, 'Sir Hugh Johnys: A Fifteenth-Century Welsh Knight', *Morgannwg*, 14 (1970)

C. J. Rogers, 'By Fire and Sword. Bellum Hostile and "Civilians" in the Hundred Years War', in M. Grimsley and C. J. Rogers (eds), *Civilians in the Path of War* (Lincoln, Nebraska, 2002)

C. J. Rogers, *War Cruel and Sharp. English Strategy under Edward III, 1327–1360* (Woodbridge, 2000)

Rous Roll: W. Courthope (ed.), *The Rous Roll* (2nd edn, Gloucester, 1980)

J. Russell, *Boke of Nurture*, in F. J. Furnivall (ed.), *Early English Meals and Manners* (Early English Text Society, 32, 1868)

F. H. Russell, *The Just War in the Middle Ages* (Cambridge, 1975)

I. J. Sanders, *Feudal Military Service in England* (Oxford, 1956)

L. F. Sandler, *Gothic Manuscripts, 1285–1385* (2 vols, Oxford, 1986)

Nigel Saul, *Knights and Esquires. The Gloucestershire Gentry in the Fourteenth Century* (Oxford, 1981)

Nigel Saul, 'Chaucer and Gentility', in *Chaucer's England. Literature in Historical Context* (Minneapolis, 1992)

Nigel Saul, *Richard II* (New Haven and London, 1997)

Nigel Saul, *Death, Art and Memory in Medieval England. The Cobham Family and their Monuments, 1300–1500* (Oxford, 2001)

Nigel Saul, 'A Farewell to Arms? Criticism of Warfare in Late Fourteenth-Century England', in C. Given-Wilson (ed.), *Fourteenth Century England, II* (Woodbridge, 2002)

Nigel Saul, *The Three Richards. Richard I, Richard II and Richard III* (London, 2005)

Nigel Saul, 'Chivalry and Art: the Camoys Family and the Wall Paintings in Trotton Church', in P. Coss and C. Tyerman (eds), *Soldiers, Nobles and Gentlemen. Essays in Honour of Maurice Keen* (Woodbridge, 2009)

Nigel Saul, *English Church Monuments in the Middle Ages. History and Representation* (Oxford, 2009)

Nigel Saul, 'The Rise of the Dallingridge Family', *Sussex Archaeological Collections*, 136 (1998)

Scalacronica: Sir Thomas Gray, *Scalacronica, 1272–1363*, ed. A. King (Surtees Society, 209, 2005)

V. J. Scattergood, 'Chaucer and the French War: *Sir Thopas* and *Melibee*', in G. S. Burgess (ed.), *Court and Poet: Select Proceedings of the Third Congress of the International Courtly Literature Society* (Liverpool, 1981)

Eleanor Searle (ed.), *The Chronicle of Battle Abbey* (Oxford, 1980)

SG: N. H. Nicolas, *The Controversy between Sir Richard Scrope and Sir Robert Grosvenor in the Court of Chivalry* (2 vols, London, 1832)

Ian Short, 'Gaimar's Epilogue and Geoffrey of Monmouth's *Liber Vetustissimus*', *Speculum*, 69 (1994)

Ian Short, 'Patrons and Polyglots: French Literature in Twelfth-Century England', in M. Chibnall (ed.), *Anglo-Norman Studies, XIV* (Woodbridge, 1991)

D. Simpkin, *The English Aristocracy at War from the Welsh Wars of Edward I to the Battle of Bannockburn* (Woodbridge, 2008)

Sir Gawain and the Green Knight: B. Stone (ed.), *Sir Gawain and the Green Knight* (2nd edn, Harmondsworth, 1974)

Sir John Paston's 'Grete Boke': G. A. Lester (ed.), *Sir John Paston's 'Grete Boke'* (Woodbridge, 1984)

Society at War: C. T. Allmand (ed.), *Society at War. The Experience of England and France During the Hundred Years War* (Edinburgh, 1973)

R. C. Stacey, 'The Age of Chivalry', in *The Laws of War. Constraints on Warfare in the Western World*, ed. M. Howard, G. J. Andreopoulos and M. R. Shulman (New Haven and London, 1994)

L. Staley, 'Gower, Richard II, Henry of Derby, and the Business of Making Culture', *Speculum*, 75 (2000)

C. Starr, *Medieval Mercenary. Sir John Hawkwood of Essex* (Chelmsford, 2007)

R. L. Storey, 'Gentleman-bureaucrats', in C. H. Clough (ed.), *Profession, Vocation and Culture in Later Medieval England* (Liverpool, 1982)

Matthew Strickland, 'Arms and the Men: War, Loyalty and Lordship in Jordan Fantosme's Chronicle', in C. Harper-Bill and R. Harvey (eds), *Medieval Knighthood, IV* (Woodbridge, 1992)

Matthew Strickland, *War and Chivalry. The Conduct and Perception of War in England and Normandy, 1066–1217* (Cambridge, 1996)

Matthew Strickland, 'A Law of Arms or a Law of Treason? Conduct in War in Edward I's Campaigns in Scotland, 1296–1307', in *Violence in Medieval Society*, ed. Richard W. Kaeuper (Woodbridge, 2000)

Matthew Strickland, 'Treason, Feud and the Growth of State Violence: Edward I and the "War of the Earl of Carrick", 1306–7', in C. Given-Wilson, A. Kettle, L. Scales (eds), *War, Government and Aristocracy in the British Isles, c. 1150–1500. Essays in Honour of Michael Prestwich* (Woodbridge, 2008)

Jonathan Sumption, *The Hundred Years War, II: Trial by Fire* (London, 1999)

Jonathan Sumption, *The Hundred Years War, III: Divided Houses* (London, 2009)

A. Sutton and L. Visser-Fuchs, '"Chevalerie . . . in some partie is worthi forto be comendid, and in some part to ben amendid": Chivalry and the Yorkist Kings', in C. Richmond and E. Scarff (eds), *St George's Chapel, Windsor, in the Late Middle Ages* (Windsor, 2001)

Michael Swanton, *English Literature before Chaucer* (Harlow, 1987)

A. J. Taylor, 'Count Amadeus of Savoy's Visit to England in 1292', *Archaeologia*, 106 (1979), reprinted in his *Studies in Castles and Castle Building* (London, 1985)

John Taylor, *English Historical Literature in the Fourteenth Century* (Oxford, 1987)

Testamenta Eboracensia: J. Raine (ed.), *Testamenta Eboracensia*, i (Surtees Society, 4, 1836)

A. H. Thompson, 'The Building Accounts of Kirby Muxloe Castle, 1480–1484', *Transactions of the Leicestershire Archaeological Society*, 11 (1913–20)

M. Thompson, 'Castles', in D. Brewer and J. Gibson (eds), *A Companion to the Gawain Poet* (Woodbridge, 1997)

J. E. Titterton, *The Grisaille and Heraldic Glass in the Chancel at Norbury, Derbyshire* (Norbury, 2004)

T. F. Tout, *Chapters in the Administrative History of Medieval England* (6 vols, Manchester, 1920–33)

Tree of Battles: G. W. Coopland (ed.), *The Tree of Battles of Honoré Bovet* (Liverpool, 1949)

B. Trowell, 'A Fourteenth-Century Ceremonial Motet and its Composer', *Musicologica*, 29 (1957)

Twenty-Six Political and other Poems, ed. J. Kail (Early English Text Society, Original Series, 124, 1904)

Christopher Tyerman, *England and the Crusades, 1095–1588* (Chicago, 1988)

Urbanus Magnus Danielis Becclesiensis, ed. J. G. Smyly (Dublin, 1939)

Juliet Vale, 'Law and Diplomacy in the Alliterative *Morte Arthure*', *Nottingham Medieval Studies*, 23 (1979)

Juliet Vale, *Edward III and Chivalry* (Woodbridge, 1982)

Juliet Vale, 'Image and Identity in the Prehistory of the Order of the Garter', in N. E. Saul (ed.), *St George's Chapel, Windsor, in the Fourteenth Century* (Woodbridge, 2005)

M. G. A. Vale, 'Sir John Fastolf's "Report" of 1435: A New Interpretation Reconsidered', *Nottingham Medieval Studies*, 17 (1973)

M. G. A. Vale, *War and Chivalry. Warfare and Aristocratic Culture in England, France and Burgundy at the End of the Middle Ages* (London, 1981)

L. Visser-Fuchs, 'Richard of York: Books and the Man', in J. Boffey and V. Davis (eds), *Recording Medieval Lives* (Donington, 2009)

Vita Edwardi Secundi: W. Childs (ed.), *Vita Edwardi Secundi* (Oxford, 2005)

Vulgate Version: H. O. Sommer (ed.), *Vulgate Version of the Arthurian Romances* (4 vols, Washington DC, 1908–16)

Wace's Roman de Brut. A History of the British, ed. J. Weiss (Exeter, 1999)

A. R. Wagner, 'A Fifteenth-Century description of the Brass of Sir Hugh Hastings at Elsing, Norfolk', *Antiquaries Journal*, 19 (1939)

A. R. Wagner, *Heralds and Heraldry in the Middle Ages* (2nd edn, Oxford, 1956)

Simon Walker, *The Lancastrian Affinity, 1361–1399* (Oxford, 1990)

Simon Walker, 'Letters to the Dukes of Lancaster in 1381 and 1399', *English Historical Review*, 106 (1991)

David Wallace (ed.), *Cambridge History of Medieval English Literature* (Cambridge, 1999)

M. Warner, 'Chivalry in Action: Thomas Montagu and the War in France, 1417–1428', *Nottingham Medieval Studies*, 42 (1998)

P. J. Watson, 'A Review of the Sources for the Battle of Barnet, 14 April 1471', *The Ricardian*, 149 (June, 2000)

J. C. Wedgwood, *History of Parliament, 1439–1509* (2 vols, London, 1936)

The Westminster Chronicle, 1381–1394, ed. L. C. Hector and B. F. Harvey (Oxford, 1982)

A. Wheatley, *The Idea of the Castle in Medieval England* (Woodbridge, 2004)

B. Whiting, 'The Vows of the Heron', *Speculum*, 20 (1952)

A. Wiggins and R. Field (eds), *Guy of Warwick. Icon and Ancestor* (Woodbridge, 2007)

Wills and Inventories: J. Raine (ed.), *Wills and Inventories of the Northern Counties, I* (Surtees Society, 2, 1835)

C. Wilson, 'The Royal Lodgings of Edward III at Windsor Castle: Form, Function, Representation', in L. Keen and E. Scarff (eds), *Windsor. Medieval Archaeology, Art and Architecture in the Thames Valley* (British Archaeological Association Conference Proceedings, 25, 2002)

C. Winston, 'An Account of the Painted Glass in the Great East Window of Gloucester Cathedral', *Archaeological Journal*, 20 (1863)

Works of Sir John Clanvowe: V. J. Scattergood (ed.), *The Works of Sir John Clanvowe* (Cambridge, 1975)

Works of Sir Thomas Malory: E. Vinaver (ed.), *The Works of Sir Thomas Malory* (3 vols, 2nd edn, Oxford, 1973)

Writings of Christine de Pizan: C. C. Willard (ed.), *The Writings of Christine de Pizan* (New York, 1993)

N. A. R. Wright, 'The *Tree of Battles* of Honoré Bouvet and the Laws of War', in C. T. Allmand (ed.), *War, Literature and Politics in the Late Middle Ages* (Liverpool, 1976)

F. A. Yates, 'Elizabethan Chivalry: the Romance of the Accession Day Tilts', *Journal of the Warburg and Courtauld Institutes*, 20 (1957)

R. F. Yeager, '*Pax poetica*: On the Pacifism of Chaucer and Gower', in *Studies in the Age of Chaucer*, 9 (1987)

Deborah Youngs, 'Cultural Networks', in R. Radulescu and A. Truelove (eds), *Gentry Culture in Late Medieval England* (Manchester, 2005)

Deborah Youngs, *Humphrey Newton (1466–1536): An Early Tudor Gentleman* (Woodbridge, 2008)

Notes

Introduction: Chivalry and History

1. Camille, *Mirror in Parchment*, pp. 49–51, where Psalm 109 should read Psalm 110. • 2. The one notable exception is Prestwich, *Armies and Warfare*. • 3. Cited by Vale, *War and Chivalry*, p. 5.

Chapter 1

1. Strickland, *War and Chivalry*, p. 1. • 2. Ibid., p. 2. • 3. Gillingham, '1066 and the Introduction of Chivalry into England', pp. 38–9. • 4. The poet narrates that Byrhtnoth's companions, after his death in the battle, 'intended then one of two things, to lose their lives or avenge their friend': *Battle of Maldon*, p. 27 (lines 207–8). • 5. As William Rufus did in 1088 when receiving the submission of the rebel garrison owing allegiance to Odo, bishop of Bayeux, at Rochester: Prestwich, *Place of War in English History*, p. 19. • 6. For discussion, see Barlow, *William Rufus*, p. 391, and Gillingham, 'Kingship, Chivalry and Love', p. 41. • 7. Quoted by Gillingham, 'Conquering the Barbarians', p. 70. • 8. Keen, *Chivalry*, pp. 23–4. • 9. For early tournaments, see Crouch, *Tournament*, ch. 1. • 10. Bradbury, 'Geoffrey V of Anjou', p. 32. • 11. Barber, *Knight and Chivalry*, p. 32. • 12. Gaimar, *Estoire des Engleis*, p. 331.

Chapter 2

1. William of Malmesbury, *Gesta Regum Anglorum*, i, pp. 557–9. • 2. Ibid., i, p. 473. • 3. Prestwich, 'War and Finance', p. 27. • 4. William of Malmesbury, *Gesta Regum Anglorum*, i, p. 559. • 5. For these examples, see Prestwich, 'War and Finance', in particular, pp. 28–36. Maine is to the south of Normandy. • 6. William of Malmesbury, *Gesta Regum Anglorum*, i, p. 549. • 7. Ibid., i, p. 745.

• **8**. For this paragraph, see Bartlett, *England under the Norman and Angevin Kings*, p. 266–9. • **9**. For this paragraph, see Prestwich, 'Military Household of the Norman Kings', pp. 1–35. • **10**. Green, *Government of England under Henry I*, ch. 4. • **11**. The esquire was John of Earley, and the poet a Frenchman, perhaps from Touraine. For a full modern edition, see *History of William Marshal*. For a lively biography, see Crouch, *William Marshal*. • **12**. Ibn al-Athir, *el-Kamil*, in *Recueil des historiens des croisades*, ii, i, p. 43. • **13**. See above, n. 12. • **14**. The best modern biography is Gillingham, *Richard I*. • **15**. This is not to suggest that Richard ever fought a war unnecessarily; he did not. As Prestwich shows, *Place of War in English History*, p. 21, he never fought on soil to which he or a member of his family had no claim, with one exception: his conquest of Cyprus. • **16**. Gillingham, 'Some Legends of Richard the Lionheart', pp. 181–92. • **17**. William of Newburgh, *Historia Rerum Anglicarum*, ii, p. 422. For discussion, see Crouch, *Tournament*, pp. 44, 53–4. • **18**. An additional attraction to Richard of the new arrangements, therefore, was the opportunity given to him to make money. • **19**. For this paragraph, see Saul, *The Three Richards*, pp. 91–3.

Chapter 3

1. The most accessible edition is Geoffrey of Monmouth, *History of the Kings of Britain*. For an edition of the Latin text, see Geoffrey of Monmouth, *The History of the Kings of Britain*, ed. M. D. Reeve and N. Wright (Woodbridge, 2007). • **2**. J. Gillingham, 'The Context and Purposes of Geoffrey of Monmouth's *History of the Kings of Britain*', pp. 99–118, reprinted in his *The English in the Twelfth Century*. • **3**. A total of 217 manuscripts of Geoffrey's *History* have been listed, a quarter of these dating from before the end of the twelfth century. For detailed discussion of the circulation of the *History*, see Crick, *The Historia Regum Britannie of Geoffrey of Monmouth, IV. Dissemination and Reception*, in particular pp. 215–25. • **4**. For Edward I and Arthurianism, see below, pp. 78–84 • **5**. *Wace's Roman de Brut*. Wace wrote in French couplets. • **6**. For the Grail legends, see below, pp. 202–203. For the Vulgate cycle, see Frappier, 'The Vulgate Cycle', pp. 295–318. • **7**. Batt and Field, 'The Romance Tradition', p. 66. • **8**. Sir Thomas Carminow: *SG*, i, pp. 49–50. • **9**. For general discussion, see Barron, *English Medieval Romance*, and Field, 'Romance in England', pp. 152–75. I am very grateful to Ros Field for generous assistance with this chapter. • **10**. In the Miller's Prologue of the *Canterbury Tales: Riverside Chaucer*, p. 67 (line. 3,179). • **11**. See the list of books, the majority of them romances, which Guy Beauchamp, earl of Warwick, deposited in Bordesley Abbey (Worcs.) in 1305: Blaess, 'L'Abbaye de Bordesley et les Livres de Guy de Beauchamp', pp. 511–18. • **12**. Short, 'Patrons and Polyglots: French Literature in Twelfth-Century

England', pp. 229–49. • **13**. Hue de Rotelande, *Ipomedon*. • **14**. Hue de Rotelande, *Protheselaus*. • **15**. Short, 'Patrons and Polyglots', p. 241. • **16**. A sword reputedly Bevis's survives in Arundel Castle to this day, affording valuable evidence of the role played by objects associated with legendary heroes in the preserving of chivalric memory. For the similar role played by objects associated with Guy of Warwick, see below, p. 302. • **17**. Mason, 'Legends of the Beauchamps' Ancestors', pp. 25–40; ead., 'Fact and Fiction in the English Crusading Tradition', pp. 81–95. Crane, *Insular Romance*, p. 18, argues against too exclusive an identification of the poem with the earls of Warwick, stressing instead the pertinence of the romance literature 'to the situation of the Anglo-Norman aristocracy as a whole'. • **18**. Barron, *English Medieval Romance*, pp. 74–80; Wiggins and Field (eds), *Guy of Warwick. Icon and Ancestor*. • **19**. Hathaway (ed.), *Fouke Le Fitz Waryn*. • **20**. Field, 'Romance in England', p. 162. • **21**. Gaimar, *Estoire des Engleis*, p. 349. • **22**. Ranulf's testimony (and he was a Lincolnshire landowner) would account for the story of Hugh d'Avranches, his grandfather, agreeing to be Rufus's staff-bearer at the Whitsun court of 1099 in Westminster Hall: ibid., pp. 325–7. • **23**. Ibid., pp. 321–3, 335. • **24**. Gillingham, 'Kingship, Chivalry and Love', p. 54. • **25**. *Jordan Fantosme's Chronicle*, pp. 51, 69, 71, 83, 151. • **26**. Strickland, 'Arms and the Men: War, Loyalty and Lordship in Jordan Fantosme's Chronicle', pp. 187–220. • **27**. Ambroise, *Crusade of Richard Lion-Heart*, pp. 410, 447 (lines 11, 171, 12,329); it was Ambroise who first called Richard the Lionheart (Coeur de Lion): ibid., p. 115 (line 2,309). • **28**. Ibid., p. 425 (line 11,648). • **29**. Ibid., pp. 37–8, 51, 69–70 (lines 192–200, 588, 1,091–1,100). • **30**. There are forty-five copies of Huntingdon's *History*: Henry of Huntingdon, *Historia Anglorum*, pp. cxix–cxliv. There are ten copies of William of Malmesbury's contemporary history: William of Malmesbury, *Historia Novella*, pp. lxix–lxxvi. Thirty-seven copies survive of William of Malmesbury's *Gesta Regum;* for its circulation, see Gransden, *Historical Writing in England c. 550 to c. 1307*, p. 179. • **31**. Gaimar, *Estoire des Engleis*, pp. 349–51. For this passage, see Short, 'Gaimar's Epilogue and Geoffrey of Monmouth's *Liber Vetustissimus*', pp. 323–43. • **32**. Bartlett, *England under the Norman and Angevin Kings*, p. 235. • **33**. Searle (ed.), *Chronicle of Battle Abbey*, p. 214. • **34**. Crouch, *Image of the Aristocracy*, pp. 222, 226–7, 231. • **35**. Keen, *Chivalry*, p. 126, quoting *Chevalier de la Charrette*, lines 5,793–812. • **36**. *History of William Marshal*, i, p. 266. • **37**. Dennys, *Heraldic Imagination*, pp. 59–62.

Chapter 4

1. Powicke, *Military Obligation*, pp. 63–81. • **2**. For the examples in this paragraph, see Sanders, *Feudal Military Service*, pp. 61–7. • **3**. Prestwich, *War,*

Politics and Finance, p. 79. • **4**. Faulkner, 'Transformation of Knighthood', pp. 1–23. • **5**. Denholm-Young, 'Feudal Society in the Thirteenth Century', pp. 83–94. • **6**. *De Nugis Curialium*, p. 8. • **7**. *Dialogus de Scaccario*, p. 111. • **8**. Crouch, *Image of the Aristocracy*, chs 4, 6 and 7. • **9**. Ibid., p. 142. • **10**. For this paragraph and the next, see Coss, *Knight in Medieval England*, pp. 79–81. • **11**. For Cogenhoe, see Coss, 'Knighthood, Heraldry and Social Exclusion', pp. 56–8. • **12**. For the thirteenth-century work at Stoke d'Abernon, see Johnston, 'Stoke D'Abernon Church', pp. 1–89, partly revised by Ralegh-Radford, 'Church of St Mary, Stoke d'Abernon', pp. 165–74.

Chapter 5

1. *Political Songs*, p. 128, probably written by the royalist chronicler Thomas Wykes, of Osney Abbey, Oxford. The 'valour' for which the Lionheart was praised refers to his crusading. • **2**. Paris, *Chronica Majora*, v, p. 557. • **3**. *Annales Monastici*, iii, p. 216. • **4**. Vale, *Edward III and Chivalry*, ch. 1, and Crouch, *Tournament*, pp. 121–6, 127–30. • **5**. Prestwich, *Edward I*, p. 60. • **6**. For the lack of earlier English involvement in crusading, see below, p. 221. • **7**. For Edward's crusade, see Tyerman, *England and the Crusades*, pp. 124–32; Lloyd, *English Society and the Crusade*. For further discussion, see below, pp. 227–9. • **8**. For the origins and early growth of the cult of Arthur, see above, pp. 40–5. • **9**. Gillingham, *Richard I*, p. 141. • **10**. Translated in Lindley, *Tomb Destruction and Scholarship*, pp. 145–6, with the Latin text at pp. 162–3. • **11**. Ibid., pp. 152–8. • **12**. Denholm-Young, 'Tournament in the Thirteenth Century', p. 248. • **13**. Paris, *Chronica Majora*, v, pp. 318–9. • **14**. Crouch, *Tournament*, pp. 117–8. • **15**. Loomis, 'Edward I, Arthurian Enthusiast', pp. 114–27, at 116–7. • **16**. Biddle and others, *King Arthur's Round Table*. The present painted decoration was applied between 1516 and 1522 in anticipation of a visit by Henry VIII and the Emperor Charles V. • **17**. The suggestion of M. Morris, 'Edward I and the Knights of the Round Table', pp. 57–76, convincingly revising Biddle and others, *King Arthur's Round Table*, where a connection with a tournament in 1290 is favoured. • **18**. *Chronicle of Pierre de Langtoft*, ii, p. 368. • **19**. For Caernarfon, see Morris, 'Architecture of Arthurian Enthusiasm', pp. 63–81. • **20**. Brown, Colvin, Taylor, *History of the King's Works*, i, pp. 369–95. • **21**. *Annales Monastici*, ii, p. 40. • **22**. Binski, *The Painted Chamber at Westminster*, pp. 19–21, 71–80, 82. Binski's argument that the paintings were commissioned by Edward I and not by Henry III, who had built the chamber, is almost certainly correct. • **23**. For the size of Edward I's armies, see Prestwich, *Edward I*, pp. 179, 190, 478–9, 485, 493, 498, 506. Knights banneret were knights entitled to the use of a square banner on which to display their arms rather than a pennon attached to the lance. They served as commanders of contingents. • **24**. Prestwich, *War, Politics and Finance*, pp. 71–3. • **25**. 'Private Indentures', pp. 35–50. • **26**. See above, p. 81. • **27**. Simpkin, *English Aristocracy at War*, pp. 22–4. • **28**. For Tiptoft and Latimer, see Prestwich, *War, Politics and Finance*, pp. 43–5. • **29**. Simpkin, *English Aristocracy at War*, pp. 24, 138, 141. • **30**. Titterton, *Grisaille and Heraldic Glass in the Chancel at Norbury*. • **31**. See above, p. 8. • **32**. In Henry III's reign, however, note the determination of the royalists to kill rather than capture Simon de Montfort at the battle of Evesham in 1265: de Laborderie, Maddicott, Carpenter, 'Last Hours of Simon de Montfort', pp. 378–412. This may actually be the exception that proves the rule: it was largely the work of the future Edward I. Moreover, there was no blood-letting after the battle: see below, p. 91. • **33**. For these cases and the legal background to them, see Bellamy, *Law of Treason*, ch. 3. • **34**. Strickland, 'Treason, Feud and the Growth of State Violence', pp. 84–113. • **35**. Fryde, *Tyranny and Fall of Edward II*, p. 61. • **36**. *Chronicon de Lanercost*, p. 244. • **37**. In the gallery of arms which Henry III had installed around the aisles of Westminster Abbey, the arms of de Montfort remained untouched. • **38**. Gillingham, 'Enforcing Old Law in New Ways', pp. 199–220. • **39**. *Vita Edwardi Secundi*, 129.

Chapter 6

1. Quoted by Rogers, *War Cruel and Sharp*, p. 229. • **2**. *LCBP*, p. 18. • **3**. Murimuth, p. 246. • **4**. Ayton and Preston, *Battle of Crécy*, p. 356. • **5**. Vale, 'Image and Identity', pp. 35–50. • **6**. Barber, *Edward, Prince of Wales*, p. 92. • **7**. Blair and Goodall, 'An Effigy at Wilsthorpe', pp. 39–48. • **8**. Vale, *Edward III and Chivalry*, pp. 87–8. • **9**. Munby, Barber, Brown, *Edward III's Round Table*. • **10**. Biddle, 'Why is the Bishop of Winchester Prelate of the Order of the Garter?', pp. 18–22. • **11**. Trowell, 'A Fourteenth-Century Ceremonial Motet and its Composer', pp. 65–75. • **12**. *Testamenta Eboracensia*, i, pp. 38–9. • **13**. Wilson, 'Royal Lodgings of Edward III', pp. 15–94. • **14**. *Cligès*, pp. 40–1 (lines 1228–71). • **15**. Barnie, *War in Medieval Society*, pp. 138–42. • **16**. *Chroniques de Jean Froissart*, viii, p. 230. • **17**. For background to this development, see Keen, 'Chivalry and English Kingship in the Later Middle Ages', pp. 250–66. • **18**. *Boke of Noblesse*, pp. 12, 20. For the examples in this and the next paragraph, see Morgan, 'Political After-Life of Edward III', pp. 856–81. • **19**. Froissart, ii, pp. 495, 558. • **20**. *Westminster Chronicle*, p. 204. • **21**. For Richard II's kingship, see Saul, *Richard II*, chs 11 and 17.

Chapter 7

1. *SG*, i, p. 166; ii, pp. 374–7. For discussion of the Scrope–Grosvenor evidence, see Keen, 'Chaucer's Knight', pp. 45–61. • **2.** *SG*, i, p. 124; ii, pp. 323–4. • **3.** Ibid., i, p. 165; ii, pp. 372–4. • **4.** Ibid., i, p. 161; ii, pp. 366–7. • **5.** Ibid., i, p. 77–8; ii, pp. 261–2. • **6.** Moor, *Knights of Edward I*, v, pp. 91–2. Valers's fine tomb effigy is in Down Ampney Church. • **7.** McFarlane, *Nobility of Later Medieval England*, p. 21. The comparison with the eighteenth-century nabobs was McFarlane's: p. 23. • **8.** The agreement is printed in translation in *Society at War*, pp. 32–4. • **9.** Powicke, *Military Obligation*, chs 8 and 10. • **10.** Goodman, 'Military Subcontracts, pp. 114–20. • **11.** *Historia Anglicana*, i, p. 272. • **12.** Prestwich, *Armies and Warfare*, pp. 103, 144. • **13.** Harriss, *Shaping the Nation*, p. 133. • **14.** For the examples in this paragraph, see McFarlane, *Nobility of Later Medieval England*, pp. 30–1; Bennett, *Community, Class and Careerism*, p. 179; Prestwich, *Armies and Warfare*, pp. 104–6. • **15.** Sumption, *The Hundred Years War, III. Divided Houses*, pp. 311, 330. • **16.** Harriss, *Shaping the Nation*, p. 180. • **17.** Prestwich, *Armies and Warfare*, p. 101. • **18.** *ODNB*, 31, pp. 952–7 (by M. Jones). • **19.** *Chronica Maiora*, p. 355. • **20.** *Knighton*, p. 161. • **21.** For Knolles, see above, n. 5; for Calveley, *ODNB*, 9, pp. 565–8 (by K. Fowler); for Mainwaring and the Cradocks, Morgan, *War and Society in Medieval Cheshire*, pp. 158, 160, 162, 176–7 • **22.** Given-Wilson and Bériac, 'Edward III's Prisoners of War', pp. 802–33. As the co-authors point out, not only was the number of battles at which rich prizes were taken relatively few, it is difficult to establish how much of the ransom agreed between captor and captive was actually collected. • **23.** *ODNB*, 19, pp. 286–7 (by P. Morgan). • **24.** Prestwich, *Armies and Warfare*, p. 107; McFarlane, *Nobility of Later Medieval England*, pp. 29–30, 126–8. • **25.** Jones, 'Sir John de Hardreshull', pp. 76–97. • **26.** *Historia Anglicana*, i, p. 265. • **27.** Ayton, 'War and the English Gentry', pp. 34–40. • **28.** Jean Froissart, quoted by Patterson, *Chaucer and the Subject of History*, p. 174. • **29.** Saul, 'A Farewell to Arms?', pp. 131–46; Yeager, 'Pax poetica', pp. 97–121. • **30.** *Riverside Chaucer*, p. 234. For discussion of *Melibee* and of Chaucer's attitude to war more generally, see Scattergood, 'Chaucer and the French War', pp. 287–96; and see below, pp. 194–5. • **31.** *Works of Sir John Clanvowe*, pp. 69–70. Clanvow's English has been modernised. • **32.** *Chronica Maiora*, p. 248. For discussion, see Ormrod, 'Knights of Venus', pp. 290–305. • **33.** *Vox Clamantis*, Book 5, ch. 8, in *Major Latin Works of John Gower*, p. 207. • **34.** Bartlett, 'Symbolic Meanings of Hair', pp. 43–60. • **35.** Keen, 'Richard II's Ordinances of War', pp. 33–48.

Chapter 8

1. Kilgour, *Decline of Chivalry*, p. 8. • **2.** On this subject, see Russell, *Just War*. • **3.** Stacey, 'Age of Chivalry', pp. 27–39. • **4.** Keen, *Laws of War*, p. 17. • **5.** Ibid., p. 21. • **6.** Interestingly, in a work of history, Sir Thomas Gray's *Scalacronica* of *c.* 1355–63, the one reference to the code of chivalry relates to a ransom case. An English knight had been captured by the French and then seized back by the English while exercising, an act which the French protested was 'against the agreement of loyal chivalry' ('countre covenaunt de loial chevalerie'). A ransom was arranged: *Scalacronica*, p. 180. • **7.** Keen, *Laws of War*, p. 25. • **8.** *Historia Anglorum*, p. 738; *Radulphi de Diceto Opera*, i, p. 374. *Lege proposita* is virtually unstranslatable, but might be rendered 'by a law proposed'. • **9.** *Gesta Stephani*, pp. 50–1. • **10.** *Ecclesiastical History of Orderic Vitalis*, iv, pp. 132–3. • **11.** *Historia Novella*, p. 75. • **12.** Strickland, *War and Chivalry*, pp. 39–54. • **13.** *Tree of Battles*, pp. 128–9, 131. • **14.** Wright, 'The *Tree of Battles* of Honoré Bouvet', pp. 12–31, at p. 20. • **15.** Edward III to Sir Thomas Lucy, on the Crécy campaign: *LC BP*, p. 22. • **16.** Contamine, *War in the Middle Ages*, p. 210. • **17.** Allmand, 'The *De Re Militari* of Vegetius', pp. 20–5. • **18.** For ownership of Vegetius's text, see Allmand, 'Fifteenth-Century English Versions of Vegetius' *De Re Militari*', pp. 30–45. • **19.** *Historie de Guillaume le Conquerant*, p. 90. • **20.** *Gesta Stephani*, pp. 186–7. • **21.** Ibid., pp. 152–5. • **22.** *Chronicon Galfridi le Baker*, p. 65. • **23.** *LC BP*, pp. 15–17. • **24.** *Anonimalle*, p. 35. • **25.** *LC BP*, pp. 50–2. • **26.** Gillingham, 'War and Chivalry in *History of William the Marshal*', pp. 227–41. • **27.** Warner, 'Chivalry in action', pp. 146–73. • **28.** Froissart, *Chronicles*, i, pp. 218, 220, 261, 264, 274, 280, 458. • **29.** Starr, *Medieval Mercenary*, pp. 23–9, 31. • **30.** Allmand, 'War and the Non-Combatant', pp. 253–72. • **31.** *Tree of Battles*, p. 125. • **32.** Ibid., pp. 153–4; and 'the good must sometimes suffer by reason of their evil neighbours': ibid., p. 125. For discussion, see Rogers, 'By Fire and Sword', pp. 33–78. • **33.** *Gesta Henrici Quinti*, p. 91. • **34.** Gillingham, 'Richard I and the Science of War', and *idem*, 'War and Chivalry in *History of William the Marshal*'. • **35.** See above, p. 97. • **36.** *Vita Edwardi Secundi*, p. 89. • **37.** *Scalacronica*, p. 100. • **38.** *Anonimalle*, p. 22. • **39.** Sumption, *Hundred Years War, II. Trial by Fire*, pp. 33–4. • **40.** Jones, 'Battle of Verneuil', pp. 375–411. • **41.** For Salisbury at Verneuil, see Warner, 'Chivalry in Action', pp. 153, 167. • **42.** The words of Ghillebert de Lannoy, quoted by Morgan, 'From a Death to a View'. Robsart, a knight in English service, was honoured with burial in Westminster Abbey. • **43.** He refused to retreat out of respect for the view that to flee from the field after the banners had been unfurled constituted an act of *lèse majesté*. • **44.** *Vita Edwardi Secundi*, pp. 91–3. • **45.** *Scalacronica*, pp. 80–2. For discussion of the *Scalacronica* as a work of chivalric history, see King, 'A Helm with a Crest of Gold', pp. 21–35. • **46**. *Chronique*, i, p. 124. • **47**. *Political Poems and Songs*, i, pp. 1–25. For the poem as a satire, see Whiting, 'Vows of the Heron', pp. 261–78. • **48**. *Scalacronica*, pp. 177, 251. Vermilion was the colour worn by Sir Galahad at the Pentecostal feast in *La Queste del Saint Graal*. It stood for the blood which a knight was prepared to shed. • **49**. Kaeuper, 'Societal Role of Chivalry in Romance', p. 98.

Chapter 9

1. *History of Parliament*, ii, pp. 790–2. • **2**. Ibid., pp. 524–32. • **3**. Saul, 'Rise of the Dallingridge Family', pp. 123–32. • **4**. *History of Parliament*, iii, pp. 152–4. • **5**. Hughes, 'Stephen Scrope and the Circle of Sir John Fastolf, p. 119. • **6**. McFarlane, *Nobility of Later Medieval England*, pp. 268–78; Saul, *Knights and Esquires*, pp. 6–29. • **7**. Crouch, *Tournament*, p. 201; Coss, *Origins of the English Gentry*, pp. 229, 244. • **8**. Ayton, 'Knights, Esquires and Military Service', p. 82. • **9**. Wagner, *Heralds and Heraldry*, pp. 125–6. • **10**. Keen, *Origins of the English Gentleman*, pp. 76–7. • **11**. Clarke, *Parochial Topography*, p. 98. • **12**. *Cal. Close Rolls 1413–19*, p. 512; Clarke, *Parochial Topography*, p. 98. • **13**. Quoted by Keen, *Origins of the English Gentleman*, p. 110. • **14**. *Boke of Noblesse*, pp. 77–8. • **15**. *De Laudibus Legum Anglie*, p. 118. • **16**. Power, 'Wool Trade', p. 53. • **17**. Wagner, *Heralds and Heraldry*, p. 79; Morgan, 'Individual Style of the English Gentleman', pp. 15–35. • **18**. Keen, *Origins of the English Gentleman*, p. 104. • **19**. Ibid., p. 103 • **20**. *Sir Gawain and the Green Knight*, lines 915–9. • **21**. Storey, 'Gentleman-bureaucrats', pp. 90–129. • **22**. Alcock and Woodfield, 'Social Pretensions in Architecture and Ancestry', pp. 51–72. • **23**. For this paragraph, and for Malory, see Maddern, 'Gentility', p. 30. • **24**. *Paston Letters and Papers*, i, p. 257. • **25**. Russell, *Boke of Nurture*. • **26**. Bornstein, *Mirrors of Courtesy*, p. 77. • **27**. Quoted by Keen, *Chivalry*, p. 150. • **28**. Ibid., p. 149. • **29**. Ibid., p. 151. • **30**. Murray, *Reason and Society in the Middle Ages*, pp. 270–7. • **31**. *Riverside Chaucer*, p. 120 (lines 1109–24). • **32**. Ibid. (lines 1152–7). • **33**. Saul, 'Chaucer and Gentility', pp. 41–55. • **34**. Hughes, 'Stephen Scrope and the Circle of Sir John Fastolf', pp. 109–46, in particular, p. 138. • **35**. For this theme, see Keen, *Origins of the English Gentleman*, p. 106. • **36**. Keen, *Chivalry*, p. 159. • **37**. Kennedy, 'Quest for Identity', pp. 84–5. • **38**. For these two quotations, see Keen, *Chivalry*, p. 160. • **39**. For Guy of Warwick, see above, pp. 47–8. The Swan Knight was the mysterious rescuer who came in a swan-drawn boat to defend a damsel, his only condition being that he never be asked his name. The story inspired Wagner's opera *Lohengrin*. • **40**. Defoe, *The Compleat English Gentleman*, p. 25. • **41**. The text is given in translation in Keen, *Origins of the English Gentleman*, p. 79. For Mille's career, see *History of Parliament*,

1439–1509, ii, pp. 593–4. Significantly, on his brass at Pulborough he is shown in civilian attire, not in armour; he never saw any active service. • **42.** A. B. Ferguson, *The Indian Summer of English Chivalry* (Durham, NC, 1960), p. 13.

Chapter 10

1. Hilton, *A Medieval Society*, p. 254. • **2.** Kaeuper, *Chivalry and Violence*, p. 136. • **3.** *Lancelot Part V*, ed. W. W. Kibler, in *Lancelot-Grail: The Old French Arthurian Vulgate and Post-Vulgate in Translation, III*, p. 197. • **4.** *Death of King Arthur*, pp. 179–80. • **5.** Ibid., p. 184. • **6.** *Crusade of Richard Lion-Heart*, p. 289 (lines 7352–60). • **7.** *History of William Marshal*, i, p. 197 (lines 3848–54). • **8.** Barbour, *The Bruce*, p. 211. • **9.** The best account of Cressy's career is Anne Curry's for the 'Medieval Soldier' project at: http://www.medievalsoldier.org/November2008.php. • **10.** To see service at such a young age was by no means unusual. All but one of the younger deponents in the Grey v. Hastings case in the Court of Chivalry in 1408 had seen service by the age of sixteen, four of them by the age of twelve (Keen, 'English Military Experience and the Court of Chivalry', p. 180). • **11.** *Calendar of Patent Rolls 1330–4*, p. 458. • **12.** *ODNB*, 36, pp. 359–61; Riddy, *Thomas Malory*, pp. 2–6. • **13.** *Chronicle of Walter of Guisborough*, p. 216. • **14.** For *Beowulf*, see Swanton, *English Literature before Chaucer*, pp. 49–65. • **15.** *Battle of Maldon*, p. 23 (lines. 103–12). • **16.** For this paragraph, see Fletcher, *Richard II. Manhood, Youth and Politics*, pp. 31–40. • **17.** Kaminsky, 'The Noble Feud in the Later Middle Ages', pp. 55–83. • **18.** Walker, *Lancastrian Affinity*, pp. 127–41. And see below, pp. 193, 251–2. • **19.** Pitt-Rivers, 'Honour and Social Status', in *Honour and Shame*, ed. Peristiany, pp. 21–73, in particular 21–9. • **20.** Walker, 'Letters to the Dukes of Lancaster in 1381 and 1399', pp. 68–79. • **21.** *Anonimalle*, p. 152. • **22.** Froissart, *Chronicles*, i, pp. 668–9; *Chronica Maiora*, pp. 168–9. • **23.** *Westminster Chronicle*, p. 409. • **24.** See above, pp. 8, 10. • **25.** *Urbanus Magnus Danielis Becclesiensis*. For discussion, see Gillingham, 'From Civilitas to Civility', pp. 267–89. • **26.** For these examples, see Strickland, 'A Law of Arms or a Law of Treason?' p. 59. • **27.** Barrow, *Robert Bruce*, p. 181. • **28.** Froissart, *Chronicles*, i, pp. 185–8. • **29.** Walker, *Lancastrian Affinity*, pp. 135–41. • **30.** For *Melibee*, see also above, p. 129. • **31.** *Riverside Chaucer*, p. 235 (lines 1680–7). For discussion, see Blamires, 'Chaucer's Revaluation of Chivalric Honour', pp. 245–69. • **32.** *Works of Sir John Clanvowe*, pp. 69–70. • **33.** 'Vox Clamantis', Book 5, ch. 8, in *Major Latin Works of John Gower*, p. 207. • **34.** *Chronica Maiora*, p. 248. • **35.** *Twenty-Six Political and other Poems*, pp. 6–9, 13.

Chapter 11

1. See above, p. 136. • **2.** Keen, *Chivalry*, p. 47. • **3.** Morris, '*Equestris Ordo*', pp. 87–96; Hehl, 'War, Peace and the Christian Order', pp. 185–228. • **4.** Kaeuper, 'Societal Role of Chivalry in Romance, pp. 97–114. • **5.** Caxton, *Book of the Ordre of Chyvalry*. • **6.** *Book of Chivalry*. See discussion of the text in Kaeuper, *Holy Warriors*, pp. 42–51. • **7.** *Death of King Arthur*, pp. 30–2; Kaeuper, 'Societal Role of Chivalry', p. 104. • **8.** *High Book of the Grail*. For discussion of these works, see Keen, *Chivalry*, pp. 59–63, and Loomis (ed.), *Arthurian Literature in the Middle Ages*. • **9.** For discussion, see Kaeuper, *Chivalry and Violence*, pp. 54–7. • **10.** Frappier, 'Le Graal et la chevalerie', pp. 165–210. • **11.** *Vulgate Version*, iii, pp. 112–7. • **12.** Denholm-Young, 'Feudal Society in the Thirteenth Century', p. 65. • **13.** Taylor, 'Count Amadeus of Savoy's Visit to England', pp. 123–32. • **14.** Denholm-Young, 'Feudal Society in the Thirteenth Century', pp. 65–6. The ceremony took place on Whit Sunday, as the ceremonial knightings at Darlington had fourteen years before. • **15.** See above, p. 106. • **16.** For general surveys of the cult of St George, see Riches, *St George*, and Good, *Cult of St George*. • **17.** For this paragraph, see Morgan, 'Banner-bearer of Christ', pp. 51–62. • **18.** Oxford, Bodleian Library, MS Douce 231, discussed by Sandler, *Gothic Manuscripts*, ii, pp. 95–6. • **19.** Oxford, Christ Church MS 92, discussed by Sandler, *Gothic Manuscripts*, ii, pp. 91–2. • **20.** Hebgin-Barnes, 'A Triumphant Image', pp. 26–8. • **21.** Good, *Cult of St George*, p. 72. • **22.** *Memorials of Henry V*, pp. 115, 121, 123–4. • **23.** Hewitt, *Organisation of War*, p. 161. • **24.** For the significance of St George's as a model of institutional religious patronage, see Burgess, 'St George's College', pp. 63–96. • **25.** Saul, *Death, Art and Memory*, ch. 3. • **26.** Catto, 'Religious Change', pp. 110–11. • **27.** The setting is said to be by 'Roi Henry'. Given the date of the manuscript, Henry V is most likely: *Gothic: Art for England*, p. 157. • **28.** Tout, *Chapters*, ii, pp. 47, 141. • **29.** Ibid., ii, p. 22. • **30.** Prestwich, *Armies and Warfare*, pp. 169–70. • **31.** 'Chronicle of Richard of Hexham', iii, p. 174. • **32.** McNab, 'Obligations of the Clergy', pp. 293–314. • **33.** Lambeth Palace Library, Register of Archbishop Arundel, i, folios. 237–8. • **34.** *Chronica Maiora*, pp. 36–7, 46. • **35.** McHardy, 'English Clergy and the Hundred Years War', pp. 171–8. • **36.** See above, p. 210. • **37.** Jones, 'English Church and Royal Propaganda', pp. 18–30 at p. 25. • **38.** Jones, 'English Church and Royal Propaganda', p. 26 • **39.** Heath, *Church and Realm*, p. 108.

Chapter 12

1. Keen, 'War, Peace and Chivalry', p. 3. • **2.** Quoted by Riley-Smith, *What were the Crusades?* p. 23 • **3.** Ibid., p. 2. • **4.** Ibid., p. 31. • **5.** *Expeditions to Prussia*. • **6.** For the size of Richard's force, see Tyerman, *England and the Crusades*,

p. 66; and see his notes 44 and 45 for the assumptions on which his calculations are based. • **7**. Ibid., p. 82. • **8**. Ibid., p. 69 • **9**. For Richard's crusaders,
see ibid., p. 67, and Gillingham, *Richard I*, p. 215. • **10**. Gillingham, *Richard I*,
p. 213. • **11**. Quoted by Gillingham, ibid., p. 215. • **12**. Oxford, Bodleian Library,
MS Dugdale 15, folio 281. • **13**. Saul, *Death, Art and Memory*, p. 12. • **14**. *Political
Songs*, p. 128. • **15**. Tyerman, *England and the Crusades*, p. 128. • **16**. Lloyd,
English Society and the Crusade, pp. 124–6. • **17**. Keen, 'Chaucer's Knight'. For
Waldegrave, see also above, p. 115. • **18**. Housley, *Later Crusades*, pp. 39–40.
• **19**. For the Scrope–Grosvenor controversy in the Court of Chivalry over
the right to bear the arms *azure a bend or*, see above, p. 115. • **20**. *SG*, i,
pp. 124–5. • **21**. Ibid., pp. 165–6. • **22**. Ibid., pp. 124–5. For Sabraham, see also
above, p. 116. • **23**. Keen, 'Chaucer's Knight', p. 54; Luttrell, 'English Levantine
Crusaders', pp. 143–53; Saul, *Death, Art and Memory*, p. 205. • **24**. For de Mézières'
activities, see Palmer, *England, France and Christendom*, ch. 11. • **25**. Clarke,
Fourteenth Century Studies, p. 288. • **26**. *Letter to Richard II*. • **27**. *Expeditions to
Prussia*; Du Boulay, 'Henry of Derby's Expeditions to Prussia', pp. 153–72.
• **28**. For the newsletters, see *Westminster Chronicle*, pp. 444–8, and *Chronica
Maiora*, pp. 278–9. For the suggestion that the interest in publicising the expedition was prompted by the succession question, see Staley, 'Gower, Richard
II', pp. 68–96. • **29**. Du Boulay, 'Henry of Derby's Expeditions to Prussia',
p. 153. • **30**. Chaplais, *Diplomatic Document*, no. 30. • **31**. Lack and Whittemor
e, 'Portfolio', pp. 402–4. • **32**. Robinson, 'Hugh Johnys', pp. 5–34.

Chapter 13

1. Fernie, *Architecture of Norman England*, pp. 53, 55. • **2**. Brown, *English Castles*,
p. 24. • **3**. Murray, *Reason and Society*, pp. 96–8. • **4**. *Ecclesiastical History of
Orderic Vitalis*, ii, pp. 218–9. • **5**. Liddiard, *Castles in Context*, pp. 15–16.
• **6**. On this theme, see Creighton, *Castles and Landscapes*. • **7**. For what
follows, see Eales, 'Royal Power and Castles', pp. 56–7; King, *Castellarium
Anglicanum*. • **8**. Brown, 'Royal Castle-Building in England', pp. 19–64. • **9**.
Prestwich, *Edward I*, p. 214. • **10**. Thompson, 'Building Accounts of Kirby
Muxloe Castle'; Brown, *English Castles*, p. 166; McFarlane, *Nobility of Later
Medieval England*, p. 93. • **11**. *Historia Novella*, p. 65. • **12**. For castle numbers
by county, see Creighton, *Castle and Landscapes*, p. 52. • **13**. For discussion of
Dover, see Coulson, 'Peaceable Power', pp. 69–95. • **14**. Emery, 'Late-Medieval
Houses', pp. 140–61, at p. 154. • **15**. For the architectural development of the
castle, see Morris, 'Architecture of the Earls of Warwick', pp. 161–74. • **16**.
See above, pp. 47–8. • **17**. Coulson, 'Some Analysis of Bodiam', pp. 51–117. It
is worth adding that Bodiam was equipped with no fewer than twenty-eight

garderobes – loos. It was a very commodious castle indeed. And almost every room had a fireplace. • **18**. *SG*, i, p. 164. • **19**. Walker, *Lancastrian Affinity*, pp. 133–4. And see above, pp. 186, 193. • **20**. Emery is surely wrong in characterising it as 'a hastily built defensive station' in his *Greater Medieval Houses, III*, p. 286. • **21**. Coulson, *Castles in Medieval Society*, ch. 3. • **22**. Wheatley, *The Idea of the Castle*, pp. 15, 21–2. • **23**. These terms are from the licences to crenellate, printed in translation in respectively *Calendar of Patent Rolls 1391–6*, p. 261, and *1377–81*, p. 596. The originals are in Latin: TNA:PRO, C66/337 m. 17 and C66/309 m. 24. In the Wardour licence the word for castle is *castrum*. • **24**. Penshurst was referred to as a 'dwelling-place' in 1341 and a 'manor' in 1392, on both occasions in licences to crenellate: *Calendar of Patent Rolls 1340–3*, p. 331; *1391–6*, p. 164. • **25**. Platt, *Medieval England*, pp. 59–60. • **26**. Coulson, 'Structural Symbolism', pp. 73–90. C. Platt, 'Understanding Licences to Crenellate', pp. 204–7, argues an unconvincing case that licences were concerned with the real needs of defence. • **27**. A. King, 'Fortresses and Fashion Statements', pp. 372–97. King emphasises that the tower house form is not unique to Northumberland. A good example from midland England is Sir William Bagot's tower house at Baginton in Warwickshire. Bagot was a counsellor of Richard II. • **28**. Creighton and Higham, *Medieval Town Walls*, pp. 165–7. The form of licences to crenellate for city walls was much the same as for gentry residences; see, for example, Coventry's: *Calendar of Patent Rolls 1361–4*, p. 417. • **29**. Liddiard, 'Castle Rising, Norfolk', pp. 169–86. • **30**. Goodall, 'Richmond Castle', pp. 148–51. • **31**. *Calendar of Close Rolls 1247–51*, p. 8. • **32**. Brieger, *English Art, 1216–1307*, p. 130. • **33**. Knight, *The Three Castles*, p. 38. • **34**. Quoted by Emery, *Greater Medieval Houses, III*, p. 289. • **35**. *Sir Gawain and the Green Knight*, lines 767–98. It is suggested that, if the Gawain poet, a north Midlander, had any castle in mind, it is likely to have been Beeston in Cheshire: Thompson, 'Castles', pp. 119–30.

Chapter 14

1. *Sir Gawain and the Green Knight*, ed. B. Stone (Harmondsworth, 2nd edn, 1974), p. 78. • **2**. Keen, *Chivalry*, p. 30. • **3**. S. Kay, 'Courts, Clerks and Courtly Love', in R. L. Krueger (ed.), *Cambridge Companion to Medieval Romance* (Cambridge, 2000), p. 86. • **4**. Bartlett, *England under the Norman and Angevin Kings, 1075–1225*, p. 559. • **5**. C. S. Lewis, *The Allegory of Love* (Oxford, 1936). • **6**. J. Gillingham, 'Love, Marriage and Politics in the Twelfth Century', in his *Richard Coeur de Lion: Kingship, Chivalry and War in the Twelfth Century* (London, 1994), pp. 243–55. • **7**. Ibid. p. 247. • **8**. H. T. Riley (ed.), *Johannis de Trokelowe et Henrici de Blaneforde Chronica et Annales* (Rolls Series, 1866), p. 27.

• **9**. N. Davis (ed.), *Paston Letters and Papers of the Fifteenth Century* (2 vols, Oxford, 1971, 1976), i, no. 332. • **10**. Keen, *Chivalry*, p. 116. • **11**. J. R. V. Barker, *The Tournament in England, 1100–1400* (Woodbridge, 1986), p. 88. • **12**. *Scalacronica*, pp. 80–2. • **13**. Keen, 'Chivalry and Courtly Love', in his *Nobles, Knights and Men-at-Arms in the Middle Ages*, p. 40. • **14**. Jean le Bel, *Chronique*, ed. J. Viard and E. Deprez (2 vols, Paris, 1904–5), i, p. 124. • **15**. Froissart, *Chronicles*, ii, p. 439. • **16**. Ibid., p. 23. • **17**. For this paragraph, see Barker, *The Tournament in England*, pp. 101–10. • **18**. D. Crouch, 'The Historian, Lineage and Heraldry, 1050–1250', in *Heraldry, Pageantry and Social Display in Medieval England*, pp. 17–37. • **19**. *Paston Letters and Papers of the Fifteenth Century*, i, no. 230. • **20**. R. E. Archer, 'Rich Old Ladies: the Problem of Late Medieval Dowagers', in A. J. Pollard (ed.), *Property and Politics. Essays in Later Medieval English History* (Gloucester, 1984), pp. 15–35. • **21**. Vale, *Edward III and Chivalry*, pp. 49–50. • **22**. A. Gibbons (ed.), *Early Lincoln Wills* (Lincoln, 1888), p. 118. • **23**. Gaimar, *Estoire des Engleis*. • **24**. J. C. Ward, 'Elizabeth de Burgh, Lady of Clare (d. 1360), in C. M. Barron and A. Sutton (eds), *Medieval London Widows, 1300–1500* (London, 1994), pp. 29–46. • **25**. Armstrong, 'The Piety of Cecily, Duchess of York: a Study in Late Medieval Culture', pp. 135–56. • **26**. J. C. Ward, *English Noblewomen in the Later Middle Ages* (Harlow, 1992), p. 145. • **27**. V. Sekules, 'Women's Piety and Patronage', in N. E. Saul (ed.), *Age of Chivalry. Art and Society in Late Medieval England* (London, 1992), pp. 126–9. • **28**. *Beauchamp Pageant*.

Chapter 15

1. Barber, *Knight and Chivalry*, p. 143. • **2**. Denholm-Young, *History and Heraldry*, pp. 112–6. For rolls of arms, see also above, p. 165 • **3**. Ayton, 'Armies and Military Communities', pp. 214–39. • **4**. *Calendar of Patent Rolls 1313–17*, p. 89. • **5**. Saul, *English Church Monuments*, pp. 221–2. • **6**. Dull, Luttrell, Keen, 'Faithful unto Death', pp. 174–90. • **7**. Saul, *Death, Art and Memory*, pp. 153–68. The tomb was probably commissioned by Cobham's widow: see above, p. 274 • **8**. Winston, 'An Account of the Painted Glass', pp. 239–53, 319–30. • **9**. For these, see Saul, *English Church Monuments*, pp. 220, 224. The armorial on the Basset tomb was recorded by Dugdale shortly before its destruction in the Civil War. • **10**. The brass, now lost, is illustrated in Nichols, *History and Antiquities of the County of Leicester*, iii, i, p. 328. Chaworth was very heraldry conscious: for his antiphonal, see above, p. 285. • **11**. See above, p. 274. • **12**. Coss, 'Knighthood, Heraldry and Social Exclusion', pp. 54–6. • **13**. Wagner, 'Fifteenth-Century Description', pp. 4, 21–8. • **14**. The vambraces and rerebraces protected the arms, while the bascinet was a form of helmet.

• **15**. Saul, *English Church Monuments*, pp. 216–18. For Hastings's career, see *ODNB*, 25, pp. 764–5 (by A. Ayton). • **16**. See above, p. 108. • **17**. For what follows, see Saul, 'Chivalry and Art', pp. 97–111. • **18**. For the grant of the crest see Blomefield, *Norfolk*, vi, pp. 77–8. • **19**. Quoted by Vale, *War and Chivalry*, p. 89. • **20**. Hughes, *Pastors and Visionaries*, pp. 29, 30, 32; *Wills and Inventories of the Northern Counties*, I, pp. 27, 41. • **21**. Wagner, 'Fifteenth-Century Description'. • **22**. For the examples in this paragraph, see Saul, *English Church Monuments*, pp. 129–30, 136. • **23**. *SG*, ii, pp. 281–2. • **24**. Ibid., p. 283. • **25**. Given-Wilson, *Chronicles*, pp. 81–2. • **26**. Morgan, 'Making the English Gentry', pp. 21–8. • **27**. British Library, Add. MS 32101. • **28**. For the Guy romance, see above, pp. 47–8. • **29**. Frankis, 'Taste and Patronage', pp. 80–93. • **30**. *Rous Roll; Beauchamp Pageant*. For the *Pageant*, see also above, pp. 279–80. • **31**. Given-Wilson, *Chronicles*, pp. 109–10.

Chapter 16

1. *Sir John Paston's 'Grete Boke'*. • **2**. Ibid., pp. 28–33. • **3**. Radulescu, *Gentry Context*, pp. 47–8. • **4**. Youngs, *Humphrey Newton*, pp. 153–200. • **5**. British Library, Royal MS 15 E vi, discussed by Dunn, 'Margaret of Anjou, Chivalry and the Order of the Garter', pp. 39–56. • **6**. British Library, Additional MS 14408. • **7**. Ackerman, 'English Rimed and Prose Romances', pp. 480–1. • **8**. Vale, 'Law and Diplomacy in the Alliterative *Morte Arthure*', pp. 31–46. • **9**. See below, p. 315. • **10**. Hahn, 'Gawain and Popular Chivalric Romance in Britain', pp. 218–34. • **11**. For a version in modern English, see *King Arthur's Death*. • **12**. It follows from this that in the debate about whether the *Morte Arthure* is critical or approving of Arthur's – and, by implication – of Edward III's wars, the views of E. Porter, 'Chaucer's Knight, the Alliterative *Morte Arthure*, and Medieval Laws of War: a Reconsideration', *Nottingham Medieval Studies*, 27 (1983), pp. 56–78, where the poet is seen as approving, are to be preferred to those of W. Matthews, *The Tragedy of Arthur* (Berkeley, California, 1960), who sees the poet as critical. • **13**. For a version in modern English, see *Sir Gawain and the Green Knight*. • **14**. For a full text, see *Works of Sir Thomas Malory*. • **15**. Meale, '"The Hoole Book": Editing and the Creation of Meaning in Malory's Text', pp. 3–35. • **16**. Riddy, *Thomas Malory*, p. 42. • **17**. Barber, 'Malory's *Le Morte Darthur* and Court Culture under Edward IV', pp. 133–55. • **18**. See below, ch. 17. • **19**. See below, p. 339. • **20**. See above, p. 338. • **21**. See below, pp. 337–8. • **22**. *Chronique*. • **23**. The main scholarly edition of Froissart's chronicle is *Chroniques de Jean Froissart*. For a full English translation, see Froissart, *Chronicles*. • **24**. Froissart, ii, p. 574. • **25**. Boffey, 'Books and Readers in Calais', pp. 67–74. • **26**. This is Stonyhurst College

MS 1, given to the college by a member of the Arundell family. The evidence for thinking that the volume was commissioned for a French patron is found in its programme of illustration, which celebrates the Valois monarchy. I am grateful to Professor P. Ainsworth for this reference. • **27**. Barron. 'Chivalry, Pageantry and Merchant Culture in Medieval London', pp. 219–42. • **28**. *LC BP*, pp. 84–139. • **29**. Ibid., p. 86. • **30**. Ibid., p. 87. • **31**. Taylor, *English Historical Literature*, p. 167. • **32**. For the pictorial *Beauchamp Pageant*, see above pp. 279–80. • **33**. Youngs, 'Cultural Networks', pp. 119–33.

Chapter 17

1. Fastolf, Sir John (1380–1459), in *ODNB*, 19, pp. 134–5 (by G. L. Harriss). • **2**. *Letters and Papers*, ii, pp. 575–85; Vale, 'Sir John Fastolf's "Report" of 1435, pp. 78–84. • **3**. McFarlane, 'William Worcester', pp. 199–224. • **4**. *Boke of Noblesse*. For discussion, see Ferguson, *Indian Summer*, pp. 143–51. • **5**. Lambeth Palace Library, MS 506, discussed by Nall, 'Perceptions of Financial Mismanagement', pp. 119–36. • **6**. Hughes, 'Stephen Scrope and the Circle of Sir John Fastolf', pp. 109–46. • **7**. *Christine de Pizan's Letter*; Scrope's translation is *Epistle of Othea*. • **8**. *Dicts and Sayings*. • **9**. Richard of York, third duke of York (1411–1460), in *ODNB*, 46, pp. 748–56 (by J. Watts). • **10**. Flugel, 'Eine Mittelenglische Claudian-Übersetzung', pp. 255–99. For discussion, see Hughes, *Arthurian Myths and Alchemy*, pp. 34–5; and Visser-Fuchs, 'Richard of York: Books and the Man', pp. 257–72. • **11**. *Paston Letters and Papers*, ii, p. 42. • **12**. Jones, 'Somerset, York and the Wars of the Roses', pp. 285–307. • **13**. *Lydgate, The Minor Poems*, ii, p. 716. • **14**. Woodville, Anthony, second Earl Rivers (*c.* 1440–1483), in *ODNB*, 60, pp. 224–7 (by M. A. Hicks). • **15**. See above, p. 329, and n. 7. • **16**. *Middle English Translation of Christine de Pisan*, where the case for identifying Woodville as the translator is made at pp. 31–6. Key passages of the French original are translated into modern English in *Writings of Christine de Pizan*, pp. 275–91. • **17**. Tiptoft, John, first earl of Worcester (1427–1470), in *ODNB*, 54, pp. 833–6 (by B. Kohl). • **18**. Mitchell, *John Tiptoft*, pp. 215–41. • **19**. See above, pp. 174–5. • **20**. For this paragraph, see Barber, 'Malory's *Le Morte Darthur*', pp. 142–4. • **21**. Ibid., p. 138. • **22**. Anne's father had died at the siege of Saint-Denis in 1435. For her and William Chamberlain, see King, 'Anne Harling Reconsidered', pp. 204–22. • **23**. See above, p. 306. For his career, see W. Dugdale, *The Antiquities of Warwickshire* (2nd edn., 2 vols (London, 1730), i, p. 110. • **24**. Beltz, *Memorials of the Order of the Garter*, pp. lxx–lxxi, where 27 February 1477 should read 27 April 1476. • **25**. Kidson, 'The Architecture of St George's Chapel'. • **26**. Hughes, *Arthurian*

Myths and Alchemy, pp. 131–6. • **27**. *Literae Cantuarienses*, iii, p. 282. • **28**. *Crowland Continuations*, pp. 133–5. • **29**. Ibid., p. 137. • **30**. Radulescu, *Gentry Context*, pp. 9–10. • **31**. Sutton and Visser-Fuchs, "'Chevalerie . . .'", pp. 107–34, p. 109.

Chapter 18

1. Girouard, *The Return to Camelot*, p. 290. • **2**. Barber, *Knight and Chivalry*, p. 381. • **3**. *Chivalry in the Renaissance*, p. xii. • **4**. Knowles, *Religious Orders, III*, p. 6. • **5**. James, 'Concept of Order', pp. 272–307, 320. • **6**. Given-Wilson and Bériac, pp. 802–33, and the references there cited. • **7**. *Chronicon Galfridi le Baker*, pp. 81–2. • **8**. Carpenter, *Battles of Lewes and Evesham*, pp. 65–6. • **9**. *Chronica Maiora*, pp. 328–9. • **10**. Ibid., p. 328. • **11**. Boardman, *Battle of Towton*, pp. 139–41 and the references there cited. • **12**. Boardman, 'Historical Background', pp. 15, 23–4. • **13**. Watson, 'Review of the Sources', pp. 59–60. • **14**. Commynes, *Memoirs*, p. 195. • **15**. Keen, *Laws of War*, p. 104; Stacey, 'Age of Chivalry', pp. 32–8. • **16**. Commynes, *Memoirs*, p. 353. • **17**. Ibid., p. 89. • **18**. Goodman, *Wars of the Roses*, pp. 163–5. • **19**. Bradbury, *Medieval Archer*, pp. 108–33. • **20**. Prestwich, *Armies and Warfare*, p. 134. • **21**. *Chronica Maiora*, p. 328. • **22**. *Chronicon Galfridi le Baker*, pp. 81–2. • **23**. Pollard, *Warwick the Kingmaker*, pp. 168–78. • **24**. Gunn, 'Sir Thomas Lovell', pp. 117–54; and *ODNB*, 34, pp. 531–2. • **25**. Gunn, 'Chivalry and the Politics of the Early Tudor Court', p. 119. • **26**. *Gothic: Art for England*, no. 9 and plate 13. It is suggested that Lovell commissioned the roundel for the gatehouse of his residence at East Harling, where in the 1730s a bust of his likeness surrounded by the Garter could still be seen. • **27**. James, 'English Politics and the Concept of Honour', pp. 308–415. Armstrong, 'Development of the Office of Arms', however, points out that developments assigned by James exclusively to the sixteenth century have their origins in the late Middle Ages.

Conclusion

1. Lincolnshire Archives Centre, 10–ANC/322. The two men communicated in French. I thank Adrian Wilkinson for this reference. • **2**. Nichols, *Progresses and Processions of Queen Elizabeth*, ii, pp. 312–29 • **3**. Yates, 'Elizabethan Chivalry', pp. 4–25; Girouard, *Robert Smythson*, pp. 210–17. • **4**. The biggest building in this part of the castle is the riding school: Girouard, *Robert Smythson*, pp. 238, 282. • **5**. Bornstein, *Mirrors of Courtesy*, p. 112. • **6**. *ODNB*, 5, pp. 489–93 (by D. J. B. Trim). • **7**. *Knighton*, p. 170.

Index